Praise from the Experts

"Dr. Patricia Cerrito, professor of mathematics at the University of Louisville, has written a very useful introduction to SAS Enterprise Miner and data mining. Dr. Cerrito is a well-known expert in data mining, and is especially well known for her research in applications of text mining. Her experience in the classroom is clearly evident in the examples and motivation of her material. She begins the text with an easy-to-follow introduction to SAS Enterprise Miner. She follows the introductory chapter with an important overview and discussion of data visualization techniques, providing clear illustrations conducted in SAS Enterprise Miner. A unique feature of this book is the early introduction of text mining, which Dr. Cerrito does in Chapter 3. The following chapters examine data summarization, association (or market basket analysis), the use of text mining in combination with association analysis, and cluster analysis. The emphasis on these exploratory or pattern recognition techniques in data mining is a helpful addition to the literature illustrating the application of SAS Enterprise Miner. Dr. Cerrito's expertise in these areas is evident. The book concludes with an excellent chapter on predictive modeling techniques and on time series techniques. The final chapter is particularly unique: Dr. Cerrito provides the student with an excellent review of technical preparation. Many students often fail to understand the importance of communicating the results of their analyses either to other scientists or senior managers. This chapter provides the student with clear examples of good report preparation.

"This is a wonderful introductory text to data mining and to SAS Enterprise Miner. I am confident that faculty, students, and business analysts will find this book to be an invaluable resource."

J. Michael Hardin, Ph.D.
Associate Dean for Research
Culverhouse College of Commerce
The University of Alabama

"*Introduction to Data Mining Using SAS® Enterprise Miner*™ is an excellent introduction for students in a classroom setting, or for people learning on their own or in a distance learning mode. The book contains many screen shots of the software during the various scenarios used to exhibit basic data and text mining concepts. In this way, the student obtains validation of correct procedures while performing the steps of the narrative or for parallel processes to complete the assignments.

"The author uses a varied and interesting set of databases for demonstration of the many capabilities of SAS Enterprise Miner. The alteration of examples based on structured data and text data sets reinforce the awareness of the need to consider all sources of information and the fact that one can process text with SAS Enterprise Miner in a quite straight-forward manner."

James Mentele, Senior Research Fellow
Central Michigan University Research Corporation

Introduction to Data Mining

Using SAS® Enterprise Miner™

Patricia B. Cerrito

The correct bibliographic citation for this manual is as follows: Cerrito, Patricia B. 2006. *Introduction to Data Mining Using SAS® Enterprise Miner™*. Cary, NC: SAS Institute Inc.

Introduction to Data Mining Using SAS® Enterprise Miner™

Contents

Preface

The increased use of computers has increased the amount of data that can be stored in them. To take advantage of the rich storehouse of knowledge that the data represent, we need to harness the data to extract information and turn it into business intelligence. Many retail businesses now use shopping cards for this purpose. Online companies have become adept at looking not only at customer purchases but at customer browsing.

However, any data set or database with a large number of observations and variables can be mined for valuable information. Organizations with information depositories that do not yet use the full resources of their databases include human resource departments, institutions of higher education, health care providers, and insurance companies.

What can you do when you have lots of data to look at and don't know where to start? This manual provides a general, practical introduction to data mining using SAS Enterprise Miner and SAS Text Miner software. It doesn't focus on specific applications such as retail sales. Instead, it provides examples from areas where data mining is not yet commonly used. Chapter 1 gives a general introduction to data mining and step-by-step instructions for navigating in SAS Enterprise Miner. The first step in looking at data is to draw pictures of the variables in the data set, and Chapter 2 provides a basic introduction to data visualization using SAS Enterprise Miner software. Because a lot of data are contained in text messages, transcribed phone calls, open-ended survey questions, and Web sites, Chapter 3 shows you how to use SAS Text Miner software to analyze text information. Chapter 4 provides an introduction to data summaries.

Chapter 5 discusses association rules, also known as market basket analysis. These rules follow the supposition that if a customer purchases item A, then there is a strong likelihood that the customer will also purchase item B. The chapter also includes some examples of the other types of data that can be examined using association rules. In addition, path analysis (or sequential association rules) is discussed.

You can use SAS Enterprise Miner software to investigate inventories, diagnostic codes, and other types of categorical information. However, many categorical fields have thousands— sometimes millions—of different levels. For example, consider the inventory of an office supply company or an online book store. Without some type of data compression, very little useful information can be extracted. SAS Text Miner software compresses nominal data (i.e., names). Techniques to compress nominal data fields are presented in Chapter 6.

Chapter 7 presents predictive modeling, which is an extension of statistical linear models. Because the data sets are typically so large that a statistical p-value has no meaning, other measures are used to judge the quality of the model, especially misclassification rates. Predictive modeling is considered supervised learning because you can use the outcome to judge the accuracy. Chapter 8 discusses cluster analysis, a form of unsupervised learning where there are no outcome variables. Clustering is a type of data compression; clustering compresses the observations into groups. Because there is no outcome variable in clustering, using a testing set to compare actual versus predicted outcomes does not work. Therefore, Chapter 8 considers methods that can be used to validate the clusters. The time series discussed in Chapter 9 uses both SAS Enterprise Miner software and the HPF procedure, which is the new High-Performance Forecasting system available in SAS.

Chapters 10 and 11 deviate somewhat from the previous chapters to provide other important user information. Chapter 10 discusses the technical writing skills needed to convey your data mining results, whether to your employer or to attendees at a professional conference. Chapter 11 details the results of the data mining analyses of the data sets used in this manual. Here, you can compare your analyses (as suggested in the exercises) with those of the author.

Remember that there is no right answer when examining data sets. You can ask many questions about the data, and each answer will start to drill down to explore the data in more detail. It is up to you as the investigator to determine what is of interest and what is important to analyze. This manual provides you with some starting points.

It is assumed that you have some basic knowledge of statistics and some familiarity with SAS. You do not need to know any data mining methods. Think of data mining as a process of exploration instead of a collection of tools to investigate the data, and then choose the methods that will extract the most information from the data.

I have been a professor of statistics for more than 25 years, and I have used SAS even longer. I started using SAS Enterprise Miner software early in its development and have developed classes in data mining using it. More recently, I started teaching data mining and SAS Enterprise Miner software in online courses at the University of Louisville. My students are required to use SAS and SAS Enterprise Miner software from the beginning. I emphasize technical writing development in every statistics course that I teach. This manual flows naturally from the material I teach in my data mining courses. I hope that you have an enjoyable experience as you explore your data.

Acknowledgments

There are many people who provided support so that I could develop and complete this book. First, I thank Judy Whatley, my acquisitions editor at SAS Press, for her assistance as the book went through its many reviews and rewrites. I also appreciate the reviewers from SAS who provided many useful comments. Many thanks also to Tom Bohannon and Randy Collica from the SAS user community for their helpful comments.

The SAS production team worked wonders with my manuscript. The team included copy editor Kathy Restivo, technical publishing specialists Candy Farrell and Jennifer Dilley, cover designer Patrice Cherry, marketing specialists Liz Villani and Shelly Goodin, and managing editor Mary Beth Steinbach.

My students' interest and enthusiasm in learning data mining formed the basis for this book. They used drafts of the book to advance their data mining skills.

Finally, I am especially grateful to my loving husband, John, for his help, and for all the meals he cooked so that I could finish this book.

x

The Basics of SAS Enterprise Miner 5.2

1.1 Introduction to Data Mining

According to Hand (1998), it is important for statisticians to become involved in data mining because statistical methods provide the glue that holds the process together. Because of its origins, data mining is a more practically oriented discipline than statistics. Therefore, it emphasizes topics that are not currently the focus of statistical research:

- Data mining deals with heterogeneous data, sometimes with complex internal structures (such as images, video, text, and signals).

- Data mining assumes that the raw data set is not of sufficient quality to apply a selected statistical methodology directly. Instead, the data set must be prepared with appropriate preprocessing techniques. That preparation can have as much or even more influence on the quality of the final results than the selected technique.

- Data mining uses flexible predictive techniques that are often based on strong algorithmic foundations but have weaker formal statistical justification (such as artificial neural networks and decision rules).

- Data mining often uses hidden (intermediate) variables as tools to perform a step-by-step compression of raw input data and presentation in more abstract form, which helps in building models for different tasks.

- Data mining attempts to find not only general, global models based on a data set but also local patterns (local models) in large data spaces, which is especially useful when the amount of data and the number of dimensions is so large that finding general models is cost prohibitive.

- Data mining has a strong emphasis on an algorithmic approach and pays attention to issues of scalability (i.e., whether the approach will work with reasonable efficiency in large data sets). Approaches that are not practical are discouraged.

Data mining concentrates on data management and optimization of data searches (with a focus on problems of preprocessing, data cleaning, algorithms, and data structures). Statistics is more oriented toward formalisms for final model representation and score function formalization in the data space to perform inference (with a focus on problems of models and principles of statistical inference). At the same time, data miners have focused on estimation and have generally ignored inferential models. Table 1.1 briefly compares statistics and data mining in terms of specific problems and tools.

Table 1.1 Comparing Statistical Methods to Data Mining Tools

Data Problem	Statistical Methods	Data Mining Methods	Similarities	Differences
Classification	Discriminant analysis and logistic regression	Artificial neural networks, rule induction and classification trees	A kernel density or nearest-neighbor discriminant analysis is equivalent to a probabilistic neural network. Most of the better data mining software packages also include logistic regression. The measure of fit depends on statistical measures such as correlation and odds ratios.	Data mining partitions the data into training, testing, and validation; statistics depends more on cross-validation techniques. The measure of fit is by misclassification rates.
Analysis of variance (ANOVA)	General linear model, mixed models	Artificial neural networks, rule induction, and classification trees	Both assess the accuracy of prediction.	Data mining tools are designed for estimation, not for inference.

(continued)

Table 1.1 Comparing Statistical Methods to Data Mining Tools *(continued)*

Data Problem	Statistical Methods	Data Mining Methods	Similarities	Differences
Estimation of probability distribution	Kernel density estimation, empirical distribution functions	None readily available	Kernel density estimation is available in SAS/STAT software. However, most statistical software packages do not yet include it as an estimation technique. Therefore, kernel density is not yet in common use as a statistical method.	It is not available directly in SAS Enterprise Miner software.
Text extraction	None readily available; still must rely on manual abstraction.	Text mining tools use singular value decomposition and text parsing in combination with classification techniques to extract information.	The primary method available for analysis is frequency counts.	Clustering and classification tools are readily available to work with text information.

Another important aspect of data analysis is the fitness and quality of data. In order to analyze the data statistically, it must first be in a format that we can analyze. According to Ferguson (1997), most organizations are drowning in data but starving for real information. As stated by Lambert (2002), many managers simply assume that the quality of the data they use is good. Unfortunately, poor quality appears to be the norm rather than the exception, and statisticians have largely ignored the issue. Poor quality data can cause more immediate harm and have other more indirect effects, according to Lambert (2002). Therefore, statisticians must consider the state of the data and the applicability of the statistical models. Working with complex data provides tremendous opportunities for statisticians who master the techniques of data mining.

Another major difference concerns the size of the data sets. In statistics, with the primary concern being inference, *p*-values and statistical significance are the primary measures of model effectiveness. However, data mining typically involves large data sets that are observational rather than random. The confidence width and effect size in such large samples decreases to 0 as the sample size increases. It is not unusual to have a regression model with every parameter statistically significant but with a correlation coefficient of almost 0. Therefore, other measures of model effectiveness are used. In data mining, the data sets are usually large enough to partition into three types: training, testing, and validation. The training data set is used to define the model, the testing data set is used in an iterative process to change the model if necessary to improve it, and the validation data set represents a final examination of the model. Depending upon the profit and loss requirements in the data, misclassification is used in supervised learning where there is a specific outcome variable.

Another issue with observational data generally is the problem of potential confounders. Although this problem can be dealt with using statistical linear models by including potential confounders in the model, in practice, the data sets collected are too small to include all confounders that should be considered. Because data mining tools can include hundreds and sometimes thousands of variables simultaneously, potential confounders can and should always be considered in the data mining process.

1.2 Introduction to SAS Enterprise Miner 5.2

SAS Enterprise Miner software streamlines the data mining process to create highly accurate predictive and descriptive models. The models are based on analysis of vast amounts of data from across an enterprise. Interactive statistical and visualization tools help you better search for trends and anomalies and help you focus on the model development process. This section discusses SAS Enterprise Miner 5.2 in detail.

Click **Log On** to start SAS Enterprise Miner software (Display 1.1).

Display 1.1 Initial SAS Enterprise Miner 5.2 Screen

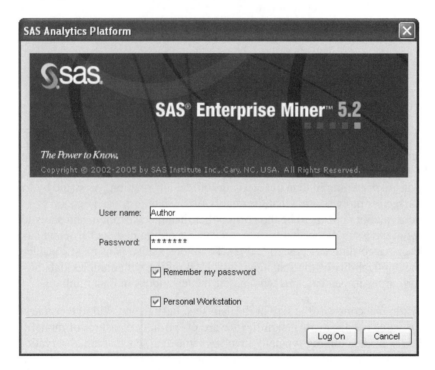

Display 1.2 shows the next screen. You can access an existing project or create a new project. If you are using the software for the first time, select **New Project**. To access an existing project, select **Open Project**.

Display 1.2 Project Screen

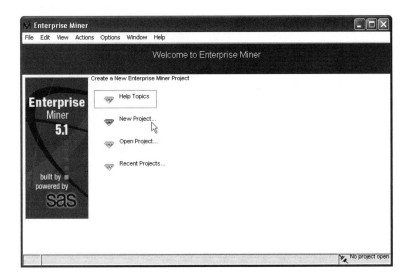

After you have selected **New Project**, the window shown in Display 1.3 prompts you for a project name.

Specify a name for the project in the **Path** field.

Display 1.3 Creating a New Project

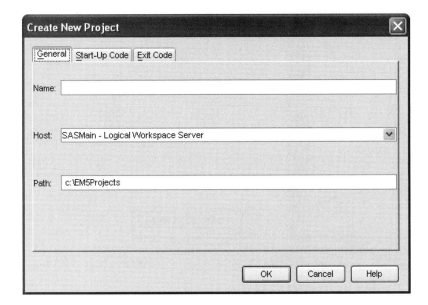

There are tabs for start-up code and for exit code. **Start-up code** allows you to enter SAS code that runs as soon as the project is open; **Exit Code** runs every time the project is closed. The **Start-Up Code** tab is generally used to define a LIBNAME statement to inform SAS Enterprise Miner where all the project data are located. Enter the following code here:

```
libname project 'C:\project_directory';
```

Once this code runs, all data sets created in the project are stored in the C:\project_directory folder. If desired, you can assign the Sasuser library name that is the default in Base SAS software. The purpose of creating a separate library name for each project is to organize the data files. Only directories defined through the LIBNAME statement are recognized in the project. Any data set you use must be located within the directory defined by the LIBNAME statement. Multiple LIBNAME statements can be used in the start-up code. However, at least one LIBNAME statement is required.

Once you have created a new project, the Enterprise Miner—Workloads window appears (see Display 1.4). The menus on the left change based on the choices you make.

Display 1.4 Initial SAS Enterprise Miner Project Screen

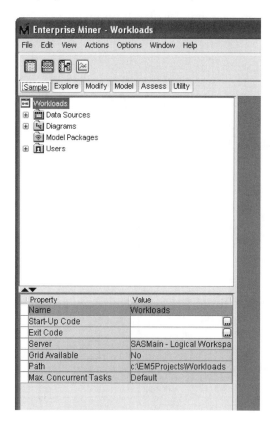

You can also access the start-up code directly through the project name menu, which is displayed by clicking the project name, to create a library name. Just click the ... button next to **Start-Up Code** in the menu on the left.

All analyses begin with a data set. SAS Enterprise Miner software is used primarily to investigate large, complex data sets with tens of thousands to millions of records and hundreds to thousands of variables. Data mining finds patterns and relationships in the data and determines whether the discovered patterns are valid.

The next step is to access a data set. First, right-click **Data Sources**.

Display 1.5 Accessing Data Sets in a SAS Enterprise Miner Project

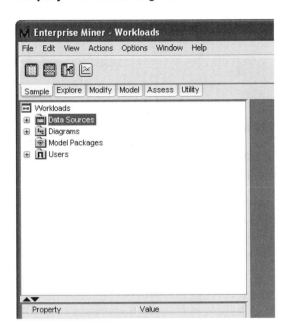

Click **Create Data Source** (Display 1.6).

Display 1.6 Creating a Data Source

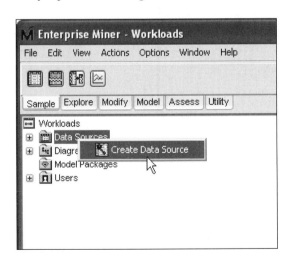

Next, a series of windows leads you through all the required steps to access a new data set in SAS Enterprise Miner 5.2.

Display 1.7 Creating a Data Source with the Data Source Wizard

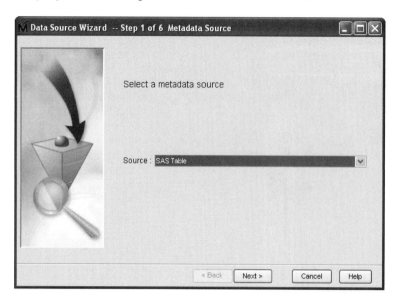

The next step is to define the SAS data table. Click **Next** to accept the default (Display 1.8).

Display 1.8 Finding the Data File

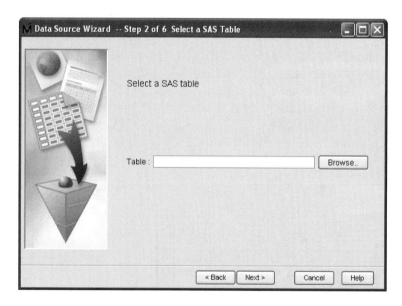

Click **Browse** to find data files contained within the defined libraries (Display 1.9).

Display 1.9 Defined Libraries

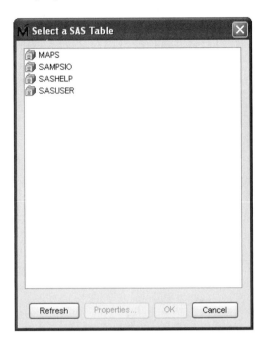

If the libraries are not visible, refresh the screen. Select the library name where the data set is located and then click **OK**. Select the file, click **OK**, and then click **Next**.

In Display 1.10, the general contents of the data file, including the number of variables and the number of observations, are listed. Display 1.10 also indicates when the data set was created and modified. Click **Next**.

Display 1.10 Data Properties

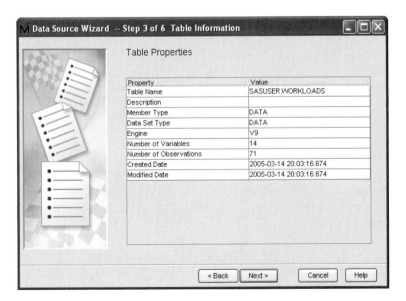

Display 1.11 prompts you to choose basic or advanced information about the data set.

You should routinely choose **Advanced**, even though the default is **Basic**.

Display 1.11 Choice of Information Type

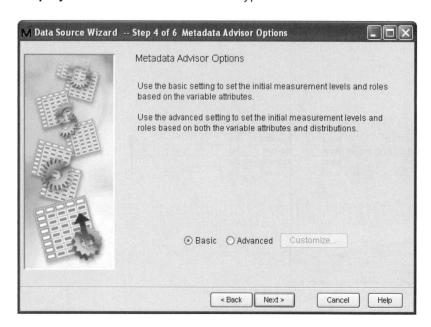

The variables in the data set are generally divided into four categories: identification, input, target, and rejected. A *rejected variable* is not used in any data mining analysis. An *input* (also called an *independent variable*) is used in the various models and exploratory tools in the software. Often, input variables are used to predict a *target value* (also called a *dependent value*). An *identification variable* is used to label a particular observation in the data set. While they are not used to predict outcomes, identification variables are used to link different observations to the same ID. Some data mining techniques require a target variable while others need only input variables.

There are other categories of variables as well that are used for more specialized analyses. In particular, a *time ID variable* is used in place of the more standard *ID variable* when the data are tracked longitudinally. A *text variable* is used with SAS Text Miner software. A raw data set is used to perform the initial analyses, unless the data are longitudinal, in which case the data set is identified as transactional.

Many of the procedures used in SAS Enterprise Miner 5.2 are also available in SAS/STAT software. However, the procedures have different names, and sometimes perform slightly different functions. For example, the regression node in SAS Enterprise Miner performs linear or logistic regression, depending upon whether the target variable is continuous or discrete. The procedure itself determines the method to use. Similarly, there is a node for clustering.

Other procedures, such as PROC NEURAL, are unique to SAS Enterprise Miner software. Methods that are available in SAS/STAT software that are not readily available in SAS Enterprise Miner can be added through a code node, which allows you to copy and paste code as needed into the SAS Enterprise Miner window. The ability to integrate SAS Enterprise Miner with SAS/STAT software and other SAS components is one of the great strengths of SAS Enterprise Miner software.

The sample data set shown in Display 1.12 identifies the role of all the variables as **Input**. However, not all the variables are listed. Use the scroll bar to access the remaining variables.

Display 1.12 Variable Properties

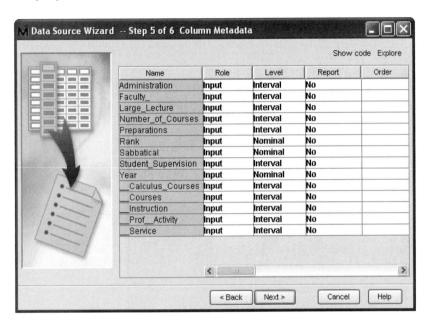

Initially, SAS Enterprise Miner 5.2 lists default role values. You can change these roles, as shown in Display 1.13.

For variables highlighted in the **Role** column, options are displayed. You can click on the role to be assigned to the variable. In this example data set, only some of the variables will be examined; others will be rejected because they are not needed.

Display 1.13 Changing Variable Roles and Levels

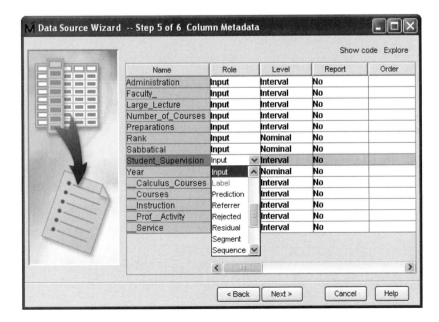

Other terms and roles can be used. However, this book focuses on the most basic and introduces others as needed.

Similarly, the level can be changed. Most of the levels in this data set are either **Nominal** or **Interval**. Not all of the data fit those levels. For example, the Number_of_Courses variable will not be **Nominal** as the variable name itself indicates that it is a number. Therefore, it will be changed to **Interval**. Display 1.14 shows the overall attributes and the role of the data file itself.

Display 1.14 Data File Attributes

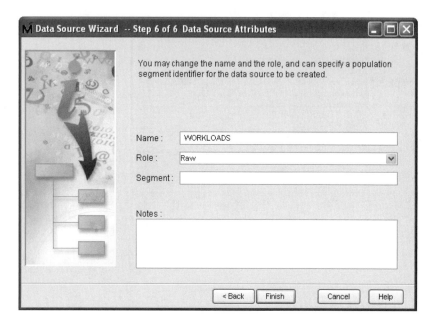

There are several roles for the data file, as shown in Display 1.15. They are explained in later chapters. For the basic analysis, the assigned role should be the default value of **Raw**.

Other possible data set roles include **Transaction**, which is used if there is a time component to the data.

Display 1.15 Possible Data File Attributes

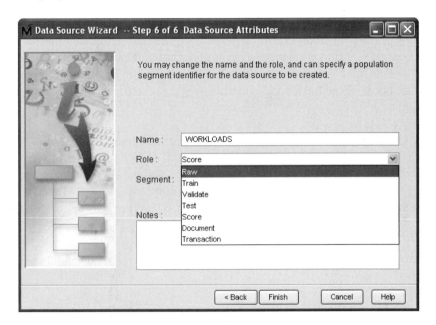

Others include **Train**, **Validate**, **Test**, **Score**, and **Document**. **Score** is used when fresh data are introduced into a model. The remaining values will not be used in this example.

It is sometimes necessary to change either a variable role or a level in the data set by selecting **Edit Variables**, which is found by right-clicking the data set name in the drop-down list (Display 1.16).

Display 1.16 Changing Variable Roles and Levels

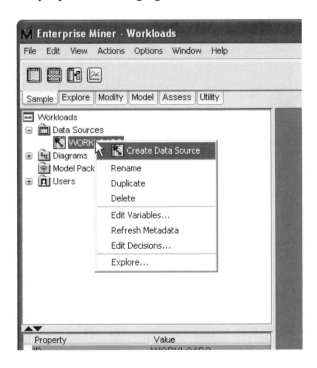

This option returns you to the window shown in Display 1.12.

1.3 Exploring the Data Set

To perform data mining, first you need to understand the data. Therefore, you must explore the data, draw some graphs of the data, and perform basic data summaries. These summaries include some tables. Some of the exploration is relatively straightforward and can be performed using a number of SAS components, including SAS/INSIGHT software, SAS/STAT software, and SAS/GRAPH software. Some of the basics are available in SAS Enterprise Miner 5.2, and are shown here.

There are a number of ways to explore a data set in SAS Enterprise Miner 5.2. The first is to click **Explore** (shown in the upper right-hand corner of Display 1.12). A second way is to select **Explore** from the menu shown in Display 1.16. A third way is to click the StatExplore icon located on the **Explore** tab. Each of these options leads to the same exploration. However, in order to use the StatExplore icon, a diagram should be defined. The other two options do not require a diagram.

Once the data set is defined in the software, a diagram can be defined. The first step is to right-click the Diagrams icon (Display 1.17).

Display 1.17 Defining a Diagram

You are then prompted to name the diagram (Display 1.18). Once you provide the name, the window on the right-hand side of the screen becomes white. The SAS Enterprise Miner diagram is constructed within that white frame.

Display 1.18 Naming the Diagram

Once you have named the diagram, move icons into the workspace area by clicking and dragging using the mouse. To explore the data using StatExplore, two icons are moved into the diagram window (Display 1.19): the data set to be explored and the StatExplore icon.

Display 1.19 Initial Diagram for the StatExplore Process

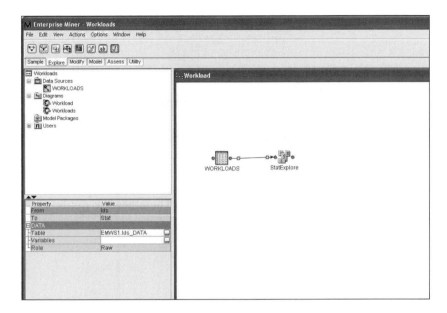

First, move the Workloads icon to the diagram window using the right mouse button. Next, move the StatExplore icon, found on the **Explore** tab, to the diagram. Using the left mouse button, move from one icon to the next, and the two will connect. Right-click the StatExplore icon to access a menu to run the exploration (Display 1.20).

Display 1.20 StatExplore Node Options

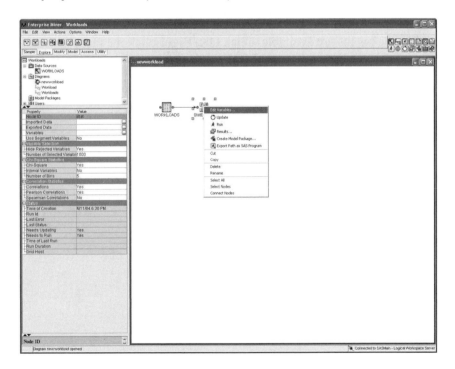

When you choose to run an icon in the diagram, SAS Enterprise Miner runs all icons that lead up to the chosen icon. A green border surrounds the icon when it is running (Display 1.21). An error has occurred if the border turns red. Once the processing has completed, you are prompted for the next step.

Display 1.21 Running the StatExplore Process

A prompt indicates that the results are available. Click OK. Right-click the menu to view the results (Output 1.1).

Output 1.1 StatExplore Results in Output Window

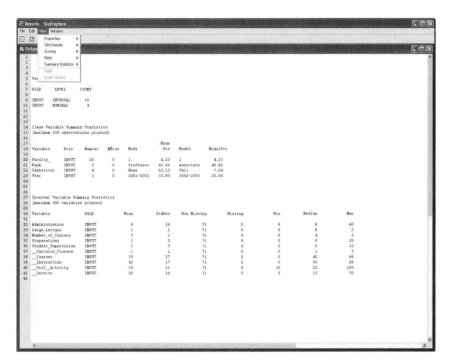

The **View** menu allows you to access more output values. The results from the StatExplore node provide a summary of the variables in the data set. Included in the **View** menu is an option to create plots of the data. These options are discussed in more detail later in this chapter.

Output 1.2 Results Using the **Explore** Button

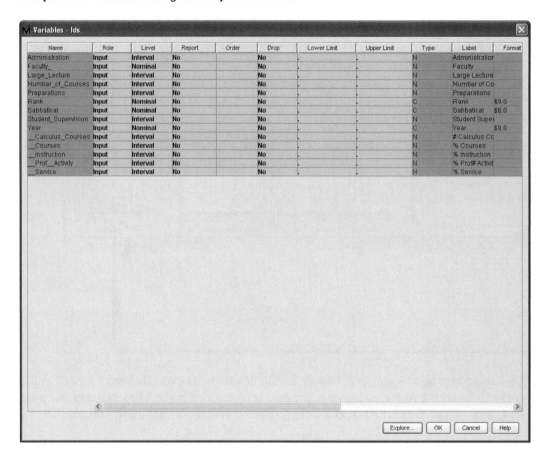

Using the **Explore** button when first defining the data set or the **Explore** option in the menu in Display 1.16, displays a summary of the data set. Clicking **Explore** yields the result in Output 1.3.

Output 1.3 Explore Button Results

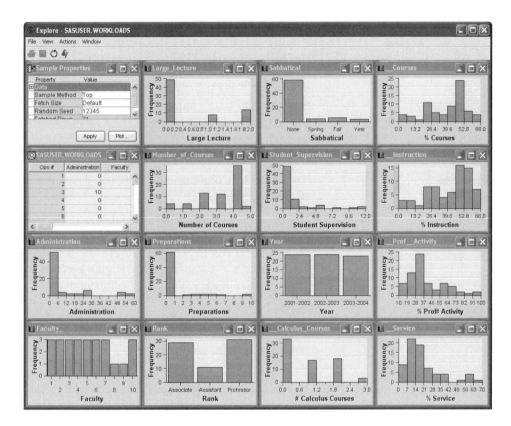

1.4 Analyzing a Sample Data Set

To explore the data well, you need to know about the domain. Therefore, it is essential to discuss the sample data set in more detail. This data set was chosen so that most readers would understand the basic domain of the data.

The data set contains the workload assignments for university faculty in one academic department for a three-year period. There are a total of 14 variables and 71 observations. There are a number of reasons to examine the data: to determine if employee resources are used efficiently and to determine whether there are longitudinal shifts in workload assignments that might impact overall productivity.

In terms of domain knowledge, it is important to understand why workloads are assigned in this fashion and why overall trends can be overlooked. Faculty members are responsible for publications, presentations, and grants at the end of the year. They are also responsible for teaching courses. As salaried employees, they have no required hours to fulfill on a daily or weekly basis. The workloads, then, are negotiated on an individual basis between each faculty member and administrative officials. Attempts to standardize workload requirements have not been entirely successful. Without standardization, trends are often missed because the data are not examined and summarized. The variable list for the data set is given in Table 1.2.

Table 1.2 List of Variables in the Workload Data Set

Variable Name	Variable Description
Faculty	Faculty members are identified only by number to preserve anonymity.
Year	This is defined as an academic year—August to May.
Percent instruction	The percentage of a full-time workload devoted to instruction. Instruction includes teaching courses, supervising students in independent study and theses, and preparation of new courses.
Percent courses	The percentage of a full-time workload devoted solely to teaching courses.
Number of courses	Course percentages have been standardized. Different percentages are allocated for 4- and 5-credit hour courses (13% and 16% respectively) while a 3-credit hour course gets a standard 10%. Higher percentages are also given for teaching large lecture courses.
Number of calculus courses	Each calculus course is allocated 18% of the workload.
Number of large lecture courses	Each large lecture course is allocated 10%+2% per recitation section.
Student supervision	The number of students supervised by a faculty member in independent study (2% each) and theses (3% each).
Preparations	If a new course is being taught, time is allocated for the extra preparation required.
Percentage professional activity	The time allocated for research activities. Faculty members are expected to publish, submit grant applications, and present at professional conferences.
Percentage service	Faculty members are also required to serve on committees or in administrative assignments.
Rank	Full-time faculty members have three possible ranks: assistant, associate, and full. Assistants are usually not tenured; associate and full faculty members usually are.
Sabbatical	Every seven years, faculty members have the potential for a half-year (at full pay) or a full-year (at half pay) sabbatical, usually related to research activities.
Administration	The percentage of service specifically allocated to administrative activities.

Rank, Sabbatical, and Year are identified as class variables, containing nominal data. The remaining variables are identified as interval variables. These assignments are made automatically by the software. To investigate these variables using the StatExplore node, examine the class variables (Display 1.22).

Display 1.22 Menu Choice for Plotting Class Variables

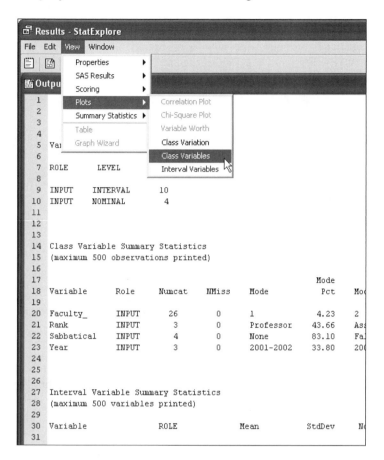

Output 1.4 shows the results of plotting class variables.

Output 1.4 Plotting Class Variables

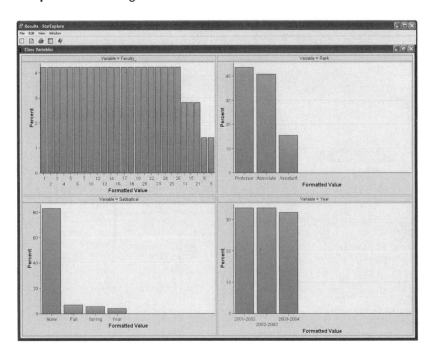

The resulting analysis indicates that the number of full and associate rank faculty members is nearly equal, with fewer at the assistant rank. The number of responses per year is about the same. Most faculty members do not have sabbaticals. In addition, half-year at full pay is more popular than full-year at half pay.

The bar charts from the output are interactive. If there are too many levels, they cannot all be displayed at once. By moving the cursor, additional parts of the charts are displayed. Variables are displayed in Output 1.5.

Output 1.5 Plotting Interval Variables

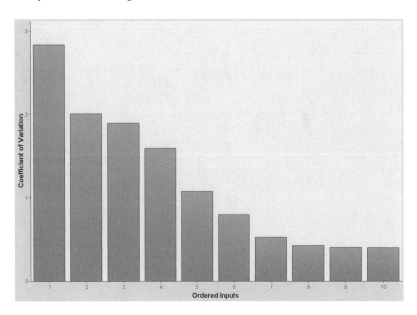

At first glance, this chart is hard to decipher. All interval variables are represented and numbered. The coefficient of variation is defined on the *y*-axis. To read the bars, move the cursor over one of them and specific information is displayed (Output 1.6).

Output 1.6 Display of Information for Interval Variables

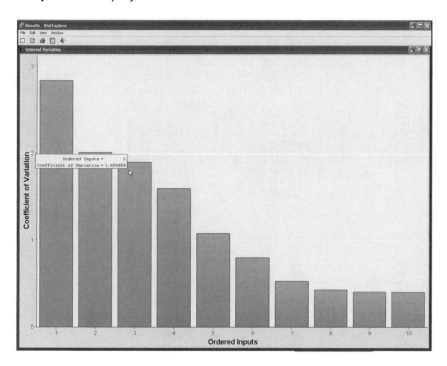

The cursor provides the variable name. Note that interval variables are displayed in the order of the magnitude of the coefficient of variation. More plots are provided with the MultiPlot node, discussed later in this section.

Other information provided in the StatExplore node includes summary statistics, means for interval variables, and frequency counts for class variables (Output 1.7 and 1.8).

Output 1.7 Summary Statistics for Class Variables

Variable	Type	Numeric Val...	Formatted V...	Frequency	Percent	Role	PLOT
Faculty_	N	11		3	4.225352	INPUT	1
Faculty_	N	22		3	4.225352	INPUT	1
Faculty_	N	33		3	4.225352	INPUT	1
Faculty_	N	44		3	4.225352	INPUT	1
Faculty_	N	55		3	4.225352	INPUT	1
Faculty_	N	66		3	4.225352	INPUT	1
Faculty_	N	77		3	4.225352	INPUT	1
Faculty_	N	1010		3	4.225352	INPUT	1
Faculty_	N	1212		3	4.225352	INPUT	1
Faculty_	N	1313		3	4.225352	INPUT	1
Faculty_	N	1414		3	4.225352	INPUT	1
Faculty_	N	1616		3	4.225352	INPUT	1
Faculty_	N	1717		3	4.225352	INPUT	1
Faculty_	N	1818		3	4.225352	INPUT	1
Faculty_	N	1919		3	4.225352	INPUT	1
Faculty_	N	2020		3	4.225352	INPUT	1
Faculty_	N	2222		3	4.225352	INPUT	1
Faculty_	N	2323		3	4.225352	INPUT	1
Faculty_	N	2424		3	4.225352	INPUT	1
Faculty_	N	2525		3	4.225352	INPUT	1
Faculty_	N	2626		3	4.225352	INPUT	1
Faculty_	N	1111		2	2.816901	INPUT	1
Faculty_	N	1515		2	2.816901	INPUT	1
Faculty_	N	2121		2	2.816901	INPUT	1
Faculty_	N	88		1	1.408451	INPUT	1
Faculty_	N	99		1	1.408451	INPUT	1
Rank	C		.Professor	31	43.66197	INPUT	1
Rank	C		.Associate	29	40.84507	INPUT	1
Rank	C		.Assistant	11	15.49296	INPUT	1
Sabbatical	C		.None	59	83.09859	INPUT	1
Sabbatical	C		.Fall	5	7.042254	INPUT	1
Sabbatical	C		.Spring	4	5.633803	INPUT	1
Sabbatical	C		.Year	3	4.225352	INPUT	1
Year	C		.2001-2002	24	33.80282	INPUT	1
Year	C		.2002-2003	24	33.80282	INPUT	1
Year	C		.2003-2004	23	32.39437	INPUT	1

The different observations for each class variable are listed, along with the frequency of each possible outcome. There are 59 values of **None** for the variable Sabbatical compared to 3 values for the year and 9 values for a semester, either fall or spring. In addition, consider the frequency for faculty rank. The total number of faculty members appears to be 71. However, because the data cover three years, it is clear that there are duplicates. For this reason, the percentages are more reliable. The percentage is given along with the frequency.

Output 1.8 Summary Statistics for Interval Variables

VARIABLE	LABEL OF F...	MEAN	STDDEV	Non Missing	Missing	Min	Median	Max	Abs C.V.	Coefficient ...	Sign	Ordered Inp...
Preparations	Preparations	1	2	71	0	0	0	10	2.835624	2.835624+		1
Student_Sup...	Student Supe...	1	3	71	0	0	0	12	2.009922	2.009922+		2
Administration	Administration	8	16	71	0	0	0	60	1.896884	1.896884+		3
Large_Lecture	Large Lecture	1	1	71	0	0	0	2	1.594357	1.594357+		4
Calculus...	# Calculus C...	1	1	71	0	0	1	3	1.076514	1.076514+		5
_Service	% Service	20	16	71	0	0	15	70	0.795939	0.795939+		6
_Prof__Acti...	% Prof# Acti...	39	21	71	0	10	32	100	0.529042	0.529042+		7
_Courses	% Courses	39	17	71	0	0	45	66	0.427766	0.427766+		8
_Instruction	% Instruction	42	17	71	0	0	50	66	0.406685	0.406685+		9
Number_of_...	Number of C...	3	1	71	0	0	4	5	0.40144	0.40144+		10

According to the summary values, the mean instruction is 41.6%, but the median is 50%. This indicates that there are a few faculty members with reduced instructional workloads of less than 50% who skew the mean downward. Similarly, the mean number of courses is equal to 3.10, but the median is equal to 5, reinforcing the fact that a small number of faculty members teach fewer courses compared to the majority.

Note that the Faculty variable is listed as an interval variable, with a mean and a standard deviation. However, numbers were used to mask faculty identity. Therefore, the level of that variable should have been changed to nominal and was erroneously left as interval. The level of the variable can be changed by returning to the data set node and selecting **Edit Variables** (Display 1.23).

Display 1.23 Changing Variable Roles

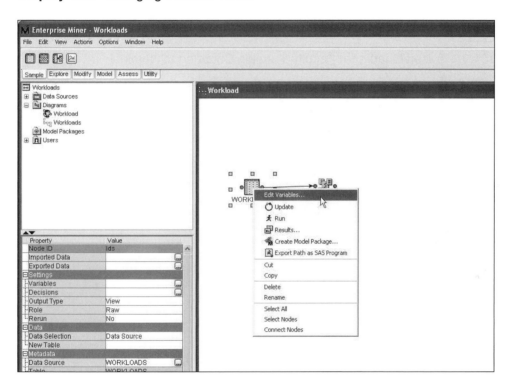

Selecting **Edit Variables** brings up Display 1.24.

Display 1.24 Edit Variables

Name	Role	Level	Report	Order	Drop	Lower Limit	Upper Limit	Type	Label	Format
Administration	Input	Interval	No		No			N	Administration	
Faculty_	Input	Nominal	No		No			N	Faculty	
Large_Lecture	Input	Interval	No		No			N	Large Lecture	
Number_of_Courses	Input	Interval	No		No			N	Number of Co	
Preparations	Input	Interval	No		No			N	Preparations	
Rank	Input	Nominal	No		No			C	Rank	$9.0
Sabbatical	Input	Nominal	No		No			C	Sabbatical	$6.0
Student_Supervision	Input	Interval	No		No			N	Student Supe	
Year	Input	Nominal	No		No			C	Year	$9.0
__Calculus_Courses	Input	Interval	No		No			N	# Calculus Co	
__Courses	Input	Interval	No		No			N	% Courses	
__Instruction	Input	Interval	No		No			N	% Instruction	
__Prof__Activity	Input	Interval	No		No			N	% Prof# Activit	
__Service	Input	Interval	No		No			N	% Service	

Right-click **Level** for **Faculty_** to change it from **Interval** to **Nominal** (Display 1.25).

Display 1.25 Changing Levels

Name	Role	Level	Report	Order	Drop	Lower
Administration	Input	Interval	No		No	.
Faculty_	Input	Nominal ⌄	No		No	.
Large_Lecture	Input	Unary	No		No	.
Number_of_Courses	Input	Binary	No		No	.
Preparations	Input	Nominal	No		No	.
Rank	Input	Ordinal	No		No	.
Sabbatical	Input	Interval	No		No	.
Student_Supervision	Input	Interval	No		No	.

Once this is changed, running the StatExplore node produces the results shown in Output 1.9.

Output 1.9 Revised Chart after Faculty Variable Changed to Nominal

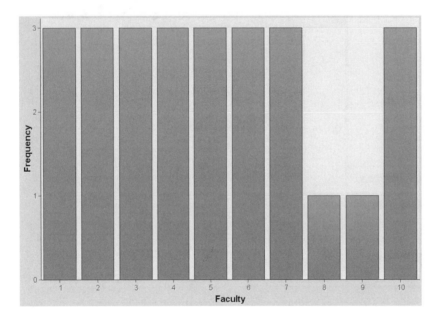

The first 10 faculty members are listed for all three years; faculty members identified as numbers 8 and 9 have two years with no teaching responsibilities.

Only the first 10 faculty members are shown in the chart. By moving the cursor to the right of 10, the remaining faculty members are shown (Output 1.10).

Output 1.10 Complete Bar Chart of the Faculty Variable

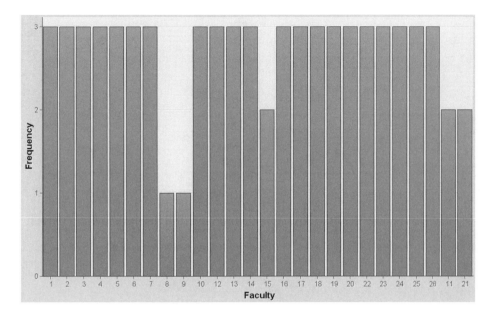

This chart indicates that there are three faculty members with no teaching responsibilities for one of the three years depicted. You will use the MultiPlot node next to examine the variables in the data set (Display 1.26).

Display 1.26 MultiPlot Node Icons in Diagram Space

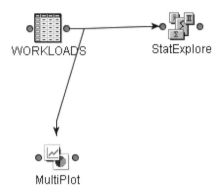

Options for the node appear in the lower left-hand corner of the window. In particular, there are options for the types of charts that can be displayed (Display 1.27).

Display 1.27 Options for Charts Using the MultiPlot Node

Property	Value
Node ID	Plot
Imported Data	
Exported Data	
Variables	
Type of Charts	Bar Charts
⊟Bar Chart Options	Bar Charts
Graph Orientation	Scatter Plots
Include Missing Values	Both
Interval Target Charts	Mean
Show Values	Yes
Statistic	Freq
Numeric Threshold	20
⊟Scatter Options	
Confidence Interval	Yes
Regression Equation	No
Regression Type	Linear
⊟Status	
Time of Creation	6/27/06 8:10 PM
Run Id	
Last Error	
Last Status	
Needs Updating	Yes
Needs to Run	Yes
Time of Last Run	
Run Duration	
Grid Host	

Both bar charts and scatter plots are available. The default is the bar chart.

To examine the workloads data, bar charts were used. There are a total of 14 charts (Output 1.11 through 1.17).

Output 1.11 First Two Charts for the First Two Variables in the Data Set

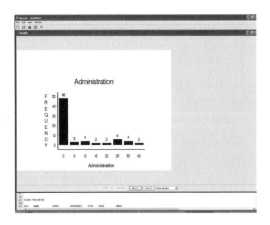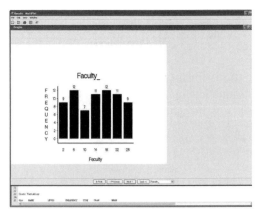

It is clear from the bar charts in Output 1.11 that most faculty members have no administrative responsibilities (a total of 48 are in the first bar). Those who do have administrative responsibilities show considerable variability in the assigned workload. Even though the variable, Faculty, has been changed to Nominal, it is still represented in a bar chart. The chart for faculty members provides no meaningful information at this point.

Output 1.12 Charts 3 and 4 for the Large_Lecture and Number_of_Courses Variables

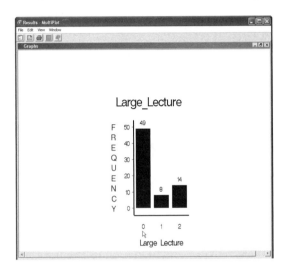
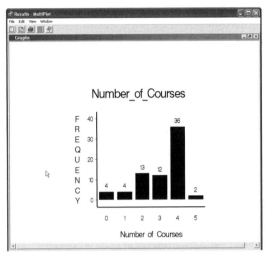

Chart 3 demonstrates that only a few faculty members teach large lecture courses with 150 or more students, with the majority teaching none. Of those teaching large lectures, almost twice as many teach two large lecture courses (14) as teach one (8). For the number of courses taught, most faculty members teach four courses in a year (two per semester). However, the graph also shows that many teach reduced loads of less than four. Only two faculty members teach more than the standard load of four courses.

Output 1.13 Charts 5 and 6 for the Preparations and Rank Variables

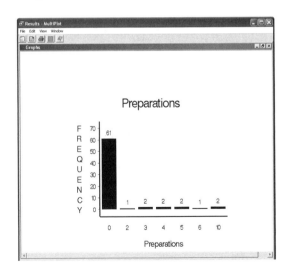
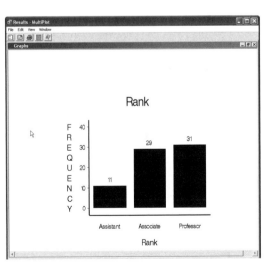

It is not common for faculty members to allocate a percentage of their workload to new course preparation. This allocation is reasonable because few courses taught in any semester are new. However, some faculty members receive time for new course preparation if they have never taught the course before. The Rank variable demonstrates what the frequency summary statistic already indicated: there are far fewer assistant rank faculty members compared to those of associate or full rank. Faculty members in this department are clearly aging.

Output 1.14 Charts 7 and 8 for the Sabbatical and Student_Supervision Variables

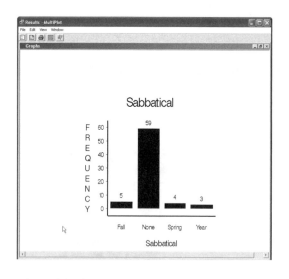
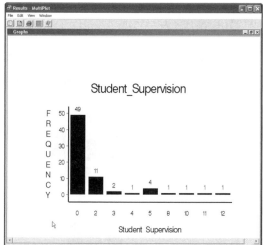

The Sabbatical variable is also nominal. The chart clearly indicates that most faculty members are not taking a sabbatical. The Student_Supervision variable offers more interesting information. Most faculty members are not working with any students on independent study or theses. However, a small number of faculty members are very active in working with students. The workload for supervision is decidedly skewed.

Output 1.15 Charts 9 and 10 for the Year and _Calculus_Courses Variables

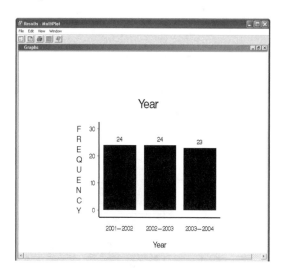
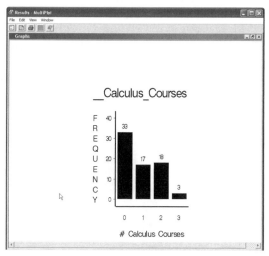

Chart 9 indicates that there is one less observation for 2003–2004 compared to the other two years, demonstrating a reduction in the number of full-time faculty. Chart 10 indicates that many faculty members teach at least one calculus course during an academic year. Slightly more teach two calculus courses during the year.

Output 1.16 Charts 11 and 12 for the _Courses and _Instruction Variables

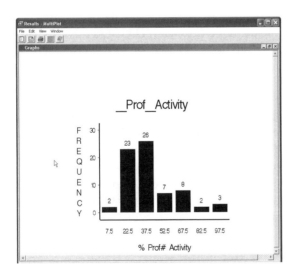
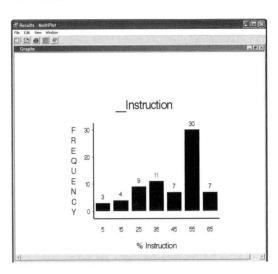

It is useful to compare courses with instruction side-by-side. The shape of the distributions differs somewhat. Therefore, some faculty members have additional instructional responsibilities that are not related to teaching courses compared to other faculty members. The peak or mode for instructional activity occurs at the 55% level for instruction and at the 55% level for courses, indicating that most faculty members have no additional instructional responsibilities other than teaching.

Output 1.17 Charts 13 and 14 for the _Prof_Activity and _Service Variables

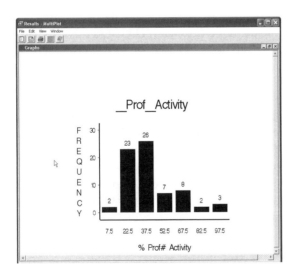
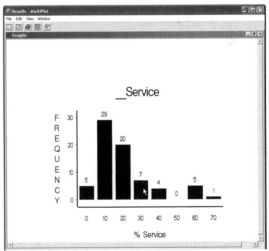

Professional activity and service have similar distributional shapes but different scales. Faculty members generally have more time allocated for research activities than for service activities. A few faculty members have large time allocations (above 50%).

Why is there so much variability in workload assignments, especially for faculty members of similar ranks? Other areas to investigate include whether there is a shift over the three-year time frame or if some of the variables are related to each other. These questions are explored in more detail in later chapters.

It is important to note that the StatExplore and MultiPlot nodes are tools to explore the data. It is up to you to use the tools and to interpret the findings. The more you are aware of domain knowledge, the more information you can extract from the data. It is particularly difficult, if not impossible, to attempt to interpret the results of a data mining investigation without any domain knowledge.

1.5 Presenting Additional SAS Enterprise Miner Icons

It is always possible to find patterns in the data. For example, flip a coin 10 times and suppose it comes up H, H, H, H, H, T, T, T, T, T. Without any attempt to verify the pattern of 5 heads followed by 5 tails, it is possible (although not valid) to conclude that every time a coin is flipped 10 times, the same pattern will occur. It is a conclusion that is easily contradicted if the coin is flipped several more times. Although this example seems somewhat absurd, other patterns seem to be accepted by many people with even less justification. Pattern recognition without validation is a reason that data mining as a method was often disparaged in statistical training.

Therefore, it is strongly recommended that you partition the data routinely into three data sets: training, validation, and testing. The training data set defines the model in SAS Enterprise Miner 5.2. The validation data set iteratively ensures that the developed model fits a fresh data set. Once the model is completed, the testing data set makes a final comparison. Because the division of a data set is so crucial to validation of the process, the software is set up so that splitting the data set into three components is almost automatic.

For a given target value, the accuracy of the final model is initially judged by the misclassification rate, where misclassification occurs when the predicted target value is not equal to the actual target value. There are additional diagnostics in the software that are discussed later.

Another difference between traditional statistics and data mining is that there are often many different models that can be used to investigate the data. Instead of choosing just one model to define a specific *p*-value, many different models are used and compared. Assessment methods have been developed to make these comparisons using the training, validation, and testing methodology.

Another important component of SAS Enterprise Miner 5.2 is the ability to score data. Scoring relates the predicted value to the actual value, and the closeness of one to the other can be examined using other statistical techniques. Scoring is particularly important when examining the likelihood of a customer making a particular purchase and the amount of the purchase. In this case, scoring assigns a level of importance to a customer. For wireless phone service, churn (meaning that a customer decides to switch phone providers) is important; the provider wants to predict in advance those who are likely to churn in order to give those customers incentives to stay. How can a business predict the likelihood of churn to offer incentives to prevent it? Scoring provides a means of making such predictions.

A number of icons on the **Sample** and **Modify** tabs are useful in investigating data. The Partition icon (Display 1.28) is extremely important and should be used almost routinely, particularly with very large data sets. This icon divides the data into three sets: train, validate, and test. For many of the models in the software, the training data set initially defines the model; the validation data set tests the model in an iterative process with the training set. The testing data set examines the overall accuracy of the model once it is complete.

Display 1.28 Partition Icon to Divide the Data Set

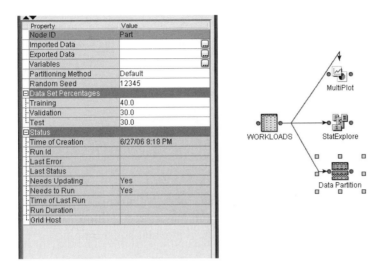

In the left-hand window, the defaults are 40% training, 30% validation, and 30% testing. These defaults can be modified by moving the cursor and changing the values.

Unless there is a good reason to change them, the defaults should be used to partition the data. The Drop icon (Display 1.29) allows you to remove specific variables from consideration as input or target variables. Specific variables might be used or dropped as models are developed to predict outcomes. While the initial list of variables might have 100 inputs, you might need to focus on just 10 for the model. In that case, the remaining 90 can be dropped for the remaining part of the analysis.

Display 1.29 Drop Icon

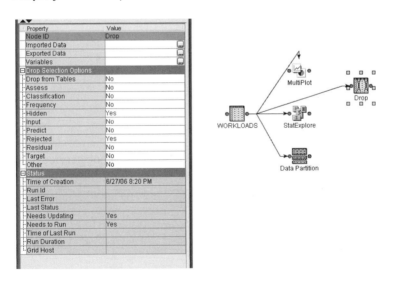

When the Drop icon is highlighted in the Diagram window, the option to drop variables is listed in the left-hand window. The same list appears by right-clicking the Drop icon to Select **Edit Variables** (Display 1.30).

Display 1.30 Drop Variables

Name	Drop	Role	Level	Type	Order	Label	Format	Informat	Length	Lower Limit
Administration	Default	Input	Interval	N		Administration			8	
Faculty_	Default	Input	Nominal	N		Faculty			8	
Large_Lecture	Default	Input	Interval	N		Large Lecture			8	
Number_of_Courses	Default	Input	Interval	N		Number of Co			8	
Preparations	Default	Input	Interval	N		Preparations			8	
Rank	No	Input	Nominal	C		Rank	$9.0	$9.0	9	
Sabbatical	Yes	Input	Nominal	C		Sabbatical	$6.0	$6.0	6	
Student_Supervision	Default	Input	Interval	N		Student Super			8	
Year	Default	Input	Nominal	C		Year	$9.0	$9.0	9	
__Calculus_Courses	Default	Input	Interval	N		# Calculus Cc			8	
__Courses	Default	Input	Interval	N		% Courses			8	
__Instruction	Default	Input	Interval	N		% Instruction			8	
__Prof__Activity	Default	Input	Interval	N		% Prof# Activit			8	
__Service	Default	Input	Interval	N		% Service			8	

Note that a **Drop** column has been added. Right-clicking any variable allows **Default** to change to **Yes** or **No** depending on whether you want to drop or keep the variable. The default indicates the assignment from the initial data set. You can use the Transform icon (Display 1.31) to modify the variables in the data set.

Display 1.31 Transform Icon

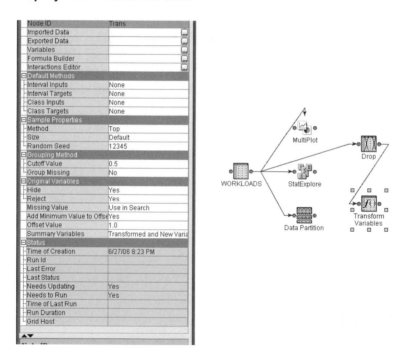

For example, interval variables can be divided into categories of values. Different options appear in the left-hand window for interval and class variables (Display 1.32).

Display 1.32 Options for Interval Inputs

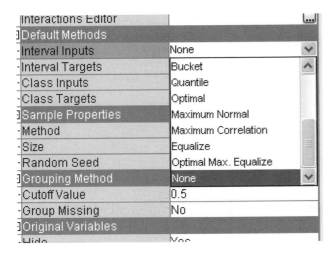

You can standardize the variables or block them into classes. The options for class inputs are listed in Display 1.33.

You can use a variety of methods to block interval inputs into categories. The default is **None**. The quintile method creates five different classes with approximately 20% of the data values in each class. It might, for example, be useful to take the variable, Age, and divide it into five classes: children, young adults, middle age, retirement age, and oldest. Examine the different methods to see what classes are defined for the variables. Target interval variables, on the other hand, are standardized to mean 0 and variance 1.

Display 1.33 Options for Class Inputs

Default Methods	
Interval Inputs	None
Interval Targets	None
Class Inputs	None
Class Targets	Group rare levels
Sample Properties	Dummy Indicators
Method	None
Size	Default
Random Seed	12345
Grouping Method	
Cutoff Value	0.5
Group Missing	No

The software automatically groups rare classes as they occur. It also creates dummy indicators if needed. Examine the data by changing options. Again, the default is to use none. However, if all of the defaults are none, there is no reason to use this node. Therefore, the transform node is used only if some of the defaults are changed to actually transform some variables.

One transformation that is of interest is the creation of interaction terms. If the Interaction Editor is selected in the transform node options, then a popup window appears (Display 1.34).

Display 1.34 Interaction Editor

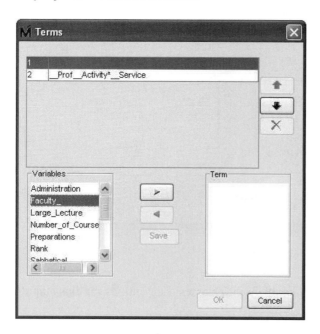

Once more than two terms are entered and saved in the Term window, they can be crossed by highlighting the terms to be crossed and clicking the cross button. Once completed, click **OK**.

The different input variables can interact with each other. For example, a faculty member with a high service component probably has a lower teaching level. Similarly, the number of courses can be related to the level of research. Interactions can be used to investigate these relationships.

To demonstrate the use of the Transformation icon, you standardize all interval inputs in the Workloads data set, and combine rare occurrences in the class variables. Also, you examine the interaction of professional activity and service. The results after running the Transformation icon appear in Output 1.18 and 1.19.

Output 1.18 Results of Transformation Node

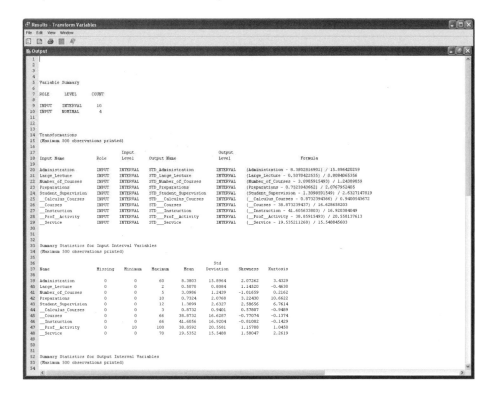

Each variable name is now preceded by STD_. The level is given as interval for the transformed variables. Use the **View** menu to display summary statistics. The output screen is expanded in Output 1.19.

Output 1.19 Transformation Output

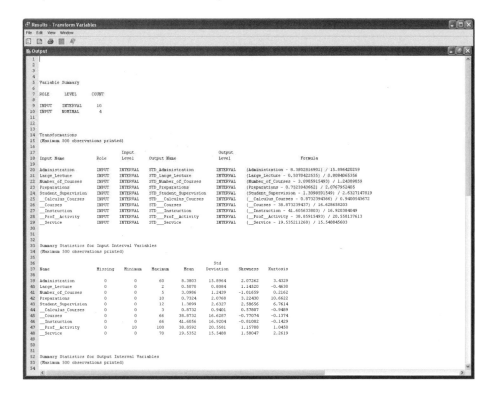

The transformation formulas are provided in the output. The interaction is also identified. To examine the interaction in more detail, connect a MultiPlot to the Transformation icon and plot the interaction (Output 1.20).

Output 1.20 MultiPlot Result after Transformation

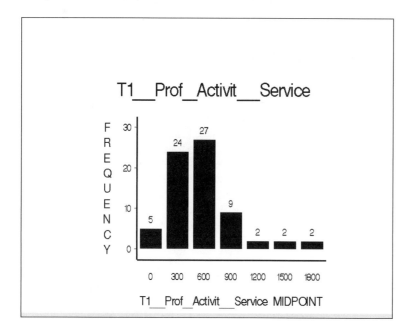

Because the scale for both professional activity and service is from 1–100, the scale for the interaction is clearly the product of the two and goes from 0 to 2,000. Note that very few faculty members have both high service and high professional activity.

Two additional icons are discussed here: Filter and Impute (Display 1.35). The purpose of the Filter icon is to remove *outliers*, or extreme values, in the data.

Display 1.35 Filter and Impute Icons

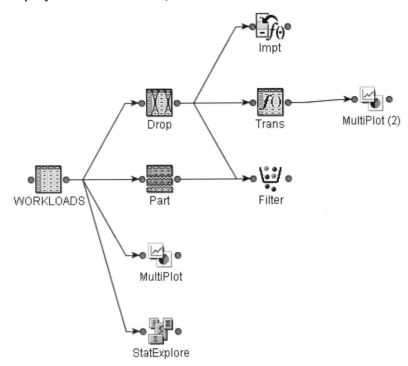

The Impute icon replaces missing values. The default is to substitute the mean for interval variables that are missing and to substitute the most frequent value for nominal data. The default results for the Filter icon are given in Output 1.21.

Be careful when using the Impute icon. If too many missing values are replaced, the outcome can become biased. If missing values are not somewhat randomized throughout the input values, the results can also become biased. Use imputation if the missing values are randomly scattered throughout the input and consist of 5% of the total number of values for any one input variable. Otherwise, imputation should be used with extreme caution. A number of imputation methods are available in SAS/STAT software. See the SAS/STAT documentation for more information.

Output 1.21 Filtered Results

```
62
63  Statistics for Original and Filtered Data
64  (Maximum 500 observations printed)
65
66  Data Role=TRAIN Variable=Administration
67
68  Statistics           Original      Filtered
69
70  Non Missing          71.0000       64.0000
71  Number Missing        0.0000        0.0000
72  Minimum               0.0000        0.0000
73  Maximum              60.0000       50.0000
74  Mean                  8.3803        6.6406
75  Std Deviation        15.8964       12.6947
76  Skewness              2.0726        2.2015
77
78
79  Data Role=TRAIN Variable=Large_Lecture
80
81  Statistics           Original      Filtered
82
83  Non Missing          71.0000       64.0000
84  Number Missing        0.0000        0.0000
85  Minimum               0.0000        0.0000
86  Maximum               2.0000        2.0000
87  Mean                  0.5070        0.5313
88  Std Deviation         0.8084        0.8159
89  Skewness              1.1452        1.0730
90
91
92  Data Role=TRAIN Variable=Number_of_Courses
93
94  Statistics           Original      Filtered
95
96  Non Missing          71.0000       64.0000
97  Number Missing        0.0000        0.0000
98  Minimum               0.0000        0.0000
99  Maximum               5.0000        5.0000
100 Mean                  3.0986        3.2500
101 Std Deviation         1.2439        1.1547
102 Skewness             -1.0166       -1.2771
103
104
```

A total of seven observations have been filtered. For the Administration variable, the maximum has been cut from 60 to 50, while reducing the mean from 8.38 to 6.64. Other variables also appear in the output.

Filtering variables reduces the impact of outliers on the variable means. In this case, the highest level of service is nearly 100%; no other value comes close. You decide whether to filter outliers. An optimal method is to perform the analyses with and without filtering to see if the outcomes are considerably different.

Note that SAS Enterprise Miner 5.2 creates new data sets as it makes the changes listed in this section. To examine these data sets, you must identify them. Consider again the diagram discussed in this section (Display 1.36). Moving the cursor to any line connecting nodes indicates what data sets are passed from one node to the next. In this example, the line connecting the Partition and Filter nodes is highlighted. On the left-hand side, three data sets are identified: EMWS.Trans_TRAIN, EMWS.Trans_VALIDATE, and EMWS.Trans_TEST. Refer to these data sets in a SAS Code node.

Display 1.36 Identifying Data Sets Passing from One Node to the Next

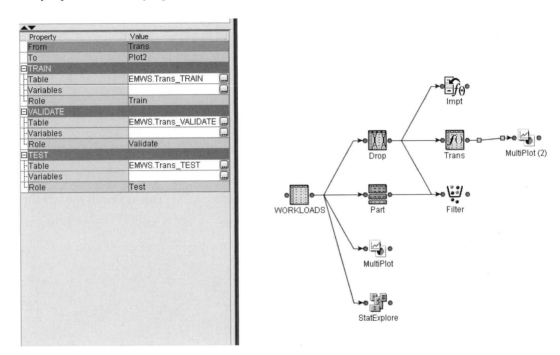

Anytime you want to examine databases created by one node, connect a SAS Code node to it, and then click on the connection.

Basic options appear on the left-hand side when the node is highlighted. To find the advanced options, select View ▶ Property Sheet ▶ Advanced (Display 1.37).

Display 1.37 Selecting Advanced Options

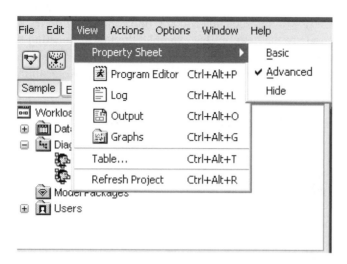

Once you have mastered the basics, you can modify some of the advanced options to see their impact.

You can adjust the diagram by selecting **Layout** (Display 1.38). This is one of the advantages of using a Java interface.

Display 1.38 Automatic Adjustment in Diagram

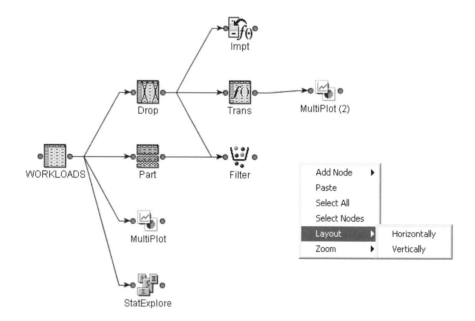

1.6 Exercises

You should investigate the Workload data set using the SAS Enterprise Miner 5.2 nodes discussed in this chapter. A second data set is provided, called Student_Survey. The variables in the list correspond to the order of the questions asked in the following survey. The variable names correspond to the questions in the survey. However, all possible responses to question 1 are listed as separate variables with a binary response. Open-ended questions were not included in the data set. Question 19 is an interval response; all others are ordinal or nominal responses. This data set is used in subsequent chapters. Therefore, you should become familiar with it by using the StatExplore and MultiPlot icons to examine the data.

As a first step, create this file as a data source in the project.

Course_____   Section _____

1. The areas of mathematics which interest me are (Check all that apply):

    _____Pure mathematics

    _____Applied mathematics

    _____Abstract algebra

    _____Number theory

    _____Topology

    _____Real analysis

    _____Discrete mathematics

    _____Differential equations

    _____Actuarial science

    _____Probability

    _____Statistics

2. I am currently enrolled in the following mathematics classes:
    _____.

3. The mathematics courses I would like to take in the spring and fall semesters are:
    _____.

4. Maple was used in the following classes:
    _____.

5. Other computer software or calculators were used in the following classes:
    _____.

6. I want [more, less *(circle one)*] use of the computer software in class.

7. The computer lab taught in calculus was [very useful, somewhat useful, of little use, totally useless, I am just starting calculus].

8. The computer lab in calculus was [very organized and well coordinated with class material, somewhat organized and partially coordinated with class material].

9. I would prefer that the applied mathematics courses focus on [concepts, computation]. Currently, they focus on [concepts, computation].

10. *(agree, disagree)* I would like to get a BS degree in mathematics.

11. *(agree, disagree)* I could not get the classes I needed to fulfill an applications area for the BS degree.

12. *(agree, disagree)* The courses I couldn't get for my applications area were in the mathematics department.

13. *(agree, disagree)* The courses I couldn't get for my applications area were in other departments.

14. I am working toward a BA degree and the reason is_____.

15. I am no longer working toward a mathematics major because _____.

16. I do not want to major in mathematics because _____.

17. *(agree, disagree)* A mathematics major is prepared only to teach after graduation.

18. *(agree, disagree)* I would like to do a co-op in an area business.

19. In comparison with other students in mathematics, I think my skills and knowledge are [very weak, weak, average, strong, very strong].

20. I usually spend _____ hours per week studying mathematics.

21. Course instructors [rarely, occasionally, frequently, usually, always] expect me to know things that were never previously covered in class.

22. Course instructors [rarely, occasionally, frequently, usually, always] expect me to know things that I remember seeing in a previous class but have forgotten.

23. There is [way too much, too much, about right, too little, way too little] material taught in mathematics courses.

24. The workload required is [way too much, too much, about right, too little, way too little].

25. *(agree, disagree)* I understand the links between the different mathematics courses in the program.

26. *(agree, disagree)* I can see the links between course content and current research in mathematics.

27. A course designed to teach how to do mathematical proofs is [of great value, of some value, of little value, of no value] to me.

28. My work habits and study methods [are inadequate, are adequate, are more than adequate] to really succeed in studying mathematics.

The variables in the data set are listed in Table 1.3.

Table 1.3 Variable Names in Survey

Variable Name	Corresponding Question in Survey
Student_Type	No question
CourseLevel	Condensed from initial question on course
Course	Initial question on course
Section	Initial question on section
Pure	Question 1
Applied	Question 1
AbstractAlgebra	Question 1
NumberTheory	Question 1
Topology	Question 1
RealAnalysis	Question 1
DiscreteMathematics	Question 1
DifferentialEquations	Question 1
ActuarialScience	Question 1
Probability	Question 1
Statistics	Question 1
_enrolled	Question 2
_wanttoenroll	Count of courses in Question 3
_maple	Question 4
_othersoftware	Question 5
Usecomputer	Question 6
Calculusmaple	Question 7
Qualitylab	Question 8
Appliedmathdoes	Question 9, first response
Appliedmathshould	Question 9, second response
BS	Question 10
Notgetclasses	Question 11
Notgetmath	Question 12

(continued)

Table 1.3 Variable Names in Survey *(continued)*

Variable Name	Corresponding Question in Survey
BA	Question 14
Quitmajor	Question 15
Notmajor	Question 16
Teachmajor	Question 17
Intern	Question 18
Comparestudents	Question 19
Hours	Question 20
Expectknownever	Question 21
Expectknowprevious	Question 22
Toomuch	Question 23
Links	Question 25
Linksresearch	Question 26
Proofs	Question 27
Workhabits	Question 28
Coursestaken	No question
Coursesnotscheduled	No question
FormNumber	No question-identifier

Note that Question 13 is omitted from the data set because the respondent was asked to write a list of courses. Therefore, it was not used when the data set was created.

There are many missing values in the data set, so imputation is required. Some errors require auditing of the data. Because most variables are similarly scaled, standardization is not required (unless the Hours variable is included in an analysis). There are approximately 190 observations, so it is reasonable to partition the data set.

You should examine the results and write a brief summary of the results and conclusions reached by examining the data using the basic summary methods outlined in this chapter.

1.7 References

Ferguson, Mike. 1997. "Evaluating and Selecting Data Mining Tools." *InfoDB* 11(2): 1–10.

Hand, David J. 1998. "Data Mining Statistics and More?" *The American Statistician* 52(2): 112–118.

Lambert, Bob. 2002. "Data Warehousing Fundamentals: What You Need to Know to Succeed." *DM Review*. Available at www.dmreview.com/master.cfm?NavID=55&EdID=1313.

Data Visualization

Data mining techniques tend to focus on estimation and pattern recognition; statistical methods tend to focus on *inference*, formulating a hypothesis, and then testing it using statistical methods. When there are hundreds and thousands of variables, you first need to understand the data set. Without an initial understanding of the data, it is impossible to determine where to focus effort in an investigation of the data.

One major estimation technique is visualization. In many cases, a simple graph can convey considerable information about the data. With visualization and data summaries (discussed in Chapter 4), you can gain real insight into the data and determine important issues that need additional exploration.

2.1 Using the StatExplore Node

The StatExplore node is a multipurpose tool used to examine distributions and basic statistics such as means and variances for the variables in the data set. To examine a data set that exists in the project, right-click the data set name in **Data Sources** in the project window and select **Explore** (Display 2.1). The Explorer node was discussed briefly in Chapter 1. This chapter focuses on the software's graphics capabilities.

Display 2.1 Exploring the Data Sets

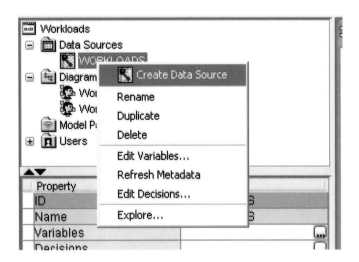

Selecting **Explore** produces the screen shown in Display 2.2. This screen includes a view table and some basic information about the variables in the data set.

Display 2.2 Basic Information

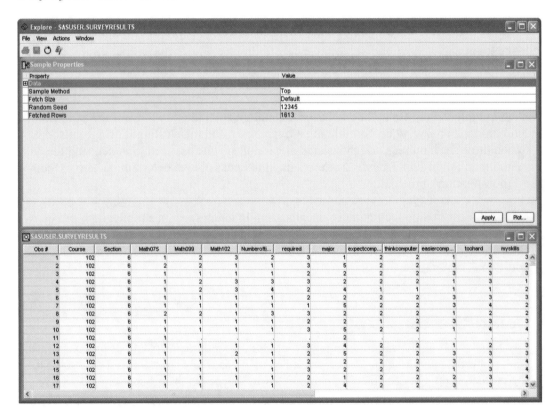

Clicking **Plot** (on the far right of Display 2.3) generates a list of choices for graphing. Bar charts, scatter plots, and basic tables are available using this selection.

Display 2.3 Graphing Options

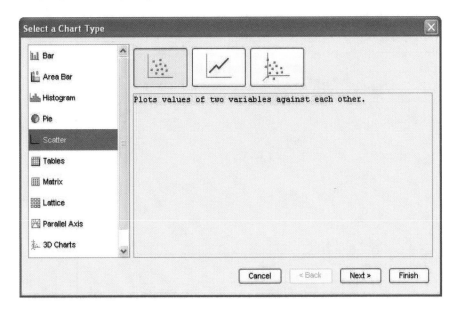

Based on these choices, investigate the student survey data set presented in the exercise in Chapter 1. Consider first the area bar chart (Display 2.4).

Display 2.4 Area Bar Chart Choices for *X* and *Y* Values

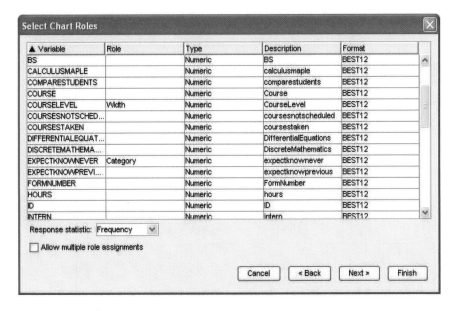

The area bar chart requires a width and category variable. Only numeric variables can be used. The screen lists default values for width and category, which you can change. Left-clicking allows you to change the variables for width and category. In this example, the **CourseLevel** variable is chosen for width and the **Expectknownever** variable is chosen for the category. This category variable charts responses to the following survey question: "Course instructors [rarely, occasionally, frequently, usually, always] expect me to know things that were never previously covered in class." Select the variables and then click **Next**. You can limit the variable categories using a Where clause (Display 2.5).

Display 2.5 Where Clause in Plots

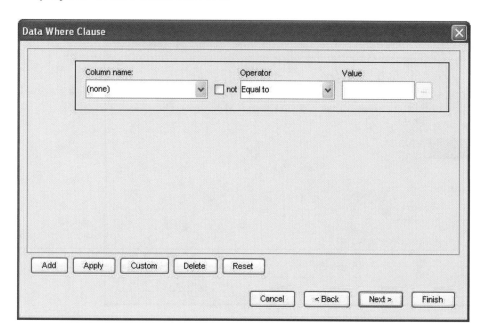

You can also use the drop-down list to identify the variable and the operator to filter the data. You can access the drop-down menu by using the cursor to click the downward arrows. Some color schemes are available (Display 2.6 and Display 2.7). You can select from the list of color schemes. Once you have finished, click **Next** to continue.

Display 2.6 Color Choices

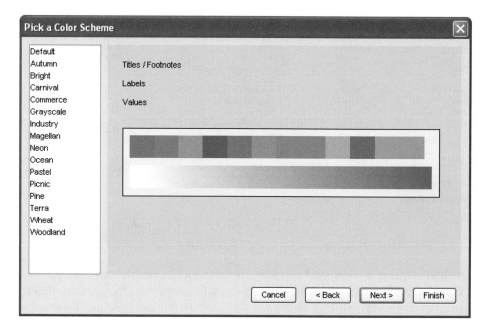

Next, you can label the chart by giving it a title, a legend name, and a footnote if desired (Display 2.7). In all cases, provide a title that is representative of the chart itself. In this example, the title is entered in the **Title** field. Output 2.1 shows the result.

Display 2.7 Labeling

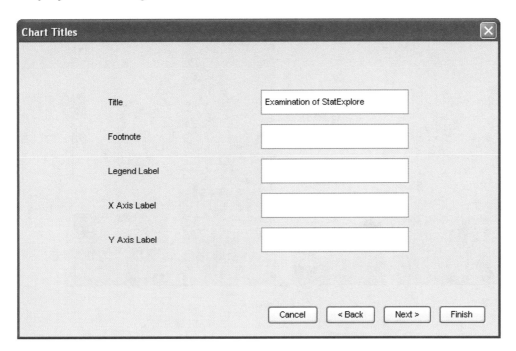

Output 2.1 Area Bar Chart

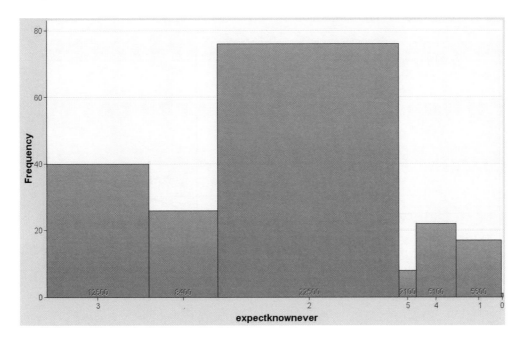

The width of the bar is determined by the value of the course level. The results indicate that the widest bar is for the response of **2**.

Compare the area bar chart to the more standard bar chart, which is another option available in the StatExplore node (Output 2.2). The area bar chart shows differences by area; the standard bar chart shows differences by length and equal widths.

Output 2.2 Bar Chart

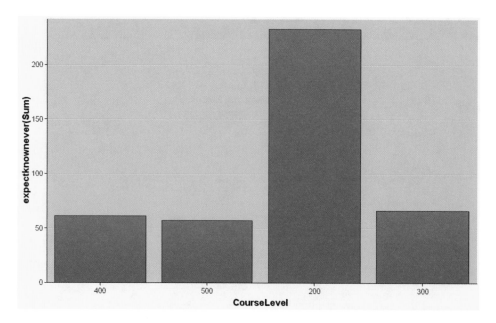

A line graph appears in Output 2.3; it is almost identical to the area bar chart, except for the shading in the area bar chart.

Output 2.3 Line Graph Representation

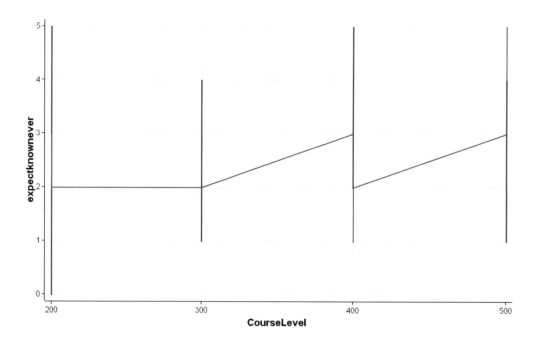

A pie chart appears in Output 2.4.

Four course levels are represented in the pie chart. The variables **Expectknownever** or **Course instructors [rarely, occasionally, frequently, usually, always] expect me to know things that were never previously covered in class** have a median value of 3 at the 200 level. The median value decreased to a value of 2 at the 300 level. The value 2 is also the median value at the 400 level. The maximum value is 5 at the 200 level, 4 at the 300 level, and 5 at the remaining two levels.

Output 2.4 Pie Chart

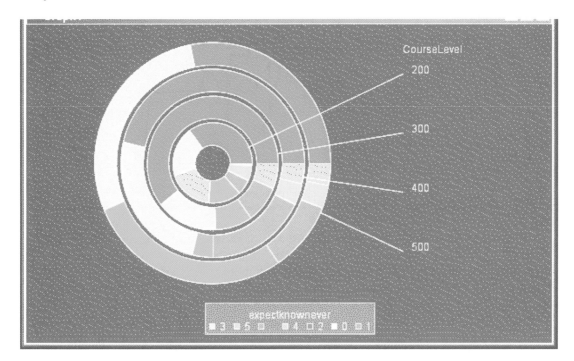

For the **Expectknownever** variable, a pie chart probably best visualizes the situation, showing a contrast across levels in the responses. The length of each colored segment can be compared by level. The red segment for the 300 level is more than half the circle; for the 200 level, it is considerably less than half the circle. Similarly, the orange segment for the 500 level is a much larger proportion of the circle than the 200, 300, or 400 levels. The pie chart enables you to compare each category more directly because there is a difference in the number of responses. It gives the proportion within each category. Area bar charts and line graphs are more appropriate for continuous data rather than the categorical data used in this example.

To show how these graphics are used for continuous data, graph the percentage of activity available in the Workloads data set discussed in Chapter 1 (Output 2.5). In this example, the *x*-axis is defined by the percentage of professional activity and the *y*-axis by the percentage of instruction. According to Output 2.5, one peak for professional activity occurs at 30%, with the percentage of instruction ranging from 40% to 60% around that peak. A second peak occurs around 70% professional activity, with a low range for the percentage of instruction. Faculty members in that segment of the graph have considerably lower percentages of instruction, ranging from 0 to 20%.

Output 2.5 Line Graph of Percentage of Effort of Professional Activity by Instruction

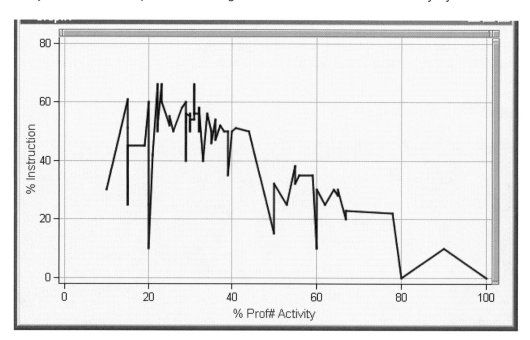

Bubble graphs (Output 2.6) allow you to see more variables simultaneously, as do matrix graphs (Output 2.6 and Output 2.7). In bubble graphs, shapes and sizes represent a third and fourth variable. In Output 2.6, both size and shape within the graph represent two variables: the continuous percentage of courses by size and the categorical rank by shape. Output 2.6 shows that assistant and full professors have the highest proportion of professional activity (60% and above), while associate professors tend to have 20% to 40% professional activity with higher levels of instruction.

Output 2.6 Bubble Graph of Instruction and Professional Activity

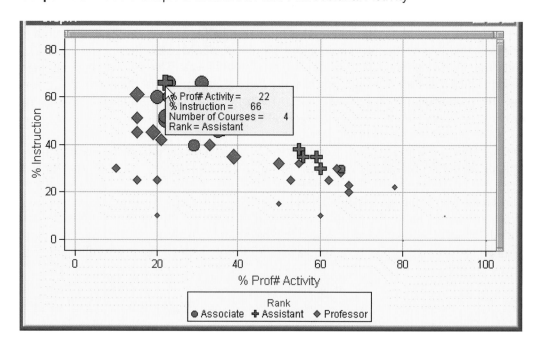

Output 2.7 shows a series of scatter plots that examine the variables two at a time. The diagonal gives the values for the *x*- and *y*-axes for each scatter plot. For example, in the first graph on the first line, the *y*-axis represents the percentage of instruction and the *x*-axis represents the percentage of professional activity. Thus, it depicts information also shown in the bubble graph. As professional activity increases, the instruction percentage decreases. There is a symmetry to the matrix plot because the variables in the *x*- and *y*-axes trade places. In the first plot in the second column, the *y*-axis represents instruction and the *x*-axis represents professional activity so that the two graphs are mirror images of each other.

Output 2.7 Matrix Graph of Three Types of Work

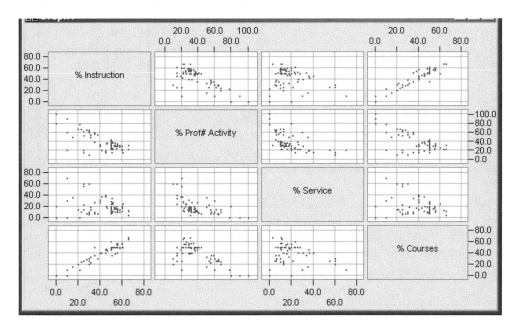

The lattice graph can be used with a variety of different plots. Output 2.8 shows the graph with a line plot. Output 2.9 shows a bar chart. The lattice plot uses three variables, showing the relationship of instruction to professional activity compared at each faculty rank. The graph shows that those with the rank of professor can vary considerably in their amount of professional activity; those at the associate and assistant rank seem to be in a similar range of instructional activity, with one outlier at the associate rank. Assistant professors, on the other hand, have higher values of professional activity, as do full professors.

Output 2.8 Lattice Graph with Line Plot

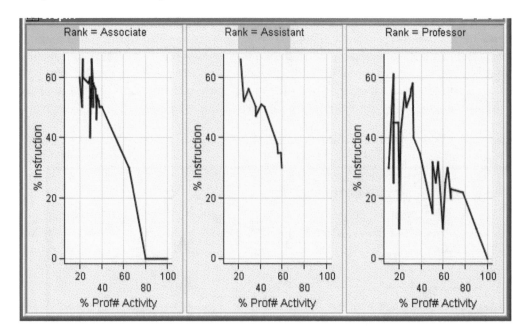

In Output 2.9, the value of the *y*-axis changes to the sum of instruction by faculty member. Because three years are represented in the data, the sum is the total instructional percentage over all three years. The *x*-axis represents the corresponding percentage of professional activity. It shows that assistant professors have higher rates of professional activity compared to associate professors.

Output 2.9 Lattice Graph with Bar Chart

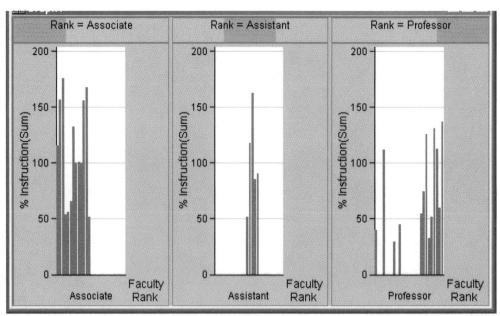

A graphic can show the relationship between variables, but it cannot identify why that relationship exists. You need to understand the domain to analyze the data completely. The Workloads data set is related to university activities. Domain knowledge indicates that assistant professors have reduced instructional workloads so that they can spend more time establishing research programs; once they advance to the level of associate rank, that reduction in the number of courses taught is no longer given since promotion is only expected for faculty who have established research programs. Domain knowledge indicates that only faculty members with continuing strong research programs are promoted to full professor. Many of those with strong research have research grants that allow them to *buy out* some of their teaching responsibilities in favor of heavier research loads. Buy out means that the department is reimbursed for 10% to 20% of a faculty member's salary in exchange for teaching one less course. In addition, domain knowledge can tell you that many full professors have administrative responsibilities that also buy out some of the instructional responsibilities.

2.2 Understanding Kernel Density Estimation

It is often assumed that the underlying distribution of a data sample is a bell-shaped (normal) curve. However, this assumption is generally valid only if the population is relatively homogeneous. Because the data sets used for data mining have a more heterogeneous population, the assumption of normality is not valid. For this reason, bar charts are often used to present the true distribution, as shown in Output 2.9. Another means of finding the true population distribution is by using the kernel density estimator, which can be considered a smoothed bar chart. As such, it is more versatile and more representative of a continuous population.

Consider the Workloads data set. Three items are of particular interest: the percentage allocated to instruction, the percentage allocated to professional activity, and the percentage allocated to service. The bar charts for these allocations appear in Figure 2.1.

Figure 2.1 Bar Charts of Workload Parameters

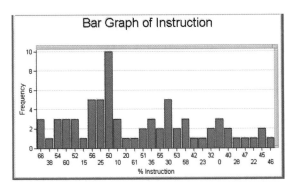

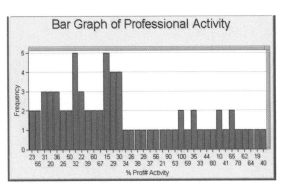

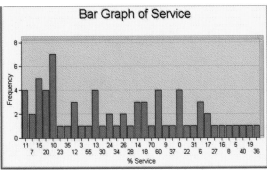

It is difficult to understand these three percentages by comparing the bar charts because they appear to be widely distributed, with several different peaks. Smoothing out the bar charts makes the distributions easier to understand. Figure 2.2 gives the kernel density estimates of these same parameters.

Figure 2.2 Kernel Density Estimates of Parameters

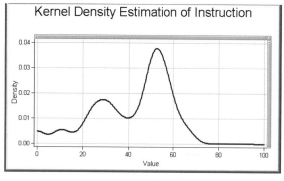

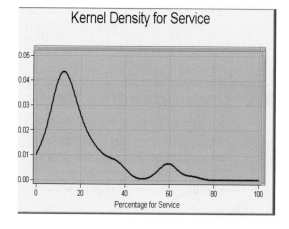

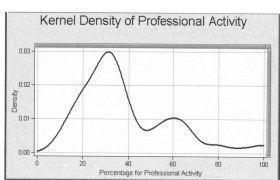

In each case, the peak, where most of the population is contained, is readily visible. For instruction, the highest peak occurs at about 55%, with a smaller peak at 30%. For professional activity, the primary peak is at 30%, with a secondary peak at 60%. Most faculty members report service around 15%. These peaks are much easier to see in the kernel density (or smoothed histogram) than they are in the bar charts in Figure 2.1.

Kernel density estimation allows graphs to be overlaid for comparison (Figure 2.3). It is not possible to overlay bar charts to convey meaningful information. As a result, kernel density provides better overall visualization.

Figure 2.3 Overlay of Kernel Density Estimators

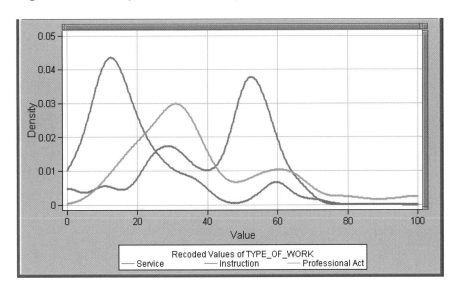

It is clear from this overlay that there is a shift in proportion of time from 15% for service to 30% for professional activity to 55% for instruction, giving a good indication of the priorities for a faculty member's time. Because the peak for professional activity is lower than the peak for the other two variables, there has to be more variability in professional activity compared to either instruction or service. That means that the graph for professional activity is slower to converge to the 0 value compared to the graphs for the other two variables.

Kernel density is not provided in a SAS Enterprise Miner node. Therefore, you must develop it in a SAS Code node (Display 2.8).

Display 2.8 SAS Code Node for Kernel Density Estimation

```
proc kde data=sasuser.transformsurvey;
   univar preference/gridl=0 gridu=10 out=sasuser.kdepreference1 bwm=2;
   run;
```

The following code appears in Display 2.8:

```
proc kde data=sasuser.transformsurvey;
  univar preference/gridl=0 gridu=10 out=sasuser.kdepreference1 bwm=2;
run;
```

The data must be stored in an output data set for each estimator; the results are entered into the project using **Create Data Source** and then examined using the StatExplore node (Display 2.9) and the scatter plot (line plot option). The Sasuser.Kdeservice data set contains four variables: **Count, Density, Value, Var**. The **Density** and **Value** variables are used for the *y*-axis and *x*-axis variables respectively in the line plot. The **Var** variable, which is the variable for the kernel density, and the **Count** variable can be disregarded.

Display 2.9 Explore Output Data

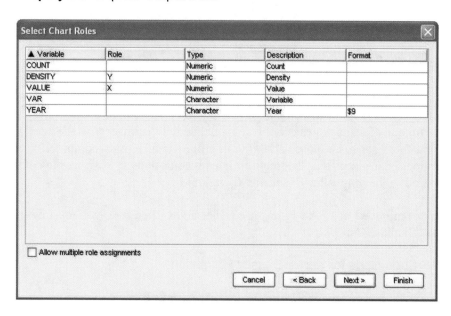

Run this code to find an optimal level of smoothing for the kernel density estimator. You can modify the level of smoothing by using the BWM=*constant* option:

```
proc kde data=sasuser.workloads;
  univar __service/gridl=0 gridu=100 bwm=2 out=sasuser.kdeservice;
run;
```

A constant value less than 1 increases the jaggedness in the curve; a constant value greater than 1 increases the smoothing. Figure 2.4 shows the resulting graph using different values of BWM. In Figure 2.4, a BWM value of 0.5 makes the curve too jagged; a BWM value of 4 makes it too smooth. For an optimal design, use a BWM value of 1 (the default) or 2. With a value of 2, the two peaks begin to merge into each other. You decide just how distinct to make the peaks in the representative graphic.

Figure 2.4 Changes in Smoothing Level

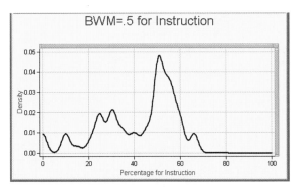

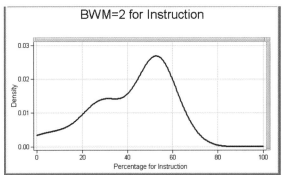

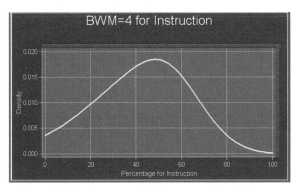

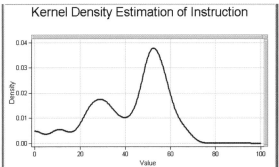

Another modification to the code allows you to investigate distributions by group, as follows:

```
proc sort data=sasuser.workloads;
   by year;
proc kde data=sasuser.workloads;
   univar __instruction/gridl=0 gridu=100;
   out=sasuser.kdeinstructionbyyear;
   by year;
run;
```

Before using the BY statement, you must sort the data by the appropriate variable. The **Year** variable is assigned the role of **Group** (Display 2.10) with the resulting graph shown in Output 2.10.

Display 2.10 Grouped Kernel Density Estimators

▲ Variable	Role	Type	Description	Format
COUNT		Numeric	Count	
DENSITY	Y	Numeric	Density	
VALUE	X	Numeric	Value	
VAR		Character	Variable	
YEAR	Group	Character	Year	$9

☐ Allow multiple role assignments

Cancel   < Back   Next >   Finish

Output 2.10 Grouped Kernel Density Graph

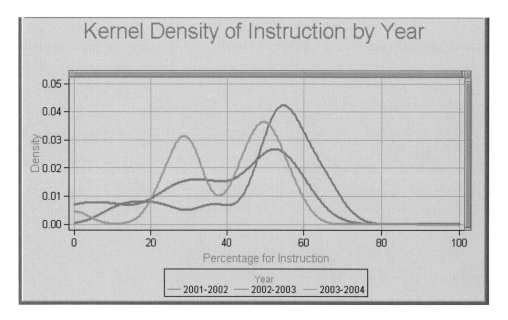

Notice that the curve for 2001–2002 has the right-most peak in the graph, indicating that the faculty had a greater percentage of instruction for that year compared to the others. In addition, a double peak is more apparent in 2003–2004, indicating that half the faculty members have a 45% teaching load while the other half have a 30% teaching assignment. The graph becomes a straight line at the 80% mark on the *x*-axis, which is why the *x*-axis should be truncated at that point. To see if the trend continues, additional data were collected for 2004–2005 and 2005–2006 on the percentage for courses (typically 10% less than the percentage for instruction). The result is given in Output 2.11.

Output 2.11 Additional Years in Grouped Kernel Density Graph for Courses

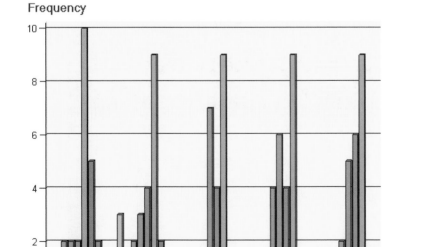

The graph for 2004–2005 is similar to that for 2003–2004, with double peaks indicating that there are two different directions in course assignments. However, for 2005–2006, there is just one peak at 40% but with a considerable amount of variance. This indicates that the allocation for instruction is continuing to decrease from the highest level in 2001–2002. Again, to show a contrast, a bar chart of the 5-year period appears in Output 2.12.

Output 2.12 Bar Chart of Percentage of Allocation for Courses

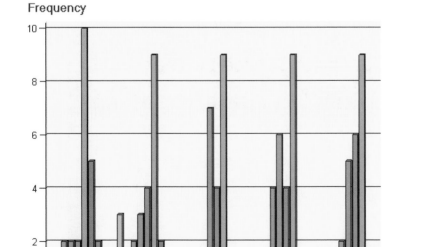

The shift downward is more difficult to see in this bar chart compared to the kernel density estimation. What can be seen is that the bar at 30% and the bar at 40% increase considerably from 2001–2002 to 2005–2006, without any real decrease in the bar at 50%.

Similar graphs were computed for the service and professional activity time allocations (Output 2.13 and Output 2.14). For professional activity, the peak remains at relatively the same place for all three years. However, the variability in 2003–2004 is much greater compared to 2001–2002. The same applies to the service percentages.

Output 2.13 Grouped Kernel Density Graph of Professional Activity

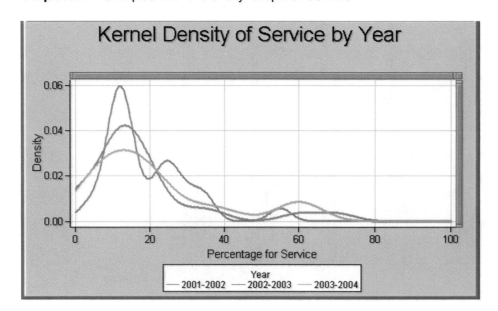

The value for 2001–2002 has the highest probability between 20% and 40% and the lowest probability of being greater than 50%. The value for 2003–2004 has the lowest probability between 20% and 40% and the highest probability between 50% and 80%.

Output 2.14 Grouped Kernel Density Graph of Service

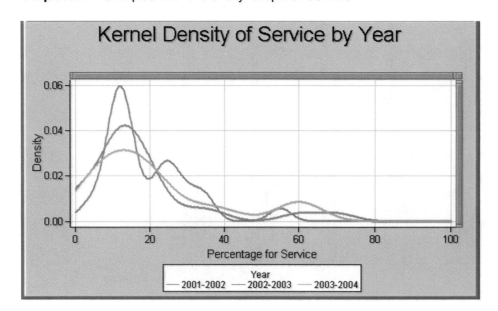

The proportion peaks for all three years at about 10%. The value for 2003–2004 has the highest probability of being between 50% and 70%.

2.3 Student Survey Example

Consider the data set provided in the exercise in Chapter 1. First, examine the **Applied** and **Pure** variables. With a bar chart, the results look similar for both variables. However, because the two variables are defined as interval, StatExplore provides summaries based upon that definition (Display 2.11 and Output 2.15).

Display 2.11 StatExplore Options for Interval Data

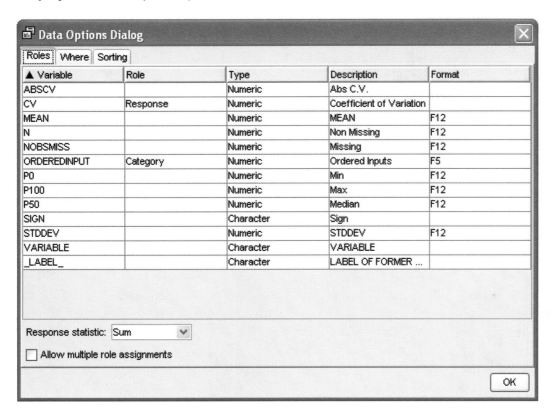

Output 2.15 Resulting Bar Chart for Interval Data

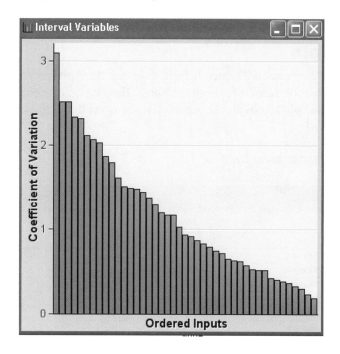

To improve the graphical display, change the variables to binary (Output 2.16).

Output 2.16 Bar Charts for Applied and Pure Variables when Defined as Binary

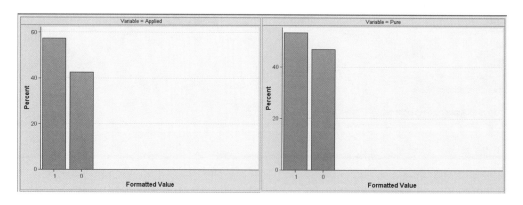

Similarly, preferences for different types of mathematics appear in Output 2.17 after changing each variables type to binary.

Output 2.17 Preferences for Types of Mathematics

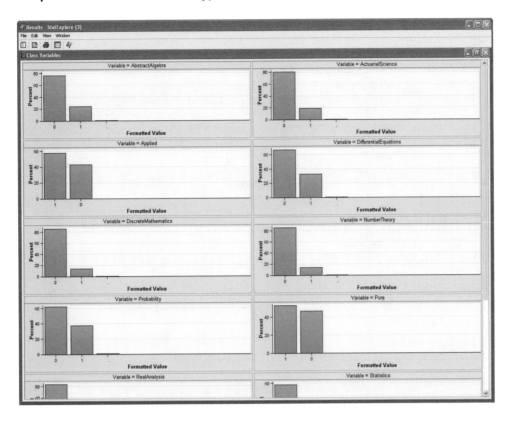

Some variables have three bars while some have two; the third bar represents missing values. Because 1 was supposed to be entered in the presence of a mark on the survey and 0 in the absence of a mark, the missing values represent data entry errors that need to be repaired. These variables can be repaired by using the Impute node discussed in Chapter 1, replacing all missing values with the constant, 0.

Another item of interest is whether students specified multiple preferences. For each mathematics type, the different values can be summed. All sums greater than 1 indicate multiple preferences.

Although it would be helpful if the first bar represented code 0 and the second bar represented code 1, the same values are not always presented first in Output 2.17. In each case the "yes" bar represented by 1 is smaller than the "no" bar represented by 0. This size difference indicates that the majority of students did not identify a preference for any type of mathematics.

Use the following code to correct data entry errors and to define a preference variable to examine how many different types of mathematics individual students indicated that they liked. This code provides an alternative method to imputing the missing values.

```
data sasuser.transformsurvey;
    set sasuser.revisedstudentsurvey;
    if abstractalgebra<0 then abstractalgebra=0;
    if actuarialscience<0 then actuarialscience=0;
    if differentialequations<0 then differentialequations=0;
    if realanalysis<0 then realanalysis=0;
    if discretemathematics<0 then discretemathematics=0;
    if statistics<0 then statistics=0;
    if probability<0 then probability=0;
    if numbertheory<0 then numbertheory=0;
    if topology<0 then topology=0;
    preference=abstractalgebra+actuarialscience+differentialequations+
    realanalysis+discretemathematics+statistics+probability+number
        theory+topology;
run;
```

The variables defined as binary in the original student survey data set are not retained as binary in the new data set; they are again defined as interval. Once changed, Output 2.18 presents the modified bar charts.

Output 2.18 Revised Outcomes from the StatExplore Node

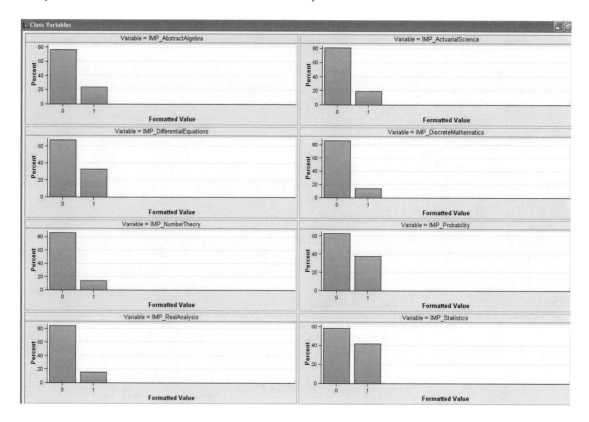

Output 2.19 shows the bar chart for the defined variable, Preference, which is the sum of the preferences of the individual students for the type of mathematics.

Output 2.19 Bar Chart of Preference

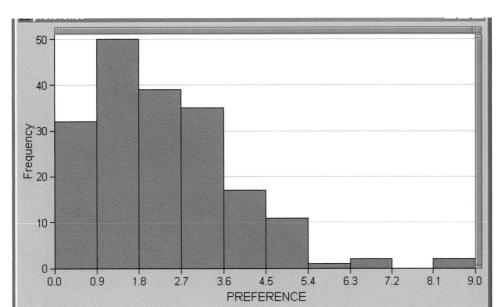

The peak occurs at the value of 1; most students indicated preference for at least one type of mathematics. One or two students indicated that they like all types of mathematics, but most differentiated between the different types.

To compare a kernel density estimation to the bar chart in Output 2.19, use the following code:

```
proc kde data=sasuser.transformsurvey;
   univar preference/gridl=0 gridu=10 out=sasuser.kdepreference;
run;
```

Output 2.20 shows the results.

Output 2.20 Kernel Density Estimation of Preference

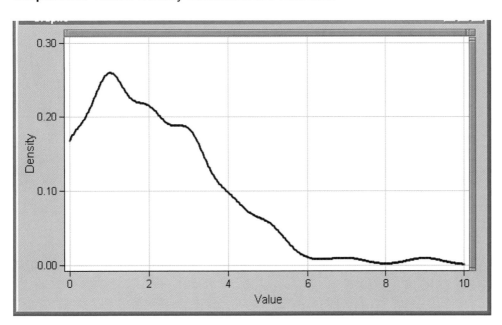

The resulting distribution looks similar, with a peak at the value of 1 and a steady decrease from that point on. However, the curve looks jagged. To smooth the curve, add `bwm=2` to the code to get the estimate in Output 2.21.

Output 2.21 Kernel Density Estimation with Smoothness Changed

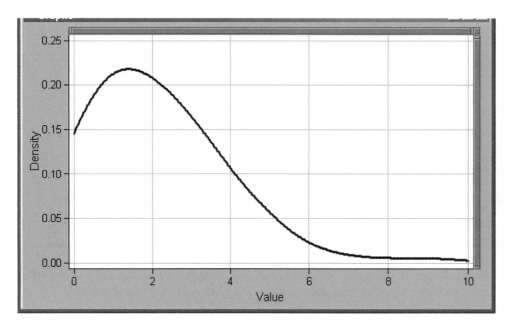

To distinguish between applied and pure preferences, two preference variables are defined. The new variables are examined using PROC KDE. To plot the values on the same graph, merge the two output data sets and then graph them (Output 2.22). To compare the applied and pure preferences, overlay the two graphs on the same axes by using the following code:

```
data sasuser.transformsurvey1;
   set sasuser.transformsurvey;
   applied=statistics+probability+actuarialscience+differential
      equations;
   pure=realanalysis+discretemathematics+topology+numbertheory;
run;

proc kde data=sasuser.transformsurvey1;
   univar applied/gridl=0 gridu=5 out=sasuser.kdeapplied;
   univar pure/gridl=0 gridu=5 out=sasuser.kdepure;
run;

data sasuser.kdemathpreference;
   length var $ 32 value 8 density 8 count 8;
   set sasuser.kdeapplied
      sasuser.kdepure
      ;
   keep var value density count;
run;
```

Output 2.22 Pure and Applied Preferences

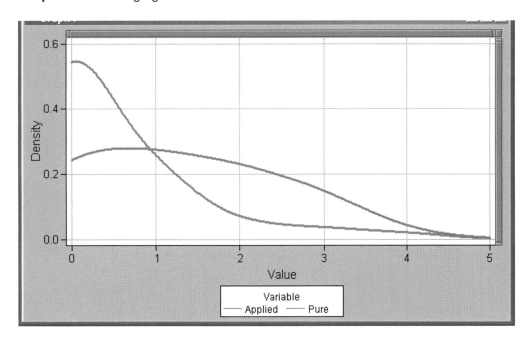

Modify the curve by adding `bwm=.7` to decrease the amount of smoothing (Output 2.23).

Output 2.23 Changing the Level of Smoothness

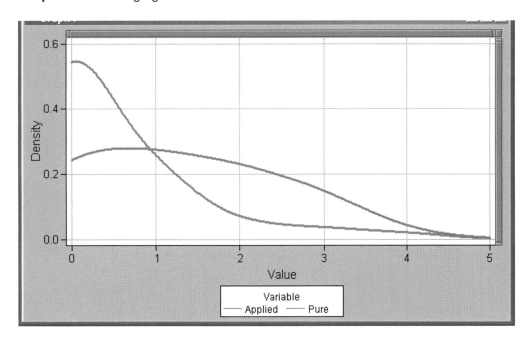

Students who indicated a preference for a pure discipline tended to indicate only one discipline; students who indicated a preference for an applied discipline were almost equally likely to indicate preferences for multiple disciplines. For this reason, the variability for the applied curve is much greater compared to the pure curve.

To examine the relationship between the two preferences, use the BIVAR command in PROC KDE, as follows:

```
proc kde data=sasuser.transformsurvey1;
   bivar applied pure/out=sasuser.kdeappliedpure;
run;
```

Bivariate density graphs should be visualized using surface plots. However, surface plots are not yet available in SAS Enterprise Miner software. Therefore, you can use SAS/GRAPH software to generate Output 2.24.

```
proc sql;
   create view work.sort616
         as select applied,density,pure from
sasuser.kdebivarappliedpure;
quit;
goptions xpixels=&_egchartwidth ypixels=&_egchartheight;
axis1
   style=1
   width=1
   minor=none
   label=(font='microsoft sans serif' height=12pt justify=right)
;
axis2
   style=1
   width=1
   minor=none
   label=(font='microsoft sans serif' height=12pt justify=center)

;
axis3
   style=1
   width=1
   minor=none
;
title;
title1 "surface plot";
footnote;
footnote1 "generated by the SAS System (&_sasservername, &sysscpl) on
%sysfunc(date(), eurdfde9.) at %sysfunc(time(), timeampm8.)";

proc g3d data=work.sort616;

   plot pure   * applied   = density /
   zaxis=axis1
   xaxis=axis2
   yaxis=axis3
xytype=0
   style=4
   grid
   rotate=70    tilt=70
   ctop=blue
   cbottom=red
;
run;
quit;
```

Output 2.24 Surface Plot of Bivariate Kernel Density Estimation

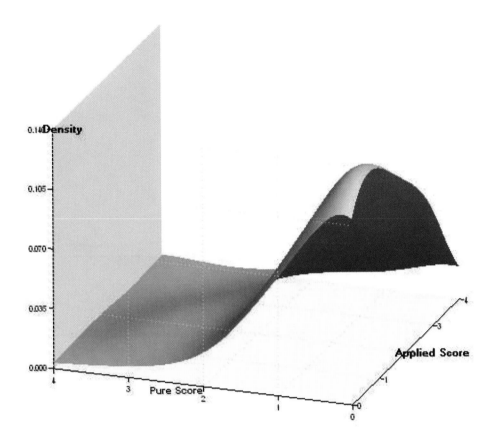

The resulting surface plot looks symmetrical. The bivariate graph shows that students tended to indicate preferences for both pure and applied mathematics disciplines in approximately equal numbers. However, the applied score is wider compared to the pure score, indicating greater variability.

To look at the relationship between student type and hours studied to see if graduate students study more hours compared to undergraduate students, use the following SAS code:

```
proc sort data=sasuser.revisedstudentsurvey;
   by student_type;

proc kde data=sasuser.revisedstudentsurvey;
   univar hours/gridl=0 gridu=40 out=sasuser.kdehours;
   by student_type;
run;
```

This produces the resulting graph in Output 2.25.

Output 2.25 Kernel Density Graph of Hours Studied by Student Type

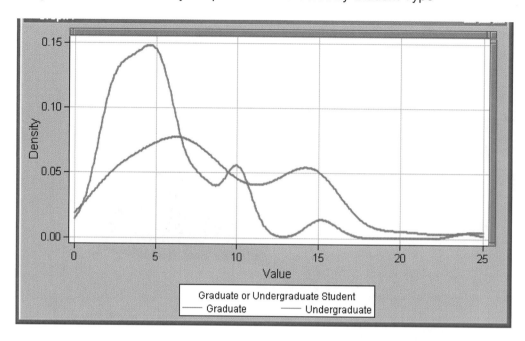

Graduate students were more likely to study 15 hours or more compared to undergraduate students. Although the graph shows a difference in study times, the reason why cannot be discerned without domain knowledge. Only with domain knowledge is it known whether the extra study is due to more difficult courses or to the fact that, generally, the better students become graduate students. To see if the pattern holds for course level, perform a second examination of the database, this time looking at the course level.

```
proc sort data=sasuser.revisedstudentsurvey;
   by courselevel;

proc kde data=sasuser.revisedstudentsurvey;
   univar hours/gridl=0 gridu=25 out=sasuser.kdehours;
   by courselevel;
run;
```

See Output 2.26 for the results.

Output 2.26 Kernel Density Graph of Hours Studied by Course Level

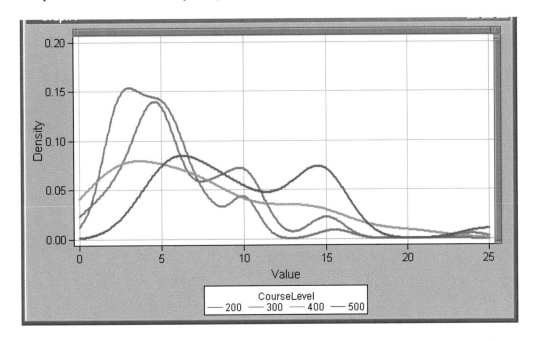

The trend continues, as shown in Output 2.26; students in 500-level and above courses were more likely to study longer. Students in 200- and 300-level courses studied the least.

2.4 Discussion

Visualization can give you a real understanding of the variables in the data. Data mining should always begin with a good look at the data and an investigation of their properties. Without such an understanding, it is difficult to take the next step to investigate patterns and relationships in the data.

Although kernel density estimation is not available in SAS Enterprise Miner software, you can use PROC KDE to examine the pattern of the entire distribution within a continuous variable instead of focusing on means and averages.

2.5 Exercises

1. Use the data set from the survey in Chapter 1 and the StatExplore node to examine the data. Also, use kernel density estimation to examine general, non-normal trends in the Hour variable.

2. Continue to examine the Workloads data set using kernel density estimation.

3. Write a summary of your findings.

SAS Text Miner Software

3.1 Analyzing Unstructured Text

In many cases, it is important to analyze text documents. A business developer might need to examine competitors' advertising. Customer service complaints might be analyzed to find patterns and relationships. Similarly, if customers call technical support with many common problems, patterns found in similar complaints might demonstrate a problem that needs to be addressed with either the documentation or the product.

In medical treatment, much patient care documentation exists in the form of chart notes. Currently, for billing and insurance requirements, hospitals and physicians must pay to manually extract information from those chart notes, a very time-consuming and costly process. Text analysis can reduce the cost of transferring that information.

Another set of documents that are often collected but rarely analyzed are comments provided as part of gathering survey data. Although the comments are read, and sometimes manually coded into categories, text analysis makes them much more meaningful.

One interesting application of text analysis is investigating the Internet, which houses millions, if not billions, of documents on a topic. It would be virtually impossible to examine all of these documents manually. With SAS Text Miner software, you can not only analyze these documents—you can automatically search the Internet for relevant documents. You can then automatically store the results of that search in a SAS data set for future analysis.

Once the documents are contained within a SAS data set and analyzed, you can use more standard statistics and data mining techniques to further investigate patterns contained within them. One way to make Internet searches more meaningful is to use a search engine. Often pages upon pages are returned in a list. A SAS macro called %TMFILTER stores the Web pages in a directory that you can then examine with SAS Text Miner software to eliminate all irrelevant pages. This chapter focuses on examining document sources to see if there are differences in information available. One critical comparison examines the availability of medical information on the Internet that can be easily accessed by patients compared to information readily available to physicians in medical journals.

3.2 Introducing the SAS Text Miner Node

The Text Miner node appears in Figure 3.1. This node can be integrated into SAS Enterprise Miner software provided that SAS Text Miner software is available.

Figure 3.1 Text Miner Node

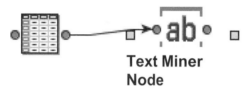

**Text Miner
Node**

To use the software, specify the data set. The Text Miner node has three section headings to examine: parse, transform, and cluster. Display 3.1 shows the first section, with node defaults.

Display 3.1 First Section of Screen (Parse)

Parse	
Parse Variable	
Language	ENGLISH
Stop List	SASHELP.STOPLST
Start List	
Stem Terms	Yes
Terms in Single Documen	No
Punctuation	No
Numbers	No
Different Parts of Speech	Yes
Ignore Parts of Speech	
Noun Groups	Yes
Synonyms	SASHELP.ENGSYNMS
Find Entities	No
Types of Entities	

There are a number of defaults to consider. A standard stoplist data set removes common words such as *and* and *the* from consideration. You can add words to the stoplist as needed or create a new list. A second default excludes consideration of words that occur in only one document because those words cannot be used to group documents together. Numbers and punctuation are ordinarily ignored when clustering text documents, so the defaults are set to **No**.

In context, a word such as *construct* or *impact* can be a noun or a verb. If **Yes** is checked for different parts of speech, they will be considered as different terms. You can change the defaults if the context of the word is not important. When you are analyzing strings of nouns (lists), change the default to **No**. You can choose whether to store the text in a SAS data set or use a variable in the data set that points to the location of the document. This second option reduces the required storage size for a SAS data set. In the second option, there is no limit on the size of each document; for the first option, the size is restricted to 10 pages.

You can focus on specific terms by listing them in a data set. Then SAS Text Miner software lists terms only from the specified data set. This step allows you to *parse* the document. Text parsing is a technical process that reduces documents to a manageable size. It also uses grammar context to identify a specific part of speech for each term used. Modifiers are often connected to nouns to define *noun groups*. If you do not want noun groups, change the default to **No**.

There are two types of output with SAS Text Miner software. On the left-hand side of the window, there is an interactive option that enables you to see the results of the parsing (Output 3.1). Three windows appear in interactive mode. The upper window displays the parsing results.

Output 3.1 Results of Parsing

	TERM	Freq	# Documents	Keep ▼	WEIGHT	Role	Attribute
	in	1402	92	☑	0.231	Prep	Alpha
	with	1006	89	☑	0.228	Prep	Alpha
	adhd	1397	86	☑	0.223	Prop	Alpha
	on	608	85	☑	0.19	Prep	Alpha
⊞	have	771	83	☑	0.23	Verb	Alpha
	information	290	75	☑	0.222	Noun	Alpha
⊞	child	1044	71	☑	0.313	Noun	Alpha
⊞	not	511	69	☑	0.294	Part	Alpha
	's	433	68	☑	0.228	Part	Unknown
	can	330	66	☑	0.288	Aux	Alpha
⊞	disorder	473	63	☑	0.312	Noun	Alpha
	other	274	62	☑	0.281	Adj	Alpha
	attention	329	61	☑	0.278	Noun	Alpha
⊞	will	203	57	☑	0.247	Aux	Alpha
⊞	treatment	280	57	☑	0.369	Noun	Alpha
⊞	parent	267	57	☑	0.285	Noun	Alpha
⊞	do	165	56	☑	0.281	Verb	Alpha

The + sign indicates that more than one word is connected to the phrase, a noun group. Click **Term** to alphabetize the words.

Notice that some of the initial terms listed are checked. Any value without a check mark is contained within the stoplist file and is not analyzed. Each term is assigned a part of speech or role. In this example, the term *ADHD* is both a preposition and a noun, and it is contained within a noun group. If *train* is labeled as a noun and as a verb, then in the Interactive model, SAS Text Miner cannot make the two terms equivalent because they are different parts of speech (Output 3.2).

You might want to preprocess the data by developing stoplists in a specific field or by correcting spelling errors. However, SAS Text Miner software is versatile enough that preprocessing is not always necessary. For large documents, correcting spelling manually can be time-consuming.

Output 3.2 Ignoring Parts of Speech

TERM	Freq	# Documents	Keep ▼	WEIGHT	Role	Attribute
in	1435	94	☑	0.225		Alpha
with	1101	91	☑	0.219		Alpha
⊞ have	799	88	☑	0.22		Alpha
adhd	1419	87	☑	0.219		Alpha
on	622	86	☑	0.186		Alpha
⊞ disorder	908	81	☑	0.249		Alpha
information	354	80	☑	0.205		Alpha
⊞ child	1226	77	☑	0.285		Alpha
⊞ other	354	76	☑	0.234		Alpha
's	523	74	☑	0.229		Unknown
⊞ do	391	74	☑	0.269		Alpha
attention	571	74	☑	0.259		Alpha
⊞ not	529	72	☑	0.284		Alpha
all	197	72	☑	0.203		Alpha
⊞ parent	394	69	☑	0.25		Alpha
can	367	68	☑	0.286		Alpha
⊞ add	500	66	☑	0.257		Alpha
⊞ site	193	66	☑	0.225		Alpha

The second part of the screen (Display 3.2) allows you to determine how to reduce the wordlist matrix to a manageable size. The default is singular value decomposition (SVD), which will be discussed in more detail later in this section. There are several possible methods to weight the value of each term in the documents.

Display 3.2 Second Section of Screen (Transform)

Transform	
Compute SVD	Yes
SVD Resolution	Low
Max SVD Dimensions	100
Scale SVD Dimensions	No
Frequency weighting	Log
Term Weight	Entropy
Roll up Terms	No
No. of Rolled-up Terms	100
Drop Other Terms	No

To see how these weights and methods affect outcomes, examine one data set and change the settings to see how the results differ.

Singular value decomposition defines a matrix of words by documents. The maximum dimensions (by default 100) limit its size. You can increase it, depending upon the number of documents. However, the larger the matrix, the more time this process takes. Instead of using SVD, use the terms with the highest frequency (called *roll-up terms*). Roll-up terms limit the wordlist to the top 100 highest-weighted terms. A menu allows you to change the weights (Display 3.3).

Display 3.3 Menu for Term Weights

Transform	
Compute SVD	Yes
SVD Resolution	Low
Max SVD Dimensions	100
Scale SVD Dimensions	No
Frequency weighting	Log
Term Weight	Entropy ∨
Roll up Terms	Entropy
No. of Rolled-up Terms	Global Frequency-Inverse Do
Drop Other Terms	Inverse Document Frequency
Cluster	Normal
Automatically Cluster	None
Exact or Maximum Numbe	Chi-Squared
Number of Clusters	Mutual Information
Cluster Algorithm	Information Gain

Entropy is the default. Terms that appear more frequently are weighted less compared to terms that appear less frequently. Therefore, entropy will give a weighting result that is very similar to the one given by Inverse Document Frequency, which weights the term in exactly the reverse order with the least-used terms given the highest weight, and the most-used term given the lowest weight.

The purpose of clustering is to define a small number of groups of documents so that documents within any one group are related and documents in different groups are not closely related. SAS Text Miner creates groups by looking at terms within each document. Documents within a group will be represented by a list of terms, and those terms will appear in most of the documents within the group.

In the third part of the screen (Display 3.4), the default for clustering is set to **No**. However, once the software completes the parsing and transformation steps, you can cluster by changing the default to **Yes** and then rerunning the node.

You can set the number of clusters and define the method on which to base the clusters. The default number of terms used to describe the cluster is 5. That number may be too small to label clusters effectively, so consider increasing this default to 20 or more terms.

DIsplay 3.4 Third Section of Screen (Cluster)

Cluster	
Automatically Cluster	No
Exact or Maximum Numbe	Maximum
Number of Clusters	40
Cluster Algorithm	EXPECTATION-MAXIMIZAT
Ignore Outliers	No
Hierarchy Levels	.
Descriptive Terms	5
What to Cluster	SVD Dimensions

There is no one correct outcome to clustering text documents. Therefore, you can change the settings to get meaningful results. You are encouraged to work with the weight defaults to determine their impact upon the results, as shown in Output 3.3.

Output 3.3 Text Mining Results

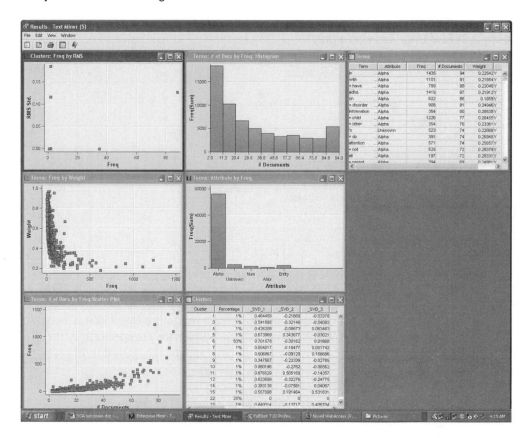

Output 3.3 displays a graphic of the terms by document frequency as well as the frequency by weight. It also includes a list of the terms.

The term by frequency graph can be queried for specific terms (Output 3.4), and the table of terms can be enlarged for viewing.

Output 3.4 Term by Frequency Matrix

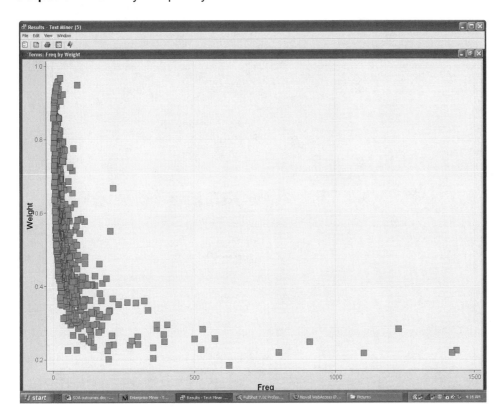

Note that most terms appear in 1 or 2 documents; only a handful appear in 500 or more.

After looking at the results screen, close it, and click on the SAS Text Miner node in the diagram window. Then, click the interactive button that is shown on the left-hand side of the diagram window. This window allows you to examine specific results from SAS Text Miner. The interactive display is shown in Output 3.5.

Output 3.5 Interactive Output with Clustering

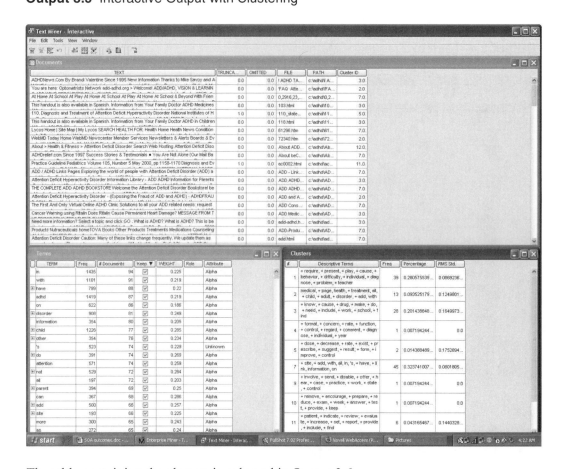

The table containing the clusters is enlarged in Output 3.6.

Output 3.6 Default Clustering with Entropy Weights

#	Descriptive Terms	Freq	Percentage	RMS Std.
Clusters				
1		35	0.251798561...	0.0
2	+ involve, + send, + disable, + offer, + hear, + case, + practice, + work, + state, + control	1	0.007194244...	0.0
3	+ university, + plan, + teach, + hear, + state, + test, + train, + resource, + site, + work	2	0.014388489...	0.1105302...
4	+ format, + concern, + rate, + function, + control, + regard, + comment, + diagnose, + year, + include	2	0.014388489...	0.1106094...
5	+ dose, + decrease, + rate, + exist, + prescribe, + suggest, + result, + form, + improve, + control	1	0.007194244...	0.0
7	+ review, + educator, + interest, + email, + issue, + study, + professional, + will, + have, + parent	1	0.007194244...	0.0
8	+ fail, + continue, + develop, + show, + know, + control, + affect, + treat, + see, + support	1	0.007194244...	0.0
9	+ college, + coach, + idea, + create, + look, + newsletter, + student, + individual, + year, + medication	2	0.014388489...	8.1308750...
10	+ face, + law, + feel, + raise, + refer, + start, + require, + follow, + know, + give	2	0.014388489...	0.1065362...
11	+ include, + cause, + diagnose, + behavior, + make, + provide, + problem, + teacher, + find, + need	19	0.136690647...	0.1534488...
12	+ link, all, with, + site, + add, + page, adhd, in, + help, on	71	0.510791366...	0.1135181...
14	+ remove, + encourage, + prepare, + reduce, + exam, + week, + answer, + test, + provide, + keep	1	0.007194244...	0.0
16	+ determine, + publication, + evaluation, + task, + create, + group, + comment, + interest, + include, + professional	1	0.007194244...	0.0

While the **Descriptive Terms** column can be extended like a spreadsheet column to see the remaining terms, it is easier to store the cluster descriptions in a SAS data set. Use the following code to store the descriptions:

```
data sasuser.adhdclusterdesctrial;
data sasuser.adhdclusterdesc (keep=_cluster_ clus_desc);
   set emws.text2_cluster;
run;

proc print;
var _cluster_ clus_desc;
run;
```

When you are clustering text, an expert with domain knowledge of the field should label each cluster. Without labels, the clusters have little value. In Table 3.1, fairly common knowledge of Attention Deficit Hyperactivity Disorder (ADHD) was used to label the clusters.

Table 3.1 Listing of Clusters

Cluster Number	Cluster Descriptors	Cluster Label
1		None
2	+ outcome, + function, + determine, + decrease, + establish, + demonstrate, + conduct, + result, + rate, + criterion, + assessment, + suggest, + indicate, + require, + evaluation, + evaluate, + process, + base, + high, + identify, + follow, + develop,	Assessment
3	+ randomize, + filter, + noise, devices, + involve, + session, + perceive, + ear, + promote, + vitamin, + contribute, + sound, + send, + improvement, + disable, + schedule, + delay, + request, + offer, + publish, + determine, + option, + process, + ind	Session
4	+ jacob, + amendment, biology, lab, devices, + master, + index, d., + ear, + letter, + university, + technology, + computer, + game, + sound, s., + word, + john, federal, + style, + advocate, + structure, + cope, + purpose, + publish, + section, + plan	University
5	+ have, + help, with, + site, + link, + add, + page, + email, + click, all, adhd, on, in, + child, information, free, + book, + right, 's, + resource, + parent, + learn, now, + not, attention, can, + will, + disorder, + treatment, web, + update, + copy	Information Resource
6	+ lose, + break, + complete, + play, + talk, + pay, + require, + activity, + continue, + evaluate, + american, such as, + set, + show, + control, + physician, + follow, + develop, often, + type, + treat, + mean, + level, before, + difficulty, + make, +	Treatment Activity
7	+ remove, + attribute, + encourage, + outline, + prepare, + reduce, + exam, + aid, + accommodation, + avoid, + model, + short, + format, + presentation, + minute, + achievement, + allow, + positive, + large, + week, + office, + peer, + schedule, + seek	Examination
8	+ trademark, + college, + choice, + begin, + subject, + coach, high school, + late, + idea, + create, + look, + newsletter, + system, + doctor, + end, + visit, + student, + trouble, + son, during, + individual, + program, might, + see, + year, + disabi	School

For example, the terms outcome, demonstrate, assessment, and evaluate all refer to ADHD testing. Therefore, Cluster 1 is labeled **Assessment**. Similarly, the terms information, book, resource, and site all indicate general information sites. Therefore, Cluster 5 is labeled **Information Resource**. This label is not unique and other labels may be even more representative. Examine the cluster descriptions to see if other cluster labels are more appropriate.

Examining the documents further, note that some common types of words were filtered out of the list (Display 3.5). The resulting clusters were found to be identical to those in Table 3.1.

Display 3.5 Filtered Types of Speech

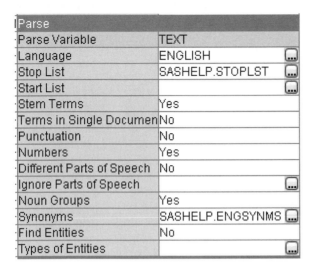

Parse	
Parse Variable	TEXT
Language	ENGLISH
Stop List	SASHELP.STOPLST
Start List	
Stem Terms	Yes
Terms in Single Documen	No
Punctuation	No
Numbers	Yes
Different Parts of Speech	No
Ignore Parts of Speech	
Noun Groups	Yes
Synonyms	SASHELP.ENGSYNMS
Find Entities	No
Types of Entities	

As Display 3.5 shows, numbers are used in the analysis, and the default, **Different Parts of Speech** is set to **No**.

The method of clustering was changed to hierarchical, with the results provided in the interactive window (Output 3.7) and written with labels in Table 3.2.

Output 3.7 Hierarchical Clustering Results

The clusters are nested because they are hierarchical. You can decide at what level to accept the tree, which determines the final number of clusters. For example, the last cluster shown in Output 3.7 is identified as Cluster 8 in Table 3.2. Similarly, Cluster (2)+ in Output 3.7 is listed as Cluster 6 in Table 3.2. As a third example, Cluster 17 in Table 3.2 is the first cluster listed in Output 3.7 and is identified as **(104)+**.

Table 3.2 Hierarchical Clustering Labels

Cluster Number	Cluster Descriptors	Cluster Label
1	+ decrease, + focus, + improvement, + involve, + compare, + vary, + represent, + abstract, + dose, + continue, + increase, + indicate, + improve, + show, + delay, + experience, + exist, + stimulant, + source, + develop, + publish, + physician, + practi	Physician Recommendations
2	+ sustain, + observation, + profile, + seat, + avoid, + publication, + tool, + detail, + engage, + content, + task, met, + note, + copyright, + measure, + play, + criterion, + function, + request, in, + adolescent, + pattern, + service, + long, + disab	Publications
3	+ human, + coach, + john, + college, + discussion, + relationship, + come, world, tips, recent, dr., general, + read, + expert, + last, + life, + board, + alternative, + subscribe, + include, + out, + help, top, + success, + interest, would, first, + r	University
4	+ site, + medication, + family, + disability, privacy, + provide, + member, + update, + reserve, + support, information, attention, + time, free, + deficit, with, + adult, in, + find, adhd, + disorder, + study, + like, + do, on, + need, + page, + quest	Medications
5	+ diagnose, + set, + indicate, + test, + function, + rate, + present, + require, + determine, + study, + concern, + develop, + problem, + conduct, + review, + criterion, + establish, + change, + increase, + control, + practice, + occur, + demonstrate,	Diagnosis
6	+ idea, + create, + newsletter, + look, + son, + back, + trouble, + choice, + doctor, + college, + coach, + link, + trademark, + begin, + late, + visit, + site, + subject, high school, + help, + learn, + student, + see, + know, + out, + end, would, + n	Newsletter
7	+ finish, + task, + complete, + class, + activity, + bad, + situation, + break, + time, + lose, into, + problem, + do, + grade, + set, + control, + answer, + make, + develop, + require, + see, when, as, + thing, + need, + teacher, + cause, + work, + gi	Completing Tasks
8	+ disable, + idea, + article, + online, federal, + resource, + law, + site, + fact, + raise, + search, + section, + teach, + program, + family, + treat, + process, + diagnose, + disability, + adult, + age, + add, + product, + cope, + evaluation, + hear	Federal Law
9	+ make, + time, + organization, common, + physician, + change, + pay, public, methylphenidate, + approach, developmental, + life, + cause, + treat, ritalin, may, + have, + copyright, + year, + american, + know, + talk, + disability, + will, before, + b	Ritalin

(continued)

Table 3.2 Hierarchical Clustering Labels (*continued*)

Cluster Number	Cluster Descriptors	Cluster Label
10	+ solution, faq, + cope, + result, + search, + download, + chemical, + prove, >, + page, info, + option, + message, + service, + site, + add, + adolescent, + interest, + press, + click, + article, side effects, + kid, + group, + find, + home, + link, +	Medication
11	+ concern, + provider, + conduct, + rate, + establish, + report, developmental, + indicate, + result, + therapy, + criterion, + function, + year, + policy, + review, + improve, + present, + change, + strategy, + increase, + relate, + show, + evaluate,	Treatment
12	+ keep, + know, + talk, + feel, + book, + cause, + list, + help, + learn, + plan, + will, + answer, + not, + read, + write, + professional, + difference, + thing, + do, + good, + time, + have, + right, + link, + give, + parent, + site, + focus, + probl	Professional Recommendation
13	ritalin, + drug, + child, side, information, + page, advice, medical, + link, + treatment, adhd, with, on, in, health, diagnosis, + doctor, more, web, + risk, + stimulant, + behavioral, + other, all, + adult, + disorder, + research, + symptom, can, as,	Ritalin
14	+ area, + good, + give, + plan, + provide, + individual, + student, + require, + develop, + teacher, + type, + difficulty, + level, + test, + program, + follow, + set, + focus, + affect, + present, + find, + result, + support, + work, + disability, + n	Schooling
15	+ email, + site, + click, + add, free, + newsletter, + link, + help, with, all, add/adhd, + book, + have, + update, 's, + right, + page, in, adhd, + will, + new, on, + resource, + other, privacy, attention, + disorder, + deficit, + read, web, informati	Resources
16	+ require, + cause, + follow, + set, + type, + include, + test, + effect, + diagnose, + behavior, + develop, + result, + make, + difficulty, + treat, + show, + symptom, + report, + individual, diagnosis, + plan, + affect, + need, + drug, + provide, + p	Behavior
17	+ have, + do, + child, + disorder, + parent, + other, + help, + not, in, + learn, + include, with, adhd, on, + treatment, + work, + site, + make, + school, information, + adult, + link, attention, 's, + deficit, + add, + will, all, + find, can, + page,	Information

Again, you need to know the domain to label the clusters. Consider Cluster 7, with **task**, **complete**, **activity**, **time**. These four words seem to relate to the difficulty children with ADHD have in completing what they start. Similarly, Cluster 9 contains several medications plus the term **physician**. Cluster 13 contains similar terms. You could combine the two clusters because of the similarity in terms. Cluster 14—containing the terms **student**, **teacher**, **difficulty**, and **test**—seems to relate to education. Again, consider labeling these clusters.

From the differences in Tables 3.1 and 3.2, it is clear that there is no one correct answer. Clusters are meaningful if they are plausible, and one sign of their plausibility is the ability to write meaningful labels.

3.3 Crawling the Web with the %TMFILTER Macro

Next, you need to find a suitable data set for text analysis. The %TMFILTER macro has been developed to *crawl* through the Internet to find documents related to an initial Internet site. By *crawl*, we mean that %TMFILTER begins with a designated Web site, finds all links from that Web site, and then puts the Web pages in a directory on the local machine. If an abstract database uses URLs instead of frames, you can investigate abstracts identified by specific keywords. If the documents are already in electronic format, including Microsoft Word, the %TMFILTER macro can create a data set, provided the necessary documents are stored in an accessible folder.

This section discusses three examples. The first examines Internet sites related to the Avian flu vaccine using the following %TMFILTER statement to search, starting with the URL http://directory.google.com/Top/Health/Conditions_and_Diseases/Infectious_Diseases/Viral/Influenza/?tc=1 (available as of January 2004 but no longer available):

```
%tmfilter(url=http://directory.google.com/Top/Health/Conditions_and_D
iseases/Infectious_Diseases/Viral/Influenza/?tc=1,
depth=2,dir=c:\vaccine\dir,
destdir=c:\vaccine\destdir,norestrict=1,
dataset=work.vaccinewebcrawl);
run;
```

Note the DEPTH=2 option, which restricts the search to links of links. This crawl returns 1,100 documents. Increasing the depth of this search also increases the time required to crawl and the amount of storage space needed. Expanding the depth to 4 returns over 50,000 documents stored in the folder **C:\vaccine\dir**. When DEPTH=4, the relationship to the initial term, **flu vaccine**, becomes weak. Therefore, such a depth is rarely necessary. Once the %TMFILTER macro has run, use the Text Miner node, ensuring that you select **text stored externally**.

In the following example, the %TMFILTER macro crawls the site http://dmreview.com (February 2005) with a depth of 4:

```
%tmfilter(url=http://dmreview.com, depth=4,dir=c:\business\dir,
destdir=c:\business\destdir,norestrict=1,
dataset=work.business);
run;
```

This example finds a total of 4,926 documents and 27,378 terms.

Some Web sites, such as http://www.google.com, have blocked Web crawling. Because these crawls are blocked, you should use other search engines such as Yahoo or Ask.com.

Also, many electronic databases are available for crawling, including PubMed (http://www.pubmed.gov) for medical documents, Lexis Nexis (http://global.lexisnexis.com for news documents, and ERIC (http://www.eric.ed.gov/ERICWebPortal/Home.portal) for education documents.

Another example of Web crawling searches the site of the SAS Global Forum's online proceedings (available as of February 2005 at http://support.sas.com/events/sasglobalforum/ index.html). To complete a Web crawl on data mining, run the following SAS program:

```
%tmfilter(url=http://www.sas.com/technologies/analytics/datamining/
index.html, depth=4,dir=c:\sugi\dir,
dataset=sasuser.sugiwebcrawl);
run;
```

In this case, the depth is increased because the search returns a large list. A depth of 4 ensures that the documents that were most responsive to the keyword search are included in the resulting crawl. This search returns 3,105 documents, with 85,208 different terms.

One Web search engine of particular interest is PubMed, provided by the National Library of Medicine. Some programming tools are available from SAS Institute to automatically store abstracts from this source to place in a SAS data set. These tools can be downloaded from SAS. Once they are installed, you can use the program to extract abstracts. To start the program, run TMPUBMED.EXE. A screen similar to Display 3.6 appears.

Display 3.6 TMPUBMED.EXE Screen

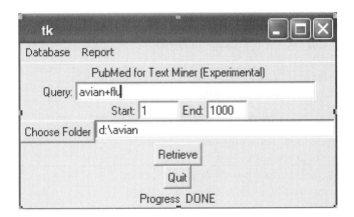

Insert terms for a keyword search through PubMed and enter the name of a folder to store the results. Decide how many documents you want to search. The higher the number, the more time the search requires. For this example, all relevant abstracts are stored in fetch.xml in the **D:\avian** directory. You can retrieve them from `fetch.xml` using the following SAS code:

```
filename fetch 'd:\Avian';
filename SXLEMAP 'E:\M2004 CD\tmpubmed\pubmed.map';

libname fetch2 xml xmlmap=SXLEMAP access=READONLY;

run;
```

Once this step is completed, the directory is stored in the Fetch2 SAS library.

3.4 Clustering Text Documents

An earlier clustering example using expectation maximization returned 20 clusters. However, some of the clusters contained only a small number of documents. Therefore, the example was rerun with the choice of exactly 10 clusters (Table 3.3).

Table 3.3 Results of Clustering of HTML Documents from http://www.dmreview.com

Cluster Number	Cluster Descriptors	Number of Documents
1	Isi, +trial, register, medical, education, +page, +field, internet, services, research, clinical, centerwatch, researchsoft, +program	1005
2	Guides, la crosse, room, immediate, papers, release, +will, tech, press, mail, resource, +enterprise, automation, +organization, editorial +industry, +form	357
3	Users, +analysis, +reference, +tax, +product, +line, +professional, +brand, +advance, +cover, +law, home, most, comprehensive, +feature, +service	662
4	Support, below, real-time, +turn, equity, customer, +decision, +support, analytical, e-mail, corporate, +client, +company, trading, management, +meetin +integrate	238
5	Profound, insite, +desk, +event, information, +search, +world, property, +selection, dialog, newsedge, data +authoritative, +portal, +aid, +online	135
6	+resource, +material, scientific, find, statement, room, +program, career, legal, +advance, corporation, financial, +learn, copyright, home, regulatory, learn	591
7	Service, +reserve, server, find, support, shadow, options, +page, customer, request, +application, +environment, +user, all, +support, +integration, documentation	456
8	Contacts, releases, faqs, market, find out, presentations, rooms, all, history, scientific, classified, manager, advertiser, group, +reserve, snapshot	546
9	Training, site, successful, + want, type, +copyright, more +level, +success, culture, +reach, +alumnus, +put, +big, development, other, news, healthcare, +stay	636
10	+copyright, +full, room +investor, +map, legal, +notice, across, information, +career, healthcare, financial, advanced, + tax, +product, full product catalog	300

Cluster 1 contains several terms related to medicine. Therefore, label the cluster as medical and clinical information. Suggested cluster labels are medical, mail and organization, tax, products, training, copyright information, customer support, news, professional resources, customer service, and new releases and contacts.

To eliminate documents not related to business relations, many of the terms in the list were removed. The remaining terms appear in Table 3.4.

Table 3.4 Reducing Terms Using the KEEP Option

Term	Freq.	No. of Documents	Keep	Links	Weight	Role	Attribute
business	1497	946	Y	5	0.198	Prop	Alpha
financial	1674	1252	Y	5	0.172	Prop	Alpha
+ product	1688	1038	Y	5	0.195	Noun	Alpha
accounting	1000	836	Y	4	0.215	Prop	Alpha
market	783	726	Y	4	0.224	Prop	Alpha
customer	785	651	Y	3	0.242	Prop	Alpha
financial	1414	956	Y	0	0.211	Adj	Alpha
client application	6	6	Y	0	0.788	NOUN_GROUP	Entity
advertisement	2	2	Y	0	0.918	Prop	Alpha
client investment counseling	4	4	Y	0	0.836	NOUN_GROUP	Entity
client component	2	2	Y	0	0.918	NOUN_GROUP	Entity
advertising/marketing	4	4	Y	0	0.836	Prop	Unknown
client tax	2	2	Y	0	0.918	NOUN_GROUP	Entity
client location	2	2	Y	0	0.918	NOUN_GROUP	Entity
client data using	2	2	Y	0	0.918	NOUN_GROUP	Entity
client services	4	4	Y	0	0.836	NOUN_GROUP	Entity
client management	2	2	Y	0	0.918	NOUN_GROUP	Entity
client information	4	4	Y	0	0.836	NOUN_GROUP	Entity
client requirements	4	4	Y	0	0.836	NOUN_GROUP	Entity

These terms generated the clusters in Table 3.5 using expectation maximization.

Table 3.5 Clusters Generated Using the Reduced Term List in Table 3.4

Cluster Number	Cluster Descriptors	Freq.
1	accounting, market, business, client data using, financial, advertising/marketing, customer, financial	752
2	client requirements, client location	1485
3	client tax, financial, market, business, financial, advertising/marketing, accounting, customer, + product	682
4	+ product, customer, advertisement, client component, client application, financial	919
5	client services, financial, client information, + product, financial, accounting, customer, business, market	276
6	financial, client investment counseling, client management, + product, client information, client application, customer, accounting, financial, market, business	590

Suggested labels are accounting, client needs, financial information and services, product marketing, client financial services, and product investing.

Consider another example where the clusters were identified from the **flu vaccine** Web crawl search (Table 3.6) as completed using the %TMFILTER macro.

Table 3.6 Clusters Identified in SAS Text Miner Software for **flu vaccine**

Cluster Number	Cluster Descriptors	Percentage
1	most, + forum, + improve, global, + subscribe, + trademark, information, + girl, + email, + newsletter, + food, + feed, + kid, + pediatrician, + age, privacy policy, + fact, + see, + death, + teen, + boy, + report, + index, + register, + doctor, + reserve, + result, + right, now, + problem, + user, + library, + policy, advice, inc., + article, + flu, privacy, + child, + topic	25
2	+ year, severe, + cause, influenza, + season, + complication, + occur, + virus, + illness, vaccine, + vaccination, + infection, + outbreak, + vaccine, + develop, during, + flu, + patient, + high, + week, + lung, + risk, + day, + symptom, + death, but, + give, + prevent, + have, when, + drug, + month, + system, + work, + know, into, + do, over, + disease, + see	15
3	+ therapy, + board, + condition, clinical, + friend, + expert, + physician, + woman, today, + newsletter, + professional, privacy, + contact, + man, + medicine, + lifestyle, free newsletter, + diagnosis, + disclaimer, + trial, always, healthcare, + healthy, + substitute, + diet, nutrition, + click, + tip, + member, + center, medical, + life, + subscribe, free, + service, + symptom, + drug, advice, more, health	14
4	regional, viewing, + science, + order, human-edited, related, + help, + history, software, + business, own, + computer, google, directory, alphabetical, + consumer, + content, + directory, + web, only, + enhance, related categories, + modify, + project, following, in, + sport, + art, + job, + recreation, pagerank, view, employment, + society, open, web, open, alphabetical order, + category, + technology	14
5	google, + directory, + large, + search, + job, health, + editor, + location, + submit, could, + list, + send, + help, + have, + do, within, website, + term, suggested category, requested category, + help, + add, + find, + will, + account, + submission, on, + build, + page, + advertise, + web, + not, + likely, + project, + copyright, + move, + site, human-edited, netscape, + category	19
6	help, + job, alphabetical, + modify, viewing, search, + order, + web, alphabetical order, + science, pagerank, + society, view, + page, web, infectious, human-edited, + support, related, education, press, + infection, + resource, + organization, + treatment, + category, + project, + disease, google, information, + editor, + technology, + large, + study, + build, + directory, open, + publication, + submit, national	13

For example, Cluster 5 has the initial keywords **google**, **directory**, **large**, **search**. These words clearly relate to Internet searching, and not to the flu. Similarly, Cluster 6 contains **help**, **job**, **alphabetical**, **modify**, **viewing**, and **search**, again suggesting Internet searching. In contrast, Cluster 2 contains **year**, **severe**, **cause**, **influenza**, and **season**, strongly indicating that the documents contained in this cluster are related to the flu.

A brief inspection of the remaining clusters indicates that only Cluster 2 contains terms that are related to vaccines. Cluster 3 seems to contain documents about women's health. This clustering indicates one of the problems with using the %TMFILTER macro. Web crawling includes many unrelated documents. Therefore, always perform a preliminary clustering to filter out irrelevant clusters. Many of the other documents are clearly unrelated. From the file menu, it is possible to save the data set containing a field, **Cluster ID**. The data set can then be filtered to only those documents where Cluster ID=2. This filtered data set containing 148 documents can be reclustered (Table 3.7). This is discussed in more detail in Chapter 6.

Table 3.7 Clusters Identified from 148 Documents Filtered from the Original Cluster 2

Cluster Number	Cluster Descriptors	Percentage
1	+ code, + picture, flu, information, + outbreak, virus, american, + pandemic, influenza, + article, news, + world, influenza virus, + die, + flu, + epidemic, + state, into, + fact, information, + virus, through, + page, + appear, + large, + site, + activity, + death, + report, + community, including, influenza, + bad, + disease, + email, in, + 's, cdc, + symptom, on	26
2	therapeutic, diagnostic, management, + issue, + product, + resistance, cme, acute, + research, + diagnosis, + introduction, sars, + tract, + population, + syndrome, + emerge, + agent, b., + journal, + diagnose, infectious, annual, + therapy, infectious diseases, respiratory, + issue, + base, + laboratory, influenza, + infection, current, + publication, clinical, + test, + disease, + impact, + section, viral, + disclaimer, inc.	19
3	+ district, + rage, + shroud, + blaze, + tanker, + pollutant, + tackle, + brunei, + burn, + moderate, + wildfire, + fire, + forest, + rain, + russia, + forest, + rage, + battle, + satellite, + close, + fire, + declare, + burn, + ignore, + spot, + threaten, + land, + join, + town, + offer, + release, + refuse, + center, + image, + urge, + big, + return, + authority, + email, + discuss	1
4	+ age, + treat, + person, + old, + cause, + doctor, + high, + illness, + give, + good, + day, + child, + effect, + receive, + do, can, + risk, + not, + have, + reduce, only, common, + make, + week, + show, + help, + develop, + prevent, + infection, + work, + complication, + occur, + problem, may, + drug, should, such as, + include, but, + month	47
5	medicine, microbiology, epidemiology, national, + meeting, + society, diseases, + serve, molecular, + contribute, infectious, + john, + student, + publication, infectious diseases, + conference, + science, + update, + program, + research, infectious, + update, + network, + organization, national, + recommendation, current, + immunization, + disease, clinical, privacy, + study, + service, health, centers for disease control and prevention, + relate, + practice, + member, + trial, + medium	15
6	+ rover, + accuse, + election, + crowd, + deny, + resign, + mark, + fly, + decade, + seek, + nation, + official, + approve, + alert, monitor, + consumer, australian, google, + hour, + stay, organization, + version, online, + american, + kill, federal, + directory, + job, international, + network, + age, + begin, world, press, + particle, + relate, out, general, + web, health	1

Of the six clusters identified in Table 3.7, only Clusters 3 and 6 seem unrelated to vaccines, indicating that the original Cluster 2 contained most of the relevant vaccine documents discovered on the Internet. Moreover, these two clusters contain only two documents. The key is to define the cluster labels. Table 3.8 contains proposed labels for the clusters in Table 3.7.

Table 3.8 Labels for Clusters in Table 3.7

Cluster Number	Label
1	Community Impact
2	General Management of vaccines
3	Not Applicable
4	Treatment and risk
5	Infectious Diseases
6	Not Applicable

Never underestimate the importance of labeling. If clusters are too difficult to label, the relationships in the clusters are not clear and probably of little value.

If the clusters are unsatisfactory, you can try different ways to improve them. One is to change the transformation method. A second is to add to the stoplist, which can be done by toggling the list of terms to remove unnecessary ones as discussed in Table 3.5.

Table 3.9 gives the clusters determined by a Web crawl through SAS Global Forum (http://support.sas.com/events/sasglobal forum/) with a depth of 4. There were 3,105 returned documents, with 85, 208 different terms.

Table 3.9 Clusters Resulting from Web Crawl through SAS Global Forum

Cluster Number	Cluster Descriptors	Freq.
1		51
2	+ strategy, + deliver, + help, + decision, privacy, data, as, + provide, + contact, + need, + system, inc., + enterprise, + see, + institute, + enable, can, + industry	1010
3	+ warrant, + limitation, + exclude, + grant, + govern, + damage, + imply, + copy, + permit, + provision, + representation, + license, + end user, + law, + authorize	39
4	en, de, + grant, + law, + copy, + warranty, + transfer, + usage, + law, + condition, +modify, + limit, + indicate, + install, + obtain, + supplier, + device, + relate	101
5	web, + service, privacy policy, all, + job, education, + download, + product, + announcement, accessibility, software piracy, + forum, + investor, + community,	532
6	+ support, + email, no, with, + user, + book, + version, sas, + statement, + include, u.s., + institute, + training, + home, + contact, + register, information, + office	1372

A total of 51 documents that could not be clustered were placed in Cluster 1. Cluster 3, with the terms **warrant**, **exclude**, **damage**, appears to focus on warranties and copyright, and the documents are not related to actual analyses of data. Similarly, terms listed in Cluster 4 are not related to analyses. Cluster 5, with **privacy**, **piracy**, and **download** defines restrictions on use, and Cluster 6 documents offer information on training. Terms in Cluster 2 primarily relate to actual papers on data mining, so the documents in that cluster were filtered and reclustered (Table 3.10).

Table 3.10 Filtered and Reclustered Documents

Cluster Number	Cluster Descriptors	Number	Label
1	+ product, + analysis, + result, success stories, + success, + industry, web, + cost, + time, + not, + manager, stories, + allow, + search, + challenge, success, + soluti	82	Success Stories
2	+ patient, care, + improve, + center, + employee, + area, + year, + find, + search, + implement, stories, + do, success stories, + develop, now, + time, + result, + syste	220	Health care
3	+ release, news, fortune, + feature, institute, + magazine, + press, + contact, sas, + leader, + center, + site, + drive, + subscribe, analytics, e-newsletters, sas com m	186	SAS advertisement
4	+ program, + school, + student, + partner, + event, + support, + user, + work, + contact, sas, + world, software, legal information, information, news, legal, + high, + 1	431	Partners
5	+ development, healthcare, + insurance, + training, + street, + link, internetweek, editorial calendar, + service, + medium, + salary, computing, roi, + resource, + trend	91	Business Intelligence

The documents were filtered again to Cluster 5 to concentrate on Business Intelligence. These remaining documents are discussed next in Section 3.5.

3.5 Using Concept Links

Another examination of relationships between words is provided by SAS Text Miner software through the use of concept links. Right-click on a term and scroll down to **View Concept Links** in the interactive screen (Display 3.7).

Display 3.7 View Concept Links

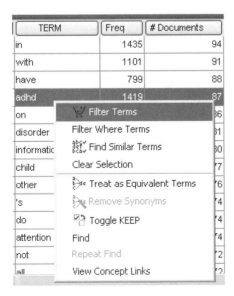

Not all terms have potential links. The first time you view concept links, a column appears in the Term window identifying the number of potential links. Sort this column by clicking on **links** to find the terms with the maximum number of links.

The concept link appears in a separate browser window as an HTML document. In SAS Enterprise Miner 5.2, the concept link remains in the results screen instead of opening a new browser window. The link can be animated by moving the cursor. All the lines connected to words are themselves connected to related words that can be discovered by moving the cursor around. Clicking one of the words connects to another browser window providing the documents that comprise the link. The algorithm used to define the concept links is that of association rules.

Association rules define the strength of association between different terms in the word list. The relationship between terms is highly significant (the chi-square statistic is greater than 12). Both terms occur in at least n documents. The default value of n is MAX(4, $A/100$, B), where A is the largest value of NUMDOCS for the subset of terms that are used in concept linking, B is the 1,000th largest value of NUMDOCS for the subset of terms that are used in concept linking, and NUMDOCS is the number of documents that a term appears in. For example, for 13,000 documents, every term in the term set must occur in at least 130 documents. See Chapter 5 for more detail.

Consider the concept links from the first example from http://dmreview.com for the term **financial** (Figures 3.1 and 3.2).

Figure 3.1 Concept Links for **financial**

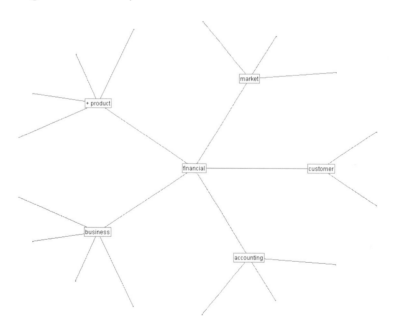

The linked terms are **product**, **material**, **customer**, **business**, and **accounting**. You can click any of these terms to find the corresponding table of documents that contain both terms.

Figure 3.2 Concept Links for **product**

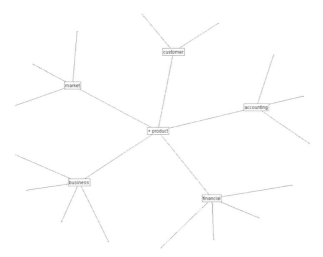

In this example, **product** is related to **market**, **customer**, **accounting**, **financial**, and **business**. You can examine the specific documents that pertain to the marketing of a product. In this way, the Text Miner node can refine the results of a keyword or a Web crawl.

By filtering down to Cluster 5 from Table 3.10, the remaining concept links relate to business intelligence.

Figure 3.3 illustrates the concept map related to the term **flu** from Table 3.7. It was developed from documents found on the Web from a search of **flu vaccine**.

Figure 3.3 Concept Links for **flu**

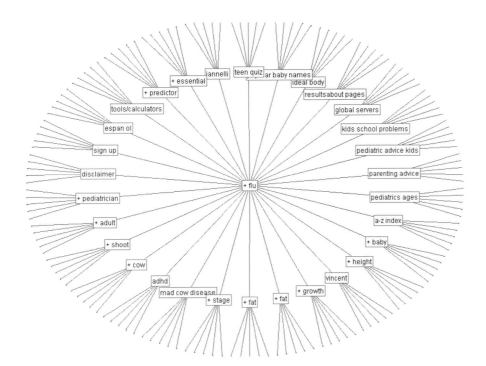

Note: The concept links will include misspellings if they occur in the original document.

There are many different links to the term **flu** because so many documents on the Internet discuss it.

Some of the links are not obvious (for example, **parenting advice** and **baby**). They need further analysis. Several of the links are related to the flu in children; other links are related to other types of diseases. The concept links for **risk** appear in Figure 3.4.

Figure 3.4 Concept Links for **risk**

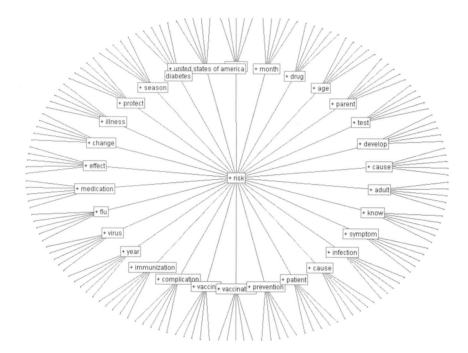

Some sites are related to the risk in children, specifically those linked to the term **parent**. Several links focus on the risk of infection; others focus on the risk of vaccination.

The secondary links from Figure 3.4 are given in Figure 3.5 for **risk** connected to **vaccine**.

Figure 3.5 Secondary Links to **risk** and **vaccine**

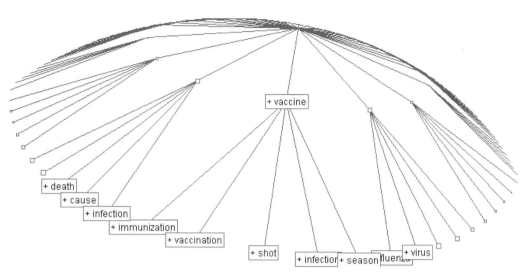

The initial concept map can be moved to find the secondary links. In this diagram, **risk** and **vaccine** are linked to **immunization**, **vaccination**, **shot**, and **infection**.

Two terms were used to define concept links: **school** and **Ritalin** (methylphenidate) for ADHD (Figure 3.6).

Figure 3.6 Concept Links for **school**

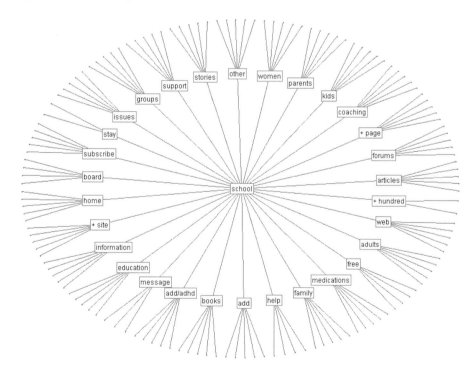

There are many connections to **school**, which is not unexpected since improvement in school performance is probably the most often cited reason for treating ADHD with medications.

There are also a number of links to **support**. Another connection of interest relates to **adult**, probably providing information on ADHD in adults.

Secondary concept links for **medications** are examined in Figures 3.7 and 3.8.

Figure 3.7 Concept Links for **school>medications**

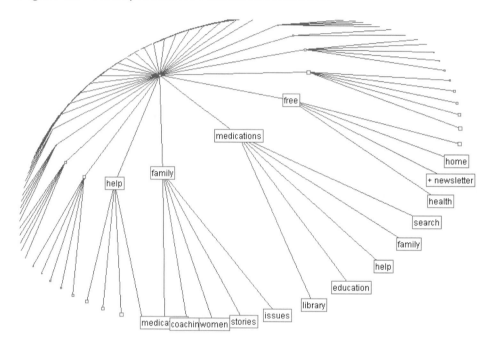

Note that one of the connections to **medications** is not the term **side effects**. Because any medication has some side effects, the problems associated with the use of Ritalin should be examined in detail. Documents linking **school** to **medications** can be listed by clicking **medications**. In contrast, direct links to the term **methylphenidate** are relatively sparse (Figure 3.8).

Figure 3.8 Concept Links for **methylphenidate**

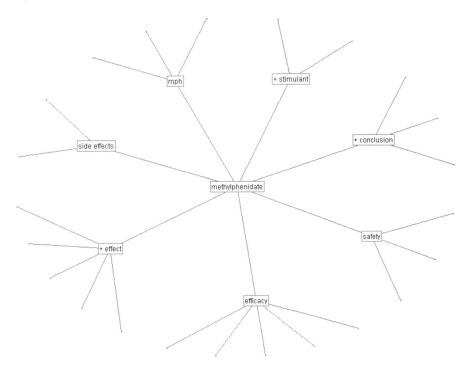

Although two related papers discuss side effects, none relate **methylphenidate** to its more common reference **Ritalin**. Using the concept links clearly demonstrates that very little information exists in any of the databases concerning the side effects of Ritalin. Therefore, you have to search deeply into the Internet literature to find relevant information. The keyword search can be expanded to include the phrase **side effects Ritalin** in all databases.

3.6 Interpreting Open-Ended Survey Questions

One reason to examine open-ended survey questions is to look for differences by sources. In the early to mid-1990s, a fictitious university operated a small daycare center. The center was outsourced in 1995. Because of deteriorating quality, the center was closed in 1997. To increase student recruitment and retention, the university debated reopening the center under the auspices of the Department of Education's Early Childhood Learning program. To determine interest, a survey was generally distributed to students, staff and faculty members. Space was reserved at the end of the survey for open-ended comments. A total of 274 respondents provided comments: 64 faculty members, 155 staff, and 55 students. These comments were made publicly available on the Web and analyzed using SAS Text Miner software. Concept links were used to find linkages between terms in the comments.

From the different sample sizes, it was inferred that the daycare center was of more interest to staff than to faculty members and students. The Text Miner node divided the 274 comments into 7 clusters (Table 3.11).

Table 3.11 Clusters Defined through Text Analysis

Cluster Number	Cluster Descriptors	Frequency	Label
1	Out, same, pay, income, teach, week, class, place, money, mom, husband, near, during, evening	30	Cost of Childcare
2	Number, size, employer, employee, childcare, institution, academic, provide, area, type, excellent	44	University should provide
3	School, school age, elementary school, summer, close proximity, holiday, close	37	Concern for school age children to be included in plans
4	Establish, student body, childcare facility, administration, facility, trust, interest	32	University should provide good quality care
5	Recruitment, childcare problems, retention, career, stay, young, work, regular, young children	24	Enable University to recruit and retain young parents
6	Answer, schedule, important, need, support, future, benefit, personally	73	Do need the childcare nearby
7	Enroll, program, child development program, drop-in, job, education	34	Need to schedule care around classes, including drop-in

An examination of the comments reveals that most respondents support a daycare facility, including those who have no children or no inclination to enroll their children. University constituencies differed over primary concerns; cost was more of a factor for students. As Table 3.12 illustrates, there is a statistically significant relationship between the cluster membership and the respondent status (faculty, staff, students) as shown by performing a chi-square analysis ($p=0.0007$).

Table 3.12 Chi-Square Analysis of Clusters by University Constituency

Cluster Number	Faculty	Staff	Student
1	5 (7.8%)	10 (6.4%)	15 (27.7%)
2	11 (17.2%)	26 (16.8%)	7 (12.7%)
3	7 (10.9%)	24 (15.5%)	6 (10.9%)
4	11 (17.2%)	12 (7.7%)	9 (15.4%)
5	4 (6.2%)	19 (12.3%)	1 (1.8%)
6	15 (23.4%)	43 (27.7%)	15 (27.3%)
7	11 (17.2%)	21 (13.6$)	2 (3.6%)

More than a quarter of students are concerned about cost; the interest in cost was minimal for faculty members and staff (Cluster 1). Students are also concerned about good quality and close proximity. Faculty members tended to comment more abstractly that such a program would be good for the university recruitment and retention. One of the major concerns of the staff was staff provision for school-age children, particularly during summer and holidays. A concept map was created for the term **program** (Figure 3.9).

Figure 3.9 Concept Links for **program**

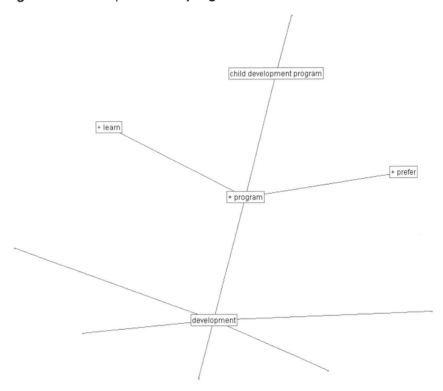

Only four terms related to this word, indicating that few comments addressed specifics about a program. However, the term **development** has a number of links, and a second concept link was centered on that word (Figure 3.10).

Figure 3.10 Concept Links for **development**

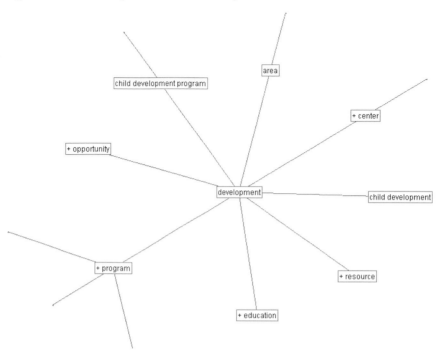

A total of 8 links were identified. The survey respondents who made a comment concerning program and development included a comment about educational resources. Quality is an issue for some.

Because there are relatively few concept links, you can increase them by changing the default settings (Figure 3.11).

Figure 3.11 Concept Links for **development** after Changing Settings

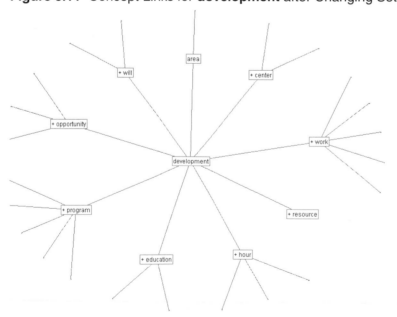

A link to **work** has been added, as well as links to **hour** and **will**.

Here is a second example of open-ended survey questions. Consider a study on the quality of life in a community. Respondents were asked to rate specific items using a 5-point Likert Scale. Mean scores ranged from 3+ to 4+ on various items such as community environment, health, and leisure. However, none of the items were ranked in the order of importance to the respondents. At the end of the survey, respondents were given the opportunity to identify strengths and weaknesses of the community through brief open-ended responses. There were a total of 286 responses for weaknesses and 190 responses for strengths. The clusters for community strengths appear in Table 3.13.

Table 3.13 Comments on Community Strengths

Cluster Number	Cluster Descriptors	Freq.
1		96
2	live, safe, safe place, place, environment, work, natural, + good	9
3	+ value, economic, safety, in general, stability, + family	13
4	health, health care, mental, care, + system	7
5	+ do, + program, living, + not	6
6	+ citizen, giving, both, + adult, community leaders, diversity, friendly, + issue, + community, involved, + care, growth, + leader, willingness, people	21
7	low, crime, unemployment	5
8	+ need, all, caring, address, when, + meet, + community, + opportunity, people	11
9	+ area, + clean, + school, progressive, + company, in, government, + resource, natural, great, + good	25
10	non-profit, non-profit sector, strong, sector, + community	7
11	ethic, work ethic, work	2
12	+ business, + activity, + lot, easily, climate, committed, base, variety, leadership, excellent, support, + service, great, in	24
13	fox, size, geographic, cities, workforce, college, + quality, many, + facility, feeling, + learn, life, with, + service, + opportunity, + community, people	26
14	+ job, availability, + opportunity	7
15	all, people, working, + work, willingness	13
16	education, culture, + road, + good, recreation	14

Summarizing, the strengths of major interest are as follows:

- Safety—low crime rate   14
- Economic value   37
- Health care   7
- Good schools   65
- Employment opportunities   14
- Caring community   38
- Work ethic   15

The clusters for community weaknesses appear in Table 3.14.

Table 3.14 Comments on Community Weaknesses

Cluster Number	Cluster Descriptors	Freq.
1	discrimination, racial, zoning, much	26
2	diverse, increasing, + family, support, + number, low-income	11
3	+ property, + tax, many, long-term	13
4	downtown, revitalization, loss, retail, + old, downtown area, + business, + area, appleton, in, lack	12
5	youth, low, no, have, + resource, social, + activity, + service, + not, with	23
6	public, recreation, easy, + trail, + public school, county, + teen, ban, + wage, + desire, + limit, street, + issue, + need to, need, funding, + opportunity, + address, + service, + need	49
7	growth, up, rapid, keeping, infrastructure, support, availability, workforce, rapid growth, with, quality, + community, in	17
8	health, affordable, housing, affordable housing, health care, dental, mental, care, + parent, adequate, especially, + cost, + wage, elderly, access, all, young, have, + child, quality	26
9	+ woman, + run, office, highway, treatment, apathy, on, + school, safety, traffic, people, education, diversity, into, + ability, tolerance, high school, + member, council, should	44
10	+ culture, different, other cultures, help, + concern, other, as, integration, people, + need, + address, + minority, with, + not, + community, lack	13
11	planning, + law, + not, poor, + government, land, + city, + do, development, + activity, on, + community, in	22
12	water, air, drinking, pollution, + supply	7
13	public, race relations, + relation, participation, lack, + official, + group, + race, concern, transportation, development, + good, + area, support, in, diversity, with, + community	23

Summarizing, the weaknesses of major interest are as follows:

- Racial discrimination and race relations   62
- Property taxes   13
- Downtown revitalization   23
- Public recreation   49
- Affordable housing and health care   26
- Government planning   22
- Pollution   7
- Infrastructure support   17
- Schools and youth programs   67

You can examine the relationship between the tables of cluster terms and the conclusion. Note that there are more clusters than categories because some of the clusters have been combined. To use the clusters on a new set of text data, use the Scoring node (Figure 3.12).

Figure 3.12 Program for Scoring Text Mining Results

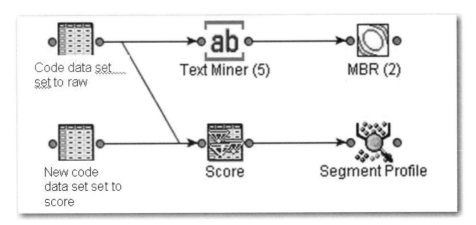

Include the most essential variables only as inputs. In the memory-based reasoning node, you are prompted to specify one target variable. Change the settings as follows:

1. Add an Input Data Source and use this data set as raw data. Set the text field as an input and some other field in the data as a target.

2. Add another Input Data Source and use a new text file. Instead of raw, it must be set to score. Again, the text field is an input variable and the target used in the Input Data Source must be defined as a rejected variable. In the Score node, in the left margin, select **testing set**.

3. Run the process from the Segment Profile node. All other nodes will be run first.

Once complete, click the connector to the Segment Profile node to find the names of the data sets.

Use the emdata data set in a PROC KDE as it was defined in Chapter 2 to compare actual to predicted interval outcomes, particularly on the validation set.

3.7 Revisiting the Federalist Papers

One of the earliest attempts at text mining was to determine the authorship of several of the Federalist Papers (Mosteller and Wallace, 1964). Since that study, other approaches have been used (http://www.cs.wisc.edu/~gfung/federalist.pdf). The Web site http://www.law.ou.edu/hist/federalist/ contains all 85 of the Federalist Papers. Each one was saved into a directory. The following code uses the %TMFILTER macro to link to documents in a folder. The first 16 results are listed:

```
%tmfilter (dir=C:\Documents and Settings\Administrator\My
Documents\FederalistPapers, dataset=sasuser.fedwebcrawl);
run;
```

```
 1 FEDERALIST NO. 1 General Introduction For the Independent Jo
 2 FEDERALIST No. 10 The Same Subject Continued (The Union as a
 3 FEDERALIST No. 10 The Same Subject Continued (The Union as a
 4 FEDERALIST No. 10 The Same Subject Continued (The Union as a
 5 FEDERALIST No. 10 The Same Subject Continued (The Union as a
 6 FEDERALIST No. 10 The Same Subject Continued (The Union as a
 7 FEDERALIST No. 10 The Same Subject Continued (The Union as a
 8 FEDERALIST No. 10 The Same Subject Continued (The Union as a
 9 FEDERALIST No. 10 The Same Subject Continued (The Union as a
10 FEDERALIST No. 10 The Same Subject Continued (The Union as a
11 FEDERALIST No. 10 The Same Subject Continued (The Union as a
12 FEDERALIST NO. 2 Concerning Dangers from Foreign Force and I
13 FEDERALIST No. 20 The Same Subject Continued (The Insufficie
14 FEDERALIST No. 20 The Same Subject Continued (The Insufficie
15 FEDERALIST No. 20 The Same Subject Continued (The Insufficie
16 FEDERALIST No. 20 The Same Subject Continued (The Insufficie
```

```
 1 file://C:\Documents and Settings\Administrator\My
Documents\FederalistPapers\federalist.1.htm
 2 file://C:\Documents and Settings\Administrator\My
Documents\FederalistPapers\federalist.10.ht
 3 file://C:\Documents and Settings\Administrator\My
Documents\FederalistPapers\federalist.11.ht
 4 file://C:\Documents and Settings\Administrator\My
Documents\FederalistPapers\federalist.12.ht
 5 file://C:\Documents and Settings\Administrator\My
Documents\FederalistPapers\federalist.13htm
 6 file://C:\Documents and Settings\Administrator\My
Documents\FederalistPapers\federalist.14.ht
 7 file://C:\Documents and Settings\Administrator\My
Documents\FederalistPapers\federalist.15.ht
 8 file://C:\Documents and Settings\Administrator\My
Documents\FederalistPapers\federalist.16.ht
 9 file://C:\Documents and Settings\Administrator\My
Documents\FederalistPapers\federalist.17.ht
10 file://C:\Documents and Settings\Administrator\My
Documents\FederalistPapers\federalist.18.ht
11 file://C:\Documents and Settings\Administrator\My
Documents\FederalistPapers\federalist.19.ht
12 file://C:\Documents and Settings\Administrator\My
Documents\FederalistPapers\federalist.2.htm
13 file://C:\Documents and Settings\Administrator\My
Documents\FederalistPapers\federalist.20.ht
14 file://C:\Documents and Settings\Administrator\My
Documents\FederalistPapers\federalist.21.ht
15 file://C:\Documents and Settings\Administrator\My
Documents\FederalistPapers\federalist.22.ht
16 file://C:\Documents and Settings\Administrator\My
Documents\FederalistPapers\federalist.23.ht
```

```
 1 federalist.1.html          english              1            0
 2 federalist.10.html         english              1            0
 3 federalist.11.html         english              1            0
 4 federalist.12.html         english              1            0
 5 federalist.13html.htm      english              1            0
 6 federalist.14.html         english              1            0
 7 federalist.15.html         english              1            0
 8 federalist.16.html         english              1            0
 9 federalist.17.html         english              1            0
10 federalist.18.html         english              1            0
11 federalist.19.html         english              1            0
12 federalist.2.html          english              1            0
13 federalist.20.html         english              1            0
14 federalist.21.html         english              1            0
15 federalist.22.html         english              1            0
16 federalist.23.html         english              1            0
```

Only a brief portion of each document was entered into the file, along with a link to its new location. Once the data set is defined, a field is added indicating the document's location. Next, a data set is created that has two fields, a document number, and an author. Merging the two data sets allows you to examine them using SAS Text Miner software. This analysis is designed to determine the authorship of several of the Federalist Papers with unknown authors (papers 49–57 and 62–63). A total of 20,238 terms are returned.

In this example, because there are a total of three authors, with several papers written jointly by two of the three, exactly four clusters were requested (Table 3.15).

Table 3.15 Clusters of Federalist Papers

Cluster Number	Cluster Descriptors	Freq.
1	+ diminish, + fix, + inform, + attach, + carry, + substitute, + comprehend, + defeat, + propose, + maintain, + rely, + secure, + tend, + vest, + derive, + lie, + recommen	10
2	+ calculate, + permit, + impose, + command, + combine, + demand, + pay, + object, + keep, + furnish, + see, + arise, + execute, + result, + contain, + afford, + leave, +	27
3	+ spring, + deserve, + destroy, + receive, + support, + feel, + serve, + oblige, + involve, + render, + divide, + admit, + supply, + observe, + fall, + preserve, + find,	12
4	+ unite, + hold, + relate, + determine, + suggest, + confine, + obtain, + prevail, + exercise, + possess, + prove, + know, + afford, + appoint, + regulate, + apply, + app	36

You can save the text_documents data set and then perform a table analysis to examine the relationship between cluster and author (Table 3.16).

Table 3.16 Table Analysis of Cluster by Author

Author(Author)	_CLUSTER_(Cluster ID)				Total
	1	2	3	4	
Either	1 9.09 10.00	0 0.00 0.00	0 0.00 0.00	10 90.91 27.78	11
Hamilton	0 0.00 0.00	20 39.22 74.07	7 13.73 58.33	24 47.06 66.67	51
Hamilton & Madison	0 0.00 0.00	1 33.33 3.70	2 66.67 16.67	0 0.00 0.00	3
Jay	0 0.00 0.00	3 60.00 11.11	1 20.00 8.33	1 20.00 2.78	5
Madison	9 60.00 90.00	3 20.00 11.11	2 13.33 16.67	1 6.67 2.78	15
Total	10	27	12	36	85

In this analysis, it appears that the unknown papers belong to Hamilton, not Madison, which is the exact opposite conclusion reached by Mosteller and Wallace (1964), who attribute the papers to Madison. To further examine the results, you can perform a text analysis a second time using rollup terms rather than the singular value decomposition. The results appear in Table 3.17, with the corresponding table analysis in Table 3.18.

Table 3.17 Clusters Using Rollup Terms

Cluster Number	Cluster Descriptor	Freq.
1	+ fill, + convene, + concern, + serve, + unite, + divide, + exercise, + afford, + appoint, + draw, + betray, + know, + confine, + prove, + possess, + hold, + regulate, + an	20
2	+ receive, + find, + state, + support, + feel, + danger, + oblige, + preserve, + observe, + admit, + interest, + divide, + have, + form, + involve, + part, + government, +	19
3	+ correspond, + decide, + determine, + constitute, + arise, + confide, + adopt, + feel, + affect, + restrain, + enjoy, + tend, + expose, + declare, + allow, + mean, + exten	6
4	+ carry, + create, + restrain, + propose, + maintain, + derive, + secure, + suppose, + declare, + relate, + extend, + show, + require, + provide, + lie, + leave, + regulate	40

Table 3.18 Table Analysis Using Rollup Terms

Author(Author)	_CLUSTER_(Cluster ID)				Total
	1	**2**	**3**	**4**	
Either	2 18.18 10.00	0 0.00 0.00	0 0.00 0.00	9 81.82 22.50	11
Hamilton	17 33.33 85.00	11 21.57 57.89	6 11.76 100.00	17 33.33 42.50	51
Hamilton & Madison	0 0.00 0.00	2 66.67 10.53	0 0.00 0.00	1 33.33 2.50	3
Jay	1 20.00 5.00	4 80.00 21.05	0 0.00 0.00	0 0.00 0.00	5
Madison	0 0.00 0.00	2 13.33 10.53	0 0.00 0.00	13 86.67 32.50	15
Total	20	19	6	40	85

The proportion of documents in each cluster has changed. Using rollup terms, it appears that the unknown documents are more closely related to Madison, which agrees with the findings of other studies. If mutual information is used to reweight the terms using the target value, the results appear in Table 3.19 with the corresponding table analysis in Table 3.20.

Table 3.19 Clusters Using Target Value for Mutual Information

Cluster Number	Cluster Descriptors	Freq.
1	+ have, + time, + state, + confederacy, + part, + advantage, + man, + government, + country, + danger, + make, must, most, more, but, should, all, + constitution, + view, +	5
2	+ hold, + relate, + confine, + suggest, + know, + exercise, + apply, + result, + unite, + answer, + declare, + bind, + provide, + leave, + happen, + proceed, + make, + appo	46
3	+ confederacy, + danger, + state, + interest, + war, + have, + good, + consideration, + nation, + power, + government, + force, + manner, + object, + find, + part, + britai	4
4	+ engage, + defeat, + receive, + execute, + carry, + propose, + prevent, + continue, + render, + regulate, + long, + do, + show, + do, + establish, + large, + derive, + pro	30

Table 3.20 Table Analysis Using Target Value for Mutual Information

Author(Author)	_CLUSTER_(Cluster ID)				Total
	1	**2**	**3**	**4**	
Either	0 0.00 0.00	10 90.91 21.74	0 0.00 0.00	1 9.09 3.33	11
Hamilton	5 9.80 100.00	31 60.78 67.39	0 0.00 0.00	15 29.41 50.00	51
Hamilton & Madison	0 0.00 0.00	0 0.00 0.00	0 0.00 0.00	3 100.00 10.00	3
Jay	0 0.00 0.00	1 20.00 2.17	4 80.00 100.00	0 0.00 0.00	5
Madison	0 0.00 0.00	4 26.67 8.70	0 0.00 0.00	11 73.33 36.67	15
Total	5	46	4	30	85

The last analysis using the Federalist Papers as given in Tables 3.21 and 3.22 used a different weighting function (mutual information) and the singular value decomposition.

Table 3.21 Clustering Using SVD and Mutual Information

Cluster Number	Descriptive Term	Freq.
1	+ grow, + keep, + enter, + engage, + defeat, + permit, + afford, + pay, + receive, + demand, + regulate, + render, + draw, + prevent, + continue, + arise, + secure, + see	15
2	+ occasion, + recommend, + vest, + act, + determine, + suggest, + contain, + exercise, + admit, + constitute, + declare, + arise, + depend, + pass, + know, + answer, + le	30
3	+ elect, + relate, + maintain, + secure, + betray, + follow, + possess, + proceed, + derive, + exclude, + prove, + extend, + know, + hold, + appoint, + confine, + regulat	30
4	+ spring, + deserve, + engage, + teach, + support, + feel, + serve, + involve, + oblige, + admit, + divide, + observe, + preserve, + allow, + apply, + render, + furnish,	10

Table 3.22 Table Analysis of Clusters with SVD and Mutual Information

Author(Author)	_CLUSTER_ (Cluster ID)				Total
	1	2	3	4	
Either	0 0.00 0.00	0 0.00 0.00	11 100.00 36.67	0 0.00 0.00	11
Hamilton	12 23.53 80.00	25 49.02 83.33	8 15.69 26.67	6 11.76 60.00	51
Hamilton & Madison	1 33.33 6.67	0 0.00 0.00	0 0.00 0.00	2 66.67 20.00	3
Jay	2 40.00 13.33	2 40.00 6.67	1 20.00 3.33	0 0.00 0.00	5
Madison	0 0.00 0.00	3 20.00 10.00	10 66.67 33.33	2 13.33 20.00	15
Total	15	30	30	10	85

Again, in this case, the disputed documents appear to resemble Madison's writing more than Hamilton's.

This example demonstrates that choices for weighting term and for clustering methods can affect the clustered results, so much so that the outcome can be completely different. You must validate the clusters to ensure that they are meaningful.

3.8 Exercises

1. Use the Web crawling %TMFILTER macro to explore a topic of interest from the Internet.

2. Since the links for the term **flu** were found, new concerns (for example, about the Avian flu) have appeared so the primary Web sites have changed. Redo the analysis in Section 3.3.

3. Write a summary of the results.

3.9 Reference

Mosteller, F., and D. Wallace. 1964. *Inference and Disputed Authorship: The Federalist.* Addison-Wesley.

Data Summary

4.1 Introduction to Data Summary

To mine data effectively, you first need to understand the data under review. While it is helpful to have some knowledge of the environment in which the data were collected, you can also learn about the data by using the data visualization techniques described in Chapter 2 and by doing simple frequency counts, summary statistics, and table analyses.

Consider, for example, the medication data set provided by the Agency for Healthcare Research and Quality (AHRQ). The database contains many different fields. Some are nominal, containing coded information. Others contain continuous information. According to information available at http://www.meps.ahrq.gov/PUFFiles/H59A/H59ACB.pdf, which you can download, the data contain medications by household and by individual patient. The data set also contains information concerning payment. Display 4.1 partially lists the fields contained in the data set.

Display 4.1 Medication Data Definition

```
  1     5   DUID       DWELLING UNIT ID
  6     8   PID        PERSON NUMBER
  9    16   DUPERSID   PERSON ID (DUID + PID)
 17    31   RXRECIDX   UNIQUE Rx/PRESCRIBED MEDICINE IDENTIFIER
 32    43   LINKIDX    ID FOR LINKAGE TO COND/OTH EVENT FILES
 44    44   PURCHRD    ROUND Rx/PRESCR MED OBTAINED/PURCHASED
 45    46   RXBEGDD    DAY PERSON STARTED TAKING MEDICINE
 47    48   RXBEGMM    MONTH PERSON STARTED TAKING MEDICINE
 49    52   RXBEGYR    YEAR PERSON STARTED TAKING MEDICINE
 53   102   RXNAME     MEDICATION NAME (IMPUTED)
103   132   RXHHNAME   HC REPORTED MEDICATION NAME
133   143   RXNDC      NATIONAL DRUG CODE (IMPUTED)
144   151   RXQUANTY   QUANTITY OF Rx/PRESCR MED (IMPUTED)
152   201   RXFORM     FORM OF Rx/PRESCRIBED MEDICINE (IMPUTED)
202   251   RXFRMUNT   UNIT OF MEAS FORM Rx/PRESC MED (IMPUTED)
252   301   RXSTRENG   STRENGTH OF Rx/PRESCR MED DOSE (IMPUTED)
302   351   RXSTRUNT   UNIT OF MEAS STRENGTH OF Rx (IMPUTED)
352   353   PHARTP1    TYPE OF PHARMACY PROV - 1ST
354   355   PHARTP2    TYPE OF PHARMACY PROV - 2ND
356   357   PHARTP3    TYPE OF PHARMACY PROV - 3RD
358   359   PHARTP4    TYPE OF PHARMACY PROV - 4TH
360   361   PHARTP5    TYPE OF PHARMACY PROV - 5TH
362   363   PHARTP6    TYPE OF PHARMACY PROV - 6TH
364   365   PHARTP7    TYPE OF PHARMACY PROV - 7TH
366   366   RXFLG      NDC IMPUTATION SOURCE ON PC DONOR REC
367   367   PCIMPFLG   TYPE OF HC TO PC PRESCRIPTION MATCH
368   368   CLMOMFLG   CHGE/PYMNT, Rx CLAIM FILING, OMTYPE STAT
369   369   INPCFLG    PID HAS AT LEAST 1 RECORD IN PC
370   370   DIABFLG    Rx INSULIN OR DIABETIC EQUIPMENT/SUPPLY
371   371   SAMPLE     HOUSEHLD RCVD FREE SAMPLE OF Rx IN ROUND
372   374   RXICD1X    3 DIGIT ICD-9 CONDITION CODE
375   377   RXICD2X    3 DIGIT ICD-9 CONDITION CODE
378   380   RXICD3X    3 DIGIT ICD-9 CONDITION CODE
381   383   RXCCC1X    MODIFIED CLINICAL CLASS CODE
384   386   RXCCC2X    MODIFIED CLINICAL CLASS CODE
387   389   RXCCC3X    MODIFIED CLINICAL CLASS CODE

397   403   RXMR01X    AMOUNT PAID, MEDICARE (IMPUTED)
404   410   RXMD01X    AMOUNT PAID, MEDICAID (IMPUTED)
411   417   RXPV01X    AMOUNT PAID, PRIVATE INSURANCE (IMPUTED)
418   424   RXVA01X    AMOUNT PAID, VETERANS (IMPUTED)
425   430   RXTR01X    AMOUNT PAID, TRICARE (IMPUTED)
431   436   RXOF01X    AMOUNT PAID, OTHER FEDERAL (IMPUTED)
437   442   RXSL01X    AMOUNT PAID, STATE & LOCAL GOV (IMPUTED)
443   448   RXWC01X    AMOUNT PAID, WORKERS COMP (IMPUTED)
449   454   RXOT01X    AMOUNT PAID, OTHER INSURANCE (IMPUTED)
455   460   RXOR01X    AMOUNT PAID, OTHER PRIVATE (IMPUTED)
461   466   RXOU01X    AMOUNT PAID, OTHER PUBLIC (IMPUTED)
```

There are thousands of different medications in this list. Because many of the drug names differ only slightly, the data will be difficult to examine. One of the biggest problems with these data is that there are so many levels in the categorical fields. Because so many levels have similar names, you can compress them.

However, the standard practice is to examine the levels manually and to equate similar levels. When there are too many levels, manual compression can be time-consuming. The following section describes a novel technique for compressing all these levels using SAS Text Miner software.

First, consider the data set using the StatExplore node (Output 4.1). For example, consider RXQUANTITY, an imputed value for the prescription quantity. It gives the unit measure of the strength of the medication. Most of the quantities are small.

Another difficulty is the need for domain knowledge of the data set. While some of the medications are available over the counter (for example, aspirin) and in common use, others require very specific product knowledge.

Output 4.1 StatExplore of Medication Database

	Interval Variables										
VARIABLE	LABEL OF F...	MEAN	STDDEV	Non Missing	Missing	Min	Median	Max	Abs C.V.	Coefficient ...	Sign
RXOT01X	AMOUNT PAI...	0	1	277866	0	0	0	152	78.4599	78.4599+	
RXSL01X	AMOUNT PAI...	0	5	277866	0	0	0	804	50.33068	50.33068+	
RXWC01X	AMOUNT PAI...	0	3	277866	0	0	0	366	49.40494	49.40494+	
RXOU01X	AMOUNT PAI...	0	4	277866	0	0	0	804	49.14957	49.14957+	
RXOF01X	AMOUNT PAI...	0	3	277866	0	0	0	456	47.30335	47.30335+	
RXOR01X	AMOUNT PAI...	0	5	277866	0	0	0	705	22.73231	22.73231+	
RXTR01X	AMOUNT PAI...	0	5	277866	0	0	0	440	21.88584	21.88584+	
RXVA01X	AMOUNT PAI...	2	13	277866	0	0	0	1408	8.054972	8.054972+	
RXBEGDD	DAY PERSO...	1	7	277866	0	-9	-1	31	7.95469	7.95469+	
RXBEGMM	MONTH PERS...	1	4	277866	0	-9	-1	12	7.43084	7.43084+	
RXMR01X	AMOUNT PAI...	2	16	277866	0	0	0	1033	7.393191	7.393191+	
PHARTP2	TYPE OF PH...	0	2	277866	0	-9	-1	4	6.330906	6.330906+	
DIABFLG	Rx INSULIN O...	0	0	277866	0	0	0	1	5.693995	5.693995+	
SAMPLE	HOUSEHLD R...	0	0	277866	0	0	0	1	4.645406	4.645406+	
RXMD01X	AMOUNT PAI...	7	33	277866	0	0	0	2660	4.557951	4.557951+	
RXQUANTY	QUANTITY O...	52	191	277866	0	-9	30	21600	3.708975	3.708975+	
RXPV01X	AMOUNT PAI...	17	53	277866	0	0	0	5985	3.050618	3.050618+	
RXSF01X	AMOUNT PAI...	23	51	277866	0	0	10	4995	2.173223	2.173223+	
VARPSU01	VARIANCE E...	5	10	277866	0	1	2	59	1.820586	1.820586+	
PHARTP3	TYPE OF PH...	-1	1	277866	0	-8	-1	4	1.746672	-1.74667+	
RXXP01X	SUM OF PAY...	53	76	277866	0	0	37	6000	1.448403	1.448403+	
RXBEGYR	YEAR PERS...	834	986	277866	0	-14	-1	2002	1.182106	1.182106+	
INPCFLG	PID HAS AT ...	1	0	277866	0	0	1	1	0.707595	0.707595+	
PERWT01F	FINAL PERS...	8975	5321	277866	0	0	8132	67537	0.59286	0.59286+	
PHARTP1	TYPE OF PH...	3	2	277866	0	-9	4	5	0.575149	0.575149+	
VARSTR01	VARIANCE E...	73	42	277866	0	1	68	145	0.57381	0.57381+	
RXFLG	NDC IMPUTA...	1	1	277866	0	1	1	3	0.573492	0.573492+	
CLMOMFLG	CHGE/PYMN...	1	1	277866	0	1	1	6	0.558524	0.558524+	
PHARTP4	TYPE OF PH...	-1	1	277866	0	-8	-1	4	0.556156	-0.55616+	
PID	PERSON NU...	21	11	277866	0	10	18	167	0.503954	0.503954+	
PURCHRD	ROUND Rx/P...	3	1	277866	0	1	3	5	0.457772	0.457772+	
PCIMPFLG	TYPE OF HC ...	2	0	277866	0	1	2	2	0.325834	0.325834+	
DUID	DWELLING U...	56836	17436	277866	0	40001	47743	85356	0.306784	0.306784+	
PHARTP5	TYPE OF PH...	-1	0	277866	0	-1	-1	4	0.235748	-0.23575+	
PHARTP6	TYPE OF PH...	-1	0	277866	0	-1	-1	4	0.098059	-0.09806+	
PHARTP7	TYPE OF PH...	-1	0	277866	0	-1	-1	4	0.069688	-0.06969+	

RXQUANTITY, for example, has a mean of 52 with a standard deviation of 191 and a maximum of 21,600 (which seems an excessive number of pills).

Unfortunately, this screen provides little information at this point because the outcomes of interest relate to households or individuals. You need to collect summaries for household and patient identifiers using a SAS Code node. Section 4.2 describes how to do this, while Section 4.1 gives a basic summary of the information in the data set that concerns payment and payment type.

4.2 Analyzing Continuous Data

Focus on the payment variables listed in Table 4.1.

Table 4.1 Variable Definitions

Variable Name	Variable Definition
RXSF01X	Self-pay
RXMR01X	Medicare
RXMD01X	Medicaid
RXPV01X	Private insurance
RXTR01X	TRICARE
RXOF01X	Other federal sources
RXSL01X	State and local government sources
RXWC01X	Worker's compensation
RXOT01X	Other private source of insurance
RXOU01X	Other public source of insurance
RXXP01X	Sum of payments for each prescribed medication

To compute the means, submit the following code:

```
proc means data=sasuser.medications mean std n min max median;
    var RXSF01X RXMR01X RXMD01X RXPV01X RXVA01X RXTR01X
        RXOF01X RXSL01X  RXWC01X RXOT01X RXOR01X RXOU01X RXXP01X;
    attrib _all_ label=' ';
run;
```

The result appears in Output 4.2.

Output 4.2 Summary Statistics

```
                              The MEANS Procedure

Variable        Mean         Std Dev        N        Minimum        Maximum        Median

RXSF01X      23.4490614     50.9600306    277866            0        4995.00    10.0000000
RXMR01X       2.2071100     16.3175858    277866            0        1032.90             0
RXMD01X       7.2504679     33.0472769    277866            0        2659.59             0
RXPV01X      17.4427821     53.2112619    277866            0        5985.00             0
RXVA01X       1.6351225     13.1708659    277866            0        1407.98             0
RXTR01X       0.2318036      5.0732167    277866            0     440.2200000            0
RXOF01X       0.0605027      2.8619780    277866            0     456.3500000            0
RXSL01X       0.1016831      5.1177785    277866            0     804.4600000            0
RXWC01X       0.0667224      3.2964171    277866            0     366.3700000            0
RXOT01X       0.0135300      1.0615632    277866            0     152.1500000            0
RXOR01X       0.2144482      4.8749019    277866            0     704.9900000            0
RXOU01X       0.0845890      4.1575135    277866            0     803.5300000            0
RXXP01X      52.7578228     76.4146048    277866    0.2000000        6000.00    36.5100000
```

The median is considerably different from the mean, with most median values equal to 0. The maximum, on the other hand, can be quite large. The distribution is clearly skewed, with most of the insured paying very little, if not at all, in each category. The only two exceptions are a $10 median for self-pay and a $36.51 median for the sum of payments. The sum of the medians is not equal to the median of the sum of payments.

Although central measures are important to payers, total payments are important to individuals and to households. Therefore, the distribution of payments is also of interest. To further examine the variables in relationship to the means table, use PROC KDE. The initial code to find the distributions for Medicare, private insurance, self-pay, and total pay follows:

```
proc kde data=sasuser.medications;
  univar RXSF01X/out=sasuser.kderxsf01x method=srot gridl=0
  gridu=250;
  univar RXMR01X/out=sasuser.kderxmr01x method=os gridl=0
  gridu=250;
  univar RXPV01X/out=sasuser.kderxpv01x method=srot gridl=0
  gridu=250;
  univar RXXP01X/out=sasuser.kderxxp01x method=srot gridl=0
  gridu=500;
run;
```

For RXMR01X, the method used to define the bandwidth has been changed to *os*, because the default method does not converge successfully. When there is no convergence with one method, you should try another method. The results are given in Output 4.3.

Output 4.3 Results of PROC KDE

Medicare Pay

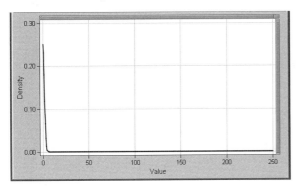

Self Pay

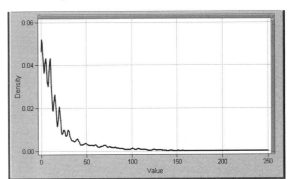

Private Pay

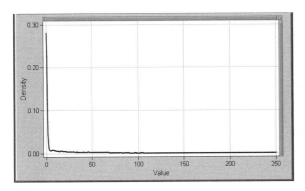

Total Pay

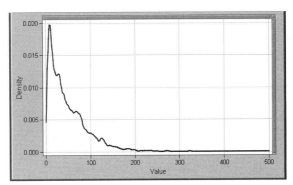

For self pay and total pay, the charts appear very jagged. For private pay and Medicare pay, the chart is almost a straight line at 0 point. The default bandwidth is too small to give a meaningful view of the population distribution. Therefore, modify PROC KDE as follows:

```
proc kde data=sasuser.medications;
  univar RXSF01X/out=sasuser.kderxsf01x method=srot bwm=10 gridl=0
  gridu=250;
  univar RXMR01X/out=sasuser.kderxmr01x method=os bwm=10 gridl=0
  gridu=250;
  univar RXPV01X/out=sasuser.kderxpv01x method=srot bwm=10 gridl=0
  gridu=250;
  univar RXXP01X/out=sasuser.kderxxp01x method=srot bwm=10 gridl=0
  gridu=500;
run;
```

The results appear in Output 4.4.

Output 4.4 Results of PROC KDE with Modified Bandwidth

Medicare Pay

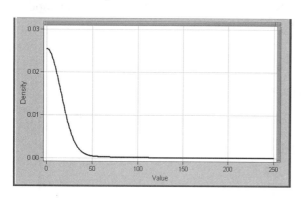

Self Pay

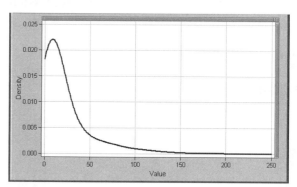

Private Pay

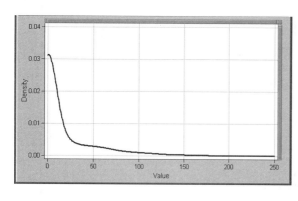

Total Pay

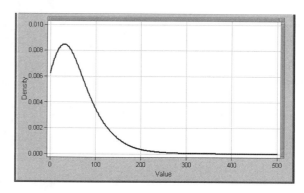

The BWM option changes the degree of smoothness by modifying the bandwidth. With BWM=10, the curves become much smoother, with wider variance at the 0 point. A higher bandwidth offers a better representation of the data because of the size of the data set. Also, the upper grid value in the kernel density can be reduced to show more of the peak and less of the tail.

According to these values, almost no prescription requires an individual to pay much more than $10, with the total cost under $200. However, that value is for prescriptions. It is more important to consider how much an individual pays in the course of a year. To make this determination, compress the data by individual or by household. Section 4.2 compresses the data by household.

4.3 Compressing Data

In data mining, it is important to be able to review multiple observations for one customer. In this example, it is important to examine the total amount that customers are paying for medications over a year. The first step to do so is to sort the data by household ID number. The second step is to use PROC MEANS to create a new data set that contains sums of the variables in the variable list. Once this data set has been created, you can examine it as you would any other data set.

```
proc sort data=sasuser.medications;
   by duid;
proc means data=sasuser.medications std n min max median;
   var RXSF01X RXMR01X RXMD01X RXPV01X RXVA01X RXTR01X RXOF01X
   RXSL01X RXWC01X RXOT01X RXOR01X RXOU01X RXXP01X;
   by duid;
   output out=sasuser.sumofmedications;
          sum=
          mean=
          /autoname;
   attrib _all_ label='';
run;
```

Once compressed, the data are summarized in Output 4.5. A total of 277,866 prescriptions were compressed to 10,630 individual households, for an average of 26.14 prescriptions per household. Again, the median is considerably different from the mean, giving a strong indication that the data are more exponential or gamma than normally distributed. In this case, the median self pay per household is equal to $255.86.

Output 4.5 Means of Compressed Data

The MEANS Procedure

Variable	Mean	Std Dev	N	Minimum	Maximum	Median
RXSF01X_Sum	612.9536124	1091.12	10630	0	30975.22	255.8650000
RXMR01X_Sum	57.6933998	365.7324733	10630	0	9943.51	0
RXMD01X_Sum	189.5257300	949.6545774	10630	0	21539.46	0
RXPV01X_Sum	455.9507131	1097.26	10630	0	54603.76	54.3750000
RXVA01X_Sum	42.7417629	291.8097481	10630	0	9707.70	0
RXTR01X_Sum	6.0592973	118.7231305	10630	0	8734.67	0
RXOF01X_Sum	1.5815268	56.9032568	10630	0	4567.09	0
RXSL01X_Sum	2.6579746	114.8763485	10630	0	11137.39	0
RXWC01X_Sum	1.7441101	115.3764048	10630	0	11205.12	0
RXOT01X_Sum	0.3536717	17.0152372	10630	0	1326.83	0
RXOR01X_Sum	5.6056312	100.9332443	10630	0	6043.38	0
RXOU01X_Sum	2.2111392	89.0615104	10630	0	6829.72	0
RXXP01X_Sum	1379.08	2064.04	10630	0.9000000	54783.76	658.1400000

To examine the entire distribution, use the following code with differing grid values to accommodate the different payment scales by different payers. Again, because the default bandwidth method would not converge, this represents an alternate method:

```
proc kde data=sasuser.sumofmedications;
    univar rxsf01x_sum/gridl=0 gridu=500 out=sasuser.kdeselfpaysum
    method=srot;
    univar rxmr01x_sum/gridl=0 gridu=500 out=sasuser.kdemedicaresum
    method=os;
    univar rxpv01x_sum/gridl=0 gridu=1000 out=sasuser.kdeprivatepaysum
    method=srot;
    univar rxxp01x_sum/gridl=0 gridu=5000 out=sasuser.kdetotalsum
    method=srot;
run;
```

The results appear in Output 4.6. The curve with the greatest variability is the self-pay group.

Output 4.6 Results of PROC KDE with Summed Data

Medicare Pay

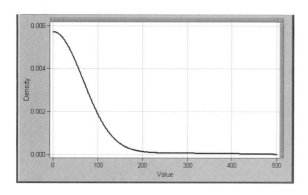

Self Pay

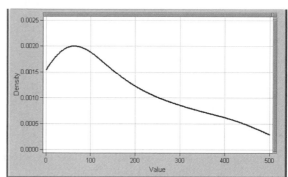

Private Pay

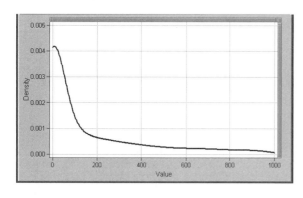

Total Pay

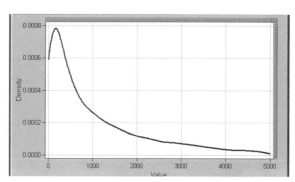

The compressed data set also contains information about the number of prescriptions per data set, defined by the _**Freq**_ field. The average number of prescriptions is equal to 26.24; the median is equal to 15.00. See Output 4.7.

Output 4.7 Kernel Density of Number of Prescriptions

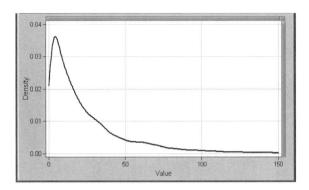

Another useful technique is to define ratios of variables. For example, the value of self pay/total pay helps determine what portion of the cost of medications is paid by the household. The code to define the ratio is shown in the following example:

```
data sasuser.ratioofpayment;
   set sasuser.sumofmedications;
   length duid 8 _type_ 8 costratio 8 _freq_ 8 RXSF01X_Sum 8 RXMR01X_Sum 8
   RXMD01X_Sum 8  RXPV01X_Sum 8 RXVA01X_Sum 8 RXTR01X_Sum 8 RXOF01X_Sum 8
   RXSL01X_Sum 8  RXWC01X_Sum 8 RXOT01X_Sum 8 RXOR01X_Sum 8 RXOU01X_Sum 8
   RXXP01X_Sum 8  RXSF01X_Mean 8 RXMR01X_Mean 8 RXMD01X_Mean 8
                  RXPV01X_Mean 8
   RXVA01X_Mean 8 RXTR01X_Mean 8 RXOF01X_Mean 8 RXSL01X_Mean 8
                  RXWC01X_Mean 8
   RXOT01X_Mean 8 RXOR01X_Mean 8  RXOU01X_Mean 8  RXXP01X_Mean 8;
      costratioselfpay= RXSF01X_Sum/RXXP01X_Sum;
      costratioprivatepay=RXPV01X_sum/RXXP01X_sum;
      costratiomedicare=RXMR01X_sum/RXXP01X_sum;
   run;
```

To visualize the data, run the following code:

```
proc kde data=sasuser.ratioofpayment;
   univar costratioselfpay/gridl=0 gridu=1
        out=sasuser.kdecostratioselfpay method=os;
   univar costratioprivatepay/gridl=0 gridu=1
        out=sasuser.kdecostprivatepay method=os;
   univar costratiomedicare/gridl=0 gridu=1 out=sasuser.kdecostmedicare
        method=os;
   run;
```

Output 4.8 shows the results.

Output 4.8 Ratios of Payment

Self Pay

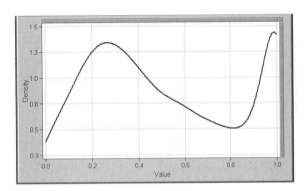

Private Pay

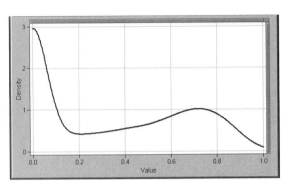

Medicare Pay

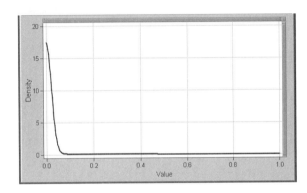

When you use ratios, the scale of the variables is the same. None of the curves can be represented by a normal distribution. It is clear that Medicare pays very little because the data were collected for 2001, prior to the addition of prescription benefits. You can overlay the charts in Output 4.8 using the following code, which combines the three data sets using PROC SQL and then plots the data using SAS/GRAPH software. Fortunately, there are alternatives to coding. See the following SAS Press title, *The Little SAS Book for Enterprise Guide*, for more information. Output 4.9 shows the results.

```
data sasuser.kdecombined;
    length var $ 32 value 8 density 8 count 8;
    set sasuser.kdecostratioselfpay
        sasuser.kdecostprivatepay;
    keep var value density count;
run;

PROC SQL;
    CREATE VIEW WORK.SORT7265 AS SELECT VALUE,DENSITY,VAR FROM
    sasuser.KDECOSTSELFANDPRIVATE;
QUIT;
```

```
GOPTIONS xpixels=&_EGCHARTWIDTH ypixels=&_EGCHARTHEIGHT;
SYMBOL1
   INTERPOL=JOIN
   HEIGHT=1
   VALUE=NONE
   CV=BLUE
   LINE=1
   WIDTH=2
   ;
SYMBOL2
   INTERPOL=JOIN
   HEIGHT=1
   VALUE=NONE
   CV=GREEN
   LINE=1
   WIDTH=2
   ;
Legend1
   FRAME
   POSITION=(BOTTOM CENTER OUTSIDE)
   LABEL=(FONT='Microsoft Sans Serif' HEIGHT=8pt JUSTIFY=Left)
   ;
Axis1
   STYLE=1
   WIDTH=1
   MINOR=NONE
   LABEL=(FONT='Microsoft Sans Serif' HEIGHT=12pt JUSTIFY=Right)
   ;
Axis2
   STYLE=1
   WIDTH=1
   MINOR=NONE
   LABEL=(FONT='Microsoft Sans Serif' HEIGHT=12pt JUSTIFY=Center)
   ;
TITLE;
TITLE1 "Line Plot";
FOOTNOTE;
FOOTNOTE1 "Generated by the SAS System (&_SASSERVERNAME, &SYSSCPL) on
%SYSFUNC(DATE(), EURDFDE9.) at %SYSFUNC(TIME(), TIMEAMPM8.)";
PROC GPLOT DATA=WORK.SORT7265;
PLOT DENSITY * VALUE=VAR
   /
   VAXIS=AXIS1
   HAXIS=AXIS2
   FRAME
   LEGEND=LEGEND1
   ;
```

Output 4.9 Overlay of Kernel Density Estimators

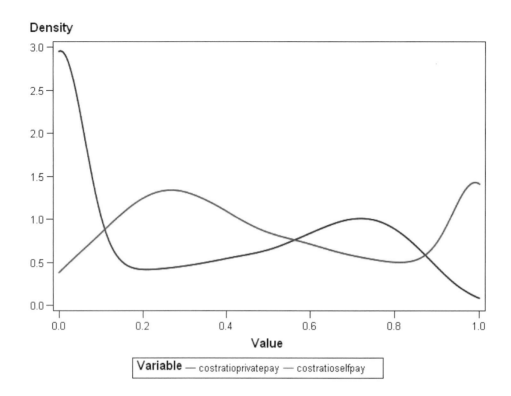

Density

Variable — costratioprivatepay — costratioselfpay

The private pay group has a greater likelihood of paying 100%, a lower likelihood of paying 0%, and an almost equal likelihood of paying 50%.

4.4 Analyzing Discrete Data

In order to examine discrete data, you can first use a simple frequency procedure. This example investigates the different categories of prescription medications as identified in the **RXNAME** field:

```
proc freq data=sasuser.medications;
   tables RXNAME;
run;
```

Output 4.10 shows the partial results of PROC FREQ.

Output 4.10 List of Medications

```
                              MEDICATION NAME (IMPUTED)

                                                        Cumulative  Cumulative
RXNAME                            Frequency   Percent   Frequency    Percent

-7                                     201     0.07         201        0.07
-9                                    3246     1.17        3447        1.24
7 CYCLES NORDETTE                        1     0.00        3448        1.24
A & D OINTMENT                          11     0.00        3459        1.24
A/B OTIC                                36     0.01        3495        1.26
ABSORBASE                                8     0.00        3503        1.26
ACCOLATE                               146     0.05        3649        1.31
ACCU-CHEK                                3     0.00        3652        1.31
ACCU-CHEK ADVANTAGE                      5     0.00        3657        1.32
ACCU-CHEK ADVANTAGE (STRIP)              8     0.00        3665        1.32
ACCU-CHEK ADVANTAGE (STRIP,2X50)         5     0.00        3670        1.32
ACCU-CHEK ADVANTAGE CARE                 6     0.00        3676        1.32
ACCU-CHEK COMFORT CURVE (STRIP)          5     0.00        3681        1.32
ACCU-CHEK COMFORT CURVE STRIPS           7     0.00        3688        1.33
ACCU-CHEK INSTANT                        1     0.00        3689        1.33
ACCU-CHEK SIMPLICITY CARE (COMPLETE MONITORING)  4  0.00  3693        1.33
ACCU-CHEK TEST STRIP                     7     0.00        3700        1.33
ACCUPRIL                              1507     0.54        5207        1.87
ACCURETIC (10X3)                        29     0.01        5236        1.88
ACCUTANE                                72     0.03        5308        1.91
ACCUTANE (RX PAK, 10X10)                42     0.02        5350        1.93
ACCUZYME                                 1     0.00        5351        1.93
ACEBUTOLOL HCL                          89     0.03        5440        1.96
ACEON                                   42     0.02        5482        1.97
ACEPHEN                                  6     0.00        5488        1.98
ACETAMIN                                19     0.01        5507        1.98
ACETAMIN W/COD                           1     0.00        5508        1.98
ACETAMIN/COD3                           28     0.01        5536        1.99
ACETAMINAPHEN                            1     0.00        5537        1.99
ACETAMINOPHEN                          358     0.13        5895        2.12
ACETAMINOPHEN (A.F.,CHERRY)              8     0.00        5903        2.12
ACETAMINOPHEN (DROPS)                    4     0.00        5907        2.13
ACETAMINOPHEN (DROPS, A.F.)              1     0.00        5908        2.13
ACETAMINOPHEN (INFANT)                   1     0.00        5909        2.13
ACETAMINOPHEN E.S.                       1     0.00        5910        2.13
ACETAMINOPHEN INFANTS                    1     0.00        5911        2.13
ACETAMINOPHEN INFANTS (DROPS,A.F.,FRUIT) 1     0.00        5912        2.13
ACETAMINOPHEN W/ CODEINE                10     0.00        5922        2.13
ACETAMINOPHEN W/COD                     36     0.01        5958        2.14
ACETAMINOPHEN W/CODEINE                 25     0.01        5983        2.15
ACETAMINOPHEN W/CODEINE #3              24     0.01        6007        2.16
ACETAMINOPHEN W/CODEINE ELIXIR           1     0.00        6008        2.16
ACETAMINOPHEN W/CODEINE#3                1     0.00        6009        2.16
ACETAMINOPHEN WITH CODEINE               1     0.00        6010        2.16
ACETAMINOPHEN/APAP                       1     0.00        6011        2.16
```

A quick review of the different medication names demonstrates that there are many medications that are virtually identical. Although drug names might appear to be standardized, there is enough discretion in data input such that there are alternative spellings and abbreviations. For example, the norm for **ACETAMINOPHEN** has a frequency count of 358, while **ACETAMINOPHEN (DROPS)** has a count of 4. **ACETAMINOPHEN W/CODEINE** is listed in many different ways. For the most part, the difference occurs because of the level of detail provided at data entry. It would be helpful to simplify the list.

You can compress these categories because of the similarity in the names of the medications using SAS Text Miner software. While you can use preprocessing to make these similar categories equivalent, SAS Text Miner software can use the stemming property of the words to do the same thing. See the process flow for SAS Text Miner in Figure 4.1.

Figure 4.1 Text Miner Node

MEDICATIONS   Text Miner (2)   Drop

To reduce the number of categories, the default changes on the left-hand side of the Text Miner node are shown in Display 4.2.

Display 4.2 Text Miner Node Settings

Property	Value
Parse Variable	RXNAME
Language	ENGLISH
Stop List	SASHELP.STOPLST
Start List	
Stem Terms	Yes
Terms in Single Document	No
Punctuation	No
Numbers	No
Different Parts of Speech	No
Ignore Parts of Speech	
Noun Groups	Yes
Synonyms	SASHELP.ENGSYNMS
Find Entities	No
Types of Entities	
Transform	
Compute SVD	Yes
SVD Resolution	Low
Max SVD Dimensions	100
Scale SVD Dimensions	No
Frequency weighting	Log
Term Weight	Entropy
Roll up Terms	Yes
No. of Rolled-up Terms	1000
Drop Other Terms	No
Cluster	
Automatically Cluster	Yes
Exact or Maximum Number	Exact
Number of Clusters	500
Cluster Algorithm	EXPECTATION-MAXIMIZAT
Ignore Outliers	No
Hierarchy Levels	.
Descriptive Terms	5
What to Cluster	SVD Dimensions
Status	

For the most part, the defaults can be used. However, to compress categories, set the roll-up terms (**Transform** section) to **Yes**. The number of roll-up terms should be large (500, 1,000) depending upon the size of the original data set.

The number of clusters (**Cluster** section) should be set to the number of categories you want after compression. Set the **Automatically Cluster** field to **Yes**.

This process can take time. In this example, the number of clusters was set to 500. The number of roll-up terms was 1,000. The number of SVD dimensions was set at 100. The interactive results (as identified in the **Property** section here) are shown in Output 4.11.

Output 4.11 SAS Text Miner Software Results

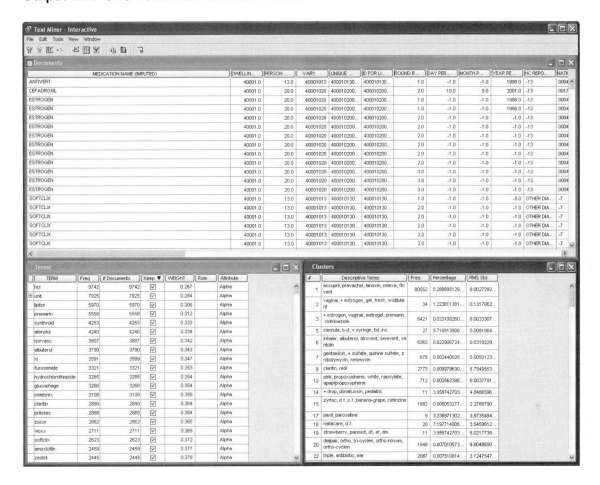

To use the compressed clusters, merge the cluster data set with the original data set. You should keep the cluster descriptive terms but not the intermediate columns used to define the text clusters.

Highlight the link between nodes. The data sets that are transferred between nodes are shown on the left-hand side of the screen (Figure 4.2 and Display 4.3).

Figure 4.2 Highlighting the Link between Nodes

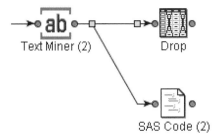

Display 4.3 Transferred Data Sets

Property	Value
From	TEXT2
To	EMCODE2
DOCUMENTS	
Table	EMWS.TEXT2_DOCUMEI...
Variables	
Role	Train
VALIDATE	
Table	EMWS.TEXT2_VALIDATE...
Variables	
Role	Validate
TEST	
Table	EMWS.TEXT2_TEST
Variables	
Role	Test
TERMS	
Table	EMWS.TEXT2_TERMS
Variables	
Role	Terms
CLUSTER	
Table	EMWS.TEXT2_CLUSTER...
Variables	
Role	Cluster
OUT	
Table	EMWS.TEXT2_OUT
Variables	
Role	Transaction

The Emws.Text2.Cluster data set contains words defining each cluster. The Emws.Text2.Documents data set contains a field assigning a cluster number to each observation in the data set.

To examine the data with reduced clusters, you must merge the two data sets. However, they contain additional fields that are not needed in any other analysis. Therefore, reduce the variable list before the merger using SAS code as shown below.

For the Text2_Cluster data set, only the cluster number, frequency, and cluster descriptor are retained. For Text2_Documents, all intermediate fields (**SVD**, **ROLL**, and **PROB**) are dropped. The size of the arrays depends upon the values used to create the text clusters.

Sort the clusters prior to the merge, as follows:

```
data sasuser.clusternamescopy (keep=_cluster_ _freq_ _rmsstd_ clus_desc);
   set emws.text2_cluster;
run;

data sasuser.desccopy (drop=_svd_1-_svd_500  _roll_1-_roll_1000
   prob1-prob500);
   set emws.text2_documents;
run;

proc sort data=sasuser.clusternamescopy;
   by _cluster_;
```

```
proc sort data=sasuser.desccopy;
   by _cluster_;
data sasuser.medicationswithdescriptionscopy2;
   merge sasuser.clusternamescopy  sasuser.desccopy;
   by _CLUSTER_;
run;
```

A partial list of the clusters and descriptors appears in Table 4.2. A total of 500 clusters were returned to create this list.

Table 4.2 Text Clusters

Original Medication Name	Cluster Number	Cluster Descriptor
ADVANTAGE MOTRIN JUNIOR (ORANGE) NIFEDIPINE CR VIDEX (MANDARIN ORANGE)	1	1 mint, + estrogen, w/dilutent, gel, u.s.p.
CEFTIN BETOPTIC S PACERONE COREG	2	celexa, ultram, avandia, lotrel, amaryl
PREMARIN CLOTRIMAZOLE MICONAZOLE VAG	3	estrogen, vaginal, metrogel, premarin, clotrimazole
CALAN SR (CAPLET)	4	sr, caplet, calan, deconamine
SERTRALINE	7	sertraline
CLARITIN	8	claritin, redi
ALBUTEROL	9	albuterol, atrovent, ventolin, proventil, difluca
ORTHO TRI -CYCLEN ORTHO TRI-CYCLEN (DIALPAK, 6X28) ORTHO TRI-CYCLEN	16	dialpak, ortho, tri-cyclen, ortho-novum, ortho-cyclen
ZESTRIL	32	zestril, lisinopril
ATENOLOL	34	atenolol, tenormin

Ensure that a subject matter expert validates the clusters by investigating their reasonableness. As an example, **Zestril** (Cluster 32) is the brand name for **lisinopril**. Similarly, **redi** is a shortened form for **Claritin Reditabs**. At first glance, Cluster 2 is not entirely logical. **Celexa** is an antidepressant, while **Avandia** and **Amaryl** are used to lower blood sugar. There are too many medications in this cluster, and the grouping is not logical. SAS Text Miner software can further subdivide Cluster 2 for a more reasonable result. Also examine the relationships between these medications to find why they were grouped together. See Chapter 6 for details.

Sometimes, the categories are defined by numeric codes rather than by names. The default in SAS Text Miner software is to ignore numbers. However, as shown in Display 4.3, the default can be changed to include numbers. If the numeric codes are already ordinal in nature, the ordering can be used to combine categories into fewer levels. However, if the numeric codes represent nominal values, SAS Text Miner can use its stemming property to compress the categories into fewer levels.

Table 4.3 shows clustering limited to 100 categories. The table is reproduced in its entirety so you can duplicate the outcome for 100 clusters.

Table 4.3 Clustering Drug List to 100 Categories

Cluster Number	Cluster Descriptors	Freq.	Percentage
1	celexa, flovent, k-dur, lorazepam, hctz/triamterene	83273	30%
2	w/applicator, + estrogen, vaginal, estrace, clotrimazole	6438	2%
3	diflucan, serevent, ventolin, diskus, advair	2880	1%
4	nestabs, accutane, nephro-vite, premesis, cbf	327	0%
5	ventolin, inhaler, intal, refill, nebulizer	3848	1%
6	diclofenac, sodium, acetaminophen/codeine, warfarin, dicloxacillin	4967	2%
7	claritin, reditabs, redi, + unit	2890	1%
8	fruit, gnp, pediatric, gantrisin, pediatric fruit	529	0%
9	zoloft	2407	1%
10	bitartrate, apap/hydrocodone, guiatuss, baby, miralax	1131	0%
11	pink, petrolatum, napsylate, apap/propoxyphene, propoxyphene	738	0%
12	fluticasone, propionate, clobetasol, prop, halobetasol	111	0%
13	srn, ml, insulin, nph, human	2174	1%
14	zyrtec, d.f.,s.f.,banana-grape, cetirizine	1682	1%
15	coumadin, kapseals, infatabs, kapseal, dilantin	2052	1%
16	cozaar, evista, hyzaar, lasix, claritin-d	7828	3%
17	caplet, pd, bromfenex, gen, calan	194	0%
18	df, strawberry, dihistine, af, strawb/pineap	90	0%
19	dialpak, ortho, tri-cyclen, ortho-novum, ortho-cyclen	1948	1%
20	+ packet, single, emla, zpak, cholestyramine	1379	0%
21	wellbutrin, cardizem, provera, maxzide, elavil	2535	1%
22	atenolol, tenormin	4549	2%
23	+ strip, ultra, natalcare, precision, test	109	0%
24	celebrex	3108	1%
25	nystatin, cherry	4	0%
26	strawberry, cefaclor, light, locholest, tannihist	121	0%
27	furosemide	3321	1%
28	hydrochlorothiazide	3285	1%
29	cromolyn, heparin, dosette, cefazolin, vial	111	0%
30	prempro, + dispenser, alesse, ez-dial, minipack	2557	1%
31	maxalt, caplet, + unit	78	0%
32	verapamil, amitriptyline, trazodone, clonidine, cyclobenzaprine	15295	6%
33	synthroid	4243	2%
34	toprol	1723	1%
35	zestril, lisinopril	2956	1%
36	metformin, xr, diltiazem	126	0%
37	+ multivitamin, compound, bactrim, anaprox, aciphex	2206	1%
38	zocor, + unit	1347	0%

(continued)

Table 4.3 Clustering Drug List to 100 Categories (*continued*)

Cluster Number	Cluster Descriptors	Freq.	Percentage
39	pilocarpine, drop-tainer	9	0%
40	ins, bd, terumo, + syringe, sodium chloride	35	0%
41	vial, p.f., albuterol, + sulfate, s.d.	722	0%
42	one, touch, + lancet, syr, point	2994	1%
43	metoprolol, tartrate, succinate, loxapine, brimonidine	1877	1%
44	ex, gelcaplet, fa, dilantin, chromagen	24	0%
45	remeron, sinemet, dynacirc, eskalith, norpace	565	0%
46	filmtab, fruit, nr, hc, s.f.	466	0%
47	patanol, hydrochloride, buspar, phoslo, codeine/promethazine	1637	1%
48	zyban, vivelle-dot, daily, vivelle, advantage	641	0%
49	prevacid	2291	1%
50	allegra	1850	1%
51	metformin, xr, effexor, adderall, glucophage	4419	2%
52	glyburide, retin-a, micro, retin-a micro, copley-d	1903	1%
53	ibuprofen, ibu, grx, motrin, berry	2496	1%
54	levoxyl	1705	1%
55	+ unit, prilosec, omeprazole, nf-omeprazole	2923	1%
56	sulfa, silver	6	0%
57	prevident, roxicet, antacid, gel-kam, therapy	2010	1%
58	paroxetine	33	0%
59	tannate, antibiotic, aid, removal, wax	2231	1%
60	vioxx, tazorac, rofecoxib, estring, nf	2759	1%
61	zocor, package, bulk, simvastatin	1948	1%
62	gum, amoxil, strawberry, amoxicillin, trihydrate	2906	1%
63	clonazepam, package, bulk, mevacor, pepcid	762	0%
64	methylprednisolone	75	0%
65	orange, carbamazepine, orange-raspberry, augmentin, cherry-banana	1290	0%
66	la, nifedipine, detrol, theophylline, adalat	3303	1%
67	histex, carmol, zantac, ointment, w/diluent	1240	0%
68	bitartrate, apap/hydrocodone, caplet	156	0%
69	valerate, medroxyprogesterone, hydrocortisone, megestrol, florinef	1455	1%
70	junior, orange, motrin	2	0%
71	prinivil, alprazolam, singulair, package, bulk	5862	2%
72	fresh, + pad, skin, ery, prep	67	0%
73	lithium, carbonate, haloperidol, oyster, atorvastatin	788	0%
74	ranitidine, n/apap, propoxy, propoxyphene-n, propoxyphene-n w/apap	69	0%
75	blister, micardis, blister card,4x7, acid, blister pack,6x28	1206	0%
76	erythromycin, mesylate, doxazosin, citrate, mononitrate	3634	1%

(continued)

Table 4.3 Clustering Drug List to 100 Categories (*continued*)

Cluster Number	Cluster Descriptors	Freq.	Percentage
77	vial, humalog, pen, ipratropium, bromide	2738	1%
78	allergy, allergy relief medicine, medicine, allergy relief, relief	24	0%
79	accupril	1507	1%
80	digoxin, lanoxin, valium, diazepam, glipizide	26	0%
81	saline, + drop, broncho, q-pap, floxin	1309	0%
82	orange, chloride, potassium chloride, penicillin, oxybutynin	2283	1%
83	+ sulfate, morphine, ferrous sulfate, quinine, ferrous	2691	1%
84	tamiflu, amerge, compack, estrostep, demulen	1707	1%
85	imitrex, nitroglycerin, glucometer, elite, care	1426	1%
86	paxil, + unit, paroxetine, orange	2361	1%
87	pravachol	1489	1%
88	caplet, depakote, d.f., glucovance, lortab	5963	2%
89	b-d, + syringe, cannula, bd, ins	27	0%
90	lipitor	5970	2%
91	formula, prenatal vitamins, wildberry, natachew, prenatal formula	373	0%
92	cough, control, mytussin, s.f.,fruit/mint, benzoyl	327	0%
93	clindamycin, phosphate, pledget, phos, clindets	154	0%
94	blister, amerge, + unit, pck, pk	1480	1%
95	non-aspirin, + child, gra, diphenhist, a.f.,fruit	108	0%
96	insulin, srn, humulin, novolin, mcg	269	0%
97	norvasc, amlodipine, besylate	3839	1%
98	dose, astelin, prednisone, pump, + meter	2983	1%
99	triamcinolone, enalapril, estradiol, tricor, micronized	3239	1%
100	guaifenesin, w/codeine, w/codeine #3, phenergan, vc	2654	1%

Ensure that a subject matter expert validates the clusters by investigating their reasonableness. Consider Cluster 55 where **Prilosec** is the brand name for **omeprazole**. This example illustrates SAS Text Miner software's ability to pick up alternate names for similar items even without defining a synonym list to equate them. Cluster 5 contains **inhaler**, **nebulizer**, and **refill**, all related to asthma medications. **Ventolin** is an asthma medication. Cluster 19 contains medications related to birth control. Cluster 53 contains **Motrin**, a brand name for **ibuprofen**. Cluster 96 contains the two brand names: **humulin** and **novolin** for insulin.

At first glance, Cluster 3 appears to contain an error because **Diflucan** is a medication used to treat yeast infections, while the remaining medications treat asthma. One of the side effects of the asthma medications, however, is oral yeast infections. Cluster 1 is also puzzling because the different medications are used for very different diagnoses.

4.5 Using the Princomp Node

Up to this point, this chapter has discussed compressing levels of a categorical variable. Now, consider compressing the number of variables in the list. This is called principal components analysis.

Principal components analysis takes a large number of variables and divides them into component parts that are orthogonal. Use it when there are too many variables in the data set to manage. The Princomp node performs principal components analysis by reducing the number of variables used in subsequent analyses. Display 4.4 shows the default menu for the Princomp node.

Display 4.4 Default Settings for the Princomp Node

Property	Value
Node ID	PRINCOMP
Imported Data	
Exported Data	
Variables	
Eigenvalue Source	Correlation
Interactive Selection	
]Eigenvalue Cutoff	
-Cumulative	0.99
-Increment	0.0010
]Max Number Cutoff	
-Apply Maximum Number	Yes
-Maximum Number	20
Reject Original Input Variabl	Yes
Hide Rejected Variables	Yes
Print Eigenvalue Source	No
]Status	

The eigenvalues determine the number of factors that are defined. You should vary the defaults to see how they impact the results. The results screen appears in Output 4.12. By default, the factor is given for each eigenvalue greater than 1.

Principal components analysis works with interval or ordinal data only. The data set in this example is the student survey data discussed in Chapter 2.

Output 4.12 Results Screen for the Princomp Node

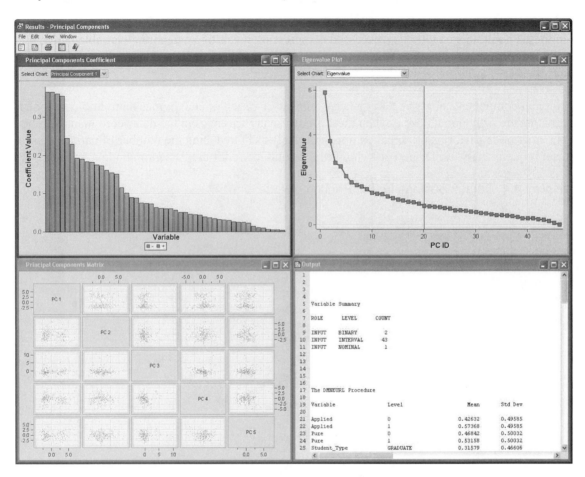

Because the default is to define components when the eigenvalue is greater than 0.99, only one component is defined from the data. The output contains other charts, including a scree plot (Output 4.13). The scree plot graphs the eigenvalues on an axes. However, both provide roughly similar information.

Output 4.13 Scree Plot

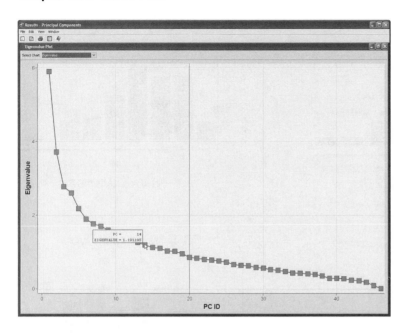

In order to examine the principal components more carefully, connect the Princomp node to the StatExplore node or the MultiPlot node. The MultiPlot node results in Output 4.14 for the student survey data. Examine the defined factors by student type (graduate or undergraduate).

Output 4.14 MultiPlot Results

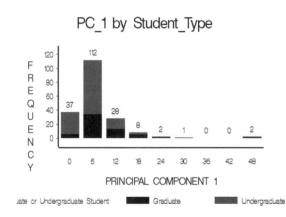

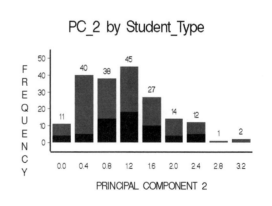

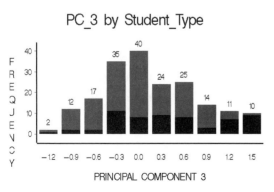

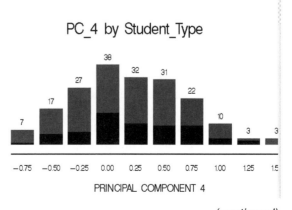

(continued)

Output 4.14 MultiPlot Results *(continued)*

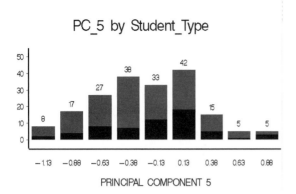

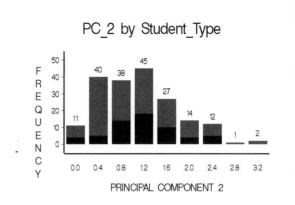

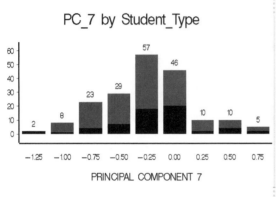

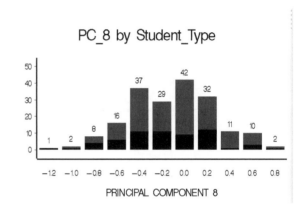

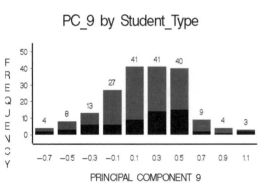

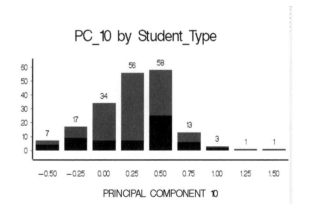

Unfortunately, although principal component analysis can compress variables into a smaller data set, the factors are not meaningful unless you can label them.

Because only the first factor has an eigenvalue greater than 1, it is the only factor you need to consider. The factor is contained in the interval from 0 to 50 and roughly defines students who generally scored high on all questions compared to students who routinely scored low.

In addition to principal components analysis, you can use SAS/STAT software's PROC FACTOR to perform a more complete factor analysis. We refer the interested reader to the following SAS Press title: *A Step-by-Step Approach to Using SAS for Factor Analysis and Structural Equation Modeling.*

4.6 Additional Example

In this example, information from a registrar's database contains all student enrollments and grades in all courses for a 5-year period. It includes information about semester of enrollment and student identification numbers so that enrollment across semesters can be tracked. There were approximately 850,000 total student enrollments during this 5-year period for almost 60,000 students. To protect student confidentiality, the student identification numbers were obscured through a random-number generator. A course catalog is provided at http://htmlaccess.louisville.edu/crseCatalog/searchCrseCatalog.cfm, so that you can identify department code abbreviations.

When approaching a new, previously unknown database, you should always use data visualization and data summary techniques to study it, and to become familiar with the values in the database. The most prominent features in this database are the field containing grades and the field containing student identification by department and by course.

Notice that grades are represented by letter codes. While A, B, C, D, F, and W are fairly self-explanatory, there are other codes represented. For example, some of the courses are graded as Pass/Fail and so a grade of P is listed. An I stands for an incomplete and an X for deferred grades. To investigate grades, stay with the basics of A, B, C, D, and F and count a W as an F. Because these grades are ordinal in nature, convert them to numbers using the following SAS code:

```
data sasuser.classes;
   set sasuser.classes;
   label GRADE_recoded = "Recoded Values of GRADE";
   select(left(trim(put(GRADE,$F2.))));
      when('') GRADE_recoded = .;
      when('A') GRADE_recoded = 4;
      when('A+') GRADE_recoded = 4;
      when('A-') GRADE_recoded = 4;
      when('AU') GRADE_recoded = .;
      when('B') GRADE_recoded = 3;
      when('B+') GRADE_recoded = 3;
      when('B-') GRADE_recoded = 3;
      when('C') GRADE_recoded = 2;
      when('C+') GRADE_recoded = 2;
      when('C-') GRADE_recoded = 2;
      when('CR') GRADE_recoded = .;
      when('D') GRADE_recoded = 1;
      when('D+') GRADE_recoded = 1;
      when('D-') GRADE_recoded = 1;
      when('F') GRADE_recoded = 0;
      when('H') GRADE_recoded = .;
      when('I') GRADE_recoded = .;
      when('NC') GRADE_recoded = .;
      when('NR') GRADE_recoded = .;
      when('P') GRADE_recoded = .;
      when('S') GRADE_recoded = .;
      when('U') GRADE_recoded = .;
      when('W') GRADE_recoded = 0;
      when('X') GRADE_recoded = .;
      otherwise;
      end;
   run;
```

All other grades are identified as missing. Once you have created this new data set, use PROC MEANS to define the average grade by university department. The summary statistics are stored in a new data set so that the results can be graphed using the visualization techniques described in Chapter 2. Output 4.15 gives the line plot for the grade averages.

Output 4.15 Line Graph of Grade Averages by Department

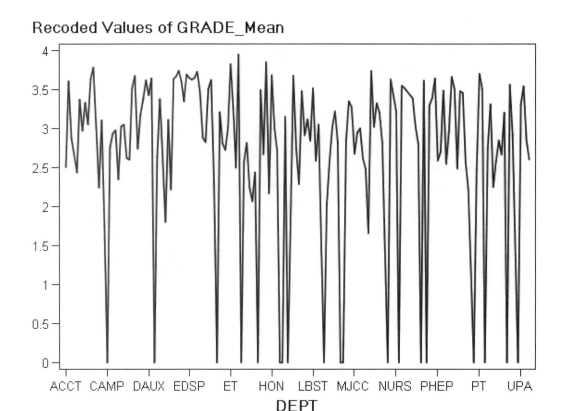

Output 4.15 shows that different departments grade differently. While some departments have an average that is close to 4.0, others are much lower. A number of departments have recorded grade averages of 0. It would seem unreasonable that these departments were failing all their students. Let's look at one of these departments more specifically to see what is happening. Because the *x*-axis does not include all departments, choose the **camp** department for drill-down purposes. The course catalog at http://htmlaccess.louisville.edu/crseCatalog/searchCrseCatalog.cfm indicates that **camp** represents a campus culture course that is required for all freshmen. A frequency count of grades for **camp** appears in Output 4.16.

Output 4.16 Grades Assigned for Campus Culture

Grade	Frequency
I	21
Nr	1
P	1803
U	359
W	170

The output indicates that a grade average of 0 was assigned because all grades were changed to missing. It is likely that the grades for other departments with a grade average of 0 also were all changed to missing. However, the lack of a grade average does not change the variability in the other departments. Remove the impact of these 0 averages by using the following code:

```
PROC SQL;
CREATE TABLE SASUSER.reducedsummarytable AS SELECT gradebydept.DEPT
    FORMAT=$F4.,
      gradebydept._WAY_,
      gradebydept._TYPE_,
      gradebydept._FREQ_,
      gradebydept.GRADEPOINT_Mean FORMAT=BEST12.,
      gradebydept.GRADEPOINT_StdDev FORMAT=BEST12.,
      gradebydept.GRADEPOINT_Min FORMAT=BEST12.,
      gradebydept.GRADEPOINT_Max FORMAT=BEST12.,
      gradebydept.GRADEPOINT_N
    FROM EC100012.gradebydept AS gradebydept
    WHERE gradebydept.GRADEPOINT_Mean>0;
QUIT;
```

A revised line graph appears in Output 4.17.

Output 4.17 Revised Line Graph of Grade Averages

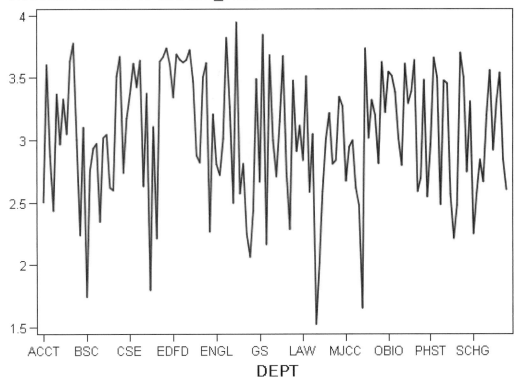

Continue to drill down into the data by averaging grades by department at the general education level (courses labeled in the 100–199 range), the undergraduate level (courses labeled in the 200–599 range), and the graduate level (courses labeled in the 500–up range). Domain knowledge is important here. Work closely with a member of the university community in order to identify salient information. Output 4.18 gives the grade averages by department for the general education level of classes.

Output 4.18 Grade Averages for General Education

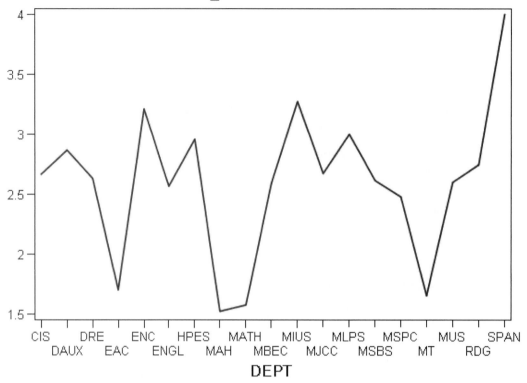

Recoded Values of GRADE_Mean

To find out which department has the lowest grade average, use filtering to remove all departments with an average grade of 2.0 or above, leaving only those departments with grade point averages less than 1.9. The results are given in Output 4.19. Only three departments remain.

```
PROC SQL;
CREATE TABLE SASUSER.lowgradeaverages AS SELECT sasuser.generaled
    FORMAT=$F4.,
        QURY5859._WAY_,
        QURY5859._TYPE_,
        QURY5859._FREQ_,
        QURY5859.GRADEPOINT_Mean FORMAT=BEST12.,
        QURY5859.GRADEPOINT_StdDev FORMAT=BEST12.,
        QURY5859.GRADEPOINT_Min FORMAT=BEST12.,
        QURY5859.GRADEPOINT_Max FORMAT=BEST12.,
        QURY5859.GRADEPOINT_N
    FROM SASUSER.QURY5859 AS QURY5859
    WHERE QURY5859.GRADEPOINT_Mean < 1.9;
QUIT;

PROC PRINT DATA=WORK.SORT6442
    OBS="Row number"
    LABEL
    ;
    VAR GRADEPOINT_Mean;
    ID DEPT;
RUN;
```

Output 4.19 Departments with Low Grade Averages in General Education

Department	Grade Average
BSC	1.74
PHCI	0.83
PHY	1.71

PHY stands for Physiology, **PHCI** for Clinical Investigations and Epidemiology, and **BSC** for Basic Science Core. All are, in fact, departments in the School of Medicine, where the 100-level courses do not represent general education courses; instead they represent the beginning level of a graduate curriculum. A similar graph was defined for the undergraduate courses (Output 4.20) after filtering out the remaining medical departments.

Output 4.20 Grade Averages by Department for Undergraduates

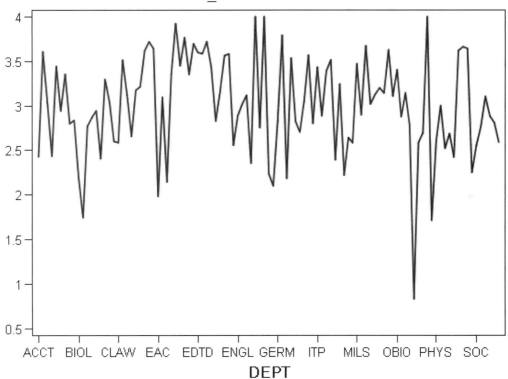

Again, note the considerable variability, which is also apparent in courses for graduate students (Output 4.21).

Output 4.21 Grade Averages for Graduate Students

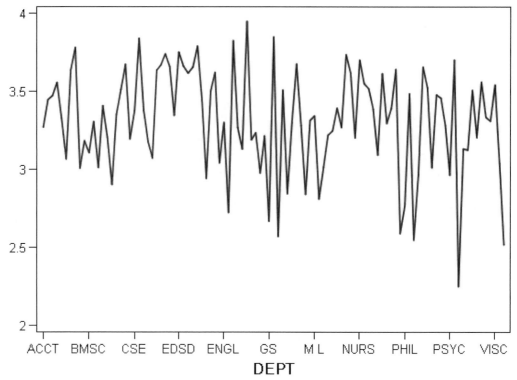

It is suggested that where decision making has no real accountability, variability will be considerable. In contrast, where there is more accountability for decisions, variability in outcome will be reduced. The question is whether some departments have more accountability (and less variability) compared to others. To investigate this question, choose three departments for drill down—English, Mathematics, and Spanish—to see if there is variability within the specific general education, undergraduate, and graduate requirements. First, filter the data again for this drill down:

```
PROC SQL;
CREATE TABLE SASUSER.QURY4670 AS SELECT classesmodified.DEPT
    FORMAT=$F4.,
        classesmodified.CRSENO FORMAT=BEST12.,
        classesmodified.SECTNO FORMAT=$F4.,
        classesmodified.CRHRS FORMAT=BEST12.,
        classesmodified.GRADE FORMAT=$F2.,
        classesmodified.AUDIT FORMAT=$F1.,
        classesmodified.STRM FORMAT=$F4.,
        classesmodified.STUID FORMAT=BEST12.,
        classesmodified.course FORMAT=$F17.,
        classesmodified.GRADEPOINT FORMAT=BEST12.
    FROM EC100043.classesmodified AS classesmodified
    WHERE ( classesmodified.DEPT IN ('ENGL', 'MATH', 'SPAN') AND
            classesmodified.CRSENO BETWEEN 100 AND 199);
QUIT;
```

At this point, kernel density becomes useful, as follows:

```
proc sort data=sasuser.genedengletc;
   by dept;

proc kde data=sasuser.genedengletc out=sasuser.kdegened;
   univar gradepoint/gridl=0 gridu=4 out=sasuser.kdegened;
   by dept;
run;
```

Output 4.22 shows the results.

Output 4.22 Kernel Density of Grade Averages for General Education

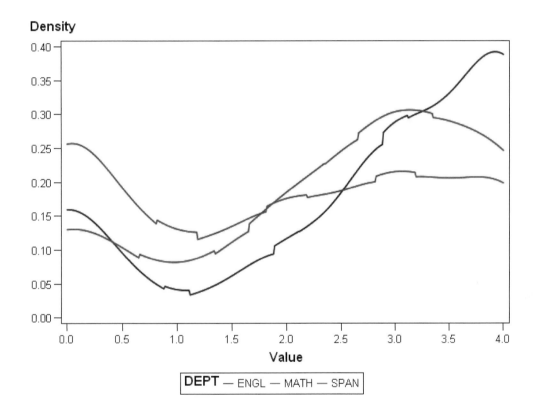

It appears that English has the most extreme distribution, while Mathematics has a distribution more approaching uniformity. Mathematics students will receive a grade of D or above in an almost uniform distribution. Undergraduate and graduate levels were compared (Output 4.23 and 4.24). For the undergraduate grades, English and Spanish coincide while the uniformity in the Mathematics grade distribution becomes more prominent.

Output 4.23 Kernel Density of Grades for Undergraduate Students

Density

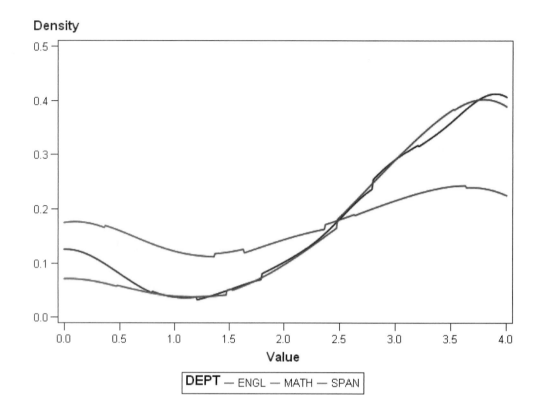

At the graduate level, the uniformity in distribution for Mathematics begins to disappear. In English and Spanish, the probability of high grades is much greater compared to Mathematics.

Output 4.24 Kernel Density of Grades for Graduate Students

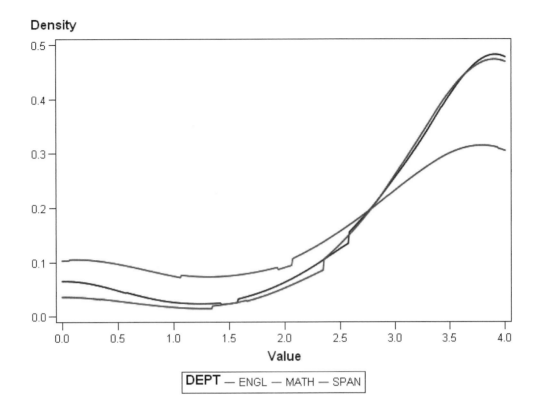

To further explore the question of variability, you can examine individual course sections and courses for one semester (Output 4.25 and 4.26). The question is whether it is the students who vary in their performance across the course sections or whether it is the instructors who vary in their grading practices.

Output 4.25 Line Graph of One Semester of English General Education

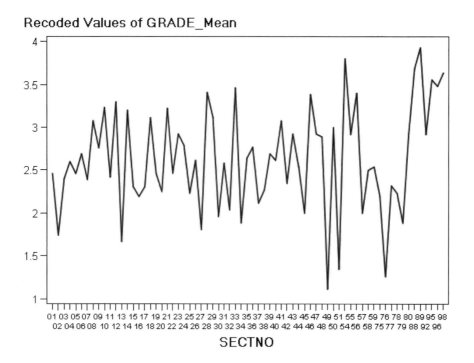

Output 4.26 Line Graph of One Semester of College Algebra

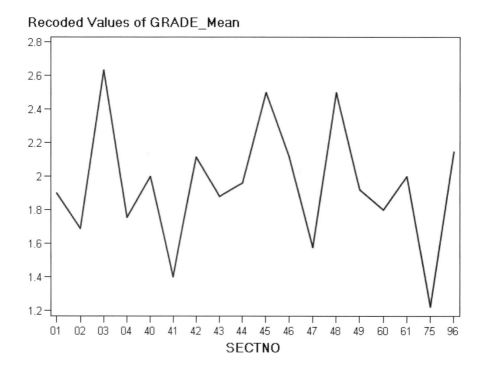

Output 4.27 shows considerable variability. The grade average by section ranges from 1 to 4. The variability is not nearly as great in College Algebra, which ranges from 1.4 to 2.7. Spanish ranges 1 grade point, from 1.8 to 2.8.

Output 4.27 Line Graph of One Semester of Introductory Spanish

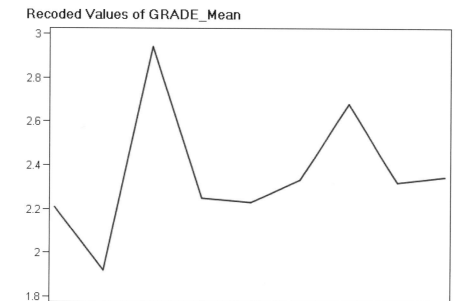

The question is whether the variability in grading results from the students enrolled in the different sections or the instructors who are teaching the courses. There are two ways to examine this question: to look at the variability across students and to look at a similar set of data where there is less variability across students. In the first way, student ACT scores (entrance examinations; see http://www.act.org/) are used to measure the competency of the students. In the second way, variability in graduate courses is examined. Because graduate courses tend to be offered on a rotational basis, many of the classes are populated by the same students, particularly 600-level courses and higher. For this reason, the variability across students is minimized. Output 4.28, 4.29, and 4.30 show the variability at the graduate level.

Output 4.28 Line Graph of Variability in Graduate Courses in English

Recoded Values of GRADE_Mean

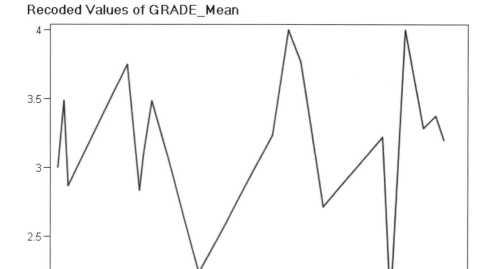

Output 4.29 Line Graph of Variability in Graduate Courses in Mathematics

Recoded Values of GRADE_Mean

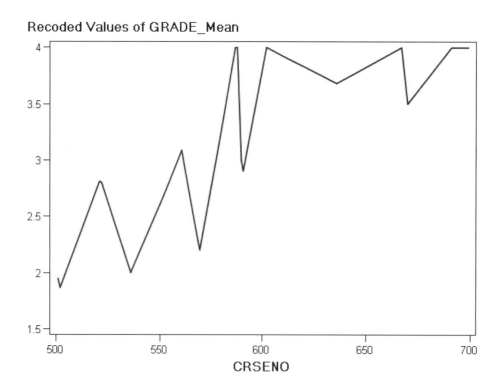

Output 4.30 Line Graph of Variability in Graduate Courses in Spanish

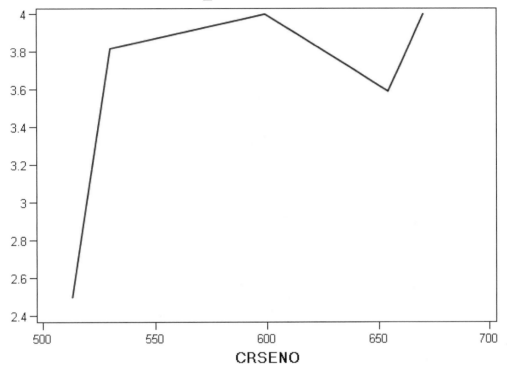

Recoded Values of GRADE_Mean

To examine ACT scores, which are available on a more limited basis, look at College Algebra. Here, course instruction is delivered in two different ways. The first is in large lecture sections of 150 students. Students have 2 contact hours of lecture with a faculty member and 2 contact hours of recitation in small sections with a graduate student. The second is in small sections of 25 students with 5 contact hours a week. As Output 4.31 shows, the type of delivery does make a difference in the grades assigned in the course.

Output 4.31 Student Grades by ACT Scores

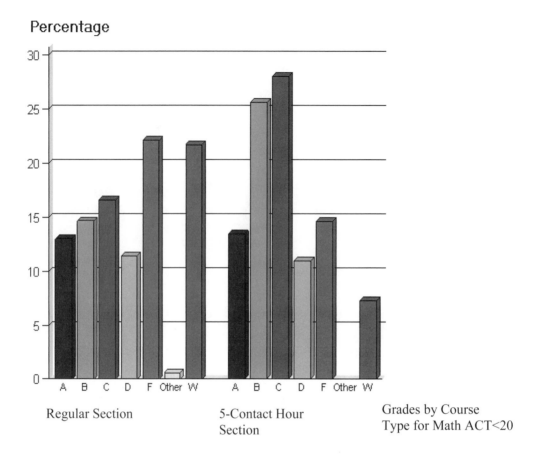

Percentage

Regular Section 5-Contact Hour Section Grades by Course Type for Math ACT<20

For students with an ACT score less than 20, there is a higher proportion of A, B, and C grades and a lower proportion of F and W scores compared to students in the regular section of College Algebra. Output 4.32 gives a similar graph for students with math ACT scores between 20 and 23.

Output 4.32 Proportion of Grades for Students with ACT Scores between 20 and 23

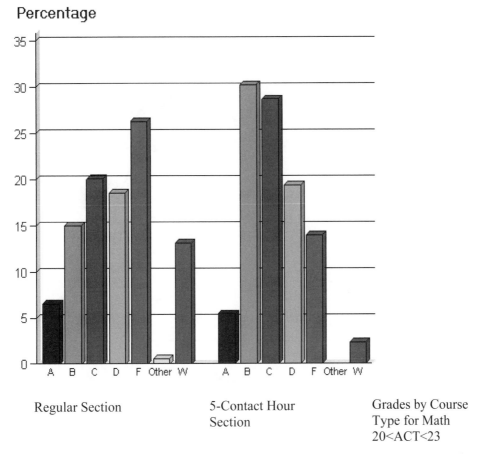

Again, there is considerable improvement in student grades in the sections with 5 contact hours. It is also interesting that there is no real difference in ACT scores for students who pass (receive an A, B, or C), and those who fail (Output 4.33).

Output 4.33 Comparison of ACT Scores for Passing and Failing Students

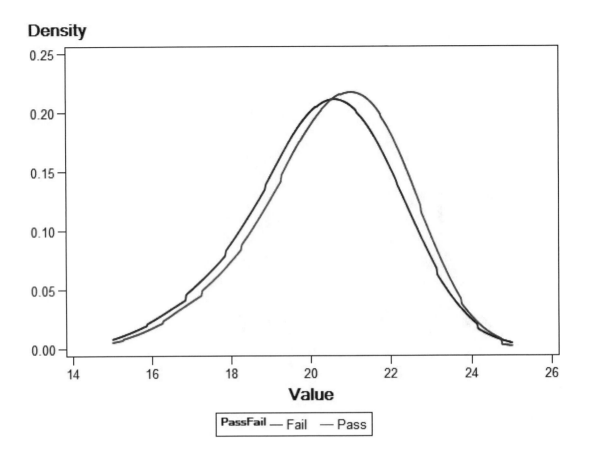

The distribution in Output 4.33 shows that preparation in the ACT scores has little to do with passing and failing in general education mathematics.

4.7 Exercises

1. The information in Sections 4.2 and 4.3 was identified by household ID. Perform similar SAS analyses using the patient ID.

2. SAS Text Miner software was used to compress the medication names to 500 categories and to 100 categories. Perform a similar analysis compressing the medication names to 250 categories. Duplicate the analysis for 100 categories.

3. RXNDC is the national drug code. Use the code numbers and SAS Text Miner software to compress the categories instead of using the drug name. See if the results are different when you use the numbers.

4. Write a brief summary of your results.

Association Node

5.1 Introduction to Association Rules

An association rule or market basket analysis is one of the most powerful and commonly used data mining techniques. This technique finds interesting associations and correlations among large sets of data items where the presence of one set of items in a transaction implies the presence of others. For example, in a grocery store, it is important to determine whether customers who purchase beef also purchase marinades for the beef and whether these items should be located close to each other. Association rules examine the strength of the purchase combinations. An association rule is of the form $X \rightarrow Y$, meaning that X and Y are related such that if a customer purchases item X, that customer will generally also purchase item Y.

In addition to the antecedent X and the consequent Y, an association rule has two numbers that express the degree of uncertainty about the rule. In association analysis, the antecedent and consequent are sets of items called item sets that are disjoint ($X \cap Y = \emptyset$). The first number is called the *support* for the rule. It is the number of times that the combination appears. The support is simply the number of transactions that include all items in the antecedent and consequent parts of the rule. The other number is known as the *confidence* of the rule. Confidence is the ratio of the number of transactions that include all items in the consequent as well as the antecedent to the number of transactions that include all items in the antecedent.

Consider a simple example. A business sells three items: red roses, blue carnations, and yellow daisies. Table 5.1 lists the number of transactions of each type. The left type is associated with the right type. In this case, the left type is the antecedent and the right type is the consequent.

Table 5.1 Purchases over a One-Year Period

LEFT TYPE	NUMBER	RIGHT TYPE	NUMBER
Yellow daisies	1648	Daisies and roses	279
Red roses	5304	Carnations and roses	128
Blue carnations	1365	Daisies and carnations	427
Total	8317		824

The confidence for antecedent and consequence appears in Table 5.2.

Table 5.2 Confidence Values

RULE	CONFIDENCE
Yellow daisies→red roses	279/1648=17%
Red roses→yellow daisies	279/5304=5%
Blue carnations→red roses	128/1365=9%
Red roses→blue carnations	128/5304=2%
Yellow daisies→blue carnations	427/1648=26%
Blue carnations→yellow daisies	427/1365=31%

The support is equal to the number in common divided by the total number of transactions (Table 5.3). The rules $X \rightarrow Y$ and $Y \rightarrow X$ can have different confidence values, but will have the same support values.

Table 5.3 Support Values

TYPE	SUPPORT
Yellow daisies→red roses	279/8317=3%
Blue carnations→red roses	128/8317=1.5%
Blue carnations→yellow daisies	427/8317=5%

The expected confidence is equal to the number of consequent transactions divided by the total number of transactions (Table 5.4).

Table 5.4 Expected Confidence

RULE	EXPECTED CONFIDENCE
Yellow daisies→red roses	5304/8317=64%
Red roses→yellow daisies	1648/8317=20%
Blue carnations→red roses	5304/8317=64%
Red roses→blue carnations	1365/8317=16%
Yellow daisies→blue carnations	1365/8317=16%
Blue carnations→yellow daisies	1648/8317=20%

The last measure of the strength of an association is the lift, which is equal to the ratio of the confidence to the expected confidence; that is, lift=confidence/expected confidence (Table 5.5).

Table 5.5 Lift Values

RULE	LIFT
Yellow daisies→red roses	17/64=0.266
Red roses→yellow daisies	5/20=0.050
Blue carnations→red roses	9/64=.140
Red roses→blue carnations	2/16=.125
Yellow daisies→blue carnations	26/16=1.625
Blue carnations→yellow daisies	31/20=1.55

Once the number of choices reaches into the hundreds or thousands, the process of calculation must be automated. Unfortunately, when there are so many choices, the confidence and support can approach 100%, while the lift becomes very small. Therefore, association works best when the choices are limited.

Note that even with the few choices in the previous example, only two combinations have a lift that is greater than 1. Care must be taken so that spurious associations are not considered to be real.

In many cases, you can reduce the number of categories by using broader classifications. For example, you might use cereal instead of corn flakes and raisin bran. There are now so many different, broad classifications in a grocery store that a market basket analysis is still difficult. For example, consider some information taken from http://amazon.com about available DVDs that are associated with *The Passion of The Christ* (as of December 2005). They are as follows:

- *The Day After Tomorrow* (widescreen edition)
- the Spider-Man feature film series
- the Harry Potter feature film series
- the Kill Bill feature film series

Even though audiences for these DVDs are different, they are identified in the same market basket. Drilling down found the following additional DVDs:

- *Shrek II*
- *The Lord of the Rings*
- *the Star Wars trilogy*
- *Cold Mountain*
- *Fahrenheit 9/11*
- *Troy*

Those who purchased *The Lord of the Rings* also purchased the following DVDs:

- the ultimate Matrix collection (*The Matrix / Reloaded / Revolutions / Revisited / The Animatrix*)
- *The Lord of the Rings* (extended edition) series
- the Harry Potter feature film series
- the Spider-Man feature film series

A pattern seems to be emerging. For *I, Robot*, the following DVDs are associated:

- *The Day After Tomorrow* (widescreen edition)
- the Harry Potter feature film series
- the Shrek series

The general category is clearly science fiction and fantasy. However, that does not explain how *Cold Mountain*, *Kill Bill*, and *Fahrenheit 9/11* entered into the association. The reliance on classes can lead to spurious associations.

Re-examining the associations provided by http://amazon.com (accessed April 2005) demonstrates a changing relationship. Associated with *The Passion of The Christ* were the following DVDs:

- *Jesus of Nazareth*
- *Crash* (widescreen edition)
- *The Ten Commandments* (50th anniversary collection)
- *Kingdom of Heaven* (widescreen edition)

Associated with *Jesus of Nazareth* were the following DVDs:

- *The Ten Commandments* (50th anniversary collection)
- *King of Kings* (1961)
- *The Greatest Story Ever Told* (movie only edition)
- *The Passion of The Christ* (widescreen edition)

Associated with *Crash* were the following DVDs:

- *Walk the Line* (widescreen edition)
- *The Constant Gardener* (widescreen edition)
- *Good Night, and Good Luck* (widescreen edition)
- *Capote*

However, with *Crash*, the movies are obviously much weaker in association since it doesn't seem to have subject content that is similar to the other films. Again, the use of larger classes can lead to such weak associations.

5.2 Using the Association Node

The Association node in SAS Enterprise Miner 5.2 is given in Figure 5.1.

Figure 5.1 Association Node

Display 5.1 lists the options available with the Association node. The first analysis should be performed with defaults, and the defaults changed as needed. In the Association submenu, you can specify the minimum level of confidence needed to list the rule. Some of the changes to the defaults are examined later in this chapter. You should investigate other changes to the defaults to find out how they impact the results.

Display 5.1 Options in the Association Node

Property	Value
Node ID	Assoc2
Imported Data	
Exported Data	
Variables	
Maximum Number of Items	100000
Rules	
Association	
Maximum Items	4
Minimum Confidence Level	10
Support Type	Percent
Support Count	2
Support Percentage	5.0
Sequence	
Chain Count	3
Consolidate Time	0.0
Maximum Transaction Dur	
Support Type	Percent
Support Count	2
Support Percentage	2.0
Rules	
Number to Keep	200
Sort Criterion	Default
Number to Transpose	200
Export Rule by ID	No
Status	

The first and second sections in the Association node (see Display 5.1) limit the size and type of rules under consideration for the default. There has to be a minimum confidence level of 1.0 before the rule will be considered. The length of the chain count is limited to 3. Also by default, the number of rules considered is limited to 200. The default criterion is to consider the lift, although options exist to consider support, confidence, expected confidence, and the number of transactions to order the first 200 rules, the only ones initially printed.

To run the Association node, the data set must include one ID variable and one target variable. The Association node examines the different purchases made by each individual customer in the data set. The results appear in Output 5.1. To run the Association Node, you must identify the data as transactional. The results show a low confidence.

Output 5.1 Results for Flower Purchases

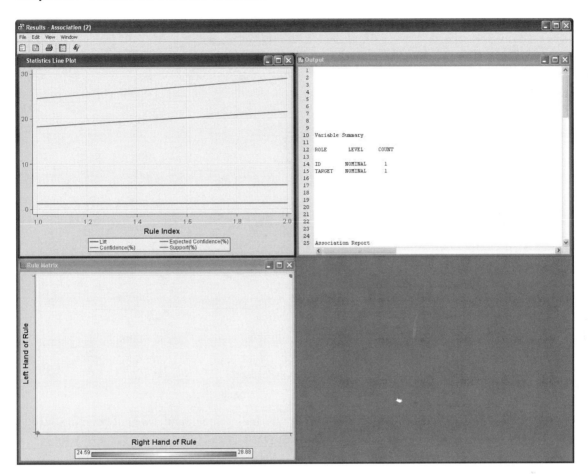

The enlarged line plot in Output 5.2 also shows low values for this example.

Output 5.2 Statistical Line Plot for Flower Purchases

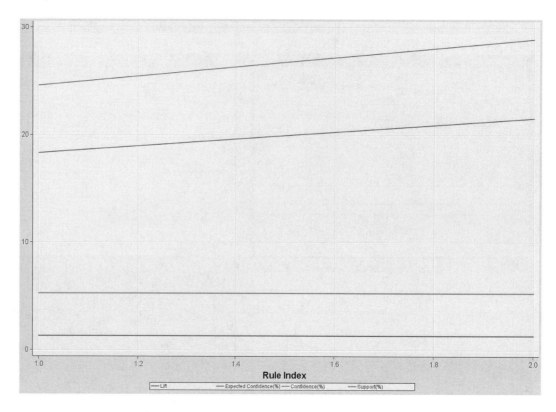

Because there are so few rules in this graph, changing the defaults will not demonstrably change the outcome. A more complex example is discussed in Section 5.3.

5.3 Using Medications

Consider the medication data set discussed in Chapter 4. That data set contains 300,000 purchases with 30,000 customers and 11,000 households. Attempting an association analysis on the entire data set results in a memory failure. There are too many values and too many possible levels in the target variable.

To complete the analysis, connect the Association node to a sample node (Figure 5.2).

Figure 5.2 Association After Sampling

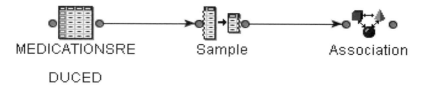

MEDICATIONSRE
DUCED

Sample

Association

To overcome the out-of-memory problem, reduce the data set to 1,000 customers. To ensure that all associations are examined, first sort the data set by customer ID. The initial results appear in Output 5.3.

Output 5.3 Results of Association Node Analysis

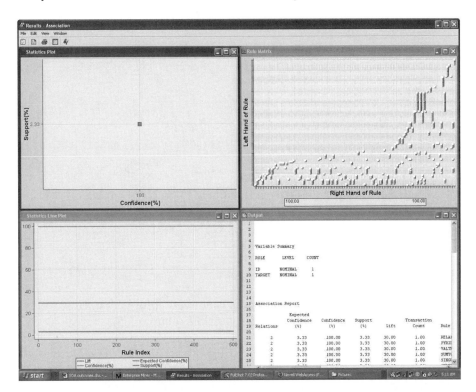

In the lower left-hand corner, a graph of the left-hand versus right-hand rules appears, giving the range of the confidence level. In the upper left-hand corner, a graph of the support, lift, and confidence for the rules is provided. The default lists the first 200 rules. Note: In this example, the first 200 rules have identical values for the three parameters. The confidence for all 200 rules remains at 100%. Output 5.4 shows an enlargement of the upper right-hand graph in Output 5.3.

Output 5.4 First 200 Association Rules for Medication Purchases

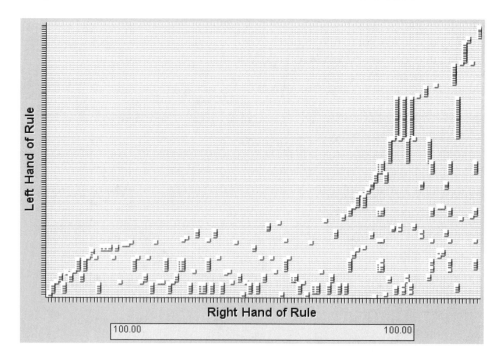

Without knowing what the rules represent, this graph is not very informative. However, you can place your cursor over any one of the rules to make it visible (Output 5.5).

Output 5.5 Rule Matrix with Cursor

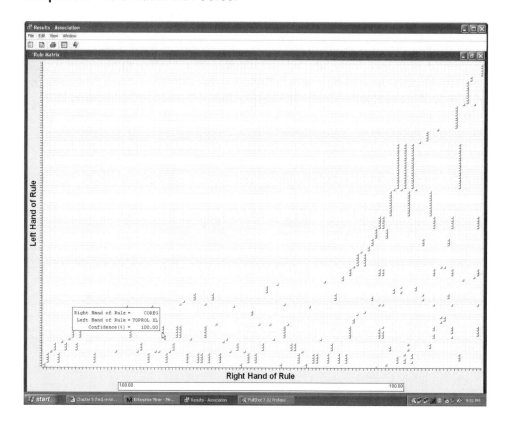

The rule depicted in Output 5.5 has 100% confidence, which is equal to the number of customers with both Avandia (to treat diabetes) and Prilosec (to treat acid reflux) divided by the number of customers with Avandia. Because this is equal to 100%, it is clear that all customers taking Avandia also take Prilosec. However, the number of individuals taking both is extremely small.

In fact, all of the first 200 rules have 100% confidence. Examining all of the rules is time-consuming, so look at the first page of the list of rules (Output 5.6).

Output 5.6 Table of Rules

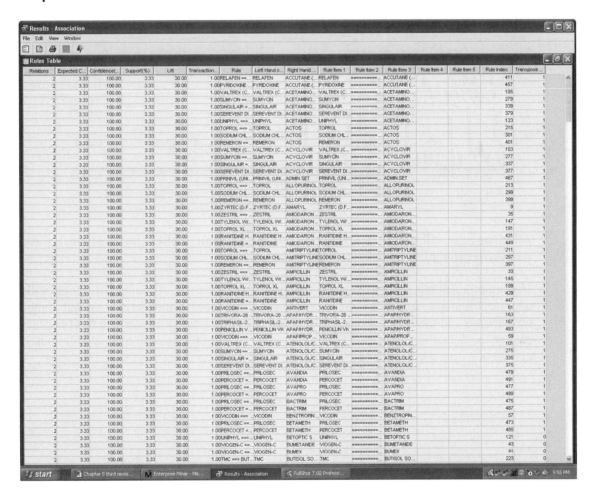

All of the first 200 rules have 100% confidence but very few transactions. Some of the rules may have 100% confidence because only one or two customers are taking those medications. You can change the default to the first 5,000 rules, as shown in Output 5.7.

Output 5.7 Rule Matrix with 5,000 Rules

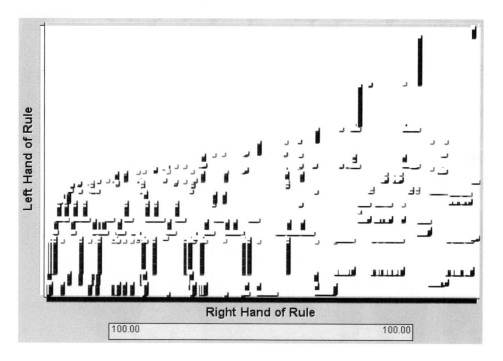

All of the rules still have 100% confidence. In this example, Keflex (for infections) is associated with Zyrtec (for allergies) and Prozac (for depression).

It is important at this point to examine the meaning of the rules. Although customers with allergies often have infections, the association itself probably follows from a small number of transactions and should most likely be discounted. To examine the most common transactions, change the default to examine the 200 rules with the highest transaction counts (Output 5.8). The confidence is no longer 100%.

Output 5.8 Rule Matrix with Highest Transaction Counts

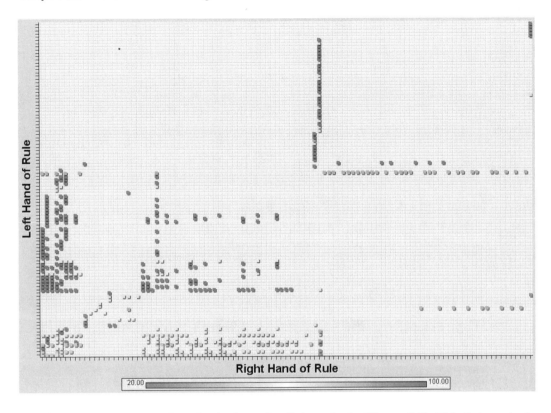

Another way to represent the rules is through a link analysis (Figure 5.3). This link analysis can be found under **View ▶ Rules ▶ Link Graph**.

Figure 5.3 Link Analysis

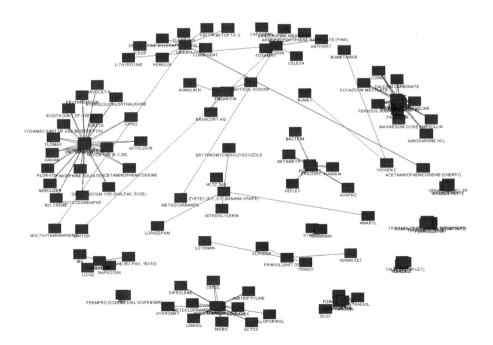

Link graphs are sometimes difficult to read, particularly when there are many nodes and many connections. Methods to help you view link graphs are discussed later in this chapter. In this example, many nodes are listed that do not have connections.

Each line represents a rule connecting one node to another. Consider the section in the lowest portion of the link graph. The connections include Amitriptyline (for depression), Lamisil (for fungal infections), Cefzil (for bacterial infections), Allopurinol (for gout), and Diprolene (for skin rashes). Antibiotics can lead to fungal infections; a side effect of the Allopruinal is a skin rash. The link analysis indicates that there is a connection between the use of antibiotics and the need for antifungal medication. Lipitor is connected to Fosamax; both drugs are used to treat elderly patients for heart problems and osteoporosis. In the center, Lorazepam (for anxiety) is connected to Nitroglycerin (for heart problems).

Because the default sort yields so many rules with so few transactions, change the default sort criterion to count, which indicates the number of transactions. Output 5.9 shows the results. Nitroglycerin is one of the medications in the center; it is mostly used for heart problems. There are small sections of connections that are related to each other.

Output 5.9 Results After Changing the Default Sort Criterion

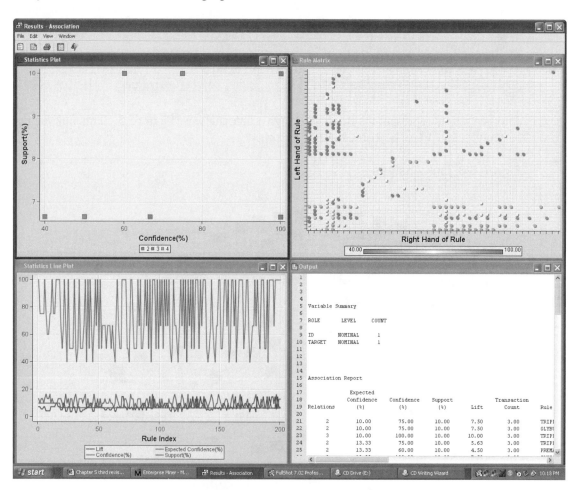

The confidence values now range from 64% to 100%. The corresponding link graph appears in Figure 5.4. The rules are now sorted by the number of transactions. The link graph also shows the differences in confidence by size and color.

Figure 5.4 Link Graph with Transactions Count

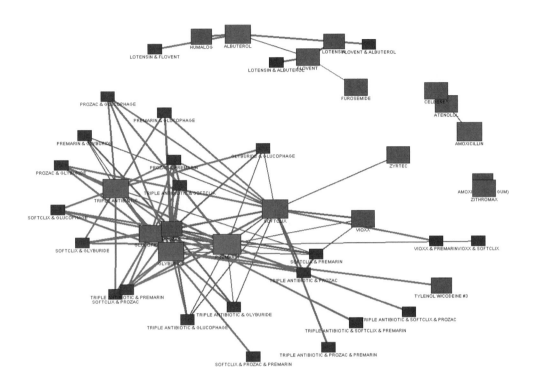

Because the link graph is so crowded, you can reduce the number of links to 50 for examination (Figure 5.5). The resulting graph is much simpler and shows a relationship between Glyburide, Glucophage, and Prozac. The first two medications treat Type II diabetes; the third treats depression. Two other links are Premarin (a hormone replacement therapy) and Vioxx (for pain and arthritis).

Figure 5.5 Link Graph with 50 Highest Transaction Counts

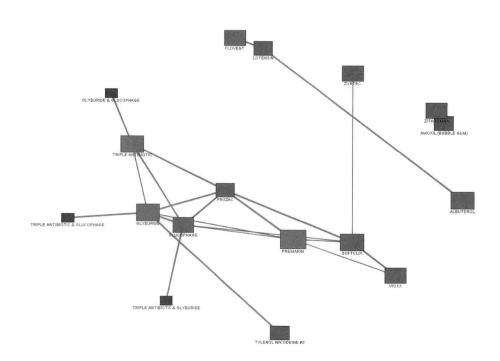

5.4 Compressing Categories

Rather than working with hundreds and thousands of categories, it is more meaningful to compress them into a few general categories. You can use cluster analysis if you do not know enough about the categories to define a set of compressed groups. Table 5.6 shows the medications in the list reduced to a total of 18 categories. Chapter 6 discusses how these categories are defined.

Table 5.6 Compressed Categories for Medications

Cluster Number	Label
1	Asthma medications
2	Upper respiratory infection
3	Post-menopause
4	Asthma medications and arthritis
5	Acute or chronic pain
6	Hypertension
7	Acne and Attention Deficit Disorder (ADD)
8	Heart condition
9	Hypertension and urinary tract infection
10	Migraine and depression
11	Hypertension
12	Type I diabetes

(*continued*)

Table 5.6 Compressed Categories for Medications (*continued*)

Cluster Number	Label
13	Congestive heart failure
14	ADD
15	Mild heart condition
16	Type II diabetes
17	ADD and aggressive behavior
18	Oral contraceptives and antibiotics

Output 5.10 shows the results using just these categories. With a small number of levels in the target variable, the entire data set can be used in the Association node rather than just a small sample.

Output 5.10 Results Using Categories of Medications

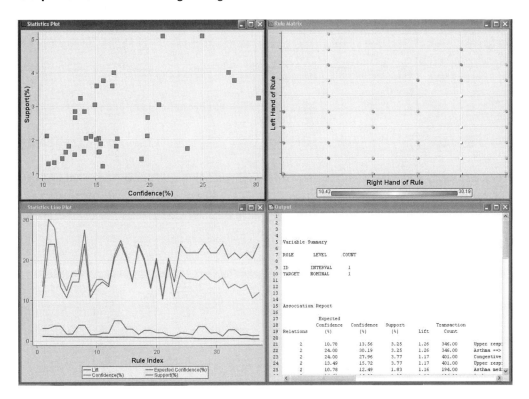

The rules are more meaningful because more transactions are involved (Output 5.12) with each of the rules in Output 5.10, where the confidence ranges from 10% to 100%. The transaction count ranges from the mid to upper 20s.

Output 5.11 Rule Matrix

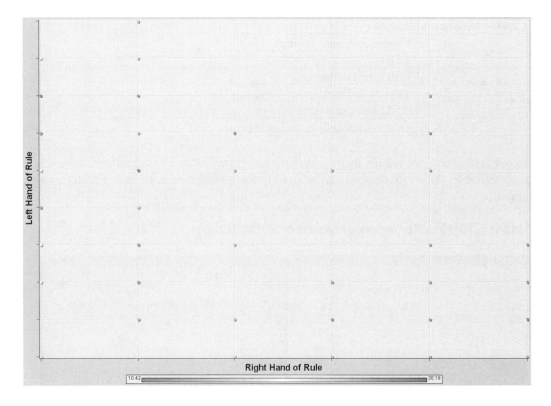

There is a right angle shape to the graph, which indicates that one cluster dominates most of the associations. Moving the cursor to highlight one of the boxes reveals what that link is. Output 5.12 gives the corresponding table of rules for the cluster associations.

Output 5.12 Table of Rules

Relations	Expected C...	Confidence(...	Support(%)	Lift	Transaction...	Rule	Left Hand o...	Right Hand...	Rule Item 1	Rule Item 2	Rule Item 3	Rule Item 4	Rule Item 5	Rule Index	Transpose ...
2	20.49	21.29	5.11	1.04	543.00	Upper respir...	Upper respir...	Acute or chr...	Upper respir...	=========	Acute or chr...			1	1
2	24.00	24.93	5.11	1.04	543.00	Acute or chr...	Acute or chr...	Upper respir...	Acute or chr...	=========	Upper respir...			2	1
2	14.61	16.70	4.01	1.14	426.00	Upper respir...	Upper respir...	Asthma medi...	Upper respir...	=========	Asthma medi...			3	1
2	24.00	27.43	4.01	1.14	426.00	Asthma medi...	Asthma medi...	Upper respir...	Asthma medi...	=========	Upper respir...			4	1
2	13.49	15.72	3.77	1.17	401.00	Upper respir...	Upper respir...	Congestive h...	Upper respir...	=========	Congestive h...			5	1
2	24.00	27.96	3.77	1.17	401.00	Congestive h...	Congestive h...	Upper respir...	Congestive h...	=========	Upper respir...			6	1
2	21.90	15.09	3.62	0.69	385.00	Upper respir...	Upper respir...	Heart condition	Upper respir...	=========	Heart condition			7	1
2	24.00	16.54	3.62	0.69	385.00	Heart conditi...	Heart condition	Upper respir...	Heart condition	=========	Upper respir...			8	1
2	10.78	13.56	3.25	1.26	346.00	Upper respir...	Upper respir...	Asthma	Upper respir...	=========	Asthma			9	1
2	24.00	30.19	3.25	1.26	346.00	Asthma ==> ...	Asthma	Upper respir...	Asthma	=========	Upper respir...			10	1
2	20.49	20.93	3.06	1.02	325.00	Asthma medi...	Asthma medi...	Acute or chr...	Asthma medi...	=========	Acute or chr...			11	1
2	14.61	14.92	3.06	1.02	325.00	Acute or chr...	Acute or chr...	Asthma medi...	Acute or chr...	=========	Asthma medi...			12	1
2	20.49	13.06	2.86	0.64	304.00	Heart conditi...	Heart condition	Acute or chr...	Heart condition	=========	Acute or chr...			13	1
2	21.90	13.96	2.86	0.64	304.00	Acute or chr...	Acute or chr...	Heart condition	Acute or chr...	=========	Heart condition			14	1
2	20.49	19.87	2.68	0.97	285.00	Congestive h...	Congestive h...	Acute or chr...	Congestive h...	=========	Acute or chr...			15	1
2	13.49	13.09	2.68	0.97	285.00	Acute or chr...	Acute or chr...	Congestive h...	Acute or chr...	=========	Congestive h...			16	1
2	20.49	19.81	2.14	0.97	227.00	Asthma ==> ...	Asthma	Acute or chr...	Asthma	=========	Acute or chr...			17	1
2	10.78	10.42	2.14	0.97	227.00	Acute or chr...	Acute or chr...	Asthma	Acute or chr...	=========	Asthma			18	1
2	21.90	14.55	2.13	0.66	226.00	Asthma medi...	Asthma medi...	Heart condition	Asthma medi...	=========	Heart condition			19	1
2	14.61	15.27	2.06	1.05	219.00	Congestive h...	Congestive h...	Asthma medi...	Congestive h...	=========	Asthma medi...			20	1
2	13.49	14.10	2.06	1.05	219.00	Asthma medi...	Asthma medi...	Congestive h...	Asthma medi...	=========	Congestive h...			21	1
2	24.00	17.03	2.05	0.71	218.00	Mild heart co...	Mild heart co...	Upper respir...	Mild heart co...	=========	Upper respir...			22	1
2	21.90	15.06	2.03	0.69	216.00	Congestive h...	Congestive h...	Heart condition	Congestive h...	=========	Heart condition			23	1
2	21.90	15.48	1.90	0.71	202.00	Hypertension...	Hypertension	Heart condition	Hypertension	=========	Heart condition			24	1
2	10.78	12.49	1.83	1.16	194.00	Asthma medi...	Asthma medi...	Asthma	Asthma medi...	=========	Asthma			25	1
2	14.61	16.93	1.83	1.16	194.00	Asthma ==> ...	Asthma	Asthma medi...	Asthma	=========	Asthma medi...			26	1
2	24.00	23.55	1.76	0.98	187.00	Migraine and ...	Migraine and ...	Upper respir...	Migraine and ...	=========	Upper respir...			27	1
2	21.90	13.91	1.67	0.63	178.00	Mild heart co...	Mild heart co...	Heart condition	Mild heart co...	=========	Heart condition			28	1
2	21.90	15.36	1.66	0.70	176.00	Asthma ==> ...	Asthma	Heart condition	Asthma	=========	Heart condition			29	1
2	10.78	12.20	1.65	1.13	175.00	Congestive h...	Congestive h...	Asthma	Congestive h...	=========	Asthma			30	1
2	13.49	15.27	1.65	1.13	175.00	Asthma ==> ...	Asthma	Congestive h...	Asthma	=========	Congestive h...			31	1
2	20.49	13.05	1.57	0.64	167.00	Mild heart co...	Mild heart co...	Acute or chr...	Mild heart co...	=========	Acute or chr...			32	1
2	24.00	11.88	1.46	0.49	155.00	Hypertension...	Hypertension	Upper respir...	Hypertension	=========	Upper respir...			33	1
2	20.49	19.27	1.44	0.94	153.00	Migraine and ...	Migraine and ...	Acute or chr...	Migraine and ...	=========	Acute or chr...			34	1
2	14.61	11.09	1.34	0.76	142.00	Mild heart co...	Mild heart co...	Asthma medi...	Mild heart co...	=========	Asthma medi...			35	1
2	20.49	10.57	1.30	0.52	138.00	Hypertension...	Hypertension	Acute or chr...	Hypertension	=========	Acute or chr...			36	1
2	24.00	15.63	1.23	0.65	131.00	Type II diabet...	Type II diabet...	Upper respir...	Type II diabet...	=========	Upper respir...			37	1

The link analysis appears in Figure 5.6.

Figure 5.6 Link Analysis Using Clusters

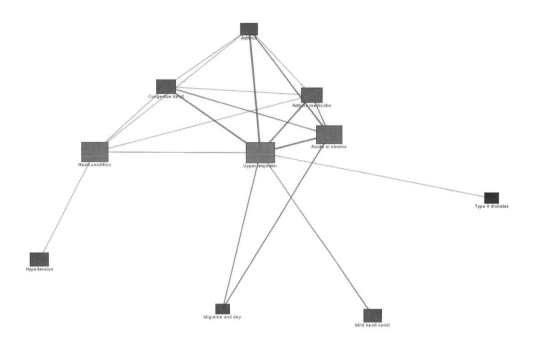

The most prominent node in the center is upper respiratory infection. It connects with many of the other clusters with varying degrees of strength, probably because these types of infection are relatively common. To discover more links, reduce the 5% default support level, as shown in Output 5.13.

Output 5.13 Rules with Reduced Support

Relations	Expected C...	Confidence(...	Support(%)	Lift	Transaction...	Rule	Left Hand o...	Right Hand ...	Rule Item 1	Rule Item 2	Rule Item 3	Rule Item 4	R...
2	20.49	21.29	5.11	1.04	543.00	Upper respir...	Upper respir...	Acute or chr...	Upper respir...	========...	Acute or chr...		
2	24.00	24.93	5.11	1.04	543.00	Acute or chr...	Acute or chr...	Upper respir...	Acute or chr...	========...	Upper respir...		
2	14.61	16.70	4.01	1.14	426.00	Upper respir...	Upper respir...	Asthma medi...	Upper respir...	========...	Asthma medi...		
2	24.00	27.43	4.01	1.14	426.00	Asthma medi...	Asthma medi...	Upper respir...	Asthma medi...	========...	Upper respir...		
2	13.49	15.72	3.77	1.17	401.00	Upper respir...	Upper respir...	Congestive h...	Upper respir...	========...	Congestive h...		
2	24.00	27.96	3.77	1.17	401.00	Congestive h...	Congestive h...	Upper respir...	Congestive h...	========...	Upper respir...		
2	21.90	15.09	3.62	0.69	385.00	Upper respir...	Upper respir...	Heart condition	Upper respir...	========...	Heart condition		
2	24.00	16.54	3.62	0.69	385.00	Heart conditi...	Heart condition	Upper respir...	Heart condition	========...	Upper respir...		
2	10.78	13.56	3.25	1.26	346.00	Upper respir...	Upper respir...	Asthma	Upper respir...	========...	Asthma		
2	24.00	30.19	3.25	1.26	346.00	Asthma ==> ...	Asthma	Upper respir...	Asthma	========...	Upper respir...		
2	20.49	20.93	3.06	1.02	325.00	Asthma medi...	Asthma medi...	Acute or chr...	Asthma medi...	========...	Acute or chr...		
2	14.61	14.92	3.06	1.02	325.00	Acute or chr...	Acute or chr...	Asthma medi...	Acute or chr...	========...	Asthma medi...		
2	20.49	13.06	2.86	0.64	304.00	Heart conditi...	Heart condition	Acute or chr...	Heart condition	========...	Acute or chr...		
2	21.90	13.96	2.86	0.64	304.00	Acute or chr...	Acute or chr...	Heart condition	Acute or chr...	========...	Heart condition		
2	20.49	19.87	2.68	0.97	285.00	Congestive h...	Congestive h...	Acute or chr...	Congestive h...	========...	Acute or chr...		
2	13.49	13.09	2.68	0.97	285.00	Acute or chr...	Acute or chr...	Congestive h...	Acute or chr...	========...	Congestive h...		
2	20.49	19.81	2.14	0.97	227.00	Asthma ==> ...	Asthma	Acute or chr...	Asthma	========...	Acute or chr...		
2	10.78	10.42	2.14	0.97	227.00	Acute or chr...	Acute or chr...	Asthma	Acute or chr...	========...	Asthma		
2	21.90	14.55	2.13	0.66	226.00	Asthma medi...	Asthma medi...	Heart condition	Asthma medi...	========...	Heart condition		
2	14.61	15.27	2.06	1.05	219.00	Congestive h...	Congestive h...	Asthma medi...	Congestive h...	========...	Asthma medi...		
2	13.49	14.10	2.06	1.05	219.00	Asthma medi...	Asthma medi...	Congestive h...	Asthma medi...	========...	Congestive h...		
2	24.00	17.03	2.05	0.71	218.00	Mild heart co...	Mild heart co...	Upper respir...	Mild heart co...	========...	Upper respir...		
2	21.90	15.06	2.03	0.69	216.00	Congestive h...	Congestive h...	Heart condition	Congestive h...	========...	Heart condition		
2	21.90	15.48	1.90	0.71	202.00	Hypertension...	Hypertension	Heart condition	Hypertension	========...	Heart condition		
2	10.78	12.49	1.83	1.16	194.00	Asthma medi...	Asthma medi...	Asthma	Asthma medi...	========...	Asthma		
2	14.61	16.93	1.83	1.16	194.00	Asthma ==> ...	Asthma	Asthma medi...	Asthma	========...	Asthma medi...		
2	24.00	23.55	1.76	0.98	187.00	Migraine and ...	Migraine and ...	Upper respir...	Migraine and ...	========...	Upper respir...		
2	21.90	13.91	1.67	0.63	178.00	Mild heart co...	Mild heart co...	Heart condition	Mild heart co...	========...	Heart condition		
2	21.90	15.36	1.66	0.70	176.00	Asthma ==> ...	Asthma	Heart condition	Asthma	========...	Heart condition		
2	10.78	12.20	1.65	1.13	175.00	Congestive h...	Congestive h...	Asthma	Congestive h...	========...	Asthma		
2	13.49	15.27	1.65	1.13	175.00	Asthma ==> ...	Asthma	Congestive h...	Asthma	========...	Congestive h...		
2	20.49	13.05	1.57	0.64	167.00	Mild heart co...	Mild heart co...	Acute or chr...	Mild heart co...	========...	Acute or chr...		
2	24.00	11.88	1.46	0.49	155.00	Hypertension...	Hypertension	Upper respir...	Hypertension	========...	Upper respir...		
2	20.49	19.27	1.44	0.94	153.00	Migraine and ...	Migraine and ...	Acute or chr...	Migraine and ...	========...	Acute or chr...		
2	14.61	11.09	1.34	0.76	142.00	Mild heart co...	Mild heart co...	Asthma medi...	Mild heart co...	========...	Asthma medi...		
2	20.49	10.57	1.30	0.52	138.00	Hypertension...	Hypertension	Acute or chr...	Hypertension	========...	Acute or chr...		
2	24.00	15.63	1.23	0.65	131.00	Type II diabet...	Type II diabet...	Upper respir...	Type II diabet...	========...	Upper respir...		
2	24.00	16.69	1.19	0.70	126.00	Type I diabet...	Type I diabetes	Upper respir...	Type I diabetes	========...	Upper respir...		
2	21.90	15.62	1.17	0.71	124.00	Migraine and ...	Migraine and ...	Heart condition	Migraine and ...	========...	Heart condition		
2	21.90	16.03	1.14	0.73	121.00	Type I diabet...	Type I diabetes	Heart condition	Type I diabetes	========...	Heart condition		
2	14.61	14.99	1.12	1.03	119.00	Migraine and ...	Migraine and ...	Asthma medi...	Migraine and ...	========...	Asthma medi...		
2	21.90	13.84	1.09	0.63	116.00	Type II diabet...	Type II diabet...	Heart condition	Type II diabet...	========...	Heart condition		
2	24.00	21.88	0.99	0.91	105.00	Hypertension...	Hypertension	Upper respir...	Hypertension	========...	Upper respir...		
2	13.49	12.97	0.97	0.96	103.00	Migraine and ...	Migraine and ...	Congestive h...	Migraine and ...	========...	Congestive h...		
2	20.49	11.81	0.93	0.58	99.00	Type II diabet...	Type II diabet...	Acute or chr...	Type II diabet...	========...	Acute or chr...		
2	20.49	13.11	0.93	0.64	99.00	Type I diabet...	Type I diabetes	Acute or chr...	Type I diabetes	========...	Acute or chr...		
3	20.49	22.77	0.91	1.11	97.00	Upper respir...	Upper respir...	Acute or chr...	Upper respir...	Asthma medi...	========...	Acute or chr...	
3	14.61	17.86	0.91	1.22	97.00	Upper respir...	Upper respir...	Asthma medi...	Upper respir...	Acute or chr...	========...	Asthma medi...	
3	24.00	29.85	0.91	1.24	97.00	Asthma medi...	Asthma medi...	Upper respir...	Asthma medi...	Acute or chr...	========...	Upper respir...	
2	10.78	11.34	0.85	1.05	90.00	Migraine and ...	Migraine and ...	Asthma	Migraine and ...	========...	Asthma		
3	20.49	21.70	0.82	1.06	87.00	Upper respir...	Upper respir...	Acute or chr...	Upper respir...	Congestive h...	========...	Acute or chr...	
3	13.49	16.02	0.82	1.19	87.00	Upper respir...	Upper respir...	Congestive h...	Upper respir...	Acute or chr...	========...	Congestive h...	
3	24.00	30.53	0.82	1.27	87.00	Congestive h...	Congestive h...	Upper respir...	Congestive h...	Acute or chr...	========...	Upper respir...	
2	20.49	17.50	0.79	0.85	84.00	Hypertension...	Hypertension	Acute or chr...	Hypertension	========...	Acute or chr...		

The highest counts suggest that the most purchases are related within each category with the highest counts for upper respiratory infections. However, there is a high count relating asthma to upper respiratory infections as well. The link graph in Figure 5.7 shows two major nodes: asthma medications and upper respiratory infection medications. The strongest links are between the two major nodes.

Figure 5.7 Link Graph Using Highest Count Option

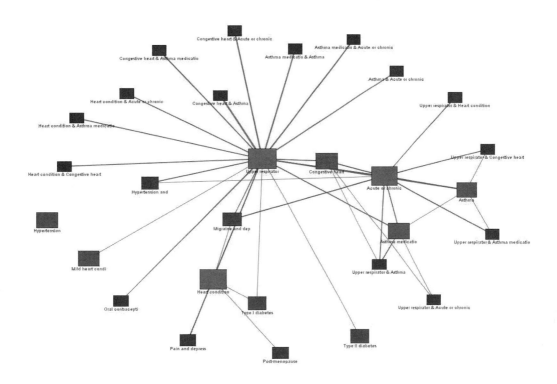

Unlike the link graph in Figure 5.6, the center contains upper respiratory and heart medications, indicating that they have the highest use. Off center is a node for asthma. Both the rule table and the link analysis indicate that the most commonly prescribed medications are for upper respiratory infections, pain, asthma, and heart conditions.

Therefore, in a large data set, you'll receive more meaningful results if you change the sort criterion default. Again, the graph is difficult to read. Another way of looking at the link graph is to select specific items to see how they connect. As shown in Display 5.2, specific values can be selected.

Display 5.2 Choosing Specific Values

The Select option brings up the screen shown in Display 5.3. Here, you can identify the value of interest.

Display 5.3 Selection Dialog Box

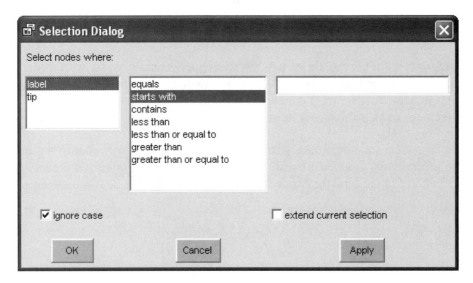

The resulting highlighted values appear in Figure 5.8.

Figure 5.8 Highlighted Values

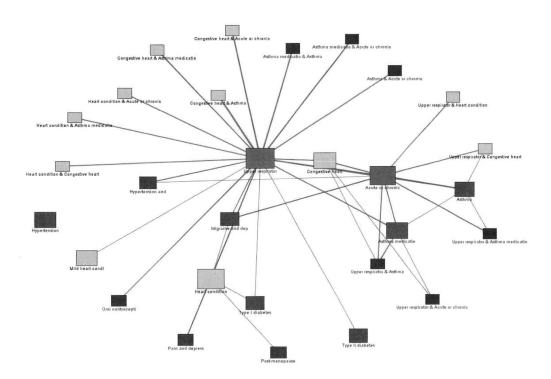

The highlighted links show that heart problems are connected to many of the other clusters.

A third example is provided by using the categories in Chapter 4, in which the medications field was reduced to a total of 500 different clusters. The results appear in Output 5.14.

Output 5.14 Results Using Reduced 500 Clusters

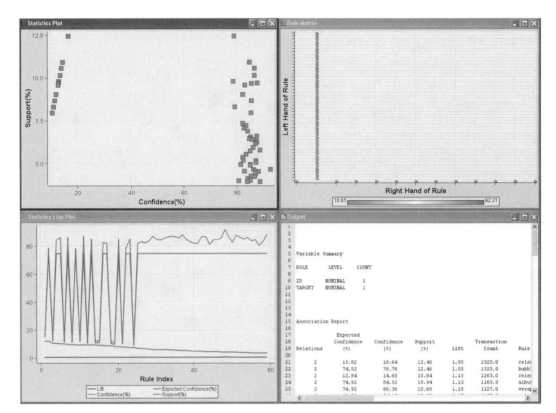

Note the odd pattern in the rule matrix with one left-hand side value. The rule matrix is enlarged in Output 5.15. Again, it shows that one cluster completely dominates the defined rules.

Output 5.15 Rule Matrix for Reduced 500 Clusters

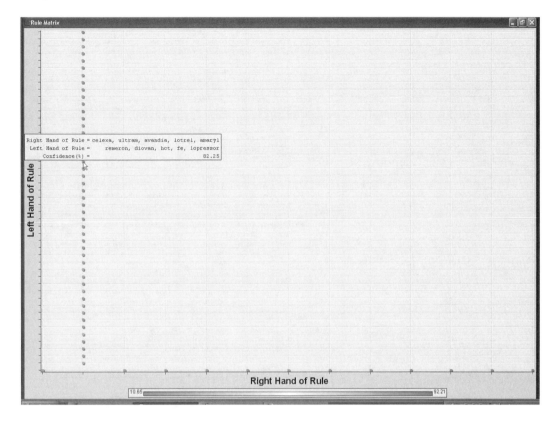

In Output 5.15, the left-hand side is equal to Acetate, Hydrocortisa, etc. (pain medications) and the right-hand side of the rule is equal to Celexa, Ultram, Avandia, Lotrel, and Amaryl (depression, pain). Unfortunately, it is not clear why the data compression created the Celexa et al. cluster as the dominant one. Output 5.16 gives the corresponding table of rules for the cluster association. Output 5.16 is a much smaller list compared to the lists we have examined previously. Here, the transaction counts enter into the hundreds instead of the thousands, indicating more commonality in the rules.

Output 5.16 Association Rules for 500 Clusters

Relations	Expected C...	Confidence(...	Support(%)	Lift	Transaction...	Rule	Left Hand o...	Right Hand ...	Rule Item 1	Rule Item 2	Rule Item 3
2	15.82	16.64	12.46	1.05	1325.0	celexa, ultra...	celexa, ultra...	bubble, gum, ...	celexa, ultra...	=========...	bubble, gum, ...
2	74.92	78.78	12.46	1.05	1325.0	bubble, gum, ...	bubble, gum, ...	celexa, ultra...	bubble, gum, ...	=========...	celexa, ultra...
2	12.94	14.60	10.94	1.13	1163.0	celexa, ultra...	celexa, ultra...	albuterol, atr...	celexa, ultra...	=========...	albuterol, atr...
2	74.92	84.52	10.94	1.13	1163.0	albuterol, atr...	albuterol, atr...	celexa, ultra...	albuterol, atr...	=========...	celexa, ultra...
2	74.92	86.36	10.60	1.15	1127.0	verapamil, hc...	verapamil, hc...	celexa, ultra...	verapamil, hc...	=========...	celexa, ultra...
2	12.28	14.15	10.60	1.15	1127.0	celexa, ultra...	celexa, ultra...	verapamil, hc...	celexa, ultra...	=========...	verapamil, hc...
2	74.92	86.35	10.18	1.15	1082.0	system, care...	system, care...	celexa, ultra...	system, care...	=========...	celexa, ultra...
2	11.79	13.59	10.18	1.15	1082.0	celexa, ultra...	celexa, ultra...	system, care...	celexa, ultra...	=========...	system, care...
2	74.92	78.38	9.82	1.05	1044.0	triple, antibioti...	triple, antibioti...	celexa, ultra...	triple, antibioti...	=========...	celexa, ultra...
2	12.53	13.11	9.82	1.05	1044.0	celexa, ultra...	celexa, ultra...	triple, antibioti...	celexa, ultra...	=========...	triple, antibioti...
2	74.92	87.33	9.73	1.17	1034.0	proscar, evis...	proscar, evis...	celexa, ultra...	proscar, evis...	=========...	celexa, ultra...
2	11.14	12.98	9.73	1.17	1034.0	celexa, ultra...	celexa, ultra...	proscar, evis...	celexa, ultra...	=========...	proscar, evis...
2	74.92	85.28	9.70	1.14	1031.0	dm, glucovan...	dm, glucovan...	celexa, ultra...	celexa, ultra...	=========...	celexa, ultra...
2	11.37	12.95	9.70	1.14	1031.0	celexa, ultra...	celexa, ultra...	dm, glucovan...	celexa, ultra...	=========...	dm, glucovan...
2	11.59	12.81	9.60	1.11	1020.0	celexa, ultra...	celexa, ultra...	+ estrogen, v...	celexa, ultra...	=========...	+ estrogen, v...
2	74.92	82.79	9.60	1.11	1020.0	+ estrogen, v...	+ estrogen, v...	celexa, ultra...	+ estrogen, v...	=========...	celexa, ultra...
2	74.92	82.04	9.07	1.10	964.00	hydrocodone...	hydrocodone...	celexa, ultra...	hydrocodone...	=========...	celexa, ultra...
2	11.05	12.10	9.07	1.10	964.00	celexa, ultra...	celexa, ultra...	hydrocodone...	celexa, ultra...	=========...	hydrocodone...
2	10.21	11.61	8.70	1.14	925.00	celexa, ultra...	celexa, ultra...	cardura, dox...	celexa, ultra...	=========...	cardura, dox...
2	74.92	85.25	8.70	1.14	925.00	cardura, dox...	cardura, dox...	celexa, ultra...	cardura, dox...	=========...	celexa, ultra...
2	10.56	11.13	8.33	1.05	886.00	celexa, ultra...	celexa, ultra...	berry, motrin,...	celexa, ultra...	=========...	berry, motrin,...
2	74.92	78.97	8.33	1.05	886.00	berry, motrin,...	berry, motrin,...	celexa, ultra...	berry, motrin,...	=========...	celexa, ultra...
2	74.92	85.14	7.98	1.14	848.00	depakote, as...	depakote, as...	celexa, ultra...	depakote, as...	=========...	celexa, ultra...
2	9.37	10.65	7.98	1.14	848.00	celexa, ultra...	celexa, ultra...	depakote, as...	celexa, ultra...	=========...	depakote, as...
2	74.92	82.06	7.36	1.10	782.00	lipitor ==> cel...	lipitor	celexa, ultra...	lipitor	=========...	celexa, ultra...
2	74.92	83.23	7.23	1.11	769.00	claritin, redi =...	claritin, redi	celexa, ultra...	claritin, redi	=========...	celexa, ultra...
2	74.92	82.48	7.08	1.10	753.00	lanoxin, vico...	lanoxin, vico...	celexa, ultra...	lanoxin, vico...	=========...	celexa, ultra...
2	74.92	83.83	6.92	1.12	736.00	phenytoin, w...	phenytoin, w...	celexa, ultra...	phenytoin, w...	=========...	celexa, ultra...
2	74.92	87.24	6.62	1.16	704.00	metocloprami...	metocloprami...	celexa, ultra...	metocloprami...	=========...	celexa, ultra...
2	74.92	84.95	6.59	1.13	700.00	ferrous, ferr...	ferrous, ferr...	celexa, ultra...	ferrous, ferr...	=========...	celexa, ultra...
2	74.92	84.44	6.48	1.13	689.00	single, + pac...	single, + pac...	celexa, ultra...	single, + pac...	=========...	celexa, ultra...
2	74.92	85.61	6.43	1.14	684.00	celebrex ==>...	celebrex	celexa, ultra...	celebrex	=========...	celexa, ultra...
2	74.92	86.97	6.34	1.16	674.00	rofecoxib, vi...	rofecoxib, vi...	celexa, ultra...	rofecoxib, vi...	=========...	celexa, ultra...
2	74.92	87.21	6.28	1.16	668.00	softclix, point...	softclix, point...	celexa, ultra...	softclix, point...	=========...	celexa, ultra...
2	74.92	86.79	6.18	1.16	657.00	buspirone, al...	buspirone, al...	celexa, ultra...	buspirone, al...	=========...	celexa, ultra...
2	74.92	85.91	5.96	1.15	634.00	potassium, c...	potassium, c...	celexa, ultra...	potassium, c...	=========...	celexa, ultra...
2	74.92	88.52	5.80	1.18	617.00	labetalol, hcl, ...	labetalol, hcl, ...	celexa, ultra...	labetalol, hcl, ...	=========...	celexa, ultra...
2	74.92	84.81	5.78	1.13	614.00	adderall, effe...	adderall, effe...	celexa, ultra...	adderall, effe...	=========...	celexa, ultra...
2	74.92	83.36	5.56	1.11	591.00	cardizem, w...	cardizem, w...	celexa, ultra...	cardizem, w...	=========...	celexa, ultra...
2	74.92	82.09	5.39	1.10	573.00	atenolol, teno...	atenolol, teno...	celexa, ultra...	atenolol, teno...	=========...	celexa, ultra...
2	74.92	82.25	5.23	1.10	556.00	remeron, dio...	remeron, dio...	celexa, ultra...	remeron, dio...	=========...	celexa, ultra...
2	74.92	86.95	5.20	1.16	553.00	u.s.p., enalap...	u.s.p., enalap...	celexa, ultra...	u.s.p., enalap...	=========...	celexa, ultra...
2	74.92	86.88	5.11	1.16	543.00	allegra, cartia...	allegra, cartia...	celexa, ultra...	allegra, cartia...	=========...	celexa, ultra...
2	74.92	81.26	4.98	1.08	529.00	synthroid ==...	synthroid	celexa, ultra...	synthroid	=========...	celexa, ultra...
2	74.92	84.75	4.97	1.13	528.00	prednisone =...	prednisone	celexa, ultra...	prednisone	=========...	celexa, ultra...
2	74.92	84.81	4.94	1.13	525.00	hydrochlorot...	hydrochlorot...	celexa, ultra...	hydrochlorot...	=========...	celexa, ultra...
2	74.92	86.01	4.68	1.15	498.00	fosinopril, ch...	fosinopril, ch...	celexa, ultra...	fosinopril, ch...	=========...	celexa, ultra...
2	74.92	92.21	4.68	1.23	497.00	furosemide =...	furosemide	celexa, ultra...	furosemide	=========...	celexa, ultra...
2	74.92	86.83	4.59	1.16	488.00	cozaar, prinz...	cozaar, prinz...	celexa, ultra...	cozaar, prinz...	=========...	celexa, ultra...
2	74.92	82.68	4.58	1.10	487.00	norvasc, aml...	norvasc, aml...	celexa, ultra...	norvasc, aml...	=========...	celexa, ultra...
2	74.92	87.84	4.55	1.17	484.00	k-dur, loraze...	k-dur, loraze...	celexa, ultra...	k-dur, loraze...	=========...	celexa, ultra...
2	74.92	86.76	4.44	1.16	472.00	citrate, nasa...	citrate, nasa...	celexa, ultra...	citrate, nasa...	=========...	celexa, ultra...
2	74.92	85.05	4.28	1.14	455.00	nitrolingual, fl...	nitrolingual, fl...	celexa, ultra...	nitrolingual, fl...	=========...	celexa, ultra...
2	74.92	86.42	4.25	1.15	452.00	prevacid ==>...	prevacid	celexa, ultra...	prevacid	=========...	celexa, ultra...

Output 5.16 contains a total of 59 different rules, all with numerous transactions. The rules are shown as a link graph in Figure 5.9. Note the circular nature of the link graph. The center is the category including Celexa et al. It appears that the medications in this cluster are commonly prescribed and are at the center of all links.

Figure 5.9 Link Graph for 500 Clusters

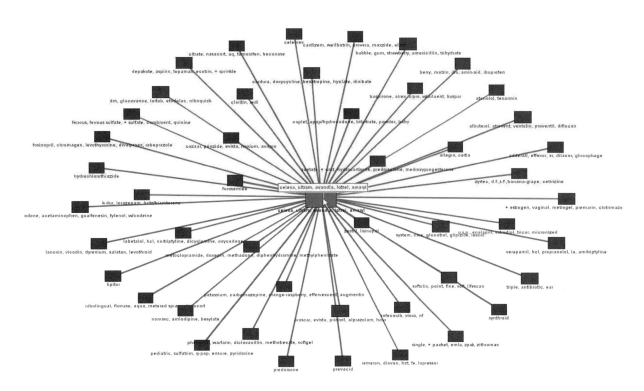

This link graph explains the shape of the rule matrix. It includes many left-hand values but only one right-hand value. The next step is to split the dominant cluster into its component medications and then recluster. Or you could just eliminate this cluster and reanalyze the data set. The choice is up to you.

5.5 Additional Examples

The University of Louisville maintains its course catalog at
http://htmlaccess.louisville.edu/crseCatalog/searchCrseCatalog.cfm (June 2006). Each course is identified by a four-letter department abbreviation and a three-digit course number. You can use the registrar's database of all course enrollments for 2000 to 2004 to examine patterns of student course choices. There are thousands of courses and course combinations for students to choose from. Students in some majors have more choices than students in other majors. During this period, there were approximately 850,000 different enrollments for almost 60,000 students. Not all students were enrolled during the entire period of time under study. Output 5.17 gives the rule matrix for the default value of the highest lift.

Output 5.17 Rule Matrix for Highest Lift Course Associations

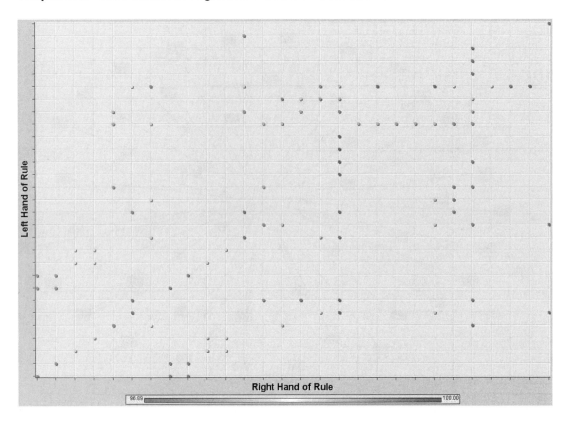

The output shows a scattered pattern in the rules increasing from left to right. Most of the courses in these rules seem to be related to the School of Law, with a few others related to the School of Medicine (Figure 5.10).

Figure 5.10 Link Graph of Rules

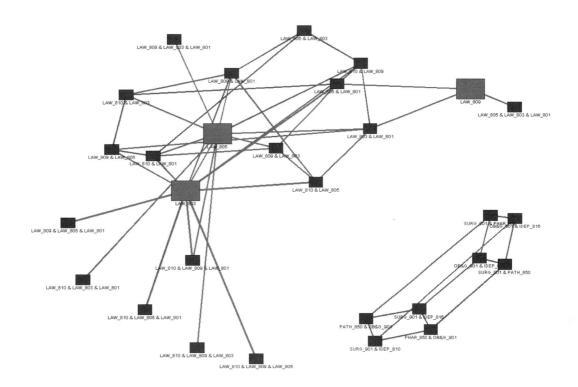

In the graph, both the upper and lower segments are related to law; the small link at the right is related to surgery. These two course patterns are determined primarily by the course of study; students in the College of Arts and Sciences have many more choices, so the links will not show such high confidence. Therefore, the default of confidence is changed to the count (Figure 5.11).

Figure 5.11 Link Graph of Rules for Highest Count

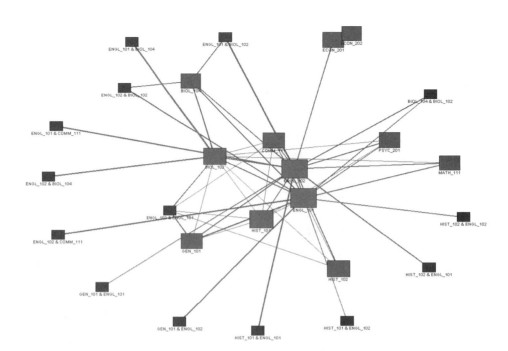

By using the links with the highest support, the link graph has captured patterns for general education requirements. Thus, the highest confidence is for graduate courses of study; the highest counts are for undergraduate general education courses. At the center are English 101 and 102, required for all undergraduates. Also at the center are History 101 and 102, Math 111 (college algebra), and Communications 111. Math 111 is a smaller link because there are other mathematics courses that also count for general education. Figure 5.11 contains some interesting links; for example, Political Science 201 is connected to Psychology 201.

Figure 5.12 shows the link graph for the top 200 rules based on the highest confidence. In this example, again, rules that are related to medicine and to law are prominent. However, the pattern is different compared to the highest lift in Figure 5.10.

Figure 5.12 Confidence Link Graph

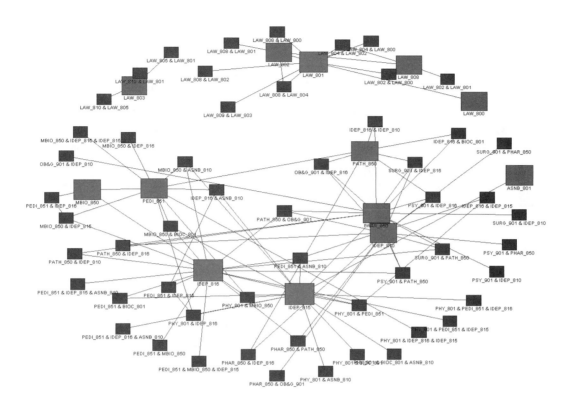

More rules appear in Figure 5.12. The center contains PHY (Physiology), IDEP (Family Medicine), and PATH (Pathology), which are basic science courses required for all medical students.

In contrast, as shown in Figure 5.13 with the expected confidence, the center of the links is English 101, a required course for all undergraduate students. Again, because the graph is dense, you need some way to make it more meaningful.

Figure 5.13 Expected Confidence Link Graph

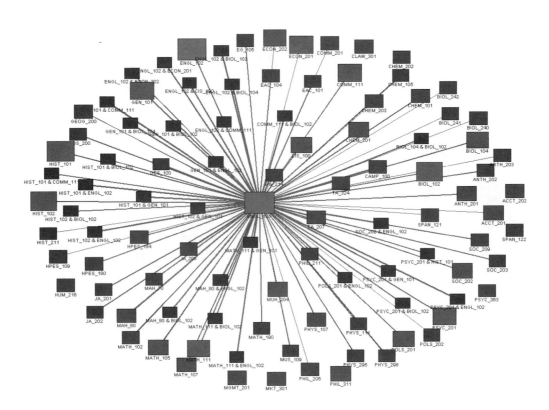

SAS Enterprise Miner 5.2 has added the ability to drill down into a small part of the link graph (Display 5.4). The menu shown is accessed by right-clicking with the mouse.

Display 5.4 Using the Action Mode to Drill Down into the Link Graph

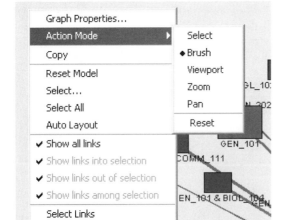

Once you have selected **Viewport**, you can mark the section of the graph to get a closer look (Figure 5.14).

Figure 5.14 Creating a Viewport

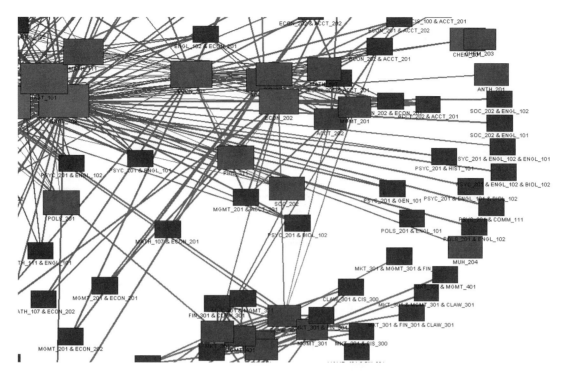

This segment of the graph highlights the relationship between courses in the School of Business. Marketing courses are linked to management courses; both are linked to economics. Other courses in the link include English 101 and Psychology 201 as well as Math 107, which are the general education courses favored by business majors. Another popular course is Sociology 202.

Another way to make the association analysis more meaningful is to filter down to a class or category. The following SAS code filters to general education courses; that is, it filters to 100-level courses. The variable Crseno represents the course number, Stuid is the student's identification code, and Course represents a concatenation of the department (Classes.Dept) and the course number.

```
PROC SQL;
   CREATE TABLE SASUSER.gened AS SELECT classes.DEPT FORMAT=$F4.,
      classes.CRSENO FORMAT=BEST12.,
      classes.STUID FORMAT=BEST12.,
      classes.course FORMAT=$F17.
   FROM EC100007.classes AS classes
   WHERE classes.CRSENO<=199;
QUIT;
```

The link graph in Figure 5.15 uses the count to define the rules.

Figure 5.15 Link Graph for General Education Courses

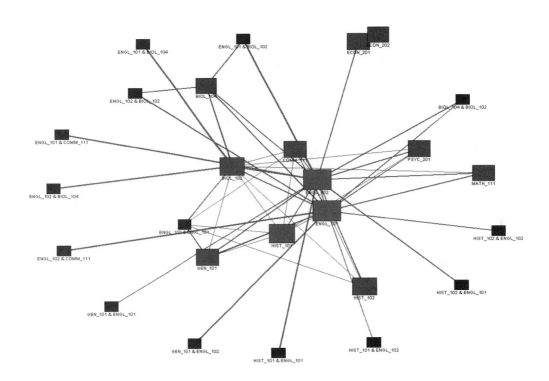

The central part of the graph shows the courses that are required for general education (Figure 5.16). Other courses are part of a required category (mathematics, biology) from which students can choose a variety of different options. Specific courses in the center are history, English, mathematics, and biology. Gen. 101, a campus culture course required for Arts and Sciences majors, is also prominent, again looking at transaction counts.

Figure 5.16 Viewport Link into General Education Courses

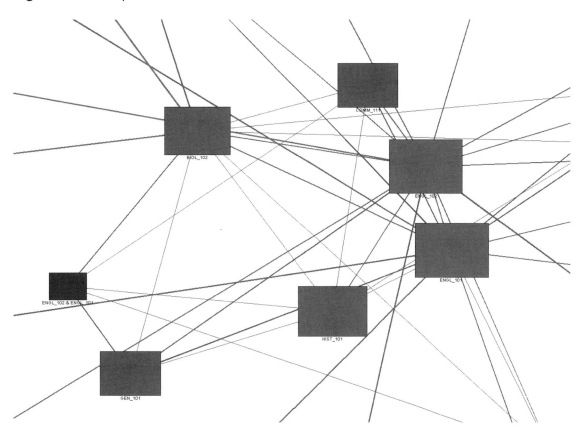

Where a science course is required, the highest transaction counts are for biology. For mathematics, the largest transaction is for Math 111, which is College Algebra.

Another way to analyze the data involves filtering out all mathematics majors to see what general courses they take. To do this, first you must identify the mathematics majors. Then, you must isolate courses taken by mathematics majors. The coding for this process is done in two steps. In the first step, assume that any student taking advanced mathematics courses can be identified as a mathematics major. Although this assumption includes some students who are not math majors, it ensures that all math majors are included.

```
PROC SQL;
CREATE TABLE SASUSER.mathstudents AS SELECT classes.DEPT FORMAT=$F4.,
      classes.CRSENO FORMAT=BEST12.,
      classes.STUID FORMAT=BEST12.,
      classes.course FORMAT=$F17.
   FROM EC100012.classes AS classes
   WHERE (classes.DEPT='MATH' AND classes.CRSENO>299);
QUIT;
```

The second step uses a left join to merge the file containing only the mathematics courses to all courses that include the same student identification numbers as those in the mathematics file:

```
PROC SQL;
CREATE TABLE SASUSER.mathstudentcourses AS SELECT QURY5093.DEPT
FORMAT=$F4.,
       mathstudents.CRSENO FORMAT=BEST12.,
       mathstudents.STUID FORMAT=BEST12.,
       mathstudents.course FORMAT=$F17.,
       classes.DEPT FORMAT=$F4. AS DEPT1,
       classes.CRSENO FORMAT=BEST12. AS CRSENO1,
       classes.STUID FORMAT=BEST12. AS STUID1,
       classes.course FORMAT=$F17. AS course1
    FROM SASUSER.QURY5093 AS QURY5093
LEFT JOIN EC100014.classes AS classes ON (mathstudents.STUID=
classes.STUID);
QUIT;
```

A left join includes all observations in the mathstudentcourses data set and only those courses in the general file that have the same student identification number as an observation in the mathstudentscourses data set. The link analysis for the default of the greatest lift appears in Figure 5.17.

Figure 5.17 Link Graph for Mathematics Majors

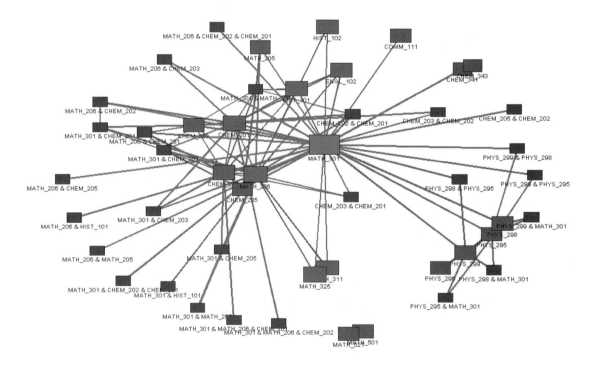

Math 301 is in the center of the link graph. It appears to be the one course that defines mathematics majors (Calculus III). In other words, students in Calculus I and II are not necessarily math majors; once in Calculus III, they tend to continue their mathematics education. The lower right-hand side shows associations to physics courses. The upper left-hand side shows associations to chemistry courses. As shown in previous link graphs, the general preference for science is Biology. Mathematics majors trend differently. When the number of links shown is increased from 200 to 500 (Figure 5.18), the associations between mathematics and chemistry and mathematics and physics become more pronounced.

Figure 5.18 Link Graph with 500 Rules

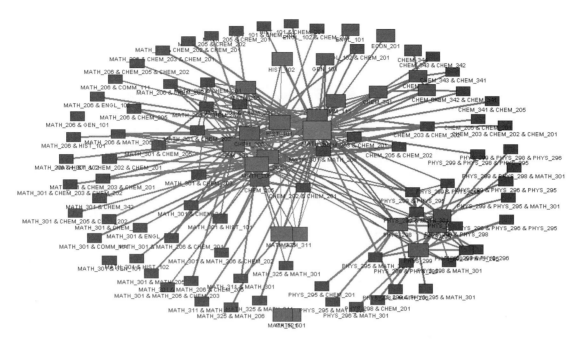

An enlargement of the center of the link graph in Figure 5.18 appears in Figure 5.19.

Figure 5.19 Center of Link Graph for Mathematics Majors

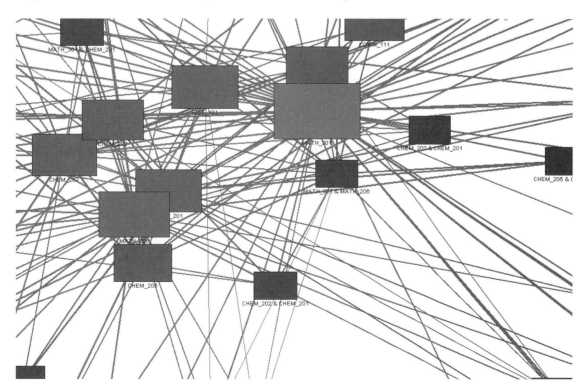

Math 301 (Calculus III) is closely linked to Chemistry 202 and Chemistry 206.

To examine the relationships of graduate students, filter the database to include 500- and 600-level courses and perform the association on the department instead of the course (Figure 5.20).

Figure 5.20 Link Analysis for Graduate Students

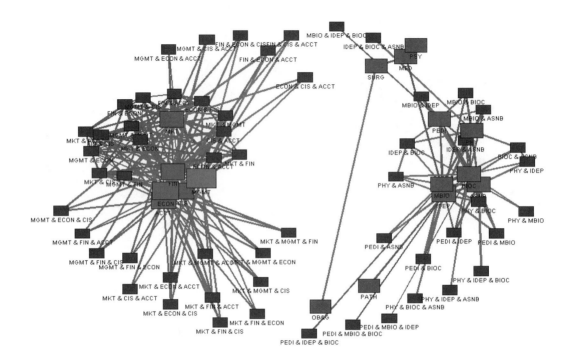

The primary relationships occur across departments in the College of Business and across basic science departments in the School of Medicine. The link graph indicates that graduate majors rarely take classes outside their own department. If you restrict the filtering to departments in the College of Arts and Sciences, only one link is found (Figure 5.21).

Figure 5.21 Graduate Links in Arts and Sciences

Art, history, and humanities are related; no other interdisciplinary work is identified. If the support is decreased to 1.0, more links are found (Figure 5.22).

Figure 5.22 Decreased Support for More Arts and Sciences Links

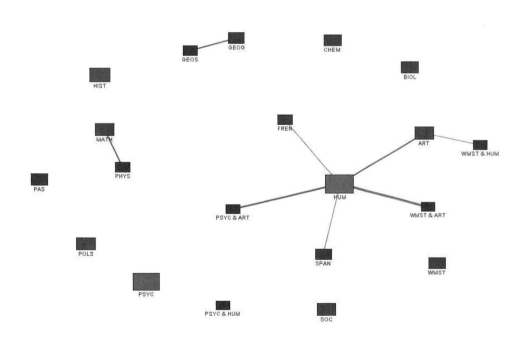

There is a small link between mathematics and physics. There are other links across several departments in the humanities. Otherwise, Figure 5.22 clearly demonstrates that very few graduate students in the College of Arts and Sciences will cross departmental lines.

5.6 Using the Path Analysis Node

The Path Analysis node, a special case of association rules, is designed to examine how Internet users navigate through the links provided (Figure 5.23).

Figure 5.23 Path Analysis Node

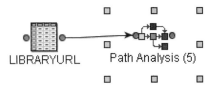

LIBRARYURL   Path Analysis (5)

The defaults for the Path Analysis node appear in Display 5.5.

Display 5.5 Default Values for Path Analysis

Property	Value
Node ID	Path5
Imported Data	
Exported Data	
Variables	
Training Mode	
Data Sorted	No
Maximal Paths	No
Longest Only	No
Maximum Number of Items	2
Backup Limit	5
Keep Reload	No
Maximum Visits	1000
Minimum Visits	0
Maximum Number of Items	100000
Support	
Support Type	Percent
Count Support	
Percentage Support	5.0
Rules	
Number to Keep	200
Sort Criterion	DEFAULT
Pattern Match	No
Match LHS	No
Number to Transpose	200
Export Rule by ID	No
Data Sets	
Restricted Paths	
Transition Probabilities	
Funnel Counts	
Recount Paths	
Scoring Rules	

Note the default value of 1,000 for the maximum number of visits and the default value of 100,000 for the maximum number of items to process. These values are probably too small for most jobs. It is recommended that you increase them routinely.

A second field in the data set is for the User ID. A third field must be defined in the data set because it is essential for path analysis, and it must be a sequencing field. The URLs must be labeled sequentially. If a date and time are provided in the data set instead of a sequence label, the following code defines the sequence:

```
      /* Sort the data on USER_ID.                              */
proc sort data= sasuser.librarysubset data out=work.ls;
   by user_id;
run;

      /* Create a SAS datetime value from the character DATETIME */
      /* field.                                                  */
data ls2;
   set ls;
   date_time=compress(date_time,'[/');
   sas_date_time=input(date_time,datetime.);
   format sas_date_time datetime18.;
   where user_id ne ' ';
run;

      /* Sort the data on both USER_ID and SAS_DATE_TIME to prepare */
      /* for sequencing.                                            */
proc sort data=ls2;
   by user_id sas_date_time;
run;

      /* Assign the SEQUENCE_NUM.                                */
data ls3;
   set ls2;
   by user_id sas_date_time;

   if first.user_id then sequence_num=0;
   sequence_num+1;
run;
```

In this example, the campus library stores information on electronic database use. All off-campus users must log in using their user ID. A data file containing user IDs and dates and times of URLs accessed was collected monthly. Data from a one-month period were examined using path analysis. After defining sequence numbers, the default values were used in the Path Analysis node (Output 5.18); the corresponding link graph appears in Figure 5.24. The first pass in the analysis shows several focal points. Unfortunately, they point to login screens, menu screens, and images. The output from the analysis reinforces that result, providing a count of the most accessed URLs.

Output 5.18 Path Analysis for Library Data

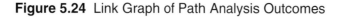

Note the line in the Items plot, which indicates that there is one Web site in the Web link that is required for use. That link can be seen in the link graph (Figure 5.24).

Figure 5.24 Link Graph of Path Analysis Outcomes

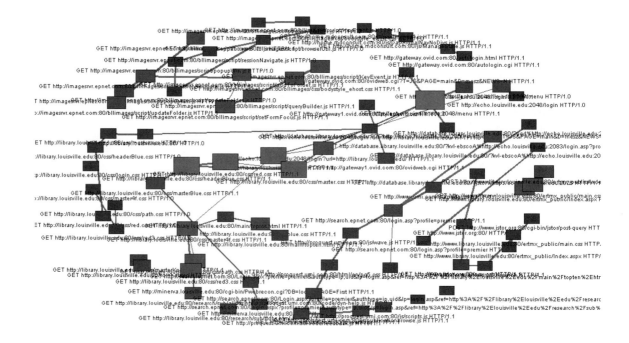

Many of the links include a login screen; others include headers and colors, as clearly identified in the path analysis output (Output 5.19). The link analysis is difficult to read because of the length of the URLs.

Output 5.19 Results of Path Analysis

```
    1227       103613     GET http://echo.louisville.edu:2048/menu HTTP/1.1
    1066        76345     GET http://library.louisville.edu:80/css/headerBlue.css
HTTP/1.1
    1000        76338     GET http://library.louisville.edu:80/css/master.css HTTP/1.1
     989        76371     GET http://library.louisville.edu:80/ HTTP/1.1
     985        76316     GET http://library.louisville.edu:80/css/red.css HTTP/1.1
     735        76314     GET http://library.louisville.edu:80/css/red3.css HTTP/1.1
     684        76336     GET http://library.louisville.edu:80/css/master4f.css HTTP/1.1
     663        76320     GET http://library.louisville.edu:80/css/path.css HTTP/1.1
     583        13280     GET http://www.library.louisville.edu:80/ertmx_public/main.css
HTTP/1.1
     546        13288     GET
http://www.library.louisville.edu:80/ertmx_public/Index.aspx HTTP/1.1
     537       104121     GET
http://echo.louisville.edu:2048/login?url=http://library.louisville.edu/ HTTP/1.1
     526        78565     GET
http://imagesrvr.epnet.com:80/bllimages/css/bodystyle_ehost.css HTTP/1.1
```

The URLs with the highest counts are described here. The first URL is for the menu, the second is for a header, and the third is for a logo. To define a more meaningful analysis, these URLs need to be filtered out of the data set. Use the count list to cut and paste the URL code to be filtered out into a SAS program. After removing these URLs, the outcomes of the second path analysis appear in Output 5.20 and Figure 5.25.

Output 5.20 Outcomes for Second Path Analysis

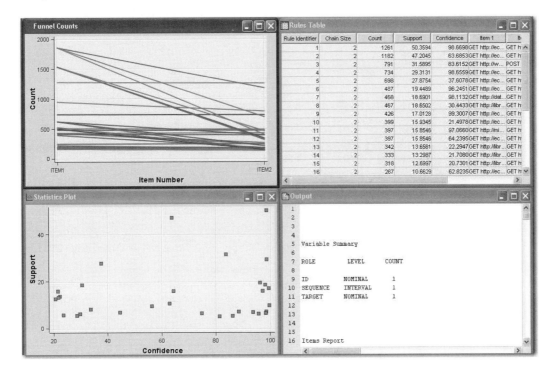

The *funnel count*, new in SAS Enterprise Miner 5.2, shows the drop off from Link A to Link B. In this example, the drop off for some of the values is relatively steep while for others it is almost nonexistent. There are fewer rules defined once the more standard links have been filtered out.

Figure 5.25 Link Graph for Second Path Analysis

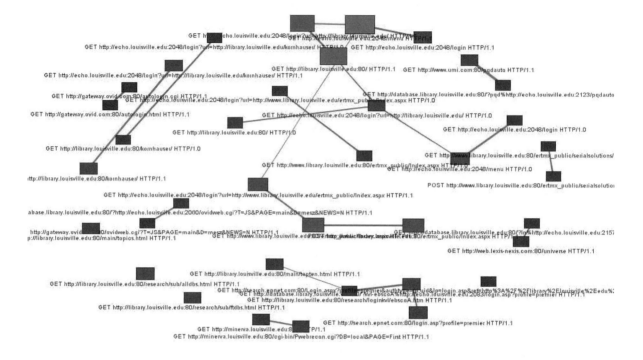

Although fewer rules are defined, there are similar levels of support and confidence. Nevertheless, as shown in Output 5.21, login screens are still included in the analysis.

Output 5.21 Second Set of URLs

```
GET
http://database.library.louisville.edu:80/?abi%http://echo.louisville.edu:2123/pqdauto
HTTP/1.1  126      5.0319
GET
http://database.library.louisville.edu:80/?http://echo.louisville.edu:2060/ovidweb.cgi
?T=JS&PAGE=main&D=mesz&NEWS=N HTTP/1.1  182      7.2684
GET http://database.library.louisville.edu:80/?kvl-
ebscoA%http://echo.louisville.edu:2083/login.asp?profile=premier HTTP/1.1 477   19.0495
GET
http://database.library.louisville.edu:80/?ln%http://echo.louisville.edu:2157/universe
HTTP/1.1  186      7.4281
GET
http://database.library.louisville.edu:80/?pqd%http://echo.louisville.edu:2123/pqdauto
HTTP/1.1 246      9.8243
GET http://echo.louisville.edu:2048/login HTTP/1.0   166        6.6294
GET http://echo.louisville.edu:2048/login HTTP/1.1   506        20.2077
GET http://echo.louisville.edu:2048/login?url=http://library.louisville.edu/ HTTP/1.0
425      16.9728
GET http://echo.louisville.edu:2048/login?url=http://library.louisville.edu/ HTTP/1.1
1278      51.0383
```

The first URL here is the home login to a proxy server, echo.louisville.edu. The second and third URLs are more meaningful and lead to electronic databases. However, some login screens still remain and need to be filtered out. Output 5.22 and Figure 5.26 show the final path analysis after these values are filtered out. Again, the support and confidence remain at the same level.

Output 5.22 Path Outcomes After Second Filtering

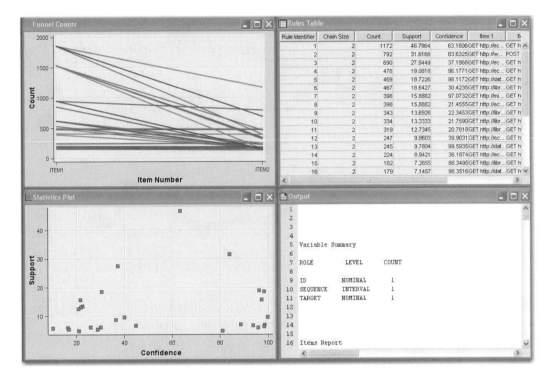

Although the number of rules has continued to decrease, the support and confidence remain roughly the same. Therefore, the more important links remain in the analysis.

Figure 5.26 Link Graph after Second Filtering

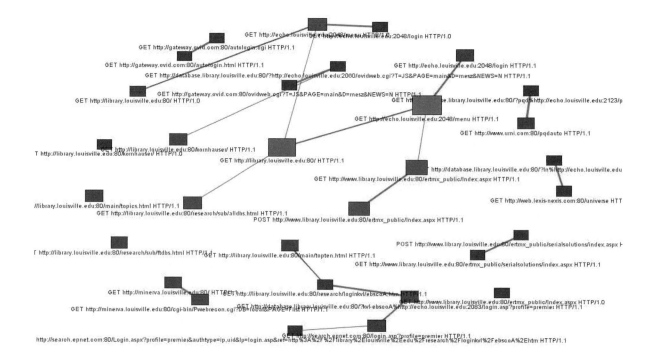

It is on the third attempt that some meaningful links are defined. In addition to Ovid, the URL location of Pqdaute is frequently used, as is rtmx-public and serial solutions.

The following path analysis considers courses taken by mathematics majors. This example uses a slightly different approach from that in Section 5.5, where the sequencing of courses was not considered. Use the following code to define the sequencing for the data file:

```
data sasuser.mathgradssequenced;
    set sasuser.mathematicsgrads;
    by stuid crseno;

    if stuid_id then sequence_num=0;
    sequence_num+1;
run;
```

The item report from the output file appears in Output 5.23.

Output 5.23 URL Counts for Mathematics Majors

Transaction Target Item	Transaction Count	Support(%)
Math 501: Introduction to Analysis I	198	33.9041
Math 502: Introduction to Analysis II	60	10.2740
Math 505: Introduction to Partial Differential Equations	38	6.5068
Math 521: Modern Algebra I	180	30.8219
Math 522: Modern Algebra II	60	10.2740
Math 550: Advanced Euclidean Geometry	70	11.9863
Math 551: Geometry	54	9.2466
Math 560: Statistical Data Analysis	175	29.9658
Math 561: Probability	99	16.9521
Math 562: Mathematical Statistics	80	13.6986
Math 570: Foundations of Actuarial Science	32	5.4795
Math 572: Theory of Interest	49	8.3904
Math 590: History of Mathematics	84	14.3836
Math 591: Selected Topics in Mathematics	83	14.2123
Math 601: Real Analysis I	38	6.5068
Math 635: Mathematical Modeling I	33	5.6507
Math 660: Probability Theory	39	6.6781
Math 681: Combinatorics and Graph Theory I	43	7.3630
Math 693: Seminar in Teaching Mathematics	55	9.4178

Notice that the second semester of a number of the 600-level course sequences is missing, indicating that there is a considerable drop off from the first to second course in certain sequences. Similarly, while Math 521 appears 180 times, Math 522 falls to 60. However, Math 570 (Foundations of Actuarial Science) occurs less than its successor course, Math 572. The funnel count graph (Output 5.24) reinforces that result by showing a steep slope.

Output 5.24 Funnel Counts for Mathematics Graduate Students

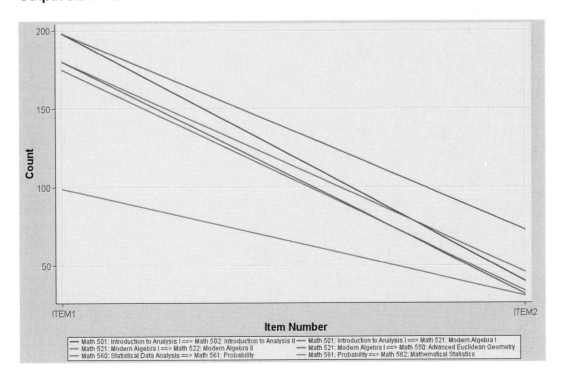

The link graph appears in Figure 5.27.

Figure 5.27 Sequential Link Graph for Mathematics Graduate Students

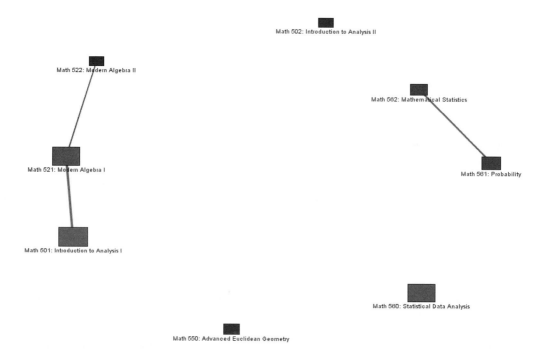

Using the default support levels, there are very few connections in the analysis. Reducing the support limit from 2.0 to 1.0 provides more links (Figure 5.28).

Figure 5.28 Link Analysis with Lower Support

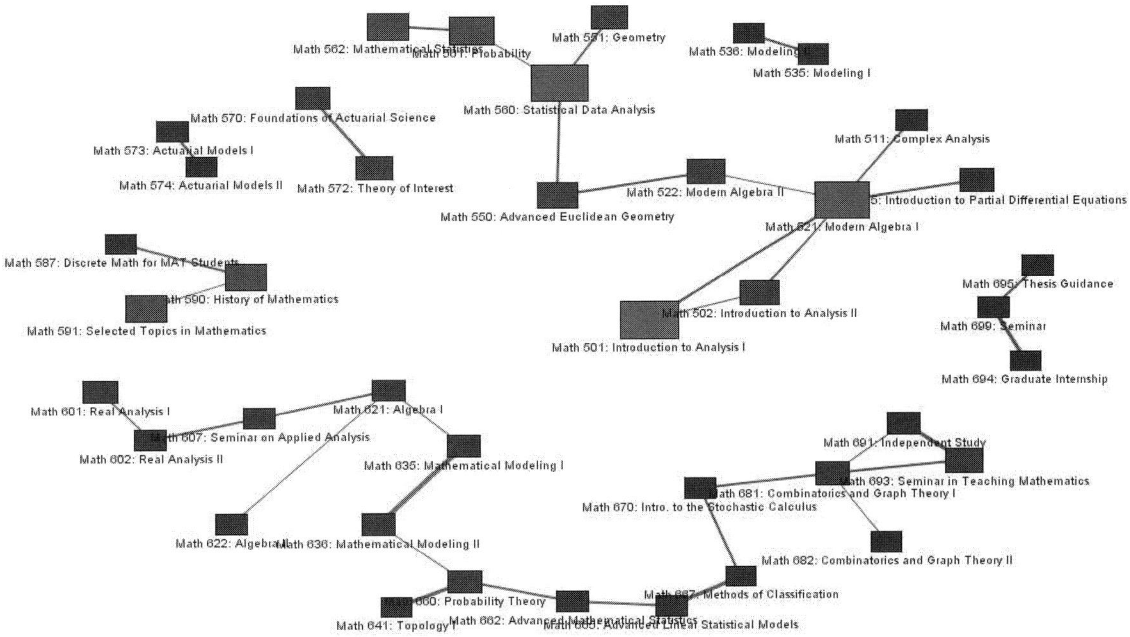

One of the relationships that appears in Figure 5.28 is between modeling courses and probability and statistics courses. However, because you need to reduce the support to find these links, they are not very strong. Math 550 (Geometry) is weakly linked to Algebra II (Math 522) but also to Statistical Data Analysis (Math 560). Math 550 is strictly for mathematics majors. This connection shows the other courses math majors take to complete their degree.

5.7 Discussion

Association rules work well for data sets with many transactions per client and when clients have similar purchasing patterns. However, if there are too many different possible purchases (different items), the transactions get too thin, resulting in rules that apply only to one or two transactions. When this occurs, you must reduce the number of different categories. You can do this manually if classes of categories are used instead of the categories themselves. Otherwise, you can reduce the categories using SAS Text Miner software.

5.8 Exercises

1. Use the medication list reduced to 250 categories to examine the association rules.
2. Shift to medications by patient rather than medications by household and investigate using association rules.
3. Write a summary of your results.

SAS Text Miner Software
with the Association Node

6.1 Introduction to SAS Text Miner

Chapter 4 illustrated how to reduce the number of similar items with slightly different wording in a list. This chapter expands on the software's power to work with lists. Consider again the list of medications described in Chapter 4. In order to use SAS Text Miner software, you must change the observable unit from medication order to individual patient or household. In other words, each patient defines one record in SAS whereas the original data set defines each medication order as a SAS record. Instead of more than 270,000 observations in the data set, there will be slightly less than 11,000 different observations (representing households). To make this change, you must combine all medications related to one patient as a text string. This text string is a collection of nouns. The associations between items are defined through these text strings.

To distinguish between an item that uses more than one word and a new item in the text string, connect all words for one item using underscores. Each individual patient or household should have one associated text string.

6.2 Creating Linkages with SAS Text Miner

SAS Text Miner software provides a number of ways for you to analyze your data. To define linkages, you need to preprocess some data. All medications for one household (or one patient, depending upon your interest) must be linked, and the observational unit must be changed from medication to household. The following code makes these changes. The first code example sorts the data by the household identifier, **duid**. One medication name is connected through underscores:

```
proc sort data=sasuser.originaldata out=work.sort_out;
   by duid rxname;
run;

data work.sort_out1;
   set work.sort_out;
   rxname = translate(left(trim(rxname)),'_',' ');
run;
```

This code example shifts all medications for one household into a series of fields; one observation per household remains:

```
proc transpose data=work.sort_out1
               out=work.tran (drop=_name_ _label_) prefix=med_;
   var rxname ;
   by duid
run;
```

The following code concatenates the fields created by the TRANSPOSE procedure and creates one long text string to contain the multiple medications per household:

```
data work.concat(keep=duid rxname);
   length rxname $32767;
   set work.tran;

   array chconcat {*} med_:;

   rxname=left(trim(med_1));
   do i=2 to dim(chconcat);
        rxname=left(trim(charges)) || ' ' ||
        left(trim(chconcat[i]));
   end;
run;

proc sql;
   select max(length(rxname)) into :rxname_LEN from work.concat;
quit;
```

This last code example finds the longest text string to use to define the final data set:

```
%put rxname_LEN=&rxname_LEN;

data sasuser.medstextstrings;
   length rxname $ &rxname_LEN;
   set work.concat;
run;

proc contents data=sasuser.medtextstrings;
run;
```

A new SAS function available in SAS®9 simplifies the concatenation of the text list, **catx**. It automatically trims leading and trailing blanks, so the do-loop listed here can be replaced by the following statement:

```
rxname=catx(' ',med[i]).
```

Once you have run this code, an initial household record provided in the data set (see Table 6.1) is modified (see Table 6.2).

Table 6.1 Household Record

DUID	RXNAME
40001	SOFTCLIX
40001	ANTIVERT
40001	SOFTCLIX
40001	SOFTCLIX
40001	SOFTCLIX
40001	SOFTCLIX
40001	SOFTCLIX
40001	SOFTCLIX
40001	ESTROGEN
40001	ESTROGEN
40001	CEFADROXIL
40001	ESTROGEN
40001	ESTROGEN
40001	ESTROGEN
40001	ESTROGEN
40001	ESTROGEN
40001	ESTROGEN
40001	ESTROGEN
40001	ESTROGEN
40001	ESTROGEN

Table 6.2 Modified Patient Record

DUID	RXNAME
40001	ANTIVERT CEFADROXIL ESTROGEN ESTROGEN ESTROGEN ESTROGEN ESTROGEN ESTROGEN ESTROGEN ESTROGEN ESTRO BETAMETH KEFLEX
40007	ACCUTANE_(RX_PAK,_10X10) ACCUTANE_(RX_PAK,_10X10) ACCUTANE_(RX_PAK,_10X10) ALBUTEROL BENZAMYCIN B
40010	ALBUTEROL APAP/PROPOXYPHENE_NAPSYLATE_(PINK) BENZTROPINE_MESYLATE CARDEC_DM_SYRUP ERYTHROMYCIN/SU

Medications that use multiple words are linked by underscores to preserve the entire name. The software then redefines the data set to find the relationships on those text strings. The SAS Enterprise Miner process flow is shown in Figure 6.1. The SAS Code node is linked to the Text Miner node so that all of the data sets created by the software can be identified and examined using SAS/STAT code, as discussed in Chapter 3.

Figure 6.1 Icons for Text Mining to Reduce Clusters

The resulting clusters appear in Table 6.3.

Table 6.3 Clusters of Medications

Cluster Number	Cluster Descriptor	Cluster Label
1	glucophage, furosemide, zestril, synthroid, softclix	Diabetes, heart
2	allegra, claritin, flonase, nasonex, hydrochlorothiazide	Allergies
3	lipitor, vioxx, allegra, claritin	Cholesterol, arthritis, allergies
4	augmentin	Children's antibiotic
5	vicodin, apap/hydrocodone_bitartrate, celexa, naproxen, vioxx	Pain
6	zoloft, triple_antibiotic, paxil, zyrtec, naproxen	Depression, allergies
7	synthroid, premarin, augmentin, zithromax, amoxicillin	Post-menopause, antibiotics
8	levoxyl, synthroid, premarin, lipitor, zoloft	Post-menopause, cholesterol, depression
9	hydrochlorothiazide, lipitor, norvasc, furosemide, zestril	Cholesterol, hypertension
10	estradiol, prednisone, prempro, zocor, zyrtec	Post-menopause, allergies, cholesterol
11	glyburide , aspirin, glucophage, lisinopril, simvastatin	Diabetes, cholesterol
12	lanoxin, coumadin, pravachol, furosemide, norvasc	Heart, cholesterol
13	atenolol, hydrochlorothiazide, lipitor, zestril, premarin	Heart, cholesterol
14	fosamax_(unit_of_use, blister_pck, fosamax_(unit_of_use), fosamax, celebrex	Ulcer, arthritis

(continued)

Cluster Number	Cluster Descriptor	Cluster Label
15	fluoxetine_hcl, prozac, zithromax, augmentin, cephalexin	Antibiotic, depression
16	singulair_(unit_of_use), albuterol, serevent, flovent, singulair	Asthma
17	celebrex, ultram, hydromet, vioxx, ibuprofen	Arthritis
18	premarin, medroxyprogesterone_acetate_(unit_of_use), allegra, triple_antibiotic, cephalexin	Post-menopause, antibiotics
19	prevacid, cephalexin, amoxicillin, ibuprofen, celebrex	Ulcer, antibiotic, arthritis
20	triple_antibiotic, augmentin, ibuprofen, motrin, amoxicillin	Antibiotic, pain
21	paxil, paxil_(unit_of_use), alprazolam, lorazepam, amoxicillin	Depression, antibiotic

The clusters represent combinations of diagnoses. Remember that the examination is by household, and different household members may have different diagnoses. Also, patients with severe, chronic illnesses often suffer from related co-morbidities. For example, patients with diabetes often have heart problems. Patients with arthritis can have gastric problems related to their arthritis medications. Note also that cluster 8 includes two medications for thyroid, so the cluster label could be changed to post-menopause, cholesterol, depression, and thyroid. Cluster 14 begins with the drug fosamax, which is used to treat osteoporosis. The cluster label could also have been osteoporosis.

As emphasized in Chapter 3, it is important to label the clusters. Because these clusters are related to medications, you might want to ask a pharmacist or another subject matter expert in medications when considering labels.

After these text strings are created, you can't use the Association node, which uses multiple occurrences of the same ID, because there is now only one occurrence of each ID. Therefore, you must use the concept links in SAS Text Miner software to perform any link analysis.

6.3 Using Concept Link Analysis

You can link terms without using clusters by using the SAS Text Miner concept link. The linkages in concept links are determined through text strings. In this example, if one person in a household has diabetes, then all medications required for that household are listed in the text string (insulin, softclix). The concept link picks up the most prominent combinations of medications in the text strings for individuals with diabetes. Because insulin is a major requirement for diabetics, you can use that term to view concept links (Figure 6.2). To ensure that you have an accurate link map, you should alphabetize the term set first, and make all medications starting with *insulin* equivalent. In this example, one term in the list was written in reverse order (novolin_insulin) and was included in the concept link.

Figure 6.2 Concept Links for Insulin

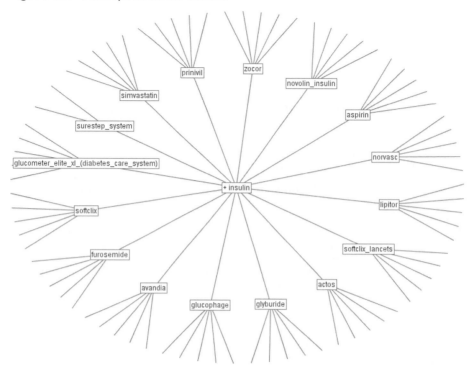

Other medications related to insulin include Lipitor and Simvastatin for cholesterol and Glucophage and Glyburide for Type II diabetes; the concept link also includes devices such as Softclix used to test blood sugar levels.

6.4 Using Concept Links with the Association Node

Once the concept link identifies links that are related to one term of interest (insulin), you can return to the original data set and filter out all terms except those related to the concept link. The following SAS code performs this filtering:

```
PROC SQL;
CREATE TABLE SASUSER.filteredmedications AS SELECT
medications.DUID FORMAT=BEST12.,
    medications.PID FORMAT=BEST12.,
    medications.RXNAME FORMAT=$F50.,
 FROM EC100007.medications AS medications
 WHERE medications.RXNAME IN ('ACTOS', 'AVANDIA', 'ASPIR 81', 'ASPIR-
LOW', 'ASPIRIN', 'ASPIRIN (E.C.)', 'ASPIRIN (ENTERIC COATED)',
'ASPIRIN (ENTERIC-COATED)', 'ASPIRIN (UNBOXED)', 'ASPIRIN ADULT LOW
STRENGTH', "ASPIRIN CHILDREN'S", "ASPIRIN CHILDREN'S (ORANGE)",
'ASPIRIN E.C.', 'ASPIRIN EC', 'ASPIRIN TRI-BUFFERED',
'ASPIRIN/BUTALBITAL/CAFFEINE', 'ASPIRIN/BUTALBITAL/CAFFEINE/CODEINE',
'ASPIRIN/CAFFEINE/ORPHENADRINE', 'ASPIRIN/CARISOPRODOL',
'FUROSEMIDE', 'GLUCOPHAGE', 'GLUCOPHAGE XR', 'GLUCOSAMINE',
'GLUCOSE', 'GLUCOMETER ELITE XL (DIABETES CARE SYSTEM)', 'GLUCOMETER
ELITE', 'GLUCOMETER', 'GLYBURIDE', 'GLYBURIDE (UNIT OF USE)',
'GLYBURIDE 2.5MG(NOVOPH-M*100', 'GLYBURIDE 5 (COPLEY-D)', 'GLYBURIDE
MICRO', 'GLYBURIDE MICRONIZ', 'GLYBURIDE MICRONIZE', 'LIPITOR',
'NORVASC', 'NOVOLIN', 'NOVOLIN 70/30', 'NOVOLIN 70/30
(SRN,PREFILLED)', 'NOVOLIN 70/30 (VIAL)', 'NOVOLIN 70/30 INSULIN',
'NOVOLIN INSULIN', 'NOVOLIN N', 'NOVOLIN N (VIAL)', 'NOVOLIN N
```

```
(VIAL)', 'NOVOLIN N PENFILL (SRN)', 'NOVOLIN NPH', 'NOVOLIN R',
'NOVOLIN R (VIAL)', 'PRINIVIL', 'PRINIVIL (25X31 UNIBLISTER)',
'PRINIVIL (BULK PACKAGE)', 'PRINIVIL (UNIT OF USE)', 'PRINIVIL (UNIT
OF USE, 12X90)', 'SIMAVASTATIN', 'SOFT TOUCH LANCETS', 'SOFTCLIX',
'SOFTCLIX LANCET', 'SOFTCLIX LANCETS', 'SURESTEP', 'SURESTEP
(GLUCOSE)', 'SURESTEP CONTROL SOLN', 'SURESTEP SYSTEM', 'SURESTEP
TEST STRIP', 'ZOCOR', 'ZOCOR (BULK PACKAGE)', 'ZOCOR (UNIT OF USE)');
QUIT;
```

The list defined by the WHERE clause is determined from an alphabetic list based on the terms identified in the concept link (Figure 6.2). You can filter this easily using SAS Enterprise Guide, where you can create the list through a point-and-click interface. Once you have reduced the data set, you can import it as a new data set in SAS Enterprise Miner software. It is then linked to the Association node, with the filtered item list as the target variable and individual identification as the ID variable. The results for insulin terms appear in Output 6.1.

Output 6.1 Results for Filtered Insulin Terms

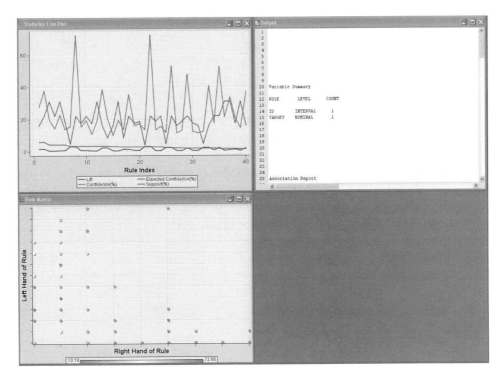

Remember that the blue and brown lines represent lift and support, respectively, in the line plot; the green and red lines represent confidence and expected confidence. Although initial rules have high confidence, that confidence diminishes quickly in the rule set. The same can be seen in the rule matrix. A visualization of these rules appears in the link graph in Figure 6.3.

Figure 6.3 Link Graph of Rules in Relationship to Insulin

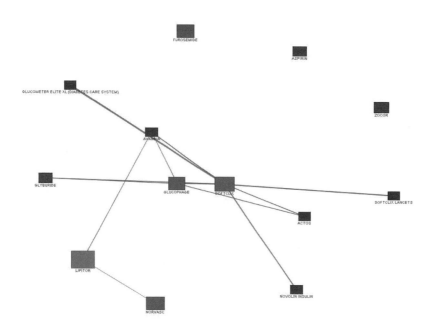

Using just the values in the original data set without any additional preprocessing eliminates any mention of the initial term, insulin. At the center of the link graph are the terms Softclix, Glucophage, and Avandia. Softclix and Softclix Lancets represent the same item, but they are identified differently in this data set. Some of the medications initially connected in Figure 6.2 are no longer connected using the Association node. You can rerun the association analysis using the transaction count instead of the confidence level, but the result will be almost identical. You can now modify the list using the Text Miner node (see Figure 6.4).

Figure 6.4 Modifying the Word List

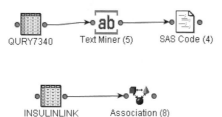

The SAS Code node in Figure 6.4 contains the following code needed to define the clusters:

```
proc print data=emws.text5_cluster;
  var clus_desc;
run;

data sasuser.insulinlink1 (keep=_cluster_ _freq_ _rmsstd_
  clus_desc);
  set emws.text5_cluster;
run;
```

```
data sasuser.insulinlink2 (drop=_svd_1-_svd_500  _roll_1-_roll_1000
prob1-prob500);
   set emws.text5_documents;
run;

proc sort data=sasuser.insulinlink1;
   by _cluster_;

proc sort data=sasuser.insulinlink2;
   by _cluster_;
run;

data sasuser.insulinlink;
   merge sasuser.insulinlink1  sasuser.insulinlink2  ;
   by _CLUSTER_;
run;
```

Using the process developed in Chapter 4, you can use SAS Text Miner software to combine terms that are similar (Output 6.2).

Output 6.2 Text Miner Clusters for Insulin Concept Links

#	Descriptive Terms	Freq	Percentage	RMS Std.
3	aspirin, avandia, actos, aspirin/carisoprodol, strength	2894	0.097869462...	0.0
6	copley-d, micro, microniz, glyburide	1675	0.056645248...	2.3584958...
2	furosemide	3321	0.112309773...	0.0
4	glucophage, xr	3240	0.109570510...	0.0
13	lipitor	5970	0.201893811...	0.0
10	norvasc	3803	0.128610077...	0.0
7	novolin, insulin, vial, srn, penfill	1097	0.037098410...	0.0
5	prinivil, bulk, package, uniblister, glyburide	801	0.027088265...	0.0090159...
11	prinivil, unit	692	0.023402096...	1.7098113...
1	softclix, + lancet, soft touch lancets, soft, touch	2633	0.089042948...	0.0
12	system, glucometer, elite, care, diabetes	606	0.020493743...	0.0
9	unit, zocor, bulk, package	1366	0.046195468...	0.0045464...
8	zocor	1472	0.049780182...	1.0916071...

Although most of the clusters contain related terms, there are some discrepancies. For example, Prinivil is not similar to Glyburide, yet they appear in the same cluster (5). Similarly, Avandia is more related to Glyburide than it is to aspirin, and yet they are also in the same cluster. The question is whether these discrepancies will have a major impact on the results of the Association node (Output 6.3 and Figure 6.5).

Output 6.3 Results of Association of Clusters Results

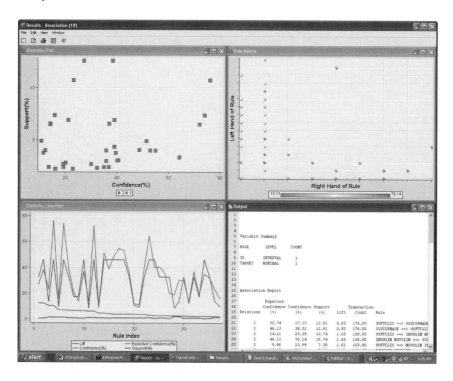

This outcome displays considerable variability in confidence and support. The pattern here is similar to that shown in Figure 6.3. The link graph also shows that more rules were developed (Figure 6.5) in contrast to Figure 6.3.

Figure 6.5 Link Graph of Clustered Associations

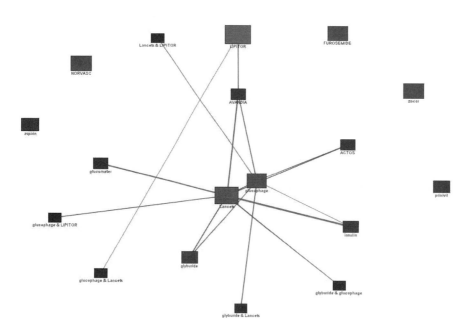

Three remaining medications are not linked to any other medications: Zocor, Furosemide, and Norvasc. However, insulin is now at the center of the link graph, along with Glucophage and Lancets. The link graph now shows links to heart medications such as Lipitor and aspirin.

A third approach is to use SAS Text Miner software's ability to equate terms before clustering. Once this is done, clustering is performed a second time. However, as shown in Figure 6.6, equating like terms can change the association rules.

Figure 6.6 Link Graph of Association Rules After Equating Like Terms

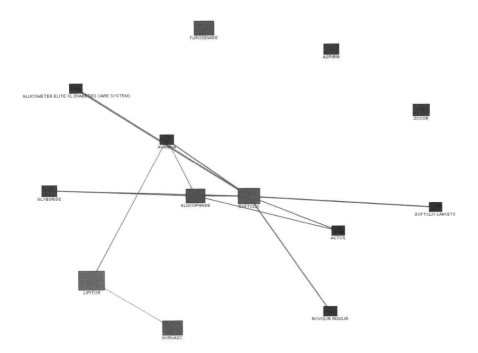

Again, note that several terms are not connected. Also, insulin is no longer in the center of the graph. Another way to make terms equivalent is to use PROC SQL, as follows:

```
PROC SQL;
 CREATE TABLE SASUSER.QURY3402 AS SELECT qury7340.DUID
 FORMAT=BEST12.,
    (CASE qury7340.RXNAME
    WHEN 'ASPIR 81' THEN 'aspirin'
    WHEN 'ASPIR-LOW' THEN 'aspirin'
    WHEN 'ASPIRIN' THEN 'aspirin'
    WHEN 'ASPIRIN' THEN 'aspirin'
    WHEN 'ASPIRIN (ENTERIC COATED)' THEN 'aspirin'
    WHEN 'ASPIRIN (ENTERIC-COATED)' THEN 'aspirin'
 .
 .
 .

    WHEN 'GLUCOMETER' THEN 'glucometer'
    WHEN 'GLUCOMETER ELITE' THEN 'glucometer'
    WHEN 'GLUCOMETER ELITE XL (DIABETES CARE SYSTEM)' THEN
'glucometer'
    WHEN 'GLUCOPHAGE' THEN 'glucophage'
    WHEN 'GLUCOPHAGE XR' THEN 'glucophage'
    WHEN 'GLYBURIDE' THEN 'glyburide'
    WHEN 'GLYBURIDE (UNIT OF USE)' THEN 'glyburide'
 .
```

```
       .
       .
       .
       WHEN 'NOVOLIN' THEN 'insulin'
       WHEN 'NOVOLIN 70/30' THEN 'insulin'
       WHEN 'NOVOLIN 70/30 (SRN,PREFILLED)' THEN 'insulin'
       .
       .
       .

       WHEN 'PRINIVIL' THEN 'prinivil'
       WHEN 'PRINIVIL (25X31 UNIBLISTER)' THEN 'prinivil'
       .
       .
       .

       WHEN 'SOFT TOUCH LANCETS' THEN 'Lancets'
       WHEN 'SOFTCLIX' THEN 'Lancets'
       WHEN 'SOFTCLIX LANCETS' THEN 'Lancets'
       WHEN 'SURESTEP' THEN 'Lancets'
       WHEN 'SURESTEP (GLUCOSE)' THEN 'Lancets'
       .
       .
       .

       WHEN 'ZOCOR' THEN 'zocor'
       WHEN 'ZOCOR (BULK PACKAGE)' THEN 'zocor'
       WHEN 'ZOCOR (UNIT OF USE)' THEN 'zocor'
       ELSE qury7340.RXNAME END) AS CC1,
       ('') AS RXNamecopy
  FROM EC100006.qury7340 AS qury7340;
QUIT;
```

The results of the association rule once the terms are made equivalent appear in Output 6.4 and Figure 6.7.

Output 6.4 Results of Association for Reduced Terms

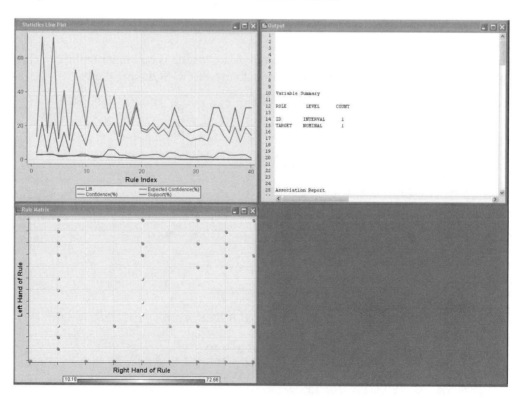

The confidence and support retain their variability in this modified output.

Figure 6.7 Link Analysis of Final Terms

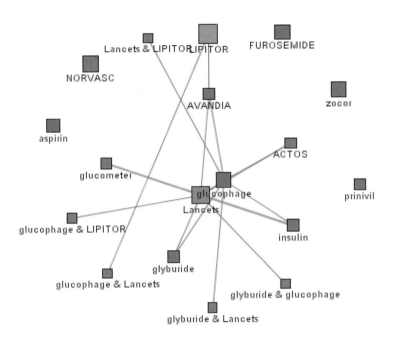

Once you make similar terms identical, the link analysis remains centered at insulin, Lancets, and Glucophage. A number of medications are still not linked, including Furosemide, Zocor, and Prinivil. Yet, in the text analysis, all three were linked to insulin. This example shows again that you can use different approaches to data mining, and you must validate the results in some way. Figure 6.7 looks like Figure 6.5 before similar terms were made equal. This suggests that SAS Text Miner software can preprocess terms before you use the Association node.

6.5 Using Clusters to Summarize Additional Variables

One additional class of variables included with this data set is the cost of medications by type of payer (for example, self-pay, insurance, Medicare). Figures 6.8 through 6.17 show the total paid by each patient (or third party) in the 21 defined clusters, as well as the kernel density estimators of several selected clusters, to examine the entire distribution of payment.

The highest self-pay, as shown in Figure 6.8, is for patients with ulcers and arthritis. A number of recently introduced medications to treat these illnesses are not yet on third-party formularies, which would account for this finding. Patients with diabetes and heart problems represent the cluster with the next highest payment. The highest average self-pay for a year among this group is $1,300 per year. The highest average payment by private insurance is $1,400 per year.

Figure 6.8 Payment by Customers for Medications by Cluster

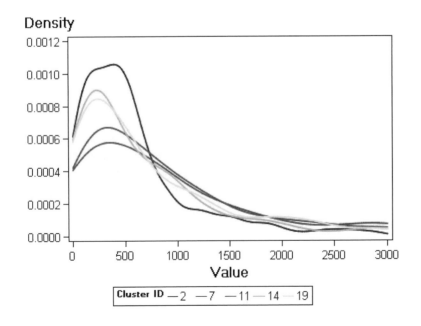

You can use kernel density estimation to examine differences within clusters (see Figure 6.9). In particular, Cluster 2 (allergies) has a high probability of low self-payments. In contrast, Cluster 14 (arthritis and ulcers) has a fairly high probability of payment in the $500–$1,000 range.

Figure 6.9 Kernel Density Estimation of Selected Clusters for Self-Pay

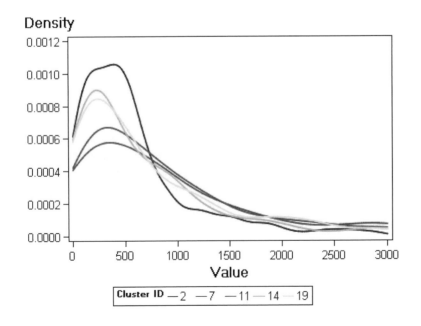

The two highest payments by private insurance are for ulcers and arthritis or for arthritis alone. The next highest cluster is for allergies. See Figure 6.10.

Figure 6.10 Average Yearly Payment by Cluster by Private Insurance (Primary Insurer)

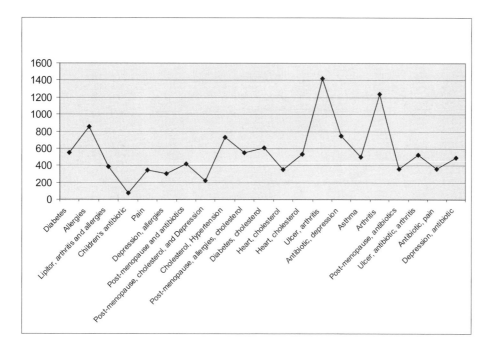

Insurance payments for post-menopause and antibiotics are relatively small but consistent across insurers. There is also similarity for diabetes and cholesterol (Cluster 11) and antibiotics (Cluster 19), as noted in Figure 6.11. However, for arthritis and allergies, the payments by different insurers vary widely.

Figure 6.11 Kernel Density Estimation of Selected Clusters for Private Insurance

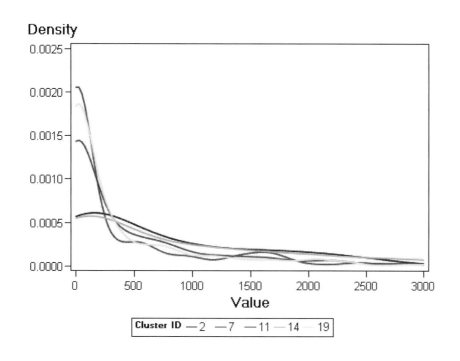

As noted in both Figures 6.12 and 6.13, Medicare pays for very few medications; its highest average payment is for post-menopause. You should compare results before and after the passage of legislation to include post-menopause medications in Medicare coverage.

Figure 6.12 Average Yearly Payment by Cluster by Medicare

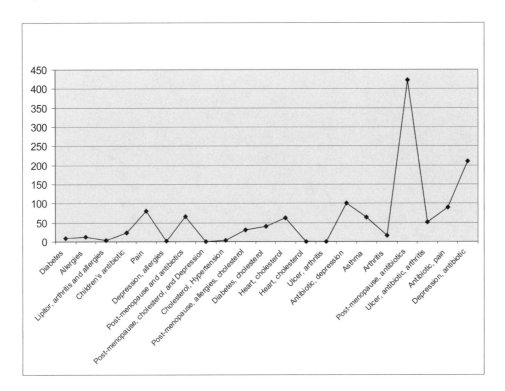

Figure 6.13 Kernel Density Estimation of Selected Clusters by Medicare

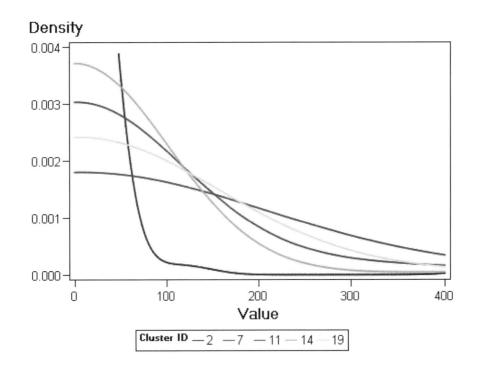

For Medicaid payments, the highest payments are also for arthritis and ulcers. The second highest is for pain. See Figures 6.14 and 6.15.

Figure 6.14 Average Yearly Payment by Cluster by Medicaid

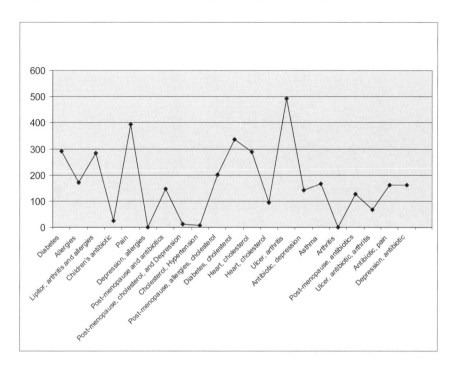

Figure 6.15 Density Estimation of Selected Clusters by Medicaid

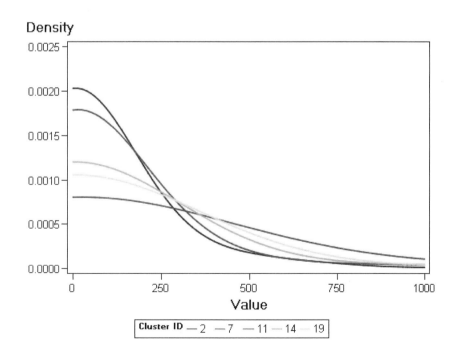

For total payments, the highest payments are again for ulcers and arthritis. The peak payment for a year is under $1,000. These results are depicted in Figures 6.16 and 6.17.

Figure 6.16 Average Yearly Payment by Cluster from All Sources

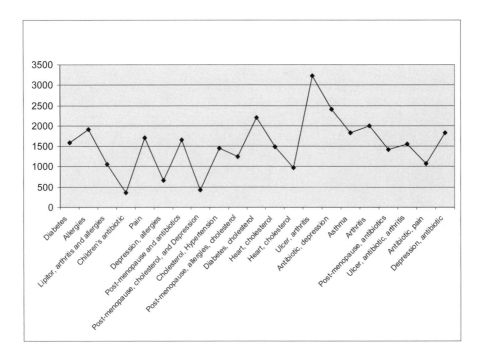

Figure 6.17 Density Estimation of Selected Clusters by All Sources

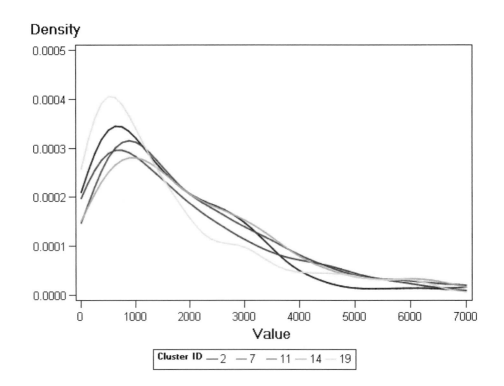

You must ensure that you validate the clusters. The validation method discussed in Section 6.6 compares other values in the data set by cluster. Section 6.5 illustrates a second method that uses link analysis.

6.6 Using SAS Text Miner with Coded Information

Nominal data can be in text format, or it can be identified through numeric codes. These codes often have stemming properties resembling words and text. Therefore, SAS Text Miner software can cluster numeric codes in the same way that it clusters lists. Using the code in Section 6.4, you can change the default in the first settings section of SAS Text Miner as shown in Chapter 3. You can use numbers to parse the text, which is particularly useful when examining information identified by numeric codes.

The numeric codes must have a *stemming* property, in which some digits identify a general category and other digits identify a more specialized category. An example is provided in the codes that define patient illnesses. For example, there are 51 codes related to diabetes. Consider just the following five:

1. 250—Diabetes mellitus
2. 25000—Type II diabetes mellitus without mention of complications
3. 25001—Type I diabetes mellitus without mention of complications
4. 25002—Type II diabetes mellitus without mention of uncontrolled complications
5. 25003—Type I diabetes mellitus without mention of uncontrolled complications

For each patient, all codes relating to multiple illnesses are combined into one text string as described in Section 6.2. For example, the string **4271 42731 42781 4019 41401 412 2724** refers to a patient who suffers from unspecified paroxysmal tachycardia, atrial fibrillation, cardiac dysrhythmia, unspecified essential hypertension, coronary atherosclerosis, old myocardial infarction, and lipoid metabolism disorder. A second patient has a diagnosis represented by the string **4271 412 4280 2724 4019 27800** or unspecified paroxysmal tachycardia, old myocardial infarction, congestive heart failure, lipoid metabolism disorder, unspecified essential hypertension, and obesity. These two examples demonstrate that certain of these numerical codes (called ICD-9 codes) tend to be associated. Based on the way the codes are defined, you can examine these text strings for patterns. More information on these codes can be found at http://icd9cm.chrisendres.com/.

Similarities between codes can be related to similarities in patient conditions, taking full advantage of the stemming properties contained within the codes. SAS Text Miner software was used on a database for 14,734 patients to create the clusters in Table 6.4.

Table 6.4 Clusters Identified Using Text Mining, Along with the Most Frequent Codes Found in the Clusters

Cluster Number	ICD-9 Codes	ICD-9 Risk Factors	Freq.	Label
1	3051, 2724, 4111, 4439, 4019, 4140, 5990, 496	tobacco abuse, hypergammaglobinemia, intermediate coronary syndrome, unspecified peripheral vascular disease, coronary atherosclerosis, urinary tract infection, other chronic airway obstruction	1682	Mild general risk factors
2	4271, 4139, 9971, 2500, 4019, 5180, 4107, 2724, 2859	tachycardia, supraventricular paroxysmal, unspecified angina, surgical cardiac complication, uncomplicated diabetes, essential hypertension, pulmonary collapse, acute myocardial infarction, unspecified anemia	3187	More severe general risk
3	5849, 4104, 4280, 4273, 7855, 9975, 3940, 4260, 3051	acute renal failure, acute myocardial infarction, congestive heart failure, atrial fibrillation, cardiogenic shock, surgical urinary complication, endocarditis, complete atrioventricular shock, tobacco abuse	1139	Complications after surgery
4	5533, 2449, 5308, 4241, 2780, 4412, 4939, 1464, 3000	diaphogmatic hernia, hypothyroidism, esophageal reflux, endocardium disease, obesity, ruptured aortic aneurysm, asthma, congenital aortic valve insufficiency	1133	Unrelated risk factors and aortic problems
5	25001, 2780, 2766, 5939, 4101, 2768, 7855, 3620, 25050, 25060	IDDM diabetes, obesity, fluid disorder, kidney disease, acute myocardial infarction, unspecified shock, retinopathy, ophthalmic manifestations of diabetes, neurological manifestations of diabetes	1469	IDDM diabetes with complications

(*continued*)

Table 6.4 Clusters Identified Using Text Mining, Along with the Most Frequent Codes Found in the Clusters (*continued*)

Cluster Number	ICD-9 Codes	ICD-9 Risk Factors	Freq.	Label
6	7159, 5121, 4139, 2500, 2780, 4140, 4019, 4294, 4111	osteoarthrosis, iatrogenic pneumothorax, unspecified angina, diabetes, obesity, chronic ischemic heart disease, unspecified hypertension, functional heart disturbance, intermediate coronary syndrome	907	Moderate risk with specific factors
7	5121, 4140, 2768, 2506, 4294, 9981, 4273, 4148, 4278	iatrogenic pneumothorax, chronic ischemic heart disease, fluid disorder, neurological manifestations of diabetes, functional heart disturbance, hemorrhage, atrial fibrillation, heart ischemia, cardiac dysrhythmia	4159	Severe risk and severe complications after surgery
8	5180, 5119, 9973, 6826, 4242, 4240, 4239, 9981, 4410	pulmonary collapse, pleural effusion, respiratory surgical complications, cellulites and abscess, endocardium disease, hemopericardium, hemorrhage, aneurysm and dissection	586	Very severe complications after surgery
9	4448, 4440, 2875, 389, 4442, 5185, 4402, 5601, 486, 9974	arterial embolism and thrombosis (aorta abdominal, extremities, other artery), unspecified thrombocytopenia, hearing loss, pulmonary insufficiency following surgery, atherosclerosis, paralytic Ileus, unspecified pneumonia, digestive system complication	1856	Severe complications after surgery

Consider Cluster 6, which contains osteoarthrosis, angina, diabetes, and heart disease, suggesting that these patients have several different diseases. Cluster 5 contains patients who are insulin-dependent and have very severe diabetic complications, such as kidney disease or retinopathy. The codes that are related to diabetes (25000) appear in Figure 6.18.

Figure 6.18 Diagnosis Codes Related to Diabetes

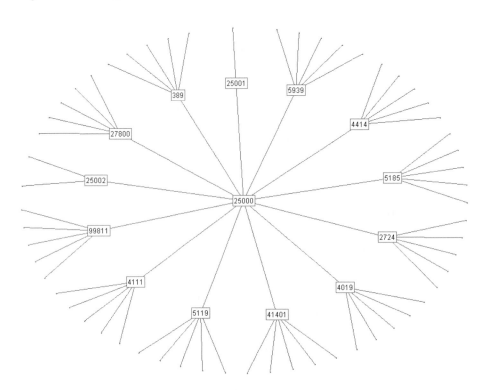

Several codes begin with 250 and are related to diabetes, including 25001 and 25002, which identify patients treated with insulin and without insulin. Other codes include 4111 and 4414, which identify heart problems.

Using the drop-down menu for the terms (as shown in Chapter 3), you can use the **Treat as equivalent terms** feature to make all codes beginning with 250 related to diabetes equivalent (Figure 6.19). The software finds all co-morbidities that are related to diabetes using concept links.

Figure 6.19 Revised Concept Links after Making All Codes for Diabetes Equivalent

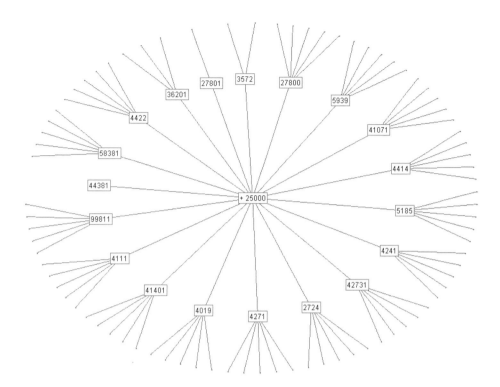

Some of the related health problems include the following:

- 27800 (obesity)
- 44200 (aneurysm)
- 44300 (other peripheral vascular disease)
- 41100 (other ischemic heart disease)
- 36200 (diabetic retinopathy)

There are two other outcomes you can examine in relations to coded information. First, examine the uniformity of code reporting. Second, examine the relationship of the text clusters to the outcomes. Reduce the total number of clusters to four to define a severity ranking. Order the four clusters in terms of severity. Then, compare patient length of stay across the four clusters to determine the relationship of patient outcome to severity ranking (Figure 6.20).

Figure 6.20 Kernel Density Estimation of Patient Length of Stay by Cluster

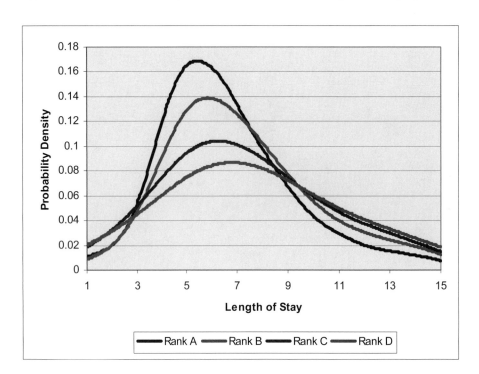

The peak value drifts to the right as the severity ranking increases. At approximately Day 9, the curves cross so that the most severe patients (Rank D) have the greatest probability of staying longer.

Figure 6.20 strongly indicates that the severity ranking defined by the text analysis does classify patients in terms of risk. Figure 6.21 compares the cluster rank by total charges billed by the hospital.

Figure 6.21 Kernel Density Estimation of Total Charges by Cluster Rank

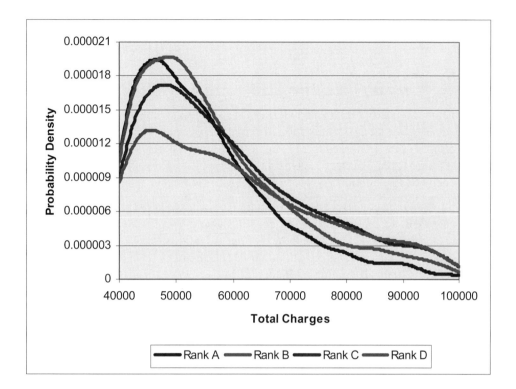

Again, the peak shifts to the right as the severity rank increases. The crossover point occurs just under $60,000, so that the patients with the higher ranking have a greater probability of incurring higher costs.

6.7 Additional Examples

The example in this section deals with student enrollment from 2000 through 2004. In this data set, the courses are identified by department and by number. These data were examined in Chapter 5 using the Association node. Adapting the code in Section 6.2, you can use SAS Text Miner software to identify the text clusters in Table 6.5. A total of 33 clusters are defined. The first 10 are reproduced here. The cluster labels appear in Table 6.6.

Table 6.5 Clusters of Classes from Enrollment Text Strings

Cluster Number	Classes in Cluster	Number of Students	Label
1	math_501, psyc_585, edem_597, ecpy_660, padm_601, exp_502, art_106, elfh_341, hist_542, edem_596, soc_303, biol_360, elfh_312, pt_605, elfh_316, engl_309, edtd_312, hpes_104, hpes_108, span_141, plan_500, edtd_411, hpes_118, edem_511, plan_600	2369	Math & Science
2	imba_610, acct_401, acct_302, imba_620, acct_320, acct_310, acct_301, acct_202, acct_415, acct_303, acct_315, acct_411, acct_205, acct_353, fin_304, econ_431, cis_390, anth_319, mkt_301, cis_201, fin_301, math_107, anth_325, acct_201	649	Accounting
3	asl_102, arth_591, art_307, anth_314, span_123, arth_542, asl_202, asl_101, ahc_300, anth_305, airs_102, edsd_606, ecpy_607, anth_327, anth_320, art_407, edsd_608, edem_507, audi_604, chem_105, arth_392, biol_260, audi_600, ed_603, airs_312	3784	Humanities, Art
4	asnb_601, ielp_92, hist_521, ielp_95, airs_151, airs_101, asnb_606, ielp_91, asnb_605, arth_203, asnb_603, cis_100, ielp_93, muh_204, math_350, isdp_101, math_521, biol_102, econ_201, cis_205, cis_115, mgmt_201, cecs_288, cis_110, anth_325	2352	Anatomical Sciences
5	idep_901, soc_604, mus_400, neur_901, fmed_905, mus_500, hist_602, med_902, nurs_655, obio_601, imba_652, ie_699, mgmt_689, phci_621, phci_610, nurs_690, nurs_645, obio_606, dxgd_900, med_905, psyc_603, mus_691, mus_509, psyc_609, obio_619	1279	Nursing
6	law_848, law_803, law_821, law_826, law_828, law_832, law_865, law_853, law_823, law_822, law_850, law_810, law_884, law_818, law_829, law_806, law_825, law_805, law_809, law_872, law_859, law_804, law_827, law_870, law_873	905	Law
7	art_301, biol_465, chem_344, chem_645, math_405, edem_596, chem_625, biol_347, cis_397, phys_561, cmds_572, biol_390, chns_101, chem_105, fren_121, chem_343, cmds_610, chem_206, art_331, biol_355, comm_112, fren_122, cmds_564, chem_320, cis_398	1776	Chemistry

(continued)

Table 6.5 Clusters of Classes from Enrollment Text Strings (*continued*)

Cluster Number	Classes in Cluster	Number of Students	Label
8	eac_100, emcs_101, chem_203, biol_240, eac_101, soc_450, chem_205, chem_202, chem_207, cee_205, pols_399, ece_289, para_310, chem_201, emcs_104, emcs_102, eg_105, eac_102, cee_307, eac_104, biol_329, cee_254, ahc_300, math_205, che_253	1062	Basic Engineering and Science
9	bmsc_807, bmsc_802, bmsc_800, obio_501, bmsc_805, dspr_832, dspr_833, bmsc_861, dspr_811, asnb_675, bmsc_804, bmsc_806, bioc_640	574	Basic Medical Sciences
10	ie_541, ie_600, em_515, em_646, ie_570, em_570, em_590, ie_550, em_, em_693, ie_480, ie_650, ie_430, ie_499, em_682, em_560, ie_, ie_516, em_510, em_683, em_550, ie_241, em_699, ie_590, ie_563	370	Industrial Engineering

Table 6.6 Labels for Clusters

Cluster Number	Cluster Label	Cluster Number	Cluster Label
1	Math & Science	18	Chemical Engineering
2	Accounting	19	Communication
3	Humanities, Art	20	Basic Core & Remedial Courses
4	Anatomical Sciences	21	English
5	Nursing	22	General Business
6	Law	23	MS, Computer Engineering
7	Chemistry	24	Medical Sciences
8	Basic Engineering & Science	25	Social Work
9	Basic Medical Sciences	26	Social Work
10	Industrial Engineering	27	Nursing & Biology
11	Management	28	Educational Counseling
12	Education	29	Computer Engineering
13	Basic Science Education	30	Anthropology
14	Computer Engineering	31	MS, Justice Administration
15	Basic Business	32	Anthropology & Biology
16	MBA	33	EDD Education
17	Justice Administration		

This example clusters the courses using another method. Each course has a department code. The 100-level courses and below are remedial and general education courses; 200- to 500-level courses are for undergraduates (500-level course are also for graduate students); and 600-level courses and above are for graduate students. Some of the concept links defined using the software are listed here. They can be contrasted with the link analysis in Chapter 5 for the same data (Figures 6.22 through 6.24).

Figure 6.22 Concept Links for English 101

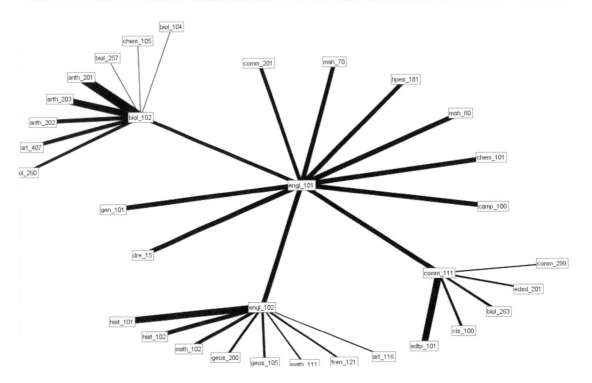

As seen in the association link graphs, English 101 is at the center because it has the most connections with undergraduate programs generally. Here, there are fewer connections, mostly related to other general education courses. However, the initial links can be expanded to other links.

Figure 6.23 Concept Links for Math 111

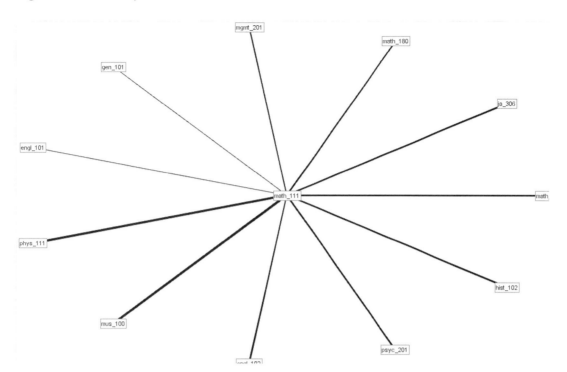

The primary general education mathematics course (College Algebra) is related to another mathematics course, Introduction to Calculus (Math 180), and to a management course. There are no associations with other humanities courses.

Figure 6.24 Concept Links for General Education Biology

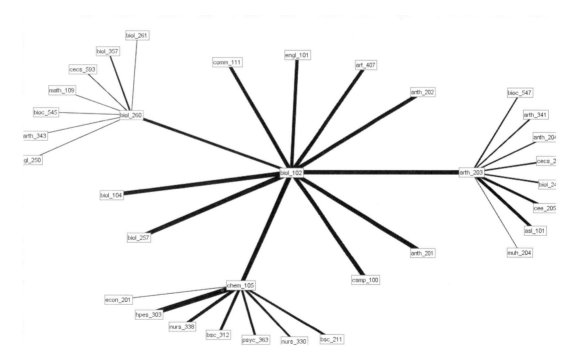

The general education biology course is related to several other biology courses, as well as to chemistry and basic English. This outcome suggests that students who start in the basic biology course like the subject well enough to enroll in additional biology courses. You can filter down the entire data set to one of the clusters and examine it using the Association node. As shown in Chapter 4, you must merge the data sets defining the text clusters with the original data set, as follows:

```
data sasuser.courseclusternames (keep=_cluster_ _freq_ _rmsstd_
    clus_desc);
    set emws.text_cluster;
run;

data sasuser.descourses (drop= _svd_1-_svd_100 prob1-prob100);
    set emws.text_documents;
run;

proc sort data=sasuser.courseclusternames;
    by _cluster_;

proc sort data=sasuser.descourses;
    by _cluster_;
run;

data sasuser.courseclusters;
    merge sasuser.courseclusternames sasuser.descourses;
    by _cluster_;
run;

PROC SQL;
  CREATE TABLE SASUSER.QURY9620 AS SELECT classes.DEPT FORMAT=$F4.,
    classes.CRSENO FORMAT=BEST12.,
    classes.STUID FORMAT=BEST12.,
    classes.course FORMAT=$F17.,
    courseclusters._CLUSTER_ FORMAT=F4.,
    courseclusters._FREQ_ FORMAT=F7.,
    courseclusters._RMSSTD_,
    courseclusters.clus_desc,
    courseclusters.classname FORMAT=$F17.,
    courseclusters.STUID FORMAT=BEST12. AS STUID1,
    courseclusters._DOCUMENT_,
    courseclusters._SVDLEN_
  FROM sasuser.courseclusters AS courseclusters
      LEFT JOIN sasuser.courseclusters AS courseclusters ON
(classes.STUID = courseclusters.STUID);
QUIT;
```

Once the data are merged, you can filter out one specific cluster for additional analysis using the Association node. Clusters 10 (Industrial Engineering), 22 (General Business), and 33 (Education) are shown in Figures 6.25 through 6.27.

In Figure 6.25, virtually all of the courses within the cluster are Industrial Engineering classes. Students identified in this cluster take courses within this department. The associations indicate that Industrial Engineering majors have relatively fixed course pathways.

Figure 6.25 Association Link Graph for the Industrial Engineering Cluster

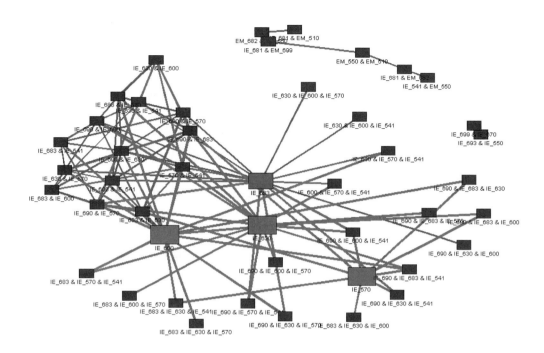

In Figure 6.26, many of the nodes in the General Business cluster contain general education English. Two mathematics courses are contained within many of the links as well: Math 111 and Math 107. Students in general business also take courses in Computer Information Systems (CIS), a department within the College of Business. At the center of the graph are the economics courses. Except for basic biology, no science courses exist in the graph.

Figure 6.26 Association Link Graph for the General Business Cluster

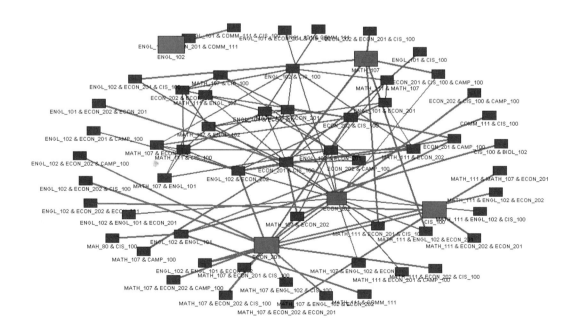

The links in Figure 6.27 suggest that the cluster is probably mislabeled. Courses depicted are in the Department of Special Education, which is what the cluster should be relabeled. Association rules, then, can serve as a means to validate the text clusters.

Figure 6.27 Association Link Graph for the Education Cluster

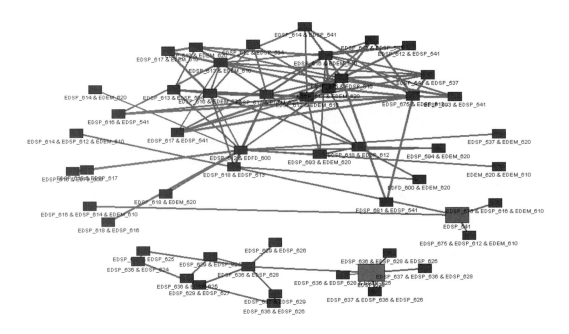

6.8 Exercises

1. Using the enrollment database, define clusters of courses using SAS Text Miner software. Reduce the total number of clusters to 15. Use the Association node with one of the clusters.

2. Here are some additional concept links using the medications database. Use the Association node on the reduced data to find the link graph of associations.

a. Vioxx

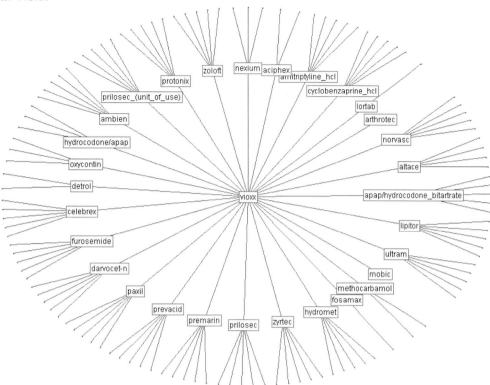

b. Zithromax

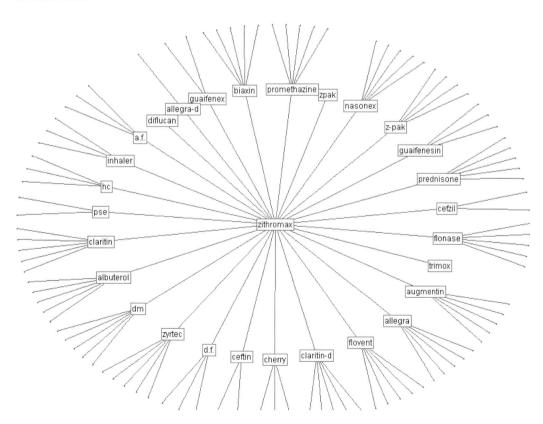

Predictive Modeling

7.1 Introduction to Classification and Predictive Modeling

Classification, a form of predictive modeling, is an important part of data mining because it defines groups within the population. Classification helps businesses identify which customers are likely to drop their services, physicians predict which patients are at high risk for heart attacks and strokes, and insurers determine which clients are at high risk for fraud.

There are many different methods of classification. SAS Enterprise Miner software uses neural networks, decision trees, and regression to classify data. With so many different methods, comparing results to determine the best means of classification for a problem is critical. You can compare the rates of correct classification and choose the technique with the highest rate. Unfortunately, accuracy tends to be inflated when data are used to define the model. It is possible, for example, to define a predictive model that is 100% accurate on a training set but 0% accurate on a validation set. Therefore, validation is essential.

Data mining uses classification methods that are similar, if not identical, to those used for statistical inference. However, while data mining uses many different models and then compares the results on a testing set, statistical inference tends to examine a single model, measuring its effectiveness by the *p*-value and by adherence to model assumptions. While cross-validation is used to examine some of the models, holdout samples are rare. A holdout sample reserves a portion of the data to be used to test the accuracy of the model after the model has been defined. Data mining, on the other hand, focuses less on model assumptions and more on the model's ability to actually predict outcomes. Assumptions are not as important as outcomes.

Classification focuses primarily on inclusion or exclusion in a small set of specific categories. However, all classification techniques work equally well to predict the outcome of a continuous variable. Therefore, this chapter also discusses continuous prediction.

The three primary SAS Enterprise Miner nodes that perform classification are Regression, Neural Network, and Decision Tree (Figure 7.1). In Version 5, there are two different algorithms for each of the major types.

Figure 7.1 SAS Enterprise Miner Nodes for Classification

A relatively recent method not included in these categories is memory-based reasoning (MBR) (Figure 7. 2). Each method is discussed later in this chapter.

Figure 7.2 SAS Enterprise Miner Classification Code

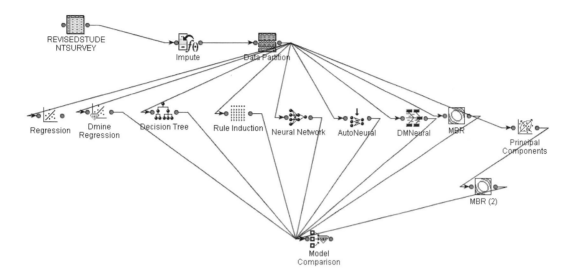

Examine several classification methods and then assess the best one. There must be enough data to partition into training, testing, and validation sets so that the methods can be compared and the results validated. This chapter uses the student survey data defined in Chapter 1 to demonstrate each method. It assigns Student_Type as the target variable to predict whether the respondent is a graduate or undergraduate student.

7.2 Using the Regression Node

The Regression node uses either linear or logistic regression, depending on the type of target variable. It is similar to the LOGISTIC and REG procedures in SAS/STAT software. The regression equation is equal to $Y = \alpha X + \varepsilon$, where ε is normally distributed for linear regression and discrete for logistic regression. If the outcome variable is nominal, it uses logistic regression; if it is an interval variable, it uses linear regression. If Y is ordinal, linear regression is used if the number of categories exceeds eight; otherwise, logistic regression is used. The Regression node can accept only two possible outcomes if the data are nominal.

The default options for regression appear in Display 7.1.

Display 7.1 Regression Defaults

Property	Value
Node ID	Reg
Imported Data	
Exported Data	
Variables	
Equation	
Main Effects	Yes
Two-Factor Interactions	No
Polynomial Terms	No
Polynomial Degree	2
User Terms	No
Term Editor	
Class Targets	
Regression Type	Logistic Regression
Link Function	Logit
Model Options	
Suppress Intercept	No
Input Coding	Deviation
Min Resource Use	D
Model Selection	
Selection Model	None
Selection Criterion	Default
Use Selection Default	Yes
Selection Options	
Sequential Order	No
Entry Significance Level	0.05
Stay Significance Level	0.05
Start Variable Number	0
Stop Variable Number	0
Force Candidate Effects	0
Hierarchy Effects	Class
Moving Effect Rule	None
Maximum Number of Steps	0
Optimization Options	
Technique	Default
Default Optimization	Yes
Max Iterations	0
Max Function Calls	0
Maximum Time	1 Hour
Convergence Criteria	
Default	Yes
Absolute	-1.34078E154
Absolute Function	0
Absolute Function Times	1
Absolute Gradient	1.0E-5
Absolute Gradient Times	1
Absolute Parameter	1.0E-8
Absolute Parameter Times	1
Relative Function	0.0
Relative Function Times	1

In SAS Enterprise Miner, the regression node determines whether to use logistic regression or linear regression. If the target variable is nominal, the software uses logistic regression; if the target variable is interval, linear regression is used. For ordinal data, the software uses logistic regression for a target with 2 to 7 variables; otherwise linear regression is chosen. If you use a selection model, there are a number of criterion methods that you can choose.

If you use the default, you cannot use interactions in the model. You should experiment with changes to the default to see how these changes impact the final results.

The Terms window contains the **Term** list (Display 7.2), which allows you to choose terms to include in the model.

Display 7.2 Terms Window

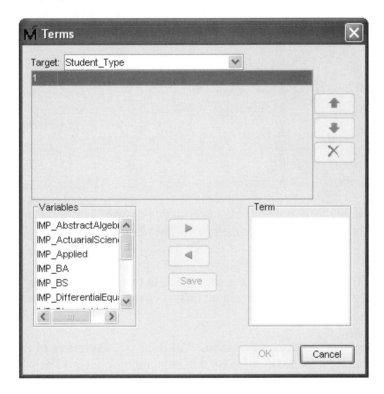

Use the **Term** list to add interactions to the model. The results appear in Output 7.1.

Output 7.1 Results of the Regression Node

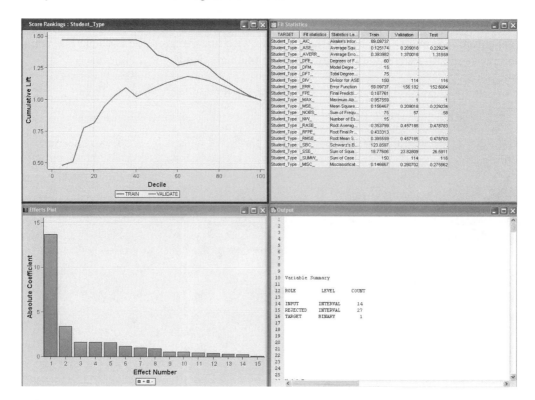

The different components of these results are discussed later in this chapter. The curve in the upper left-hand corner gives the cumulative lift for the model. See Chapter 5 for more information on lift.

The effects plot gives the r^2 value for each variable in the model. In this case, the first two factors account for most of the cumulative r^2, with the remaining factors contributing only a small amount.

The misclassification rate (shown in the last row in Output 7.2) is the best indication of the regression's accuracy. Note that the misclassification on the initial training set is 15%, which increases to 28% for the validation and testing sets. Without partitioning, regression inflates the accuracy of the results. Another measure you might consider is the Akaikes Information Criterion (AIC), which is defined by the equation, AIC $= -\ln L + p$, where L is the likelihood for an estimated model with p parameters. There is also the average error (AVERR), which is the difference between the actual and predicted target values. Average error takes the average error for all data points.

Output 7.2 Regression Fit Statistics

TARGET	Fit statistics	Statistics La...	Train	Validation	Test
Student_Type	_AIC_	Akaike's Infor...	89.09737	.	.
Student_Type	_ASE_	Average Squ...	0.125174	0.209018	0.229234
Student_Type	_AVERR_	Average Erro...	0.393982	1.370018	1.31559
Student_Type	_DFE_	Degrees of F...	60	.	.
Student_Type	_DFM_	Model Degre...	15	.	.
Student_Type	_DFT_	Total Degree...	75	.	.
Student_Type	_DIV_	Divisor for ASE	150	114	116
Student_Type	_ERR_	Error Function	59.09737	156.182	152.6084
Student_Type	_FPE_	Final Predicti...	0.187761	.	.
Student_Type	_MAX_	Maximum Ab...	0.957559	1	1
Student_Type	_MSE_	Mean Square...	0.156467	0.209018	0.229234
Student_Type	_NOBS_	Sum of Frequ...	75	57	58
Student_Type	_NW_	Number of Es...	15	.	.
Student_Type	_RASE_	Root Averag...	0.353799	0.457185	0.478783
Student_Type	_RFPE_	Root Final Pr...	0.433313	.	.
Student_Type	_RMSE_	Root Mean S...	0.395559	0.457185	0.478783
Student_Type	_SBC_	Schwarz's B...	123.8597	.	.
Student_Type	_SSE_	Sum of Squa...	18.77606	23.82809	26.5911
Student_Type	_SUMW_	Sum of Case ...	150	114	116
Student_Type	_MISC_	Misclassificat...	0.146667	0.280702	0.275862

To put the results in context, you must consider the actual group size to determine whether the prediction is valid. The misclassification rate on the testing set is approximately 28%. The proportion of graduate students is equal to 32%. That means that if you classify every student as an undergraduate, then the misclassification rate is 32%. The model's 28% is not much more accurate. Random choice also has about a 32% misclassification rate. Model accuracy must be compared to random chance.

Lift is equal to the ratio of the average target value at a given depth to the overall average target value. Generally, increasing the depth decreases the lift. For the training set, the lift is relatively high, starting to decrease at a depth of 40%. However, in the validation set, lift increases to a peak at 65%, then decreases beyond that. Again, because the training data can inflate results, it is better to examine the lift for the validation set.

The lift curve (that is, the score rankings) appears in Output 7.3.

Output 7.3 Lift Curve for Regression

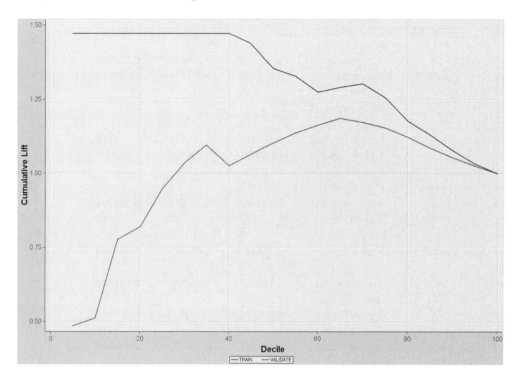

In Output 7.4, note the identification of the variables as IMP_*xxxx* because the Impute node was used to substitute for missing values. The **Estimate** column gives the linear regression equation. The **Wald Chi-Square** column gives the odds ratio. For an odds ratio greater than 1, as the *x* variable increases from 0 to 1, the *y* variable also increases from 0 to 1. If the odds ratio is less than 1, the *x* variable decreases as the *y* variable increases from 0 to 1. In this example, 1=graduate students and 0=undergraduate students.

Output 7.4 Regression Output

```
📑 Output
146
147
148                        Analysis of Maximum Likelihood Estimates
149
150                                      Standard       Wald                    Standardized
151  Parameter                  DF   Estimate    Error   Chi-Square   Pr > ChiSq    Estimate    Exp(Est)
152
153  Intercept                   1     3.3669   1.2434       7.33       0.0068                    28.989
154  IMP_AbstractAlgebra         1     1.6144   1.1389       2.01       0.1563       0.3752        5.025
155  IMP_ActuarialScience        1    -0.8633   1.0087       0.73       0.3921      -0.1867        0.422
156  IMP_Applied                 1     0.4109   0.7227       0.32       0.5696       0.1111        1.508
157  IMP_BA                      1    -1.1325   1.1662       0.94       0.3315      -0.2174        0.322
158  IMP_BS                      1    -0.9780   0.8960       1.19       0.2751      -0.2255        0.376
159  IMP_DifferentialEquations   1     0.2454   0.8895       0.08       0.7827       0.0635        1.278
160  IMP_DiscreteMathematics     1    -1.6142   1.1432       1.99       0.1580      -0.3170        0.199
161  IMP_NumberTheory            1    -1.5481   1.0909       2.01       0.1559      -0.2921        0.213
162  IMP_Probability             1    -0.3623   0.9493       0.15       0.7027      -0.0965        0.696
163  IMP_Pure                    1     0.0553   0.7381       0.01       0.9403       0.0153        1.057
164  IMP_RealAnalysis            1     0.4989   1.3484       0.14       0.7114       0.1015        1.647
165  IMP_Statistics              1     0.4982   0.8841       0.32       0.5731       0.1373        1.646
166  IMP_Topology                1    13.6838   283.1        0.00       0.9614       2.0605      999.000
167  IMP_hours                   1    -0.2782   0.1077       6.67       0.0098      -0.9897        0.757
168
169
170           Odds Ratio Estimates
171
172                          Point
173  Effect                 Estimate
174
175  IMP_AbstractAlgebra       5.025
176  IMP_ActuarialScience      0.422
177  IMP_Applied               1.508
178  IMP_BA                    0.322
179  IMP_BS                    0.376
180  IMP_DifferentialEquations 1.278
181  IMP_DiscreteMathematics   0.199
182  IMP_NumberTheory          0.213
183  IMP_Probability           0.696
184  IMP_Pure                  1.057
185  IMP_RealAnalysis          1.647
186  IMP_Statistics            1.646
187  IMP_Topology            999.000
188  IMP_hours                 0.757
189
190
191
192
```

Additional results can be found using the **View** menu. The score distributions appear in Output 7.5. For categorical targets, observations are grouped into bins based on the posterior probabilities of the event level. The valid range of posterior probabilities is [0, 1]. By default, the range of [0, 1] is divided into 20 bins so that the ranges for the first and second bins are [0.95, 1] and [0.9, 0.95], respectively. The model score of observations in the first bin is the average of 0.95 and 1=0.975, and the model score of the second bin is 0.925.

Output 7.5 Score Distributions for Regression

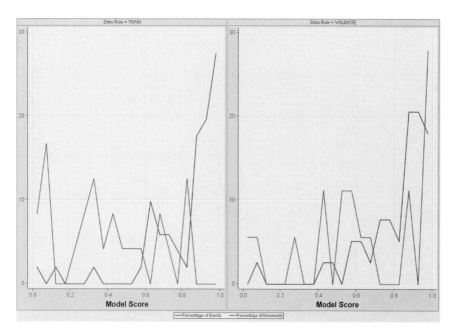

A second result available in the View window is the classification chart (shown in Output 7.6).

Output 7.6 Classification Chart for Regression

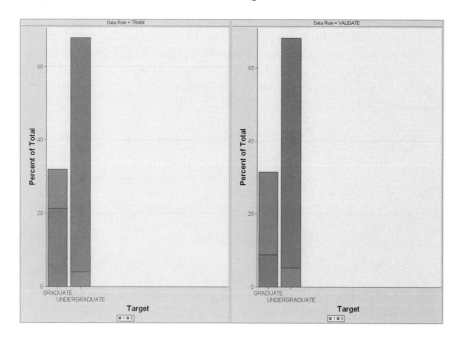

From the classification chart for the validation set, it appears that the model does not correctly classify graduate students based on the input values. In other words, all marginal values are classified as undergraduate.

The Dmine Regression node works only on binary or interval targets. It should not be used on ordinal or nominal targets with more than two outcome values. In this example, the results viewed are the same as for the Regression node. The Dmine Regression node differs from the Regression node as follows (Display 7.3):

- Computes a forward stepwise least-squares regression.
- Can use AOV16 variables, which change an interval variable into a class variable, to identify nonlinear relationships between interval variables and the target variable. The AOV16 variable allows a covariate (interval variable) with 1 degree of freedom to be considered as a nonlinear class variable with up to 16 degrees of freedom.
- Optionally uses group variables to reduce the number of levels of classification variables.
- Uses a fast algorithm for approximate logistic regression for a binary target.

Otherwise, the methodology is similar.

Display 7.3 Dmine Regression Defaults

Property	Value
Node ID	DmineReg
Imported Data	
Exported Data	
Variables	
Maximum Variable Number	3000
R-Square Options	
Minimum R-Square	0.0050
Stop R-Square	5.0E-4
Created Variables	
Use AOV16 Variables	Yes
Use Group Variables	Yes
Use Interactions	No
Print Option	Default
SPDS	Yes

The group class variables are used to determine if specific levels of a class input can be collapsed into a single group without reducing the explanation of the total variation by more than 5%.

The misclassification rates appear in Output 7.7.

Output 7.7 Misclassification Rates for Dmine Regression

TARGET	Fit statistics	Statistics La...	Train	Validation	Test
Student_Type	_ERR_	Error Function	48.19473	141.374	84.60204
Student_Type	_SSE_	Sum of Squa...	15.81116	26.54825	22.86394
Student_Type	_MAX_	Maximum Ab...	0.893507	1	0.998601
Student_Type	_DIV_	Divisor for ASE	150	114	116
Student_Type	_NOBS_	Sum of Frequ...	75	57	58
Student_Type	_WRONG_	Number of W...	8	16	15
Student_Type	_DISF_	Frequency of...	75	57	58
Student_Type	_MISC_	Misclassificat...	0.106667	0.280702	0.258621
Student_Type	_ASE_	Average Squ...	0.105408	0.232879	0.197103
Student_Type	_RASE_	Root Averag...	0.324666	0.482576	0.443963
Student_Type	_AVERR_	Average Erro...	0.321298	1.240122	0.729328

The misclassification rate for the training set is 11%, less than that for the Regression node. However, the misclassification rate of the testing set increases to 26%, only slightly better than the regression results. Nevertheless, accuracy improves somewhat using the Dmine Regression node.

7.3 Using the Neural Network Node

Neural networks act like black boxes. There is no definite model or equation and the model is not presented in a concise format available for regression. Its accuracy is examined similar to the diagnostics of the regression curve including the misclassification rate, the AIC, and the average error. The simplest neural network contains a single input (an independent variable) and a single target (a dependent variable) with a single output. Its complexity increases with the addition of hidden layers and additional input variables (Figure 7.3).

Figure 7.3 Diagram of a Neural Network

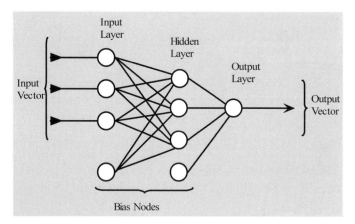

With no hidden layers, the results of a neural network analysis resemble those of regression. Each input variable is connected to each variable in the hidden layer, and each hidden variable is connected to each outcome variable. The hidden layers combine inputs and apply a function to predict outputs. Hidden layers are often nonlinear.

The model defaults appear in Display 7.4. The architecture is used to define the model. There are two major types of neural network used, the MLP and the GLIM. MLP, the multi-layer perceptron, is the default model. A perceptron is a classifier that maps an input x to an output, f(x). The GLIM represents the more standard generalized linear model used in PROC GENMOD in SAS/STAT software. You should compare these two models to see the impact on the results. You can also define your own model, although this method is not recommended for beginners.

Display 7.4 Neural Network Defaults

Property	Value
Node ID	Neural3
Imported Data	
Exported Data	
Variables	
Use Current Estimates	No
Architecture	MLP
Direct Connection	No
Model Selection Criterion	Profit/Loss
Number of Hidden Units	3
Training Options	
Maximum Iterations	20
Maximum Time	4 Hours
Training Technique	Default
User Defined Network Opt	
Randomization Distributio	Normal
Randomization Center	0.0
Randomization Scale	1.0
Input Standardization	Standard Deviation
Hidden Layer	Yes
Hidden Layer Combinatior	Default
Hidden Layer Activation Fu	Default
Hidden Bias	Yes
Target Layer Combination	Default
Target Layer Activation Fur	Default
Target Layer Error Functior	Default
Target Bias	Yes
Preliminary Training Optior	
Preliminary Training	No
Maximum Iterations	10
Maximum Time	1 Hour
Number of Runs	5
Convergence Criteria	
Default	Yes
Absolute	-1.34078E154
Absolute Function	0
Absolute Function Times	1
Absolute Gradient	1.0E-5
Absolute Gradient Times	1
Absolute Parameter	1.0E-8
Absolute Parameter Times	1
Relative Function	0.0
Relative Function Times	1
Relative Gradient	1.0E-6
Relative Gradient Times	1

Model results, summarized in Output 7.8, are similar to those from the Regression node. Because neural networks represent an iterative process, the results provide a graph of the rate of convergence to a final model.

Output 7.8 Neural Network Results

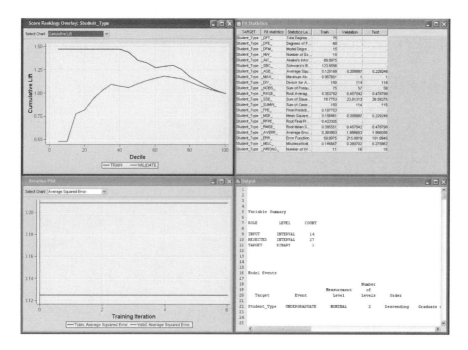

The lift curve is lower compared to that for regression. The graph's output screen shows the rate of convergence of the neural network. Although the training set converges after 20 iterations, the validation set does not seem to converge at all. The misclassification rate appears in Output 7.9.

Output 7.9 Fit Statistics for Neural Networks

TARGET	Fit statistics	Statistics La...	Train	Validation	Test
Student_Type	_DFT_	Total Degree...	75		
Student_Type	_DFE_	Degrees of F...	12		
Student_Type	_DFM_	Model Degre...	63		
Student_Type	_NW_	Number of Es...	63		
Student_Type	_AIC_	Akaike's Infor...	132.3272		
Student_Type	_SBC_	Schwarz's B...	278.3289		
Student_Type	_ASE_	Average Squ...	0.00704	0.351399	0.32746
Student_Type	_MAX_	Maximum Ab...	0.407882	1	1
Student_Type	_DIV_	Divisor for A...	150	114	116
Student_Type	_NOBS_	Sum of Frequ...	75	57	58
Student_Type	_RASE_	Root Averag...	0.083902	0.592789	0.572241
Student_Type	_SSE_	Sum of Squa...	1.055929	40.05945	37.98536
Student_Type	_SUMW_	Sum of Case ...	150	114	116
Student_Type	_FPE_	Final Predicti...	0.080955		
Student_Type	_MSE_	Mean Square...	0.043997	0.351399	0.32746
Student_Type	_RFPE_	Root Final Pr...	0.284525		
Student_Type	_RMSE_	Root Mean S...	0.209755	0.592789	0.572241
Student_Type	_AVERR_	Average Erro...	0.042181	2.206776	2.115332
Student_Type	_ERR_	Error Function.	6.327168	251.5725	245.3785
Student_Type	_MISC_	Misclassificat...	0	0.403509	0.327586
Student_Type	_WRONG_	Number of W...	0	23	19

The misclassification rates for the validation and testing sets are somewhat higher compared to those for regression. However, the rate for the training set is lower compared to regression. The AIC is twice the level compared to regression. The average error is half the size. The classification chart appears in Output 7.10. At this point in the analysis, no model has been identified as the best for classification.

Output 7.10 Classification Chart for Neural Networks

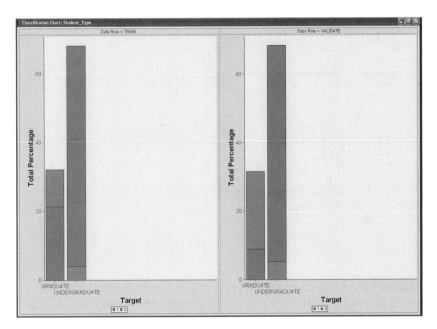

The misclassification rate for graduate students is higher in the training set compared to the regression results.

The distribution graph appears in Output 7.11. Note that the percentage of events peaks at the 80% model score.

Output 7.11 Distribution Graph for Neural Networks

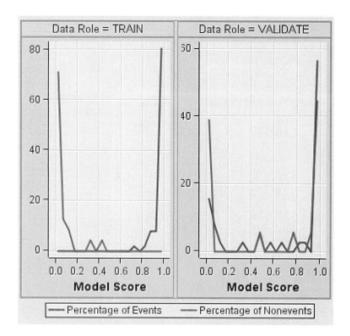

The 20% and 40% values have a much higher proportion of nonevents compared to events. However, at the 80% value, there are many more events compared to nonevents. In addition, the differential is greater for the training set compared to the validation set.

It is recommended that you study the algorithms of artificial neural networks in greater detail. Alter the defaults to see how the changes impact outcomes. Some changes to the defaults are shown in Display 7.5, with the results in Output 7.12 through 7.14.

Display 7.5 Changes to Defaults

Property	Value
Node ID	Neural
Imported Data	[...]
Exported Data	[...]
Variables	[...]
Use Current Estimates	No
Architecture	GLIM
Direct Connection	Yes
Model Selection Criterion	Profit/Loss
Number of Hidden Units	3
Training Options	
Maximum Iterations	20
Maximum Time	4 Hours
Training Technique	Quasi-Newton
User Defined Network Opt	

In this example, the architecture was changed to GLIM and the training technique was changed to quasi-Newton.

Output 7.12 Neural Network Results with Changed Architecture

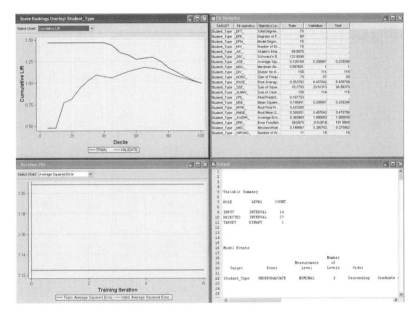

Using the GLIM architecture, the validation set squared error reaches a minimum value, at which point the convergence is optimized when compared to the result in Output 7.8. However, there is still no convergence in the validation set.

Output 7.13 Fit Statistics for Changed Architecture

TARGET	Fit statistics	Statistics La...	Train	Validation	Test
Student_Type	_DFT_	Total Degree...	75	.	.
Student_Type	_DFE_	Degrees of F...	60	.	.
Student_Type	_DFM_	Model Degre...	15	.	.
Student_Type	_NW_	Number of Es...	15	.	.
Student_Type	_AIC_	Akaike's Infor...	89.0975	.	.
Student_Type	_SBC_	Schwarz's B...	123.8598	.	.
Student_Type	_ASE_	Average Squ...	0.125169	0.208887	0.229248
Student_Type	_MAX_	Maximum Ab...	0.957601	1	1
Student_Type	_DIV_	Divisor for A...	150	114	116
Student_Type	_NOBS_	Sum of Frequ...	75	57	58
Student_Type	_RASE_	Root Averag...	0.353792	0.457042	0.478798
Student_Type	_SSE_	Sum of Squa...	18.7753	23.81313	26.59275
Student_Type	_SUMW_	Sum of Case ...	150	114	116
Student_Type	_FPE_	Final Predicti...	0.187753	.	.
Student_Type	_MSE_	Mean Square...	0.156461	0.208887	0.229248
Student_Type	_RFPE_	Root Final Pr...	0.433305	.	.
Student_Type	_RMSE_	Root Mean S...	0.395551	0.457042	0.478798
Student_Type	_AVERR_	Average Erro...	0.393983	1.886683	1.568056
Student_Type	_ERR_	Error Function.	59.0975	215.0819	181.8945
Student_Type	_MISC_	Misclassificat...	0.146667	0.280702	0.275862
Student_Type	_WRONG_	Number of W...	11	16	16

At 15%, 28%, and 27%, changing the architecture improves the results by a couple of percentage points compared to the results in Output 7.9. The AIC measure is lower as well, but the average error is slightly higher.

Output 7.14 Distribution Graph for Changed Architecture

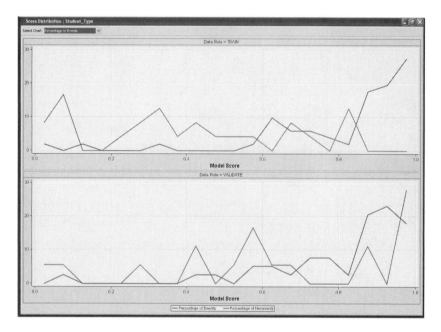

Unfortunately, using the model to differentiate between events and nonevents in both the validation and training sets is still unreliable.

Autoneural is a new technique developed for SAS Enterprise Miner 5.2. It changes defaults automatically; the Neural Network node requires you to make the changes manually. The AutoNeural node adds hidden nodes one at a time. An adjustable setting defines the maximum number of iterations in the neural network analysis. Display 7.6 shows the defaults for the AutoNeural node. Compare these defaults to those for the Neural Network node shown in Display 7.4.

Display 7.6 Default Settings for the AutoNeural Node

Property	Value
Node ID	AutoNeural
Imported Data	
Exported Data	
Variables	
Architecture	Block Layers
Termination	Overfitting
Train Action	Train
Adjust Iterations	Yes
Freeze Connections	No
Maximum Iterations	8
Number of Hidden Units	2
Tolerance	Medium
Total Number of Hidden Uni	30
Total Time	One Hour
Activation Functions	
Direct	Yes
Exponential	No
Identity	No
Logistic	Yes
Normal	Yes
Reciprocal	No
Sine	Yes
Softmax	No
Square	No
Tanh	Yes
Scoring Variables	
Hidden Units	No
Residuals	Yes
Standardization	No
Status	

The architecture for this node is defined slightly differently. The default defines a single-layer neural network. This setting specifies how hidden layers are added to the model. Again, you should change the defaults to examine the impact on outcomes. The results appear in Output 7.15 through 7.18.

Output 7.15 Results of the AutoNeural Node

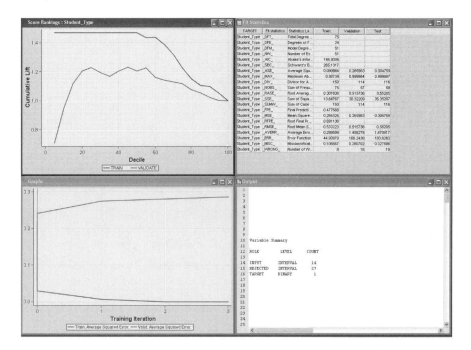

Here again, the squared error for the validation set does not converge, giving a preliminary indication that the Neural Network node provides a better model. Also, the score rankings drop quickly to the 1.0 point.

In Output 7.16, the misclassification rate on the testing set becomes very high at 33%, suggesting that the AutoNeural node does not provide a good fit to the data, even though the training set misclassification rate is 11%. The average error is also high.

Output 7.16 Fit Statistics for the AutoNeural Node

TARGET	Fit statistics	Statistics La...	Train	Validation	Test
Student_Type	_DFT_	Total Degree...	75		
Student_Type	_DFE_	Degrees of F...	24		
Student_Type	_DFM_	Model Degre...	51		
Student_Type	_NW_	Number of Es...	51		
Student_Type	_AIC_	Akaike's Infor...	146.9398		
Student_Type	_SBC_	Schwarz's B...	265.1317		
Student_Type	_ASE_	Average Squ...	0.090984	0.265983	0.304759
Student_Type	_MAX_	Maximum Ab...	0.98739	0.999984	0.999997
Student_Type	_DIV_	Divisor for A...	150	114	116
Student_Type	_NOBS_	Sum of Frequ...	75	57	58
Student_Type	_RASE_	Root Averag...	0.301636	0.515736	0.55205
Student_Type	_SSE_	Sum of Squa...	13.64767	30.32209	35.35207
Student_Type	_SUMW_	Sum of Case ...	150	114	116
Student_Type	_FPE_	Final Predicti...	0.477668		
Student_Type	_MSE_	Mean Square...	0.284326	0.265983	0.304759
Student_Type	_RFPE_	Root Final Pr...	0.691136		
Student_Type	_RMSE_	Root Mean S...	0.533223	0.515736	0.55205
Student_Type	_AVERR_	Average Erro...	0.299599	1.458279	1.670917
Student_Type	_ERR_	Error Function.	44.93979	166.2438	193.8263
Student_Type	_MISC_	Misclassificat...	0.106667	0.280702	0.327586
Student_Type	_WRONG_	Number of W...	8	16	19

The chart in Output 7.17 clearly identifies why there is such a difference between the training and validation sets. In the validation set, you can't distinguish graduate students from undergraduate students.

Output 7.17 Classification Chart for the AutoNeural Node

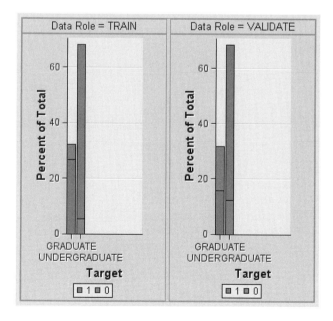

There is no clear decile at which the model clearly distinguishes between student types (Output 7.18).

Output 7.18 Distribution Graph for the AutoNeural Node

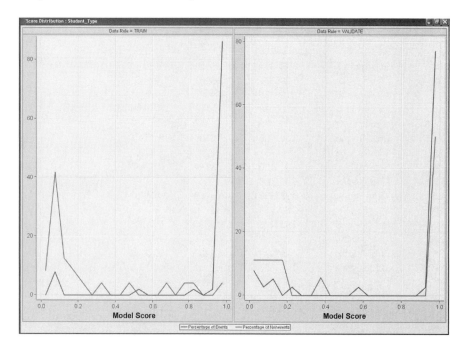

The DMNeural node offers still another method for neural network analysis. It focuses on nonlinear estimation while simultaneously reducing computing time. The defaults appear in Display 7.7.

Display 7.7 DMNeural Node Defaults

Property	Value
Node ID	DMNeural
Imported Data	
Exported Data	
Variables	
DMNeural Network	
Lower Bound R2	5.0E-5
Max Component	3
Max EigenVector	400
Max Function Call	500
Max Iteration	200
Max Stage	3
Convergence Criteria	
Abs Gradient Conv.	5.0E-4
Gradient Conv.	1.0E-8
Model Criteria	
Selection	Default
Optimization	SSE
Print Option	Default
Status	

The DMNeural node begins with a principal component analysis to determine those input variables that are most closely related to the outcome variable. The results using the defaults appear in Output 7.19 through 7.21.

Output 7.19 DMNeural Node Results

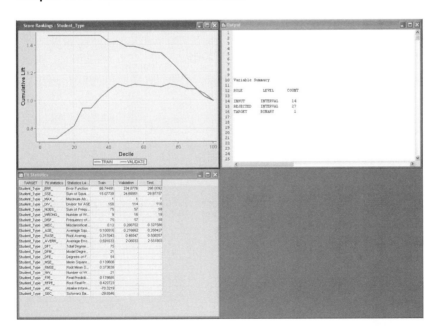

Again, the validation set does not converge in terms of the average squared error. However, the score rankings seem to be more accurate, with the cumulative lift above 1.0 for both the training and validation sets. This is similar to the results in Output 7.3 for the regression model.

Output 7.20 Fit Statistics for the DMNeural Node

TARGET	Fit statistics	Statistics La...	Train	Validation	Test
Student_Type	_ERR_	Error Function	88.74491	234.8776	296.0092
Student_Type	_SSE_	Sum of Squa...	15.07739	24.69951	29.97757
Student_Type	_MAX_	Maximum Ab...	1	1	1
Student_Type	_DIV_	Divisor for ASE	150	114	116
Student_Type	_NOBS_	Sum of Frequ...	75	57	58
Student_Type	_WRONG_	Number of W...	9	16	19
Student_Type	_DISF_	Frequency of...	75	57	58
Student_Type	_MISC_	Misclassificat...	0.12	0.280702	0.327586
Student_Type	_ASE_	Average Squ...	0.100516	0.216662	0.258427
Student_Type	_RASE_	Root Averag...	0.317043	0.46547	0.508357
Student_Type	_AVERR_	Average Erro...	0.591633	2.06033	2.551803
Student_Type	_DFT_	Total Degree...	75	.	
Student_Type	_DFM_	Model Degre...	21	.	
Student_Type	_DFE_	Degrees of F...	54	.	
Student_Type	_MSE_	Mean Square...	0.139606	.	
Student_Type	_RMSE_	Root Mean S...	0.373638	.	
Student_Type	_NW_	Number of W...	21	.	
Student_Type	_FPE_	Final Predicti...	0.178695	.	
Student_Type	_RFPE_	Root Final Pr...	0.422723	.	
Student_Type	_AIC_	Akaike Inform...	-78.3219	.	
Student_Type	_SBC_	Schwarz Ba...	-29.6546	.	

The misclassification rate for the training set is 11%, the lowest of all models studied so far; the testing misclassification rate is 33%. If misclassification is the most important measure of fit, the Neural Network node is the best model so far. If you are judging by lift, the DMNeural node provides the best fit. The AIC remains high, as does the average error.

Output 7.21 Classification Chart for the DMNeural Node

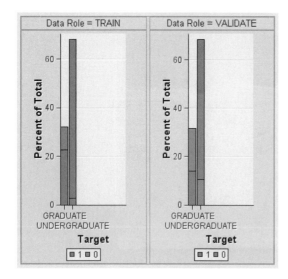

The difference between the training and validation sets is clear; the ability to classify both graduates and undergraduates declines in the validation set.

7.4 Using the Decision Tree Node

Decision trees provide a completely different approach to classification. A *decision tree* develops a series of if-then rules. Each rule assigns an observation to one segment of the tree, at which point another if-then rule is applied. The initial segment, containing the entire data set, is the *root* node for the decision tree. The final nodes are called *leaves*. *Intermediate* nodes (a node plus all its successors) form a branch of the tree. The final leaf containing an observation is its predictive value.

Unlike neural networks and regression, decision trees do not work with interval data. Decision trees work with nominal outcomes that have more than two possible results and with ordinal outcome variables. Decision tree defaults appear in Display 7.8.

Missing values can be used in creating if-then rules. Therefore, imputation is not required for decision trees, although you can use it when working with decision trees.

Display 7.8 Decision Tree Defaults

Property	Value
Node ID	Tree
Imported Data	
Exported Data	
Variables	
Interactive	
Splitting Rule	
Criterion	Default
Significance Level	0.2
Missing Values	Use in search
Use Input Once	No
Maximum Branch	2
Maximum Depth	6
Minimum Categorical Size	5
Node	
Leaf Size	5
Number of Rules	5
Number of Surrogate Rule	0
Split Size	
Split Search	
Exhaustive	5000
Node Sample	5000
Subtree	
Method	Assessment
Number of Leaves	1
Assessment Measure	Decision
Assessment Fraction	0.25
P-Value Adjustment	
Bonferroni Adjustment	Yes
Time of Kass Adjustment	Before
Inputs	No
Number of Inputs	1
Split Adjustment	Yes
Output Variables	
Variable Selection	Yes
Leaf Variable	Yes
Leaf Role	Segment
Performance	Disk

By default, missing values are used in the construction of the tree. Also by default, the size of the tree is limited to six levels; the number of rules is also limited. Again, you should change the defaults to see the impact on the outcomes. Results are provided in Output 7.22 through 7.27.

Output 7.22 Decision Tree Results

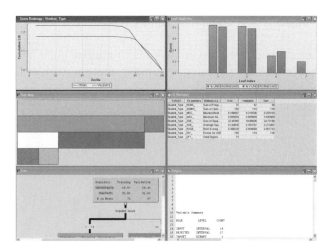

The results presented here are illustrated individually in Output 7.23 through 7.27.

The cumulative lift is above 1.0 for both the training and validation sets, indicating a reasonably accurate model. However, the cumulative lift is not much more than 1.0, so the decision tree provides only a slightly better prediction than chance.

Output 7.23 Cumulative Lift for Decision Tree

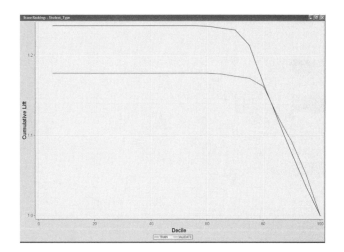

The decision tree map lists the percentage of graduate and undergraduate students at each node in the tree. Moving the cursor over any bar displays summary information (upper left-hand corner, see Output 7.24).

Output 7.24 Decision Tree Map

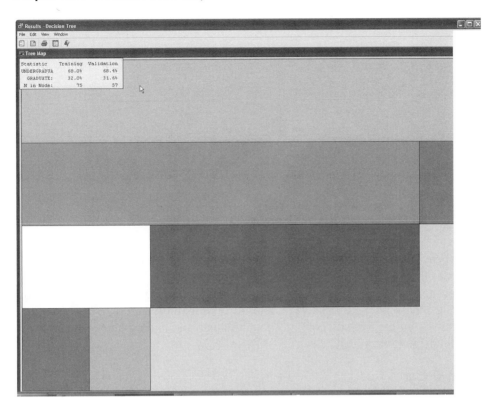

The misclassification rate for the training set is 19%, which increases to 29% for the testing set. Again, the neural network model still seems to offer the best misclassification rates.

Output 7.25 Fit Statistics for Decision Tree

TARGET	Fit statistics	Statistics La...	Train	Validation	Test
Student_Type	_NOBS_	Sum of Frequ...	75	57	58
Student_Type	_SUMW_	Sum of Case ...	150	114	116
Student_Type	_MISC_	Misclassificat...	0.186667	0.210526	0.293103
Student_Type	_MAX_	Maximum Ab...	0.840909	0.840909	0.840909
Student_Type	_SSE_	Sum of Squa...	22.44545	18.66826	24.73198
Student_Type	_ASE_	Average Squ...	0.149636	0.163757	0.213207
Student_Type	_RASE_	Root Averag...	0.386829	0.404669	0.461743
Student_Type	_DIV_	Divisor for ASE	150	114	116
Student_Type	_DFT_	Total Degree...	75	.	.

Output 7.26 is a bar chart of the sum of values for each possible outcome for each of the final leaves of the tree. It indicates how well the decision rules separate graduate from undergraduate students.

Output 7.26 Leaf Index for Decision Tree

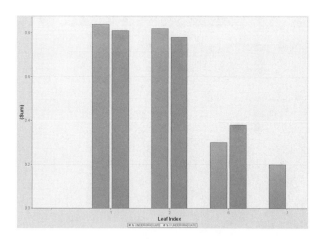

In the **View** menu, English rules are listed rather than relying on the decision tree model in this example. Notice that the first split in Output 7.27 depends on the number of hours of study. All students reporting over 11 hours are classified as graduate. Undergraduate students reporting less than 11 hours are more likely to indicate an interest in probability and pure mathematics. However, each leaf of the tree still contains both graduate and undergraduate students. The tree does not separate the groups well.

Output 7.27 Decision Tree

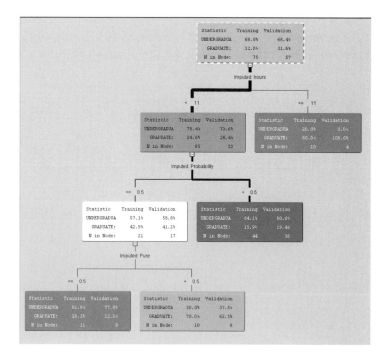

You can also use an interactive option to modify the decision tree. The interactive option is on the left-hand side with the defaults (Output 7.28). The interactive window is shown in Display 7.9.

Output 7.28 Interactive Decision Tree

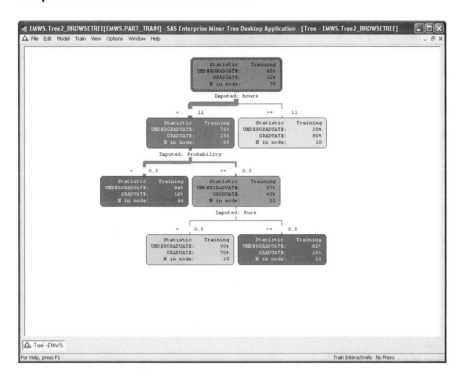

The interactive tree enables you to make changes to the decision tree. To do so, the **Model** submenu lists basic options (Display 7.9).

Display 7.9 Basic Options for an Interactive Decision Tree

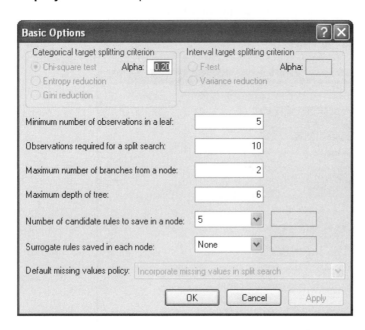

You can change the minimum number of observations contained within a leaf, the number of branches from each node, and the missing values. The defaults are listed here. Changes to the defaults appear in Display 7.10.

Display 7.10 Changes to Option Defaults

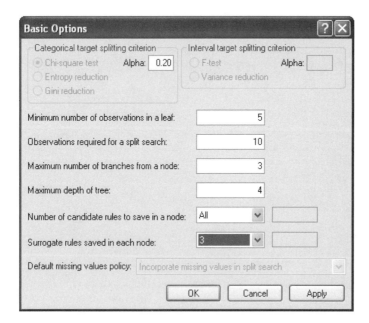

Three branches can now be defined from each node, while the depth of the tree has been reduced from 6 to 4. The result appears in Output 7.29. While three branches are permitted, they are not required in the model.

Output 7.29 Changes to the Model

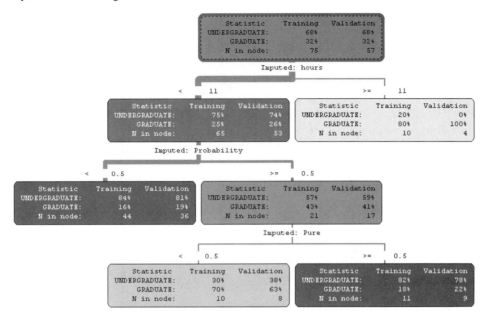

In this example, the changes to the default options did not change the results in a meaningful way. You should modify additional defaults to change the results. The **Model** submenu also contains advanced options (Display 7.11).

Display 7.11 Advanced Options for an Interactive Decision Tree

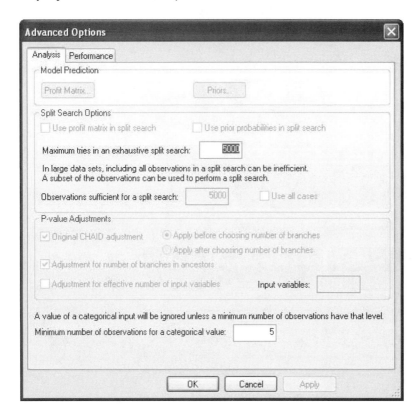

Again, you are encouraged to experiment with the basic and advanced options to see how these changes impact outcomes.

Rule induction is another tree-based algorithm for classification. It focuses primarily on the classification of rare events. It works with nominal or ordinal data only; you cannot use it with interval data. In this case, the model starts with the most rare event and moves to the most common event, creating a binary model for each level of the outcome. The defaults appear in Display 7.12.

Display 7.12 Rule Induction Defaults

Property	Value
Node ID	Rule
Imported Data	
Exported Data	
Variables	
Initial Ripping	Yes
Purity Threshold	100
Max. Number of Rips	16
Binary Models	Tree
Binary Order	Descending
Cleanup Model	Neural
Status	

The default for the binary model is a tree. A cleanup model offers a way to model all unclassified observations. Using a neural network is the default. The results appear in Output 7.30 through 7.33. The score rankings here are similar to those for the Decision Tree node. The cumulative lift remains above 1.0.

Output 7.30 Results Window for Rule Induction

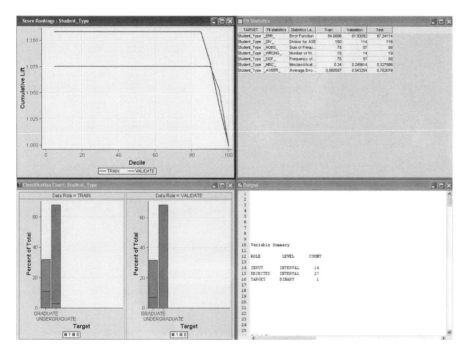

The misclassification rates for rule induction are also similar to those for the decision tree. However, the neural network analysis still remains the best model.

Output 7.31 Fit Statistics for Rule Induction

TARGET	Fit statistics	Statistics La...	Train	Validation	Test
Student_Type	_ERR_	Error Function	84.0896	61.93092	87.24114
Student_Type	_DIV_	Divisor for ASE	150	114	116
Student_Type	_NOBS_	Sum of Frequ...	75	57	58
Student_Type	_WRONG_	Number of W...	18	14	19
Student_Type	_DISF_	Frequency of...	75	57	58
Student_Type	_MISC_	Misclassificat...	0.24	0.245614	0.327586
Student_Type	_AVERR_	Average Erro...	0.560597	0.543254	0.752079

As Output 7.32 shows, undergraduate students are mostly classified correctly; graduate students are not.

Output 7.32 Classification Chart for Rule Induction

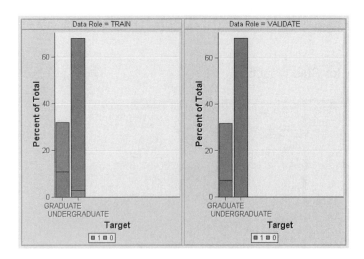

Note the discrete nature of the results using rule induction. There are only two nonzero values in either the training or validation set.

Output 7.33 Distribution Graph for Rule Induction

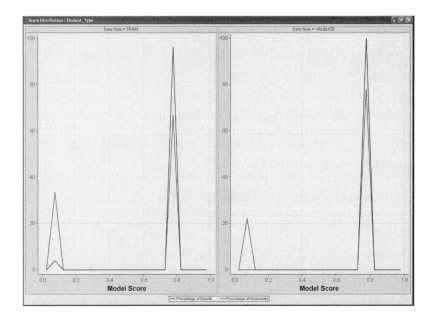

7.5 Using the Memory-Based Reasoning Node

The Memory-Based Reasoning node uses a *k*-nearest neighbor algorithm. It assumes Euclidean distance between an observation and its nearest neighbor. The outcome variable can be binary, nominal, or interval. It does not work with ordinal outcomes, although the ordinal can be identified as nominal or interval.

In addition, all input variables are assumed to be numeric, orthogonal to each other, and standardized. In order for this assumption to be valid, you can use the Princomp node first. However, you can use the Memory-Based Reasoning node to determine whether the results are reasonable without first running the principal components. The defaults are listed in Display 7.13. The results appear in Output 7.34 through 7.38. In this example, the same data were used for the Memory-Based Reasoning node without first examining the variables for orthogonality.

Display 7.13 Defaults for Memory-Based Reasoning

Property	Value
Node ID	MBR
Imported Data	
Exported Data	
Variables	
Method	Scan
Number of Neighbors	16
Epsilon	0.0
Number of Buckets	8
Weighted	Yes
Create Nodes	No
Create Neighbor Variables	Yes

The node creates a binary tree by repeatedly partitioning the observations into subsets, usually using the median. The default number of nearest neighbors is equal to 16.

Output 7.34 Results of Memory-Based Reasoning

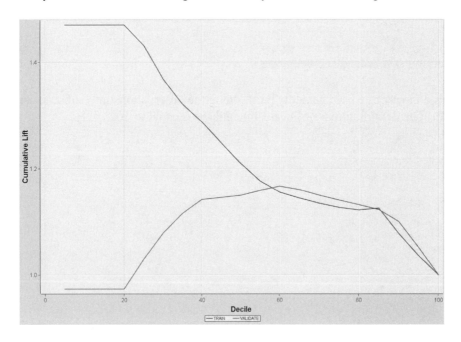

At about the 50th decile, the lifts for the validation and training sets become almost identical. The cumulative lift is just slightly above 1.0.

Output 7.35 Score Rankings for Memory-Based Reasoning

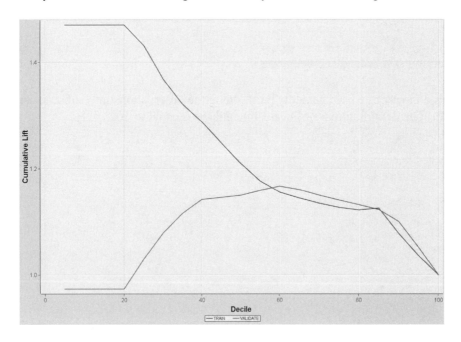

The results presented here are virtually identical to the results in Output 7.32 for rule induction.

Output 7.36 Classification Chart for Memory-Based Reasoning

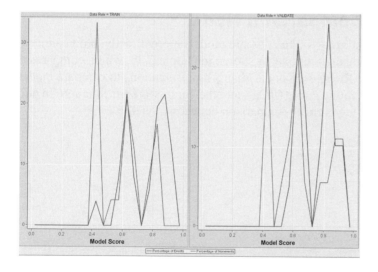

However, the distribution graph for memory-based reasoning is considerably different from that for rule induction. The training and validation sets differ in the lowest and highest decile levels.

Output 7.37 Distribution Graph for Memory-Based Reasoning

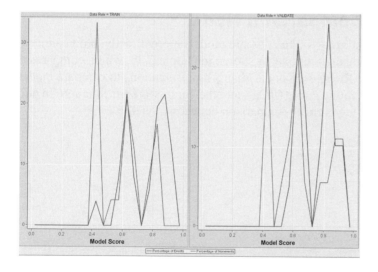

The misclassification rates for memory-based reasoning are similar to those for decision trees and neural networks. In this case, the best choice is the one with the more favorable lift chart. However, the misclassification rates remain slightly higher than those for neural network analysis.

Output 7.38 Fit Statistics for Memory-Based Reasoning

TARGET	Fit statistics	Statistics La...	Train	Validation	Test
Student_Type	_NW_		14	.	.
Student_Type	_NOBS_	Sum of Frequ...	75	57	58
Student_Type	_SUMW_	Sum of Case ...	150	114	116
Student_Type	_DFT_	Total Degree...	75	.	.
Student_Type	_DFM_		14	.	.
Student_Type	_DFE_	Degrees of F...	61	.	.
Student_Type	_ASE_	Average Squ...	0.177396	0.194901	0.202586
Student_Type	_RASE_	Root Averag...	0.421184	0.441476	0.450096
Student_Type	_DIV_	Divisor for ASE	150	114	116
Student_Type	_SSE_	Sum of Squa...	26.60938	22.21875	23.5
Student_Type	_MSE_	Mean Square...	0.21811	0.194901	0.202586
Student_Type	_RMSE_	Root Mean S...	0.467022	0.441476	0.450096
Student_Type	_AVERR_	Average Erro...	0.361667	0.377193	0.394397
Student_Type	_ERR_	Error Function	54.25	43	45.75
Student_Type	_MAX_	Maximum Ab...	0.8125	0.9375	0.9375
Student_Type	_FPE_	Final Predicti...	0.258823	.	.
Student_Type	_RFPE_	Root Final Pr...	0.508747	.	.
Student_Type	_AIC_	Akaike's Infor...	-49.7168	.	.
Student_Type	_SBC_	Schwarz's B...	-17.272	.	.
Student_Type	_MISC_	Misclassificat...	0.24	0.245614	0.310345
Student_Type	_WRONG_	Number of W...	18	14	18

You can also use the Memory-Based Reasoning node along with the Princomp node. The results are virtually identical.

7.6 Using the Model Comparison Node

The Model Comparison node allows you to compare models more directly. You connect the model nodes to the Model Comparison node, as shown in Output 7.39, which compares the Regression node to the Dmine Regression node. Visual representations to compare models are provided with the receiver operating curve (ROC) and the cumulative lift function. In addition, fit statistics allow you to make a more direct comparison between models.

Output 7.39 Model Comparison Results for Regression Nodes

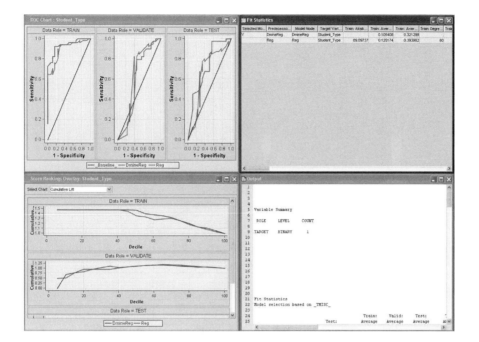

The ROC maps the sensitivity of the test against 1-specificity and indicates the overall accuracy of the model. Sensitivity is the proportion of target values that are predicted as a value of 1 and are actually equal to 1. Specificity is the proportion of observations that are predicted as a value of 0 and are actually equal to 0. The values 1 and 0 can represent the levels of a target variable with only two possible outcomes. The result for the training set appears the most accurate, with the area under the curve nearly equal to 1. Unfortunately, the ROC for the testing set shows less accuracy.

Output 7.40 ROCs for Regression Nodes

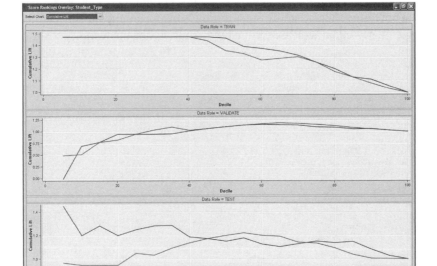

The cumulative lifts (in Output 7.41) appear similar when comparing the two different regression algorithms. A similar comparison is performed between the Neural Network node and the AutoNeural node (Output 7.42).

Output 7.41 Lift Curves for Regression Nodes

With the exception of the testing set, the two curves are relatively similar. However, in the testing set, the neural network result has a higher cumulative lift, indicating a better predictive model.

The comparison between the Neural Network and AutoNeural nodes appears in Output 7.42.

Output 7.42 Comparison of the Neural Network and AutoNeural Nodes

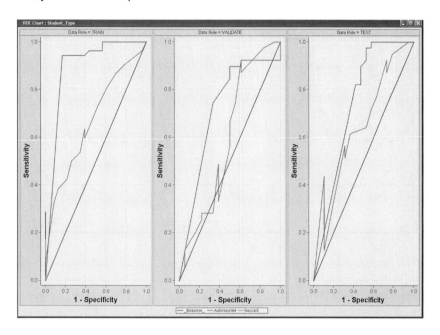

Output 7.43 adds the results from the DMNeural node.

Output 7.43 Addition of DMNeural Node Results

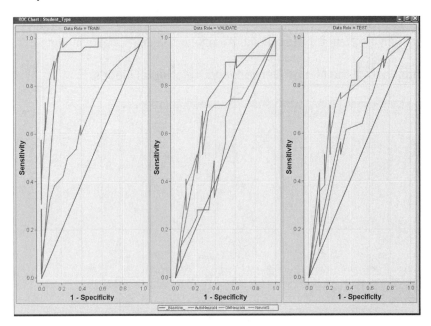

The results from the Neural Network node still appear to be more accurate compared to the other two, although the improvement is slight.

Output 7.44 compares the results of rule induction to the decision tree.

Output 7.44 Rule Induction Compared to Decision Tree

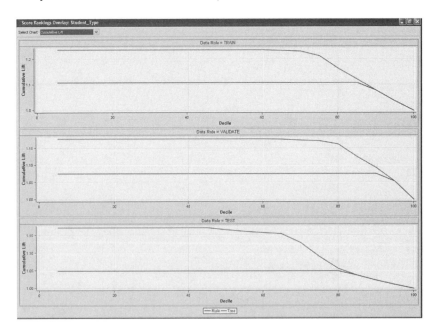

According to the results, the decision tree has a much higher cumulative lift compared to the rule induction and a lower misclassification rate. Thus, the decision tree is a better model for the data here.

Including the Memory-Based Reasoning node (Output 7.45) results indicates that the decision tree remains the better model, except perhaps in the early deciles where the results of memory-based reasoning are better.

Output 7.45 Added Comparison with Memory-Based Reasoning

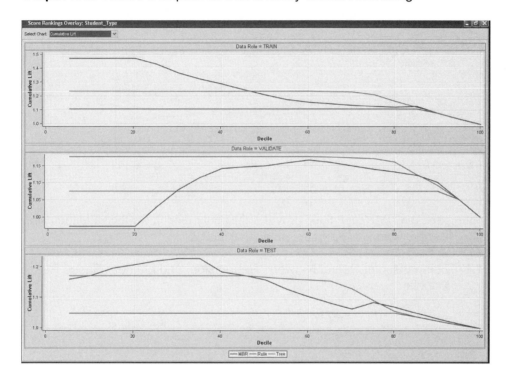

Adding the results of the Neural Network node indicates that both the rule induction and decision tree models are not as accurate at predicting outcomes as both the neural network and autoneural models. See Output 7.46.

Output 7.46 Comparison of Five Models

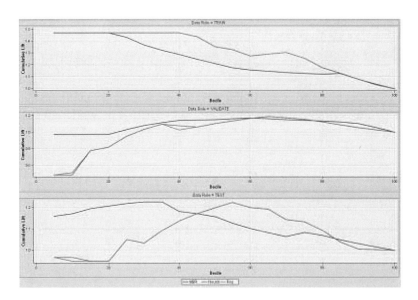

For the training set, the DMNeural node provides the better model; for the validation and testing sets, memory-based reasoning is the better predictive model.

Output 7.47 Comparison of Neural Network, Regression, and Memory-Based Reasoning Models

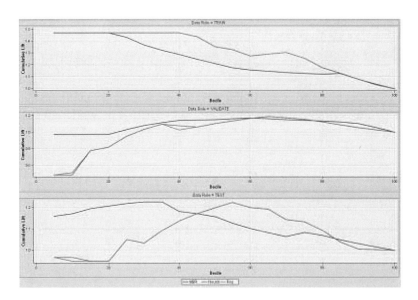

We recommend the pathway shown in Figure 7.2. First, use the Model Comparison node to determine the optimal model. Once you've chosen the optimal model, you can examine its results in detail.

7.7 Predictive Modeling Interval Data

When the target value is interval, misclassification rates are no longer included in the fit statistics. Instead, score rankings (Output 7.48) are based on the average, and the fit statistics provide additional error functions (Output 7.49). Using the same data set, the target variable has been changed to the number of hours of study; the previous target variable has been changed to an input.

Output 7.48 Score Rankings

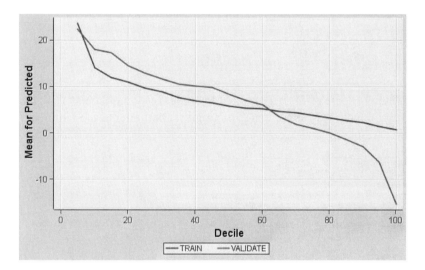

The target mean by decile is somewhat erratic; in contrast, the predicted mean is linear, as expected for a regression model. The average error function increases significantly for the testing set while remaining fairly similar for the training and validation sets (again, as expected for a regression model).

Output 7.49 Fit Statistics

TARGET	Fit statistics	Statistics La...	Train	Validation	Test
hours	_AIC_	Akaike's Infor...	272.3293	.	.
hours	_ASE_	Average Squ...	16.83014	105.0739	126.7189
hours	_AVERR_	Average Erro...	16.83014	105.0739	126.7189
hours	_DFE_	Degrees of F...	23	.	.
hours	_DFM_	Model Degre...	43	.	.
hours	_DFT_	Total Degree...	66	.	.
hours	_DIV_	Divisor for ASE	66	51	51
hours	_ERR_	Error Function	1110.789	5358.768	6462.666
hours	_FPE_	Final Predicti...	79.76022	.	.
hours	_MAX_	Maximum Ab...	16.06404	25.46168	52.83951
hours	_MSE_	Mean Square...	48.29518	105.0739	126.7189
hours	_NOBS_	Sum of Frequ...	66	51	51
hours	_NW_	Number of Es...	43	.	.
hours	_RASE_	Root Averag...	4.102455	10.25056	11.25695
hours	_RFPE_	Root Final Pr...	8.930858	.	.
hours	_RMSE_	Root Mean S...	6.949473	10.25056	11.25695
hours	_SBC_	Schwarz's B...	366.4845	.	.
hours	_SSE_	Sum of Squa...	1110.789	5358.768	6462.666
hours	_SUMW_	Sum of Case ...	66	51	51

The mean square error is a measure of the accuracy of the model. Again, the error is greatly increased for the testing set. Output 7.50 compares the regression model to the Dmine regression model. They have similar results.

Output 7.50 Comparison of Regression Node Outcomes

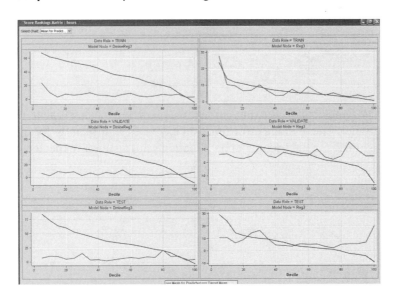

Performing a decision tree analysis for an interval variable does not result in an error; however, the results are meaningless (Output 7.51). Analyzing with rule induction does produce an error.

Although a result is given, it is essentially meaningless because the tree has no branches. This tends to be the result when the target variable is interval rather than nominal.

Output 7.51 Results from Decision Tree with Interval Target

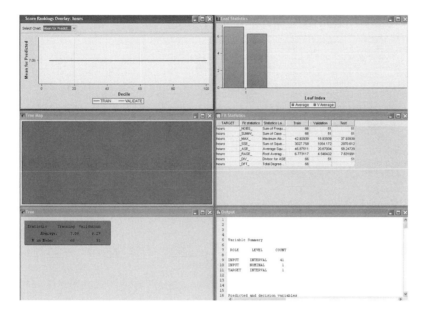

The three neural networks are shown in Output 7.52 through 7.54. The three networks are directly compared in Output 7.55.

Output 7.52 Fit Statistics for the Neural Network Node

TARGET	Fit statistics	Statistics La...	Train	Validation	Test
hours	_DFT_	Total Degree...	66	.	.
hours	_DFE_	Degrees of F...	-67	.	.
hours	_DFM_	Model Degre...	133	.	.
hours	_NW_	Number of Es...	133	.	.
hours	_AIC_	Akaike's Infor...	.	.	.
hours	_SBC_	Schwarz's B...	.	.	.
hours	_ASE_	Average Squ...	45.87511	20.67004	58.24729
hours	_MAX_	Maximum Ab...	42.93939	16.93939	37.93939
hours	_DIV_	Divisor for A...	66	51	51
hours	_NOBS_	Sum of Frequ...	66	51	51
hours	_RASE_	Root Averag...	6.773117	4.546432	7.631991
hours	_SSE_	Sum of Squa...	3027.758	1054.172	2970.612
hours	_SUMW_	Sum of Case ...	66	51	51
hours	_FPE_	Final Predicti...	.	.	.
hours	_MSE_	Mean Square...	.	20.67004	58.24729
hours	_RFPE_	Root Final Pr...	.	.	.
hours	_RMSE_	Root Mean S...	.	4.546432	7.631991
hours	_AVERR_	Average Erro...	45.87511	20.67004	58.24729
hours	_ERR_	Error Function.	3027.758	1054.172	2970.612
hours	_MISC_	Misclassificat...	.	.	.
hours	_WRONG_	Number of W...	.	.	.

The error terms are smaller for the testing set compared to the regression fit statistics, indicating a better fit. Output 7.53 lists the fit statistics for the AutoNeural node.

Output 7.53 Fit Statistics for the AutoNeural Node

TARGET	Fit statistics	Statistics La...	Train	Validation	Test
hours	_DFT_	Total Degree...	66	.	.
hours	_DFE_	Degrees of F...	-199	.	.
hours	_DFM_	Model Degre...	265	.	.
hours	_NW_	Number of Es...	265	.	.
hours	_AIC_	Akaike's Infor...	.	.	.
hours	_SBC_	Schwarz's B...	.	.	.
hours	_ASE_	Average Squ...	40.24989	34.26505	68.33474
hours	_MAX_	Maximum Ab...	34.55318	15.94354	39.05448
hours	_DIV_	Divisor for A...	66	51	51
hours	_NOBS_	Sum of Frequ...	66	51	51
hours	_RASE_	Root Averag...	6.34428	5.853635	8.266483
hours	_SSE_	Sum of Squa...	2656.492	1747.517	3485.072
hours	_SUMW_	Sum of Case ...	66	51	51
hours	_FPE_	Final Predicti...	.	.	.
hours	_MSE_	Mean Square...	.	34.26505	68.33474
hours	_RFPE_	Root Final Pr...	.	.	.
hours	_RMSE_	Root Mean S...	.	5.853635	8.266483
hours	_AVERR_	Average Erro...	40.24989	34.26505	68.33474
hours	_ERR_	Error Function.	2656.492	1747.517	3485.072
hours	_MISC_	Misclassificat...	.	.	.
hours	_WRONG_	Number of W...	.	.	.

The AutoNeural node has a higher error term for the testing set when compared to the Neural Network node. The DMNeural node's fit statistics are considered in Output 7.54. The errors are even larger.

Output 7.54 Fit Statistics for the DMNeural Node

TARGET	Fit statistics	Statistics La...	Train	Validation	Test
hours	_NOBS_	Sum of Frequ...	76	57	57
hours	_ERR_	Error Function	1270.786	12904.86	8446.52
hours	_SSE_	Sum of Squa...	1270.786	12904.86	8446.52
hours	_MAX_	Maximum Ab...	17.15475	67.66826	69.81395
hours	_DIV_	Divisor for ASE	76	57	57
hours	_ASE_	Average Squ...	16.72087	226.401	148.1846
hours	_RASE_	Root Averag...	4.089116	15.04663	12.17311
hours	_AVERR_	Average Erro...	16.72087	226.401	148.1846
hours	_DFT_	Total Degree...	76	.	.
hours	_DFM_	Model Degre...	21	.	.
hours	_DFE_	Degrees of F...	55	.	.
hours	_MSE_	Mean Square...	23.10521	.	.
hours	_RMSE_	Root Mean S...	4.806788	.	.
hours	_NW_	Number of W...	21	.	.
hours	_FPE_	Final Predicti...	29.48954	.	.
hours	_RFPE_	Root Final Pr...	5.430427	.	.
hours	_AIC_	Akaike's Infor...	256.066	.	.
hours	_SBC_	Schwarz's B...	305.0114	.	.

Output 7.55 compares all three methods.

For the testing and validation sets, the Neural Network node gives a better fit; for the training set, the DMNeural node is the better fit. However, at the lower deciles, the DMNeural node is a better fit; at the higher deciles, the Neural Network node is a better fit.

Output 7.55 Comparison of Neural Network Methods

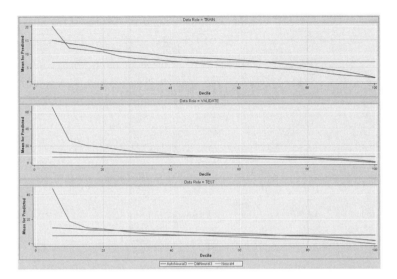

Use the Model Comparison node to compare all valid models. This node also provides a means of comparing all error terms. For this example, the Neural Network node provides the best fit with the least error on the testing set as well as on the validation set.

7.8 Scoring

When you use the Partition node, the results are already scored because predictive values are provided. Therefore, the Score node is not required with these classification models.

You must use it, however, when you use a completely new data set in the model. To demonstrate the technique, you can define the entire data set as a scoring data set as well as a raw data set. First, you must ensure that the variable identification in the data set to be scored is identical to the original data set. Then you must identify the data set as a scoring set (Display 7.14).

Display 7.14 Scoring Set

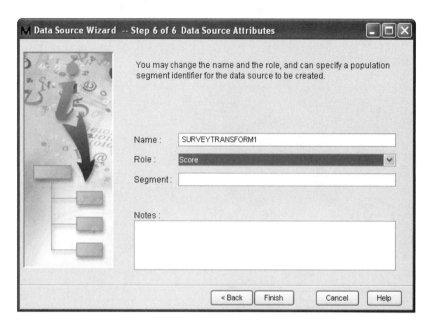

In this example, the best way to ensure that the data set has the same variable identifiers is to copy the data set, rename it, and then reset the variable Role to **Score**. Figure 7.4 is a scoring diagram of the Neural Network node. The initial results appear in Output 7.56.

Figure 7.4 Scoring Diagram

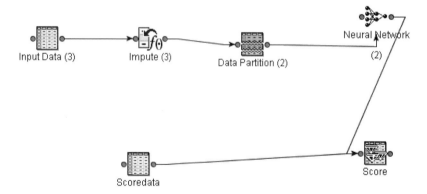

In Output 7.56, means and quantiles are used to compare the scoring results to the results of the initial data set.

Output 7.56 Results of Score Node

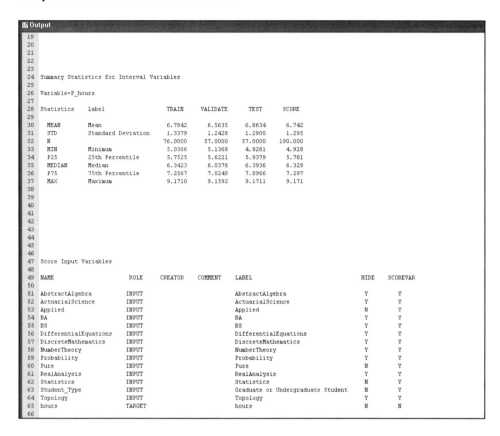

Using the **View** menu, you can recover the score code used to define the results (Display 7.15).

Display 7.15 Score Code

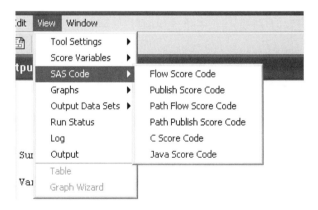

Another way to perform scoring is to use all possible predictive models with the Model Comparison node (Figure 7.5). The node chooses the best model for scoring.

Figure 7.5 Multiple Models with Scoring

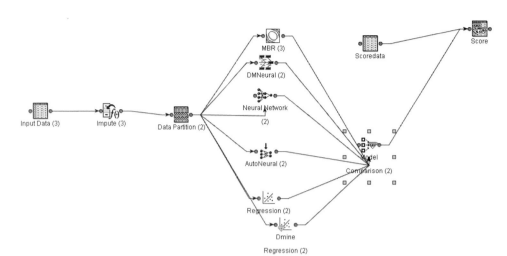

7.9 Additional Examples

Consider the 21 clusters of medications defined in Chapter 6 to see if models can predict membership clusters based on payment. To perform this operation, use the MEANS procedure to determine the sum total payment for each household and each payer. These sums are the input variables; the cluster number is the target variable, and DUID is the household ID. Not all models accept so many nominal categories. The DMNeural node requires a binary or interval target, for example. The cumulative lift curves appear in Output 7.57.

Output 7.57 Cumulative Lift Curves from Model Comparison

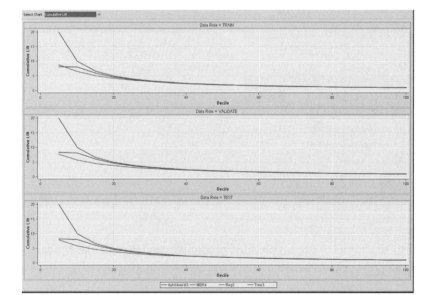

The cumulative lift reduces quickly, indicating a poor model fit. The misclassification rates are listed in Table 7.1.

Table 7.1 Model Misclassification Rates

Method	Misclassification Training	Misclassification Validation	Misclassification Testing
Neural Network	0.94	0.94	0.94
Memory-Based Reasoning	0.68	0.77	0.77
Regression	0.73	0.75	0.75
Decision Tree	0.74	0.75	0.75

The decision tree (in Output 7.58) shows why the model is such a poor fit. Each of the 21 different clusters has a small percentage of the population, which is spread too thin.

Output 7.58 Decision Tree Results

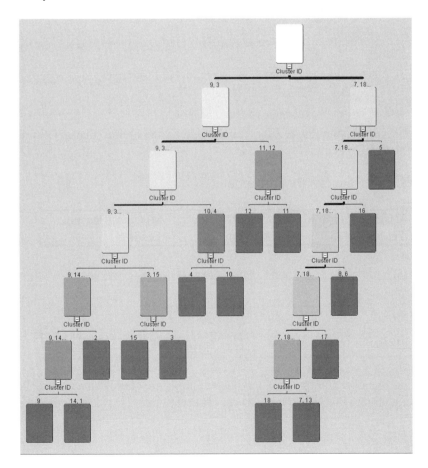

One way to resolve this issue is to isolate one or two clusters to see if the models can predict their membership. In this example, consider the diabetes clusters. You can define a variable equal to 1 if the household is in one of the diabetes clusters and 0 if not. Output 7.59 shows the model comparison results.

Output 7.59 Model Comparison for Binary Target

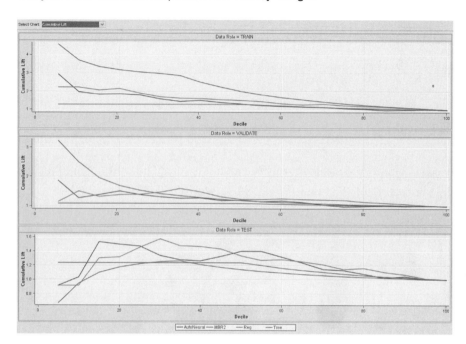

Except for the decision tree, the cumulative lift is much higher compared to that in Output 7.57. The misclassification rates are listed in Table 7.2.

Table 7.2 Misclassification Rates for Binary Target

Method	Misclassification Training	Misclassification Validation	Misclassification Testing
Neural Network	.067	.067	.067
Memory-Based Reasoning	.067	.067	.067
Regression	.067	.069	.067
Decision Tree	.067	.067	.067

The decision tree has no branches (Output 7.60). All households are classified as nondiabetes, and the models predict a target value of group 0 for all observations.

Output 7.60 Decision Tree for Binary Target

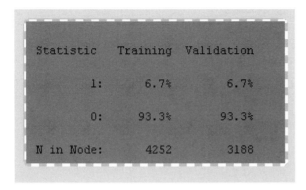

When two groups have such different sizes, predictive modeling is not effective. You can improve the fit by trying to equalize the two group sizes. First, separate code 1 households into a different data set from code 0 households. Then take a random sample of code 0 households, and append the data sets back together.

The following SAS code performs these tasks. The first section separates target variable values of 1 into a new data set; similar code separates target values of 0:

```
PROC SQL;
  CREATE TABLE SASUSER.QURY7005 AS SELECT QURY4112.Clusterrevised,
    QURY4112.DUID FORMAT=BEST12.,
    QURY4112._WAY_,
    QURY4112._TYPE_,
    QURY4112._FREQ_,
    QURY4112.RXSF01X_Sum FORMAT=BEST12.,
    QURY4112.RXMR01X_Sum FORMAT=BEST12.,
    QURY4112.RXMD01X_Sum FORMAT=BEST12.,
    QURY4112.RXPV01X_Sum FORMAT=BEST12.,
    QURY4112.RXVA01X_Sum FORMAT=BEST12.,
    QURY4112.RXTR01X_Sum FORMAT=BEST12.,
    QURY4112.RXOF01X_Sum FORMAT=BEST12.,
    QURY4112.RXSL01X_Sum FORMAT=BEST12.,
    QURY4112.RXWC01X_Sum FORMAT=BEST12.,
    QURY4112.RXOT01X_Sum FORMAT=BEST12.,
    QURY4112.RXOR01X_Sum FORMAT=BEST12.,
    QURY4112.RXOU01X_Sum FORMAT=BEST12.,
    QURY4112.RXXP01X_Sum FORMAT=BEST12.
  FROM SASUSER.QURY4112 AS QURY4112
  WHERE QURY4112.Clusterrevised = 1;
RUN;
QUIT;
```

The next code section creates a random sample:

```
PROC SURVEYSELECT DATA=WORK.SORT1389
   OUT=SASUSER.RAND176(LABEL="Random sample of SASUSER.QURY7051")
   METHOD=SRS
   RATE=0.1
   ;
   ID Clusterrevised DUID RXSF01X_Sum RXMR01X_Sum RXMD01X_Sum
RXPV01X_Sum RXVA01X_Sum RXTR01X_Sum RXOF01X_Sum RXSL01X_Sum
RXWC01X_Sum RXOT01X_Sum RXOR01X_Sum RXOU01X_Sum RXXP01X_Sum;
RUN;
```

The next code section appends the data sets again:

```
PROC SQL;
DROP TABLE SASUSER.APND7547;
DROP VIEW SASUSER.APND7547;
QUIT;

PROC SQL;
CREATE TABLE SASUSER.APND7547 AS
SELECT * FROM SASUSER.RAND176
 OUTER UNION CORR
SELECT * FROM EC100002.qury7005
;
Quit;
```

The Sampling node executes this code automatically. The revised results appear in Output 7.61.

Output 7.61 Cumulative Lift for Revised Data Set

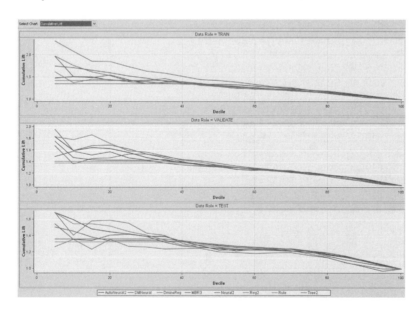

The shape of the lifts is similar to Output 7.59. The misclassification rates hover around 35% (Table 7.3).

Table 7.3 Misclassification Rates for Reduced Data Set

Method	Misclassification Training	Misclassification Validation	Misclassification Testing
Neural Network	.35	.33	.36
Memory-Based Reasoning	.35	.38	.38
Regression	.39	.34	.38
Decision Tree	.34	.35	.37

The decision tree analysis result is also much more reasonable (Output 7.62).

Output 7.62 Decision Tree for Reduced Data Set

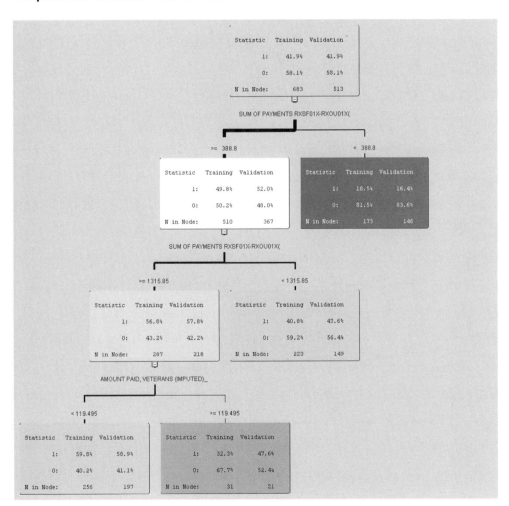

Classification into the cluster is based on payment totals.

7.10   Exercises

1. Use the faculty workload data set to investigate predictive models. Use the model comparison to find the optimal model.

2. Choose another target variable in the survey data to investigate predictive models. Again, use model comparison to find the optimal model.

3. Split the faculty workload in order to score a new data set.

4. Write a summary of your results.

Cluster Analysis

8.1 Introduction to Cluster Analysis

As a data mining process, clustering is considered to be unsupervised learning because it has no specific outcome or target variable. Clustering differs from classification because no pre-specified category defines the observations; there is no clearly defined outcome variable. Therefore, you need a different set of techniques to analyze the data.

Because there are no outcome categories, there are no right answers. Clustering focuses on determining whether the groupings found are meaningful. SAS Enterprise Miner software uses two primary clustering techniques: hierarchical and k-means clustering. Clustering with SAS Enterprise Miner software is similar to clustering with the CLUSTER and FASTCLUS procedures in SAS/STAT software.

Clustering is restricted to binary, nominal, ordinal, and interval data. Categories must be represented as numeric codes. Unfortunately, variables with large variances tend to mask the impact of other variables; therefore, some form of standardization is recommended. You can standardize the data using the Cluster node.

K-means clustering is performed on random choices of *seeds*, or central values for the clusters. A pre-specified number of clusters are assigned, and observations are placed in the clusters to minimize the total variation among the individual profiles within each cluster. Either you determine the number of clusters to begin or SAS Enterprise Miner 5.2 automatically attempts to optimize the number of clusters.

Clustering involves the following process:

- group observations or group variables
- choice of type-hierarchical or non-hierarchical
- number of clusters
- cluster identity
- validation to determine whether the clusters are reasonable

Once the number of clusters is determined, observations are moved from one cluster to another if the total variation within each cluster is reduced. The central value is then recomputed. This process continues until there are no more switches of observations into a new cluster.

Because there is no target or outcome, validating the clusters by comparing target classifications is difficult. Validation, then, is performed by examining the reasonableness of the clusters and by accessing how distinct they are. Clusters are reasonable if you can label them. Therefore, labeling the clusters is critical. It is also difficult. Labels are based on the values of the input variables within each cluster. Clusters are separated within these input variables.

For example, assume that X_1 and X_2 are used to define Clusters A and B. Suppose that the two input variables can only take the values 0 and 1. If $X_1=0$ for 90% of the values in Cluster A and $X_2=1$ for 75% of the values in Cluster B, then the clusters are distinct and a label can be defined in terms of variable X_1. However, if $X_1=1$ for 50% of the values in both Clusters A and B, but $X_2=1$ for 80% of the values in Cluster A and $X_2=0$ for 75% of the values in Cluster B, then the clusters are defined more by X_2.

Clustering results are not unique. There are many different methods of clustering, and all can give different results. Different users can find very different clusters. Different cluster results can be almost equally reasonable, which is why clustering is an exploratory—not inferential— multivariate analysis tool.

8.2 Comparing Methods

Hierarchical clustering involves grouping observations based on the distance between observations. Distance can be defined using different criteria in PROC CLUSTER. The clusters are built on a hierarchical tree structure. The closest observations are grouped together initially, followed by the next closest match. Clustering in PROC FASTCLUS is based on selecting random seed values as the centers of spheres containing all observations closest to that center. Then the centers are redefined based on the outcomes. SAS Enterprise Miner software uses PROC FASTCLUS to perform clustering. This is the same procedure available in SAS/STAT software, which offers additional hierarchical clustering techniques. You can use SAS/STAT procedures in SAS Enterprise Miner software with the SAS Code node.

The variables in the data set identifying preferences for mathematics subjects were first clustered in SAS/STAT software using the hierarchical procedure in PROC CLUSTER. To demonstrate the differences, the survey data introduced in Chapter 1 are analyzed in this example. Several distance criteria are used for comparison. In addition, the course level (200, 300, 400, 500, and above) are included.

```
proc cluster data=sasuser.studentsurvey method=density r=2;
   var courselevel pure applied abstractalgebra numbertheory
   topology realanalysis discretemathematics differentialequations
   actuarialscience  probability statistics;
   id id;
run;

proc tree horizontal spaces=2;
   id id;
run;
```

In addition to the density method, Ward's method, the centroid method, and the two-stage method were used to determine clusters (Figure 8.1), with very different results.

Figure 8.1 Methods of Clustering

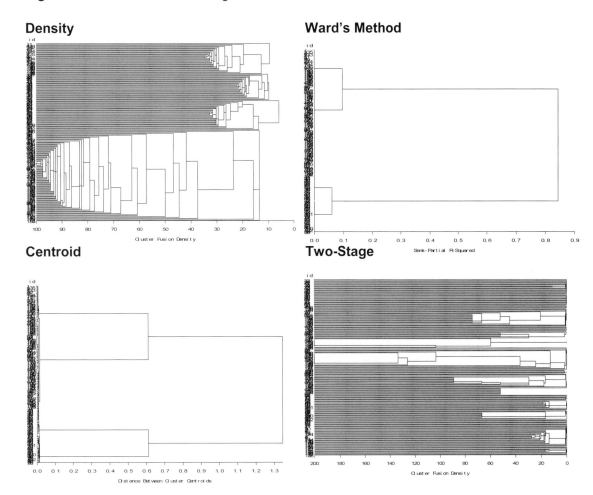

The number of clusters defined ranges from 2 to many. With so many different clusters, it is difficult to judge which is optimal. In contrast, *k*-means clustering uses the following code:

```
proc fastclus data=sasuser.studentsurveyimputed maxclusters=4 list;
   var courselevel pure applied abstractalgebra numbertheory topology
   realanalysis discretemathematics differentialequations
   actuarialscience  probability statistics;
   id id;
run;
```

In this program, you must specify the maximum number of clusters. In PROC FASTCLUS, you can create a list identifying which observations are classified into which cluster. You cannot do that with hierarchical clustering because the final clustering is uncertain. Table 8.1 lists the means of each variable by cluster.

Table 8.1 Cluster by Variable

Cluster	Pure	Applied	Algebra	Topology	Probability	Statistics
1	.68	.36	.32	.02	.18	.06
2	.28	.92	.05	.08	.43	.69
3	.36	.08	.08	.04	.88	.92
4	1.00	1.00	.76	.56	.41	.35

To validate the results, give each cluster a meaningful identity. Given the proportion of values in each cluster, you can define labels for each cluster (Table 8.2). Small percentages indicate that most of the observations in the cluster have a value of 0; high percentages indicate that most of the observations have a value of 1. A value of 0.41 indicates that most have a value of 0, but many also have a value of 1.

Note that Cluster 2 has a value of 0.92 for Applied Math and a value of 0.68 for Pure Math, with low values for specific types of mathematics.

Table 8.2 Cluster Labels

Cluster	Label
1	Pure Math
2	Applied Math
3	Statistics
4	Math Generally

There are many possibilities for cluster labels. Consider whether the labels are meaningful.

Five clusters are summarized in Table 8.3.

Table 8.3 Five Clusters in PROC FASTCLUS

Cluster	Pure	Applied	Algebra	Topology	Probability	Statistics
1	.36	.46	.07	.03	.09	.04
2	.30	.80	.48	.14	.22	.32
3	.05	.44	.02	.05	.65	.98
4	1.00	.50	.40	.05	1.00	.75
5	1.00	.90	.70	.60	.60	.40

Cluster	Label
1	Pure Math
2	Applied Math
3	Statistics
4	Somewhat Ambivalent
5	Math Generally

There is currently no clear reason to favor the five clusters defined in Table 8.3 over the four clusters defined in Table 8.1, or conversely.

8.3 Using the FASTCLUS Procedure in SAS Enterprise Miner Software

In contrast, in SAS Enterprise Miner software, specifying a maximum number of clusters is optional, not required. The software also provides some graphics to examine the data that are not readily available in SAS/STAT software. The Cluster node is illustrated in Figure 8.2.

Figure 8.2 Beginning Cluster Node

REVISEDSTUDE

NTSURVEY

Cluster

The default results appear in Output 8.1.

Output 8.1 Default Results for Cluster Node

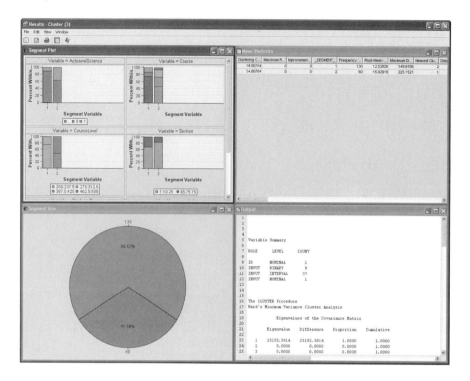

Only two groups are defined. However, scrolling down the output indicates that only two observations are used in the clustering. Most of the values have been eliminated because so many values are missing that most observations have at least one missing value in the input. It is possible that one or two inputs have almost no responses. To examine the inputs, use the multiplot tool, which indicates that no one variable should be eliminated from the analysis. Therefore, add imputation to the clustering (Display 8.1 and 8.2).

Display 8.1 View of Imputation Options

Non Missing Variables	No
Class Variables	
Default Input Method	Count
Default Target Method	None
Interval Variables	
Default Input Method	Mean
Default Target Method	None
ABW Tuning	9.0
AHUBER Tuning	1.5
AWAVE Tuning	6.2831853072
Spacing Proportion	90.0

Interval variables are imputed using the mean; nominal and ordinal variables are imputed by the most frequently occurring value. Right-click to change the imputation defaults. See Display 8.2.

Display 8.2 Imputation Choices

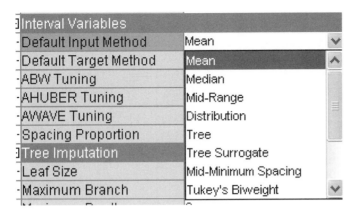

This expanded menu can be accessed by selecting **Advanced** from the **View** submenu (Display 8.3).

Display 8.3 Access to the Expanded Menu

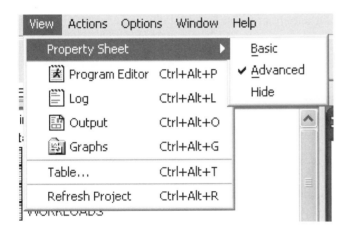

With the imputed values, the default output appears in Output 8.2.

Output 8.2 Imputed Results

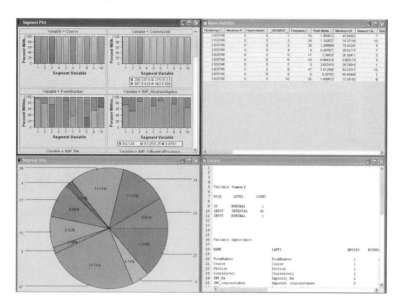

The default contains a total of 15 different clusters. Each of the four output windows can be enlarged. Output 8.3 contains an enlargement of the segment plot, which appears in the upper left-hand corner.

Output 8.3 Segment Plot

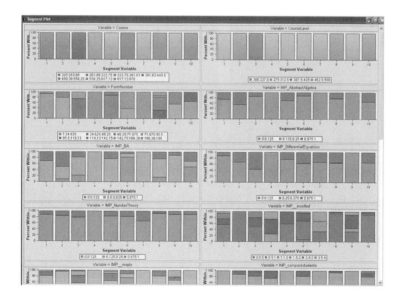

The different colors indicate how well the individual variable separates values into the different clusters. Only five input variables are used to separate the clusters. Some of the variables separate better than others (for example, the number of hours). You can use a decision tree to examine the separation in the clusters.

Display 8.4 Menu for Accessing Decision Tree

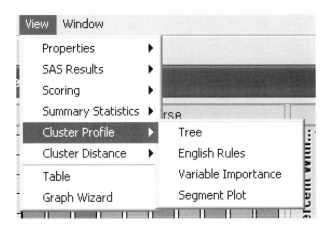

Output 8.4 Decision Tree for Clustering

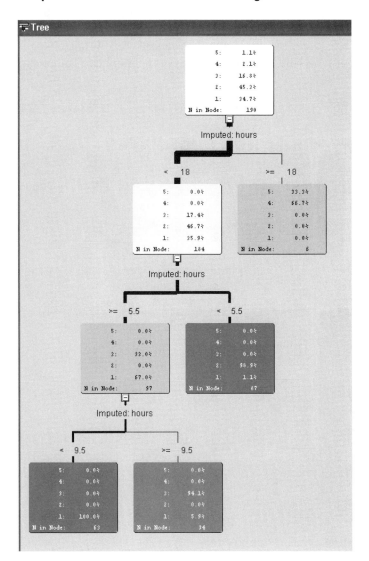

The decision tree indicates that the number of hours is the most important variable separating clusters. Another important issue in clustering is using subject matter knowledge to label the clusters (Table 8.4).

Table 8.4 Cluster Labels

Cluster	Label
1	Diligent students (more than 13 hours of study)
2	Moderately diligent students (between 5 and 13 hours of study)
3	Well-advanced students (more than 5 math courses completed)
4	Somewhat diligent students (between 6 and 10 hours of study)
5	Non-diligent students (less than 6 hours of study)

As is discussed in Section 8.4, because the scale for hours is considerably greater than 5 while most of the other variables are ordinal on a scale of 1–5, or 0–1, this one variable dominates all others just by the magnitude of its range (from 0 to 25 hours). When one variable could dominate by a magnitude larger than all other input variables, it is better to standardize all variables, which is discussed in Section 8.4. Another way of looking at the clustering is to eliminate the disparate variable, Hours. You can recluster using the Drop node to reduce the number of input variables (Output 8.5).

Output 8.5 Cluster Output with Reduced Input Variable List

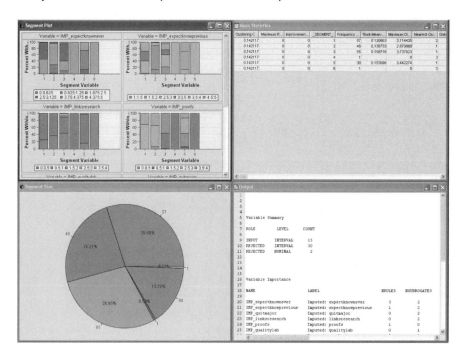

A total of six clusters are now identified. However, three of the clusters are very small while one cluster contains almost half the observations.

Only three of the clusters have any appreciable number of observations. You can change the method to user specify and the number of clusters to three or to four. If you reduce the clusters to a maximum of four, the results still show one very small cluster and three others with an appreciable number of observations (Output 8.6 and 8.7).

Output 8.6 Reducing the Number of Clusters

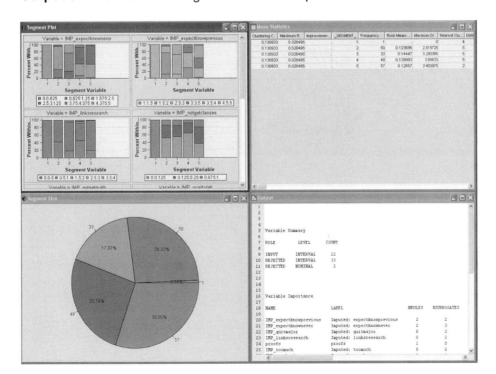

The pie chart shows a total of four clusters, but one of the clusters is negligible in size compared to the other three.

Output 8.7 Further Reducing the Number of Input Variables

Output 8.7 yields four reasonable clusters and a fifth cluster with only one value. The accompanying decision tree (Output 8.8) identifies the variables used to separate the clusters. It is clear that students who like proofs in class become the primary separator into clusters with responses to what instructors expect students to know.

Other clusters are defined by negative responses to those same questions.

Output 8.8 Decision Tree for Model in Output 8.7

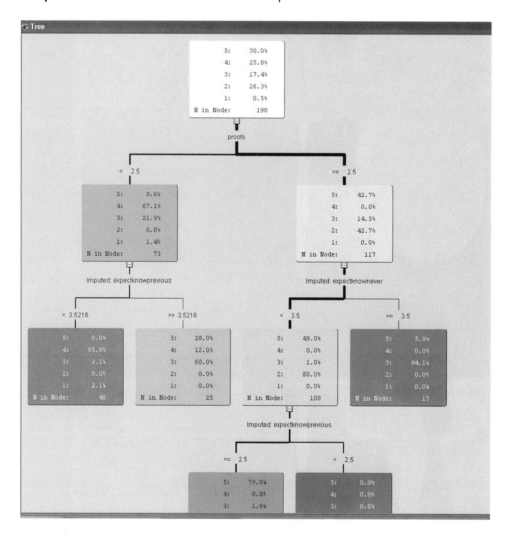

Table 8.5 Cluster Labels

Cluster	Label
1	Likes proofs
2	Does not like proofs but does not believe the instructor is too demanding
3	Instructor is too demanding of prerequisite material and expects knowledge that has been forgotten
4	Instructor is too demanding but does not expect forgotten knowledge and wants to learn real analysis
5	Instructor is too demanding but does not expect forgotten knowledge and does not want to learn real analysis

You should also examine the separation between clusters as provided in the selection path **View ▶ Cluster Distances ▶ Plot** (Output 8.9).

Output 8.9 Cluster Distances

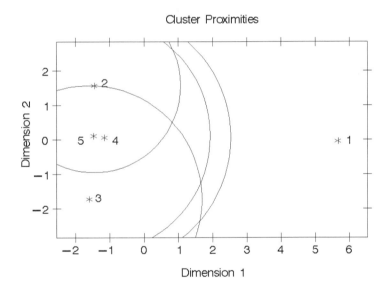

Clusters 2, 4, and 5 are close together and separated from Clusters 1 and 3. In the final analysis, it is probably better to combine the two similar clusters, 4 and 5, and to reduce the total number of clusters to three.

8.4 Standardizing Variables

If the scale of one variable is proportionally greater than that of other variables, that variable can dominate the clustering results. The dominance can mask the contributions of some variables. To prevent this, you can standardize the input variables using the Cluster node. This section re-analyzes the clustering in Section 8.3 using standardized variables. The results are considerably different (Output 8.10).

Ouput 8.10 Results after Standardization

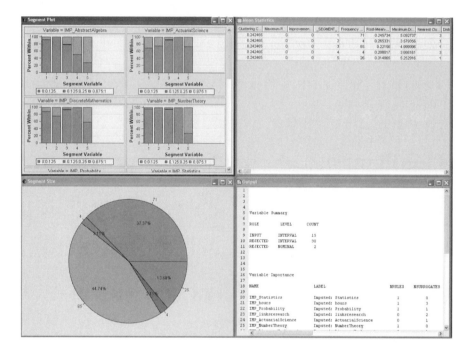

With standardization, more variables are used in the final analysis (Output 8.11). However, the results include one very large cluster, which contains more than half of the observations.

The variables used to separate the clusters tend to focus on preferences in work habits, hours, and types of mathematical disciplines. Research now becomes a variable of interest.

Output 8.11 Decision Tree for Standardized Clustering

Suggested cluster labels appear in Table 8.6.

Table 8.6 Cluster Labels

Cluster	Label
1	Studies a great number of hours
2	Likes Statistics
3	Statistics and Abstract Algebra
4	No Statistics and Number Theory
5	No Statistics and no Number Theory

The cluster distance profiles are changed as well (see Output 8.12).

Output 8.12 Distance Profiles for Standardized Variables

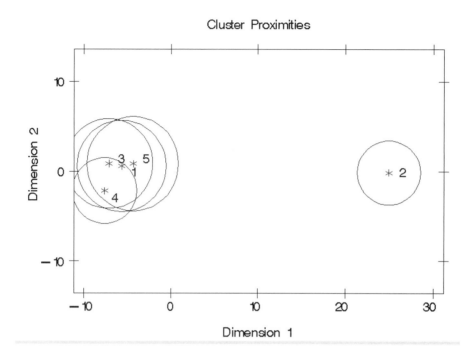

In this example, the cluster centers are poorly spaced out, and the clusters overlap. The clusters are labeled differently as well.

8.5 Clustering Specific Variables

Sometimes, you might want to determine whether there are different clusters based on specific values. This example uses only the responses to question 1 of the survey listed in the exercises in Chapter 1. It determines whether there are specific clusters related to student preferences in types of mathematics. The default results appear in Output 8.13.

Output 8.13 Default Results for Preference Variables

In this case, the default number of clusters is greater than the number of variables used in the clustering model. Thus, you need to reduce the number of clusters and rerun the analysis (Output 8.14).

Output 8.14 Reduced Number of Clusters

Once reduced in number, the clusters appear to be well spaced. The decision tree indicates the way preferences define the clusters (Output 8.15).

Output 8.15 Decision Tree for Preferences

The initial separators appear to be the pure mathematical disciplines. Table 8.7 lists the cluster labels.

Table 8.7 Cluster Labels

Cluster	Label
1	Statistics and no Abstract Algebra
2	Differential Equations and Pure Mathematics
3	Probability and Real Analysis
4	No Differential Equations and no Statistics
5	No Real Analysis and Statistics

There are real differences in observed responses.

8.6 Examining the Results

Thus far, there is no indication that the final clusters are correct. Indeed, it is not possible to define the term *correct* in relation to clusters. Instead, you need to determine whether the existing clusters are reasonable and offer meaningful information. However, you can determine whether the clusters can be sustained if new observations are collected; in other words, it is possible to validate the clusters.

There are many similar procedures in SAS/STAT and SAS Enterprise Miner software that you could use to do this. Probably the easiest approach is to partition the data into the usual training, testing, and validation sets. Then you can compare the three sets. By adding a SAS Code node and highlighting the connection (Figure 8.3), you can investigate the partitioned sets (Display 8.5 and Output 8.16).

Figure 8.3 Addition of SAS Code Node

Display 8.5 Finding Data Sets

Property	Value
From	Clus
To	EMCODE
TRAIN	
Table	EMWS.Clus_TRAIN
Variables	
Role	Train
VALIDATE	
Table	EMWS.Clus_VALIDATE
Variables	
Role	Validate
TEST	
Table	EMWS.Clus_TEST
Variables	
Role	Test
CLUSSTAT	
Table	EMWS.Clus_OUTSTAT
Variables	
Role	Cluster Statistics
CLUSMEAN	
Table	EMWS.Clus_OUTMEAN
Role	Mean Statistics
VARMAP	
Table	EMWS.Clus_OUTVAR
Role	Variable Mapping

You can examine the variables and the proportion of data in each of the data sets. First, click on the variables for the training set (Output 8.16 and 8.17). A segment variable containing the cluster number is added.

Output 8.16 Training Set Variables

Name	Role	Level	Type	Order	Label	Format	Informat	Length
Applied	Input	Interval	N		Applied	BEST12.0	F12.0	8
appliedmathdoes	Rejected	Interval	N		appliedmathd	BEST12.0	F12.0	8
appliedmathshould	Rejected	Interval	N		appliedmaths	BEST12.0	F12.0	8
calculusmaple	Rejected	Interval	N		calculusmapl	BEST12.0	F12.0	8
comparestudents	Rejected	Interval	N		comparestud	BEST12.0	F12.0	8
Course	ID	Interval	N		Course	BEST12.0	F12.0	8
CourseLevel	ID	Interval	N		CourseLevel	BEST12.0	F12.0	8
coursesnotscheduled	Rejected	Interval	N		coursesnotsc	BEST12.0	F12.0	8
coursestaken	Rejected	Interval	N		coursestaken	BEST12.0	F12.0	8
Distance	Rejected	Interval	N					8
expectknownever	Rejected	Interval	N		expectknowne	BEST12.0	F12.0	8
expectknowprevious	Rejected	Interval	N		expectknowpr	BEST12.0	F12.0	8
FormNumber	Rejected	Interval	N		FormNumber	BEST12.0	F12.0	8
hours	Rejected	Interval	N		hours	BEST12.0	F12.0	8
id	Rejected	Nominal	N			BEST12.0	F12.0	8
IMP_AbstractAlgebra	Input	Interval	N		Imputed: Abst	BEST12.0		8
IMP_ActuarialScience	Input	Interval	N		Imputed: Actu	BEST12.0		8
IMP_BA	Input	Interval	N		Imputed: BA	BEST12.0		8
IMP_BS	Input	Interval	N		Imputed: BS	BEST12.0		8
IMP_DifferentialEquations	Input	Interval	N		Imputed: Diffe	BEST12.0		8
IMP_DiscreteMathematics	Input	Interval	N		Imputed: Disc	BEST12.0		8
IMP_NumberTheory	Input	Interval	N		Imputed: Num	BEST12.0		8
IMP_Probability	Input	Interval	N		Imputed: Prob	BEST12.0		8
IMP_RealAnalysis	Input	Interval	N		Imputed: Real	BEST12.0		8
IMP_Topology	Input	Interval	N		Imputed: Topo	BEST12.0		8
IM_IMP_AbstractAlgebra	Input	Interval	N		Imputed: IMP_			8
IM_IMP_ActuarialScience	Input	Interval	N		Imputed: IMP_			8

Explore... OK

Output 8.17 Pie Chart of Clusters (_Segment_)

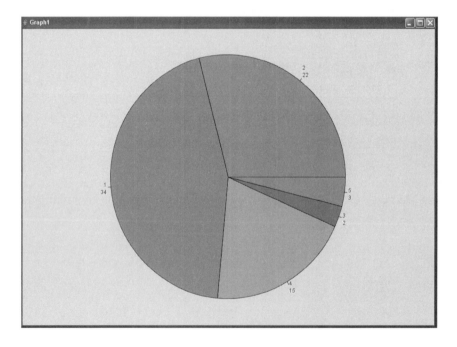

Compare this graph to the graphs for the validation and testing sets (Output 8.18 and 8.19).

Output 8.18 Pie Chart of Validation Set

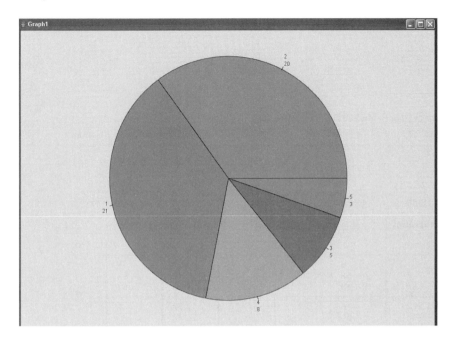

There are some variations in the data sets. You need to determine whether these differences are in the margin of error. To do this, merge the training, validation, and testing sets together. If you want to use the clusters in other analyses, the sets have to be merged as well.

Note that the Explore node does not identify the clusters with the same colors.

Output 8.19 Pie Chart of Testing Set

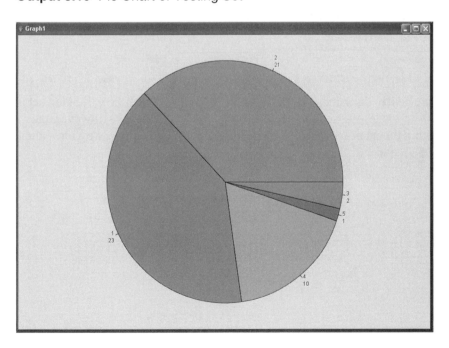

To use the clustered values, merge the data sets together by using the append code discussed in Chapter 7.

Once the data sets have been merged, you can make standard comparisons using the grouping. First, perform a chi-square analysis to see if there are differences in proportions. The results appear in Output 8.20:

```
proc freq data=Sasuser.Clustercombined;
   tables SETCODE*_SEGMENT_ / MEASURES CHISQ NOPERCENT NOROW;
run;
```

Output 8.20 Chi-Square Results

```
                         The FREQ Procedure

                   Table of SETCODE by _SEGMENT_

         SETCODE      _SEGMENT_

         Frequency|
         Row Pct  |
         Col Pct  |        1|       2|       3|       4|       5| Total
         ---------+--------+--------+--------+--------+--------+
         test     |     14 |      2 |     28 |     11 |      2 |    57
                  |  24.56 |   3.51 |  49.12 |  19.30 |   3.51 |
                  |  29.79 |  33.33 |  29.17 |  37.93 |  16.67 |
         ---------+--------+--------+--------+--------+--------+
         train    |     19 |      2 |     40 |     12 |      3 |    76
                  |  25.00 |   2.63 |  52.63 |  15.79 |   3.95 |
                  |  40.43 |  33.33 |  41.67 |  41.38 |  25.00 |
         ---------+--------+--------+--------+--------+--------+
         validate |     14 |      2 |     28 |      6 |      7 |    57
                  |  24.56 |   3.51 |  49.12 |  10.53 |  12.28 |
                  |  29.79 |  33.33 |  29.17 |  20.69 |  58.33 |
         ---------+--------+--------+--------+--------+--------+
         Total          47        6       96       29       12     190


              Statistics for Table of SETCODE by _SEGMENT_

         Statistic                     DF       Value      Prob
         ------------------------------------------------------------
         Chi-Square                      8      6.2828     0.6156
         Likelihood Ratio Chi-Square     8      5.8817     0.6605
         Mantel-Haenszel Chi-Square      1      0.1598     0.6893
         Phi Coefficient                        0.1818
         Contingency Coefficient                0.1789
         Cramer's V                             0.1286

         WARNING: 40% of the cells have expected counts less
```

The percentages are nearly the same, except for Cluster 5 with 12% in the validation set and Cluster 4 with 19% in the testing set compared to 16% in the training set. However, the differences are within the margin of error. The results can also be compared by individual variables (Output 8.21 and 8.22).

Output 8.21 Comparison of Individual Variables

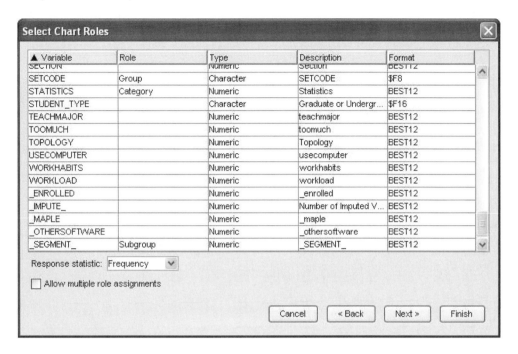

Output 8.22 Comparison of Statistics Variable

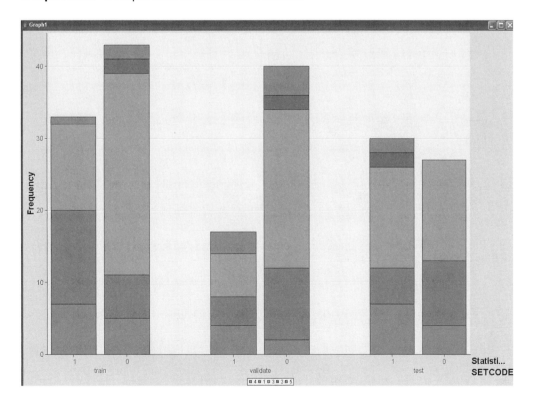

The bar chart shows that the proportions do differ slightly between testing, training, and validation sets. Segment 3 has a much higher proportion of 0 responses compared to Segment 1, which has a higher proportion of 1 responses in the training set. However, the proportion of 0 responses for Segment 1 is higher in the validation and testing sets.

Similar comparisons can be made for other variables in the data set. Once the clusters are in the data set, you can use the clustering variable in other comparisons. By connecting a SAS Code node to a Regression node, you can investigate the result (Figure 8.4).

Figure 8.4 Regression Comparison

In this example, Hours is the target variable with three input variables: Cluster, Setcode (data set), and Student Type. The results appear in Output 8.23 and 8.24.

Output 8.23 Score Rankings for Regression

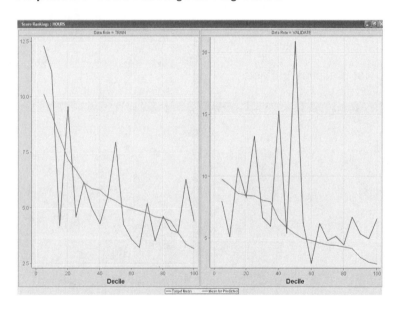

The results are somewhat difficult to interpret because the target mean changes so much. It does show that the target mean is higher at the lower deciles for the validation set.

Output 8.24 Fit Statistics

TARGET	Fit statistics	Statistics La...	Train	Validation	Test
HOURS	_AIC_	Akaike's Infor...	169.6937	.	.
HOURS	_ASE_	Average Squ...	10.16576	50.77911	70.94985
HOURS	_AVERR_	Average Erro...	10.16576	50.77911	70.94985
HOURS	_DFE_	Degrees of F...	62	.	.
HOURS	_DFM_	Model Degre...	6	.	.
HOURS	_DFT_	Total Degree...	68	.	.
HOURS	_DIV_	Divisor for ASE	68	51	49
HOURS	_ERR_	Error Function	691.2715	2589.735	3476.543
HOURS	_FPE_	Final Predicti...	12.13332	.	.
HOURS	_MAX_	Maximum Ab...	9.65543	39.54054	41.16922
HOURS	_MSE_	Mean Square...	11.14954	50.77911	70.94985
HOURS	_NOBS_	Sum of Frequ...	68	51	49
HOURS	_NW_	Number of Es...	6	.	.
HOURS	_RASE_	Root Averag...	3.188378	7.125946	8.423173
HOURS	_RFPE_	Root Final Pr...	3.483292	.	.
HOURS	_RMSE_	Root Mean S...	3.339093	7.125946	8.423173
HOURS	_SBC_	Schwarz's B...	183.0107	.	.
HOURS	_SSE_	Sum of Squa...	691.2715	2589.735	3476.543
HOURS	_SUMW_	Sum of Case ...	68	51	49

The average error is low for the training set, but it increases for the validation and testing sets. Another way of analyzing the data is to find out how the results differ in the training, testing, and validation sets by comparing predicted values to actual values (Output 8.25 through 8.27).

Output 8.25 Predicted versus Actual Hours for Training Set

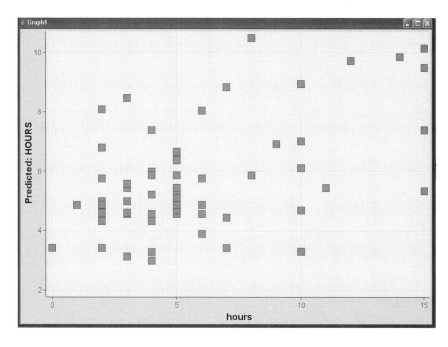

The training set indicates that as actual hours increase, so do predicted hours. The increase is fairly linear.

Output 8.26 Predicted versus Actual Hours for Validation Set

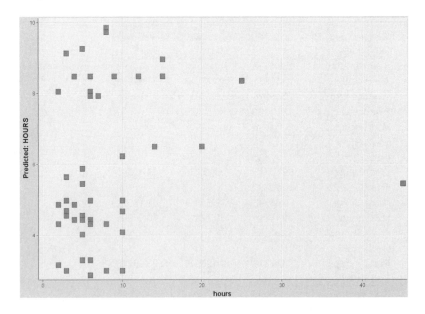

The validation set contains an extreme outlier. In addition, the number of hours is much higher compared to the predicted hours. Otherwise, the increase is fairly linear.

Output 8.27 Predicted versus Actual Hours for Testing Set

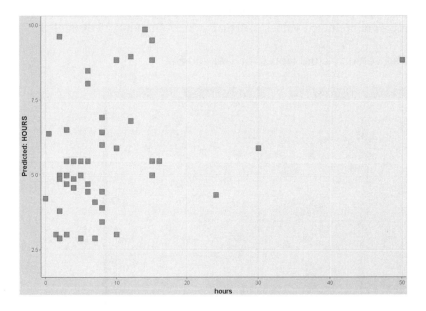

There is another outlier in the predicted hours for the testing set, but the result remains linear.

Another way of validating the clusters is to perform additional analyses with the clusters as an input variable used to predict a target variable.

8.7 Additional Examples

Consider the faculty workload data set defined in Chapter 1. This example uses faculty rank to validate the clusters instead of partitioning the data set. Using only the actual workload percentages without faculty rank produces Output 8.28 and 8.29.

Output 8.28 Clustering Faculty Workload

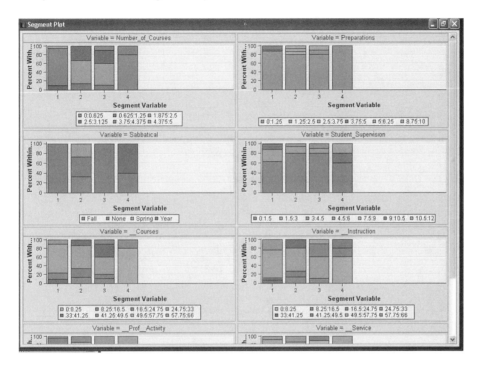

Output 8.29 Pie Chart of Clusters

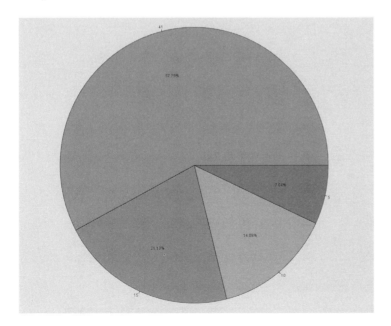

This analysis results in four clusters, with one cluster containing over half of all observations. Using the following code, you can test the clustering by examining faculty rank and cluster:

```
data sasuser.workcluster;
   set emws.clus3_train;
run;
```

The corresponding decision tree appears in Output 8.30.

Output 8.30 Decision Tree for Cluster Analysis

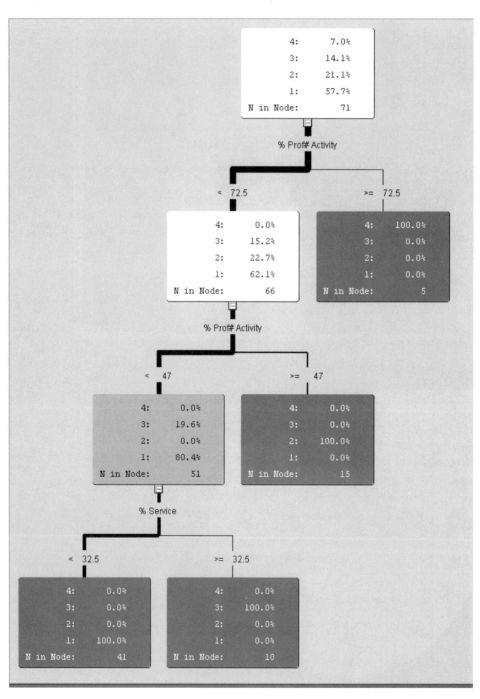

Faculty rank is predicted based on the percentage of activities. Clustering is not a predictor for rank. However, remember that the variables listed as predictors were in fact used to define the clusters. Next, use a simple table analysis to compare cluster and faculty rank (Output 8.31).

Output 8.31 Table Analysis of Cluster Results

Table of Rank by _SEGMENT_					
Rank(Rank)	**_SEGMENT_**				**Total**
	1	**2**	**3**	**4**	
Assistant	7 63.64 17.07	4 36.36 26.67	0 0.00 0.00	0 0.00 0.00	11
Associate	26 89.66 63.41	1 3.45 6.67	0 0.00 0.00	2 6.90 40.00	29
Professor	8 25.81 19.51	10 32.26 66.67	10 32.26 100.00	3 9.68 60.00	31
Total	41	15	10	5	71

Most assistant and associate faculty members are in Cluster 1; full-rank faculty members are scattered across all four clusters. To help you label the clusters, see Table 8.8, which lists the mean values by variable.

Table 8.8 Mean Values of Input Variables by Cluster

Variable	Cluster 1	Cluster 2	Cluster 3	Cluster 4
Large Lecture	0.68	0.27	0.40	0.0
Number of Courses	3.9	2.2	2.4	0.2
New Preparations	0.51	1.27	1.2	0.0
Student Supervision	1.34	0.6	0.7	4.4
Number of Calculus Sections	1.2	0.47	0.6	0.0
Percent for Courses	50.61	25.33	29.50	2.0
Percent for Instruction	53.31	27.80	32.80	6.4
Percent for Professional Activity	30.80	59.20	16.00	8.96
Percent for Service	15.88	13.60	51.20	4.0

It appears that faculty members in Cluster 1 have a standard teaching load; Cluster 2 focuses on professional activity; Cluster 3 focuses on administration; and Cluster 4 focuses on faculty members with reduced teaching loads who are on sabbatical.

Now, consider a second example that uses the medications database. You can use the payment sums to define clusters and then compare these clusters to the text clusters defined using patient conditions. The default defines nine clusters (Output 8.32 and 8.33).

Output 8.32 Variables Defining Clusters

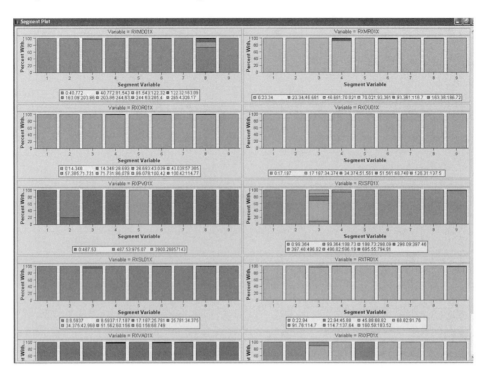

From the different color schemes, you can see that some of the payment variables separate better than others.

Output 8.33 Pie Chart of Clusters

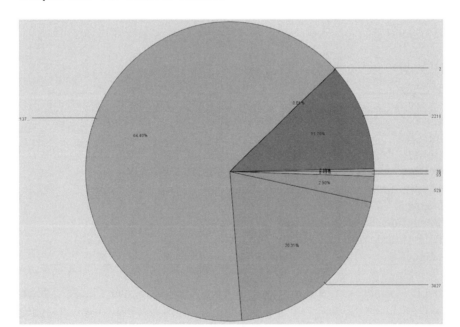

Again, consider a frequency table comparing these clusters to the clusters defined using text analysis; the text clusters compared to the clustering procedure here appear in Output 8.34.

Output 8.34 Table Analysis of Clusters

Table of _CLUSTER_ by _SEGMENT_

CLUSTER(#)	_SEGMENT_									Total
	1	**2**	**3**	**4**	**5**	**6**	**7**	**8**	**9**	
1	13 0.67 11.02	135 6.96 10.45	6 0.31 5.04	17 0.88 20.73	0 0.00 0.00	0 0.00 0.00	46 2.37 6.36	1723 88.81 20.79	0 0.00 0.00	1940
2	38 1.83 32.20	313 15.08 24.23	36 1.73 30.25	30 1.45 36.59	1 0.05 100.00	0 0.00 0.00	226 10.89 31.26	1431 68.96 17.27	0 0.00 0.00	2075
3	1 0.08 0.85	9 0.70 0.70	0 0.00 0.00	0 0.00 0.00	0 0.00 0.00	1 0.08 100.00	3 0.23 0.41	1264 98.90 15.25	0 0.00 0.00	1278
4	3 0.60 2.54	46 9.16 3.56	2 0.40 1.68	3 0.60 3.66	0 0.00 0.00	0 0.00 0.00	10 1.99 1.38	438 87.25 5.29	0 0.00 0.00	502
5	0 0.00 0.00	32 19.16 2.48	0 0.00 0.00	0 0.00 0.00	0 0.00 0.00	0 0.00 0.00	12 7.19 1.66	123 73.65 1.48	0 0.00 0.00	167
6	0 0.00 0.00	16 6.72 1.24	0 0.00 0.00	0 0.00 0.00	0 0.00 0.00	0 0.00 0.00	4 1.68 0.55	218 91.60 2.63	0 0.00 0.00	238
7	23 3.57 19.49	126 19.53 9.75	28 4.34 23.53	16 2.48 19.51	0 0.00 0.00	0 0.00 0.00	112 17.36 15.49	337 52.25 4.07	3 0.47 42.86	645
8	1 0.49 0.85	33 16.18 2.55	1 0.49 0.84	2 0.98 2.44	0 0.00 0.00	0 0.00 0.00	6 2.94 0.83	161 78.92 1.94	0 0.00 0.00	204
9	1 0.63 0.85	27 16.98 2.09	1 0.63 0.84	1 0.63 1.22	0 0.00 0.00	0 0.00 0.00	7 4.40 0.97	121 76.10 1.46	1 0.63 14.29	159
10	3 0.91 2.54	60 18.24 4.64	4 1.22 3.36	0 0.00 0.00	0 0.00 0.00	0 0.00 0.00	29 8.81 4.01	232 70.52 2.80	1 0.30 14.29	329

Table of _CLUSTER_ by _SEGMENT_

CLUSTER(#)	_SEGMENT_									Total
	1	2	3	4	5	6	7	8	9	
11	8 4.42 6.78	50 27.62 3.87	4 2.21 3.36	0 0.00 0.00	0 0.00 0.00	0 0.00 0.00	26 14.36 3.60	93 51.38 1.12	0 0.00 0.00	181
12	1 0.34 0.85	39 13.09 3.02	1 0.34 0.84	2 0.67 2.44	0 0.00 0.00	0 0.00 0.00	28 9.40 3.87	227 76.17 2.74	0 0.00 0.00	298
13	0 0.00 0.00	38 15.32 2.94	8 3.23 6.72	2 0.81 2.44	0 0.00 0.00	0 0.00 0.00	33 13.31 4.56	166 66.94 2.00	1 0.40 14.29	248
14	4 2.16 3.39	50 27.03 3.87	3 1.62 2.52	1 0.54 1.22	0 0.00 0.00	0 0.00 0.00	13 7.03 1.80	114 61.62 1.38	0 0.00 0.00	185
15	2 0.72 1.69	64 22.94 4.95	1 0.36 0.84	0 0.00 0.00	0 0.00 0.00	0 0.00 0.00	25 8.96 3.46	187 67.03 2.26	0 0.00 0.00	279
16	0 0.00 0.00	12 5.50 0.93	0 0.00 0.00	1 0.46 1.22	0 0.00 0.00	0 0.00 0.00	4 1.83 0.55	201 92.20 2.43	0 0.00 0.00	218
17	7 3.91 5.93	44 24.58 3.41	7 3.91 5.88	1 0.56 1.22	0 0.00 0.00	0 0.00 0.00	26 14.53 3.60	94 52.51 1.13	0 0.00 0.00	179
18	0 0.00 0.00	31 6.01 2.40	0 0.00 0.00	0 0.00 0.00	0 0.00 0.00	0 0.00 0.00	3 0.58 0.41	482 93.41 5.82	0 0.00 0.00	516
19	12 2.26 10.17	111 20.94 8.59	14 2.64 11.76	5 0.94 6.10	0 0.00 0.00	0 0.00 0.00	84 15.85 11.62	303 57.17 3.66	1 0.19 14.29	530
20	0 0.00 0.00	11 6.47 0.85	1 0.59 0.84	1 0.59 1.22	0 0.00 0.00	0 0.00 0.00	5 2.94 0.69	152 89.41 1.83	0 0.00 0.00	170
21	1 0.35 0.85	45 15.57 3.48	2 0.69 1.68	0 0.00 0.00	0 0.00 0.00	0 0.00 0.00	21 7.27 2.90	220 76.12 2.65	0 0.00 0.00	289
Total	118	1292	119	82	1	1	723	8287	7	10630

The first six text clusters are concentrated in Segment 8. Clusters 7 and 11 have only about half of their observations concentrated in Segment 8.

Next, look at the monetary representations of these clusters (Table 8.9).

Table 8.9 Cluster Segment Monetary Values

Payment Type	1	2	3	4	5	6	7	8	9
Medicare	119	77	928	128	0	0	265	22	0
Medicaid	28	216	381	6294	15265	0	717	57	28
Other Federal	0	4	0	0	0	0	4	1	0
Other Private	4	12	55	0	0	0	18	3	0
Other Insurance	0	0	11	0	0	0	1	0	0
Other Public	0	5	57	53	0	0	2	0	232
Private Insurance	6058	1765	593	227	244	54605	211	186	2234
Self-Pay	1838	839	5690	1564	15591	180	2487	298	1829
State & Local	0	2	94	0	0	0	0	2	0
Tricare	0	15	103	0	0	0	9	3	0
Veterans	70	61	481	7	0	0	190	20	771
Worker's Comp	0	0	94	0	0	0	8	0	0
Total	8114	2996	8487	19274	31121	54784	3913	593	21559

As expected, Cluster 8, with the largest proportion of the population, has the lowest payments for medications. The clusters with more crucial illnesses have much higher payments. In particular, Cluster 6 has the highest payments, mostly from private insurance. However, this cluster only contains one household. The next highest is Cluster 5, also containing only one household. Cluster 4 follows, with most of the remaining households in Cluster 2, or allergies. The cluster segments defined in this example can clearly be defined in terms of costs.

8.8 Exercises

1. Perform a similar clustering using the workload data set defined in Chapter 1. Reduce the number of clusters to three. First, standardize the variables.

2. Perform diagnostics to determine the effectiveness of the clustering.

3. Perform a clustering of the student survey data using other variables in the list. Test the clusters by comparing the results to student type.

4. Write a summary of your results.

Time Series Analysis

9.1 Using the Time Series Node

The Time Series node is a method of investigating *time series data*, which are data collected with a time stamp. Usually, you examine time series data to predict future results. Therefore, time series data are usually examined using very specific models. To demonstrate time series techniques, this example uses the data set outlined in Table 9.1. The data represent electricity usage for a 10-year period.

Table 9.1 Electricity Usage

Variable Name	Variable Description
Date	Dates are given on a monthly basis for a 10-year period.
Total Electric Usage	Total electricity used for all customers, including some charity customers who are not charged.
Total Sale of Electricity	Number of dollars of revenue from the sale of electricity.
Residential Electric	Total electricity used by residential customers (charged one rate).
Commercial Electric	Total electricity used by commercial (nonindustrial) firms.
Industrial Electric	Total electricity used by industrial firms.

To use the Time Series node, the data set must be identified as transactional. One interval variable must be identified as a time ID (Display 9.1). At least one target variable must also be defined.

Electricity usage is clearly seasonal: energy needs differ in winter and summer. Therefore, any useful model of these data must have a seasonal component.

Display 9.1 Transactional Data

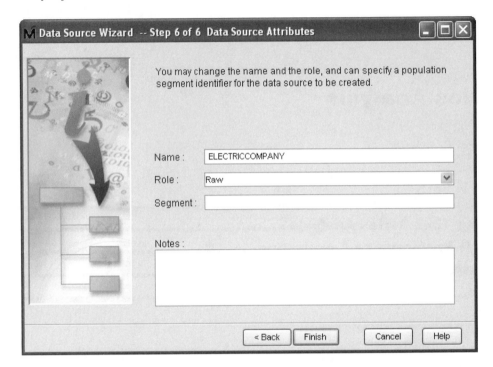

The icon for the Time Series node is found on the **Sample** tab of SAS Enterprise Miner (Figure 9.1).

Figure 9.1 Time Series Node

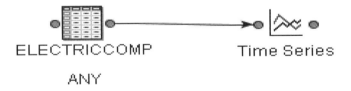

Because there are multiple targets, by default, the Time Series node analyzes the first target variable in the list, Commercial Usage.

You can change the parameters in the left-hand window or by right-clicking on the Time Series node and selecting **Edit Variables** from the pop-up menu (Figure 9.2).

Figure 9.2 Time Series Parameters

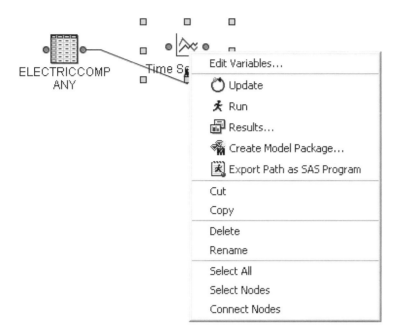

You can choose from four options for results: seasonal, trend, autocorrelations, and seasonal decomposition. You specify these options in the Time Series node (Display 9.2).

Display 9.2 Options in the Time Series Node

Property	Value
Node ID	TIME
Imported Data	...
Exported Data	...
Variables	...
Accumulation	Total
Transformation	None
Box-Cox Parameter	0.0
Apply Differencing	No
Difference Order	1
Time Interval	
Interval Selection	Automatic
Specify an Interval	
Time of Day	No
Seasonal Cycle Selection	Default
Length of Cycle	2
Missing Value	
Set Value	Missing
Constant Value for Missing	0.0
Analysis Method	
Select an Analysis	Correlation
Transpose	Yes
Seasonal Analysis	
Exported Statistics	Sum
Trend Analysis	
Exported Statistics	Sum
Use Default Number of Tir	Yes
Number of Time Periods	24
Correlation Analysis	
Exported Statistics	Autocorrelations
Use Default Number of La	Yes
Number of Lags	24
Seasonal Decomposition	
Exported Component	Trend Cycle Seasonal
Type	Default
Lambda	1600
Use Default Number of Pe	Yes
Number of Time Periods	24

These options are discussed later in this chapter and illustrated in Output 9.1 through 9.4.

Output 9.1 Seasonal Results

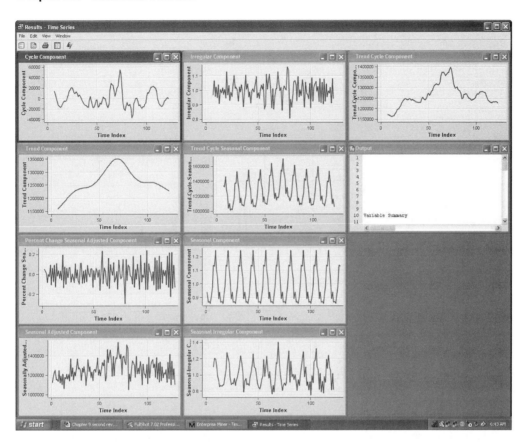

The seasonal graph plots one season of the data. In this example, the seasonal period is 12 months. Note the change of scale between the mean and sum.

Output 9.2 Trend Results

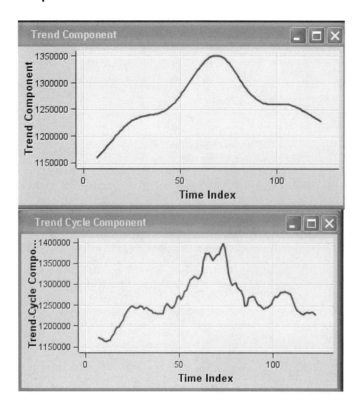

The trend gives a time index of 0 to 150. In a 10-year period, there are a total of 120 months, with time 0 indicating the beginning of the time series. Seasonal trends are easy to identify in this example. They occur at 12-month intervals. Again, the slope is similar for each of the statistical parameters; the main difference is one of scale.

Output 9.3 Correlational Plots

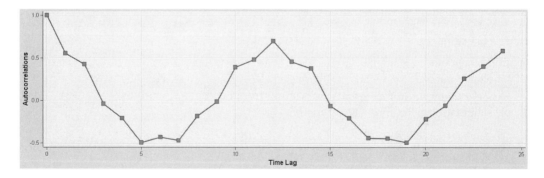

Correlational plots provide time lags. A *time lag* indicates to what extent the present depends upon the past. Consider the autocorrelations in Output 9.3. They are periodic, with a peak of 12 to indicate the seasonality of the time series. The inverse autocorrelations show that, except for seasonality, the dependence over time quickly becomes 0, so that seasonality is the main component of this time series example.

Output 9.4 Seasonal Decomposition

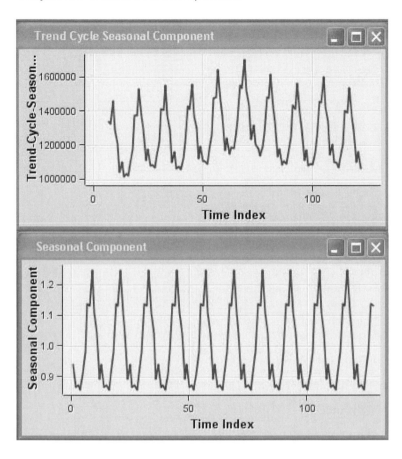

The seasonal decomposition graphs again indicate that electric usage is seasonal. More electricity is used in the peak of summer (air conditioning) than in winter (when most homes are heated with gas or oil).

9.2 Performing Time Series Analysis

A time series model takes into consideration the following characteristics of the data:

- *Autocorrelation.* A positive deviation from the mean is likely to stay positive; a negative deviation is likely to stay negative.
- *Trend.* A positive or negative trend requires a first or second difference.
- *Seasonality.* The data have a seasonal trend.
- *Transformation.* To maintain the assumption of normality, a transformation is sometimes required.

A purely autoregressive (with autocorrelations) model indicates that the current value $Y(t)$ depends on a specific number of previous values. If the number of previous values is equal to p, then an autoregression of size p is equal to

$$Y(t) = \mu + \alpha_1(Y(t-1) - \mu) + \alpha_2(Y(t-2) - \mu) + \ldots + \alpha_p(Y(t-p) - \mu) + \varepsilon(t) \qquad (9.1)$$

Estimation of the number of lags in the model is based on the autocorrelations. The moving average component expresses the current value $Y(t)$ in terms of future shocks (or errors):

$$Y(t) = \mu + \varepsilon(t) - \theta_1 \varepsilon(t-1) - \ldots - \theta_q \varepsilon(t-q) \tag{9.2}$$

In the existence of a trend, a first or second difference is used. That is, a new model $W(t)$ is defined so that

$$W(t) = Y(t) - Y(t-1) \tag{9.3}$$

and the model is then defined for the difference $W(t)$. Once this is estimated, $Y(t)$ is estimated as equal to

$$Y(t) = W(t) + Y(t-1) \tag{9.4}$$

The number of differences is defined by the parameter d. The three components (9.2), (9.3), and (9.4) make up the ARIMA model (AR=autoregressive, I=integrated, MA=moving average). It is identified as of order (p,d,q). It estimates both the autocorrelation and the trend.

Seasonality is added to the model by using an ARIMA$(p,d,q)x(P,D,Q)$ model,

where

P is the number of seasonal autoregressive terms

D is the number of seasonal differences

Q is the number of seasonal moving average terms

In the seasonal part of the model, all of these factors operate across multiples of lag s (the number of periods in a season). If the seasonality changes yearly, then the value of s is 12.

If the seasonal pattern is both strong and stable over time (e.g., high in the summer and low in the winter or vice versa), then your model should probably use a seasonal difference (regardless of whether the first, nonseasonal part uses a difference) to prevent the seasonal pattern from fading in long-term forecasts.

Sometimes a log transformation is included as part of the model. Seasonal ARIMA models are inherently additive models, so to capture a multiplicative seasonal pattern, use the log transformation with the data prior to fitting the ARIMA model. If the residuals show a marked increase in variance over time, the log transformation should be used.

Consider how the different components work to estimate the values for residential sales. Figure 9.3 shows an AR(1) model while Figure 9.4 shows an AR(2) model.

Figure 9.3 AR(1) Model

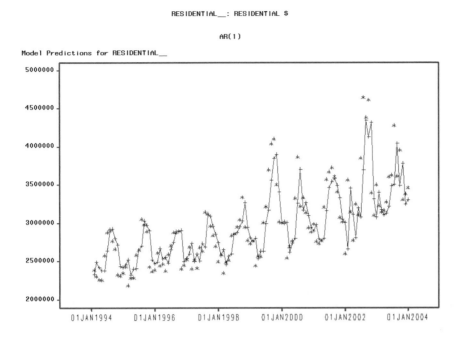

A comparison of the two figures indicates that the AR(10) model gives a better fit than the AR(1) model. The peaks become slightly more regular. Even the autoregressive component alone can show a slight increasing trend. However, the seasonality component can improve the fit, as can using other parts of the complete model.

Figure 9.4 AR(2) Model

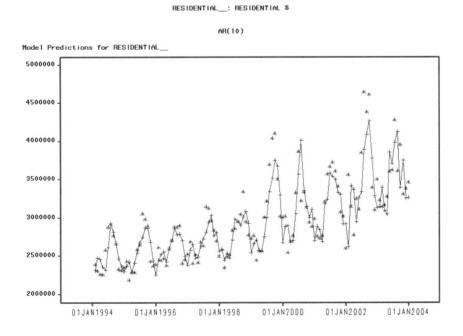

Figure 9.5 illustrates the ARIMA(1,0,1) model, which adds a moving average piece to the autoregressive component.

Figure 9.5 ARIMA(1,0,1) Model

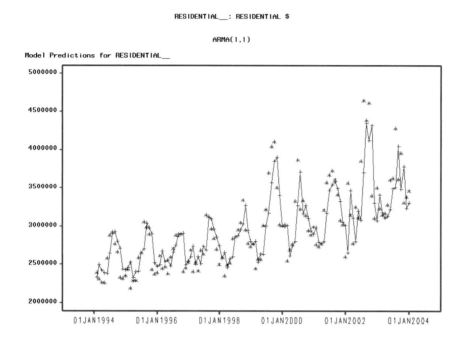

Figure 9.6 illustrates the ARIMA(10,0,5) model. Again, it is more regular compared to the ARIMA(1,0,1) model.

Figure 9.6 ARIMA(10,0,5) Model

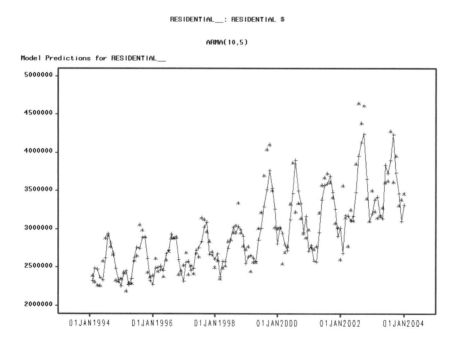

Figure 9.7 illustrates the ARIMA(1,1,1) model, which includes the addition of the trend.

Figure 9.7 ARIMA (1,1,1) Model

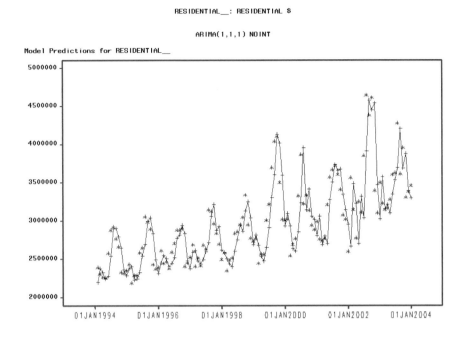

Figure 9.8 adds a seasonality component to the ARIMA (5,1,1) x (1,0,0) model.

Figure 9.8 ARIMA(5,1,1) x (1,0,0)

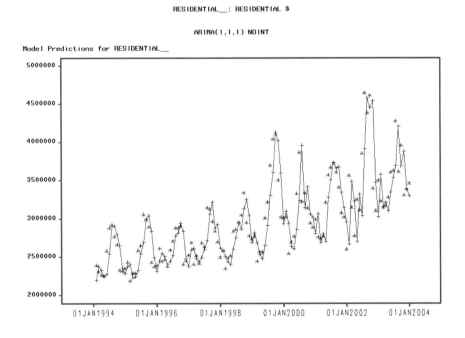

These two graphs appear to be very similar. When this occurs, choose the simpler model.

Figure 9.9 adds a log transformation to the ARIMA(1,1,1)x(1,0,0) model.

Figure 9.9 Log Transformation

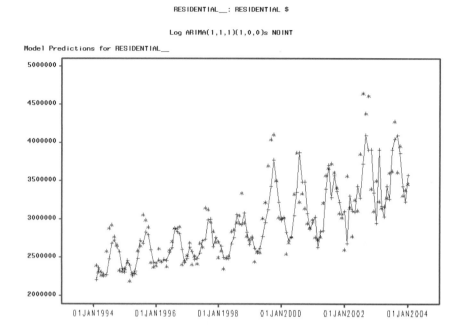

The log transformation does not account for as many outliers as does the ARIMA(5,1,1)x(1,0,0) model. Do not use the log because the model appears to be a poorer fit.

The two models that use multiplicative seasonal adjustment deal with seasonality explicitly (i.e., seasonal indices are broken out as an explicit part of the model). The ARIMA models deal with seasonality implicitly—you can't easily see from the ARIMA output how, for example, the average December differs from the average July. If isolating the seasonal pattern is important, this might be a factor in choosing among models. Once they have been initialized, the ARIMA models have the advantage because they have fewer moving parts than the exponential smoothing and adjustment models.

The optimal method for this time series as chosen by the Time Series Forecasting System (available in SAS/ETS software) uses Winter's method, which adds a smoothing component to the trend and seasonality components. This model is shown in Figure 9.10.

Figure 9.10 Winter's Method

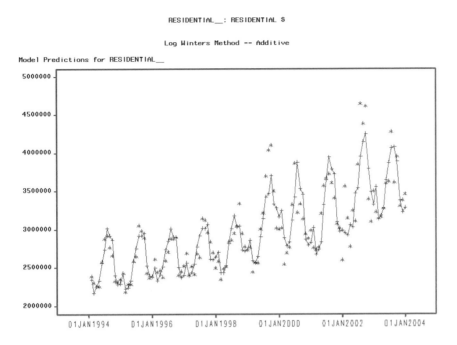

The optimal model is chosen based on the autocorrelations and the residuals.

9.3 Using High-Performance Forecasting

The HPF procedure, a relatively new procedure, is used with SAS Enterprise Miner software. Not only can it define predictions, the procedure can choose the optimal estimator. This section gives a brief introduction to PROC HPF. It is not intended to be a complete discussion of high-performance forecasting. Consult the appropriate SAS documentation for more information. To use PROC HPF, add a SAS Code node to the input data node (Figure 9.11).

Figure 9.11 Adding a SAS Code Node

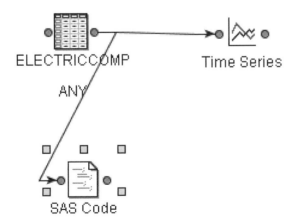

When the SAS Code node is highlighted, there is an entry in the left-hand menu for **SAS code**. Click on that menu item; then the Code window pops up. You can then enter SAS code (Display 9.3).

Display 9.3 SAS Code Node Entry

```
libname sasuser "C:\Documents and Settings\Author\My
Documents\My SAS Files\9.1";
run;
proc hpf data=sasuser.electriccompany out=sasuser.hpfoutput;
id date interval=month;
forecast _all_;
run;
```

Automatically adding the LIBNAME statement allows files to be written to the **sasuser** directory from SAS Enterprise Miner 5.2. The prediction is stored in the Hpfoutput data set. The _ALL_ option forecasts all variables in the list, excluding the date. PROC HPF returns all data in the Electriccompany data set while adding 12 months of predictions. To examine the predictions, use the **Explore** button and the Graph Wizard on the output data set, as discussed in Chapter 1. First, however, this data set must be added using Create Data Source. Once it is added, use StatExplore and the scatterplot with a line plot. We can define a WHERE clause to limit the values in the data set that are written on the graph (Display 9.4). In this example, the predicted values are highlighted.

Display 9.4 Highlighted Values

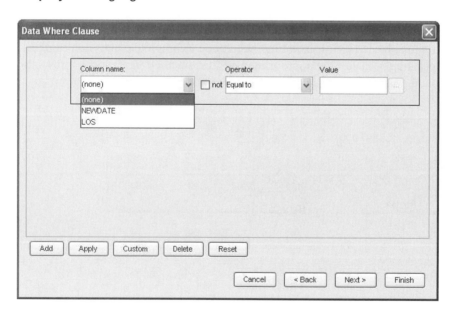

Output 9.5 contains the results. Residential usage appears to maintain a seasonal pattern in the prediction.

Output 9.5 Forecast for Residential Usage

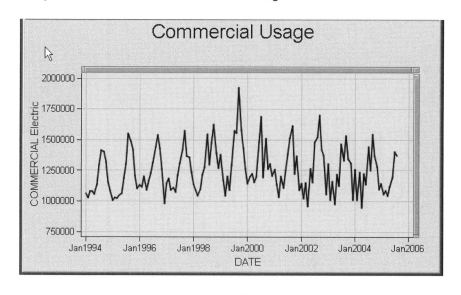

Output 9.6 and 9.7 forecast commercial and industrial usage. Commercial usage also appears to have a seasonal pattern.

Output 9.6 Forecast for Commercial Usage

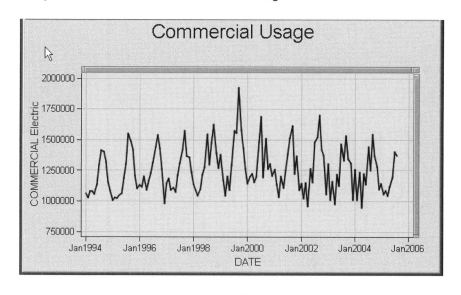

Industrial usage is predicted to have a linear decrease in the future, probably due to a decreasing manufacturing base. It is not seasonal.

Output 9.7 Forecast for Industrial Usage

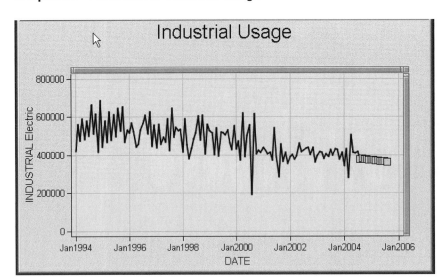

Output 9.8 and 9.9 forecast total electric usage and total sale of electricity. Total usage has a seasonal pattern as well.

Output 9.8 Total Electric Usage

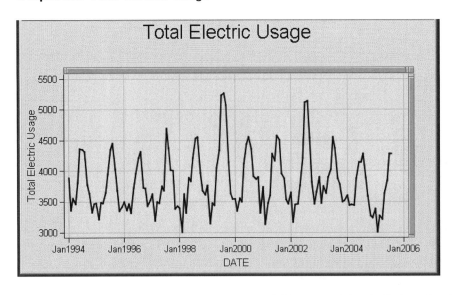

The total sale of electricity is seasonal. It could be argued that inflation should be considered, but a moving average, if needed, can easily account for the seasonality.

Output 9.9 Total Sale of Electricity

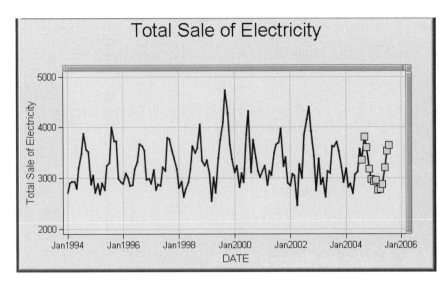

To change the amount of time predicted from the default of 12, modify the code slightly to add a LEAD= option where the number of forecast steps is predicted, as follows:

```
proc hpf data=sasuser.electriccompany out=sasuser.hpfoutput lead=18;
   id date interval=month;
   forecast _all_;
run;
```

There are a number of options for the interval values in the ID statement (Table 9.2).

Table 9.2 Interval Options

Intervals	Options
Months	Year, Semiyear, Qtr, Month, Semimonth
Weeks	Ten-day, Week, Weekday
Days	Day, Hour, Minute, Second

There are also different options for output data sets. In particular, OUTSUM=*dataset* contains the summary statistics and the forecast summation. Similarly, OUTSTAT=*dataset* contains the goodness-of-fit statistics to evaluate how well the model fits the series.

The FORECAST statement has a number of options as well. Adding a HOLDOUT option validates the forecast with fresh data, as follows:

```
proc hpf data=sasuser.electriccompany out=sasuser.hpfoutput lead=18;
   id date interval=month;
   forecast _all_/holdout=12;
run;
```

The HOLDOUT option is used only to select the best forecasting model. Then, the full time series is used for model fitting. Another important option is the ACCUMULATE option:

```
proc hpf data=sasuser.electriccompany out=sasuser.hpfoutput lead=18;
   id date interval=month accumulate=total;
   forecast _all_ ;
run;
```

The ACCUMULATE=**total** option sums all values within a month's time (using the INTERVAL option). Use this option to change the time series model from months to years by substituting the following code:

```
id date interval=year accumulate=total;
```

You can substitute the ACCUMULATE=**average** option to find average values; **total** gives sums.

9.4 Working with Transactional Data

The example in Section 9.3 has values at fixed time points; not all data are recorded in such fixed time. *Transactional data* are data collected with no fixed time points, such as customer arrival time and customer service time. The time to product failure can be at fixed time points if data are collected periodically or at random time points if the actual failure time is recorded. Data collected online often have an accompanying time stamp to record the time of data entry. Any use of these time stamps is transactional.

To examine transactional data, first collect them into fixed time units. Use the ACCUMULATE= option when the data are not entered at fixed time points. Consider the Time_Series_Example data set. In this example, customers enter into a queue for service. The total waiting time plus the time required to provide service is identified as length of service (LOS). The employee providing service is also recorded, and the time at which the customer entered the queue is provided as a day and time field. To use PROC HPF, you must first sort the data by time (Display 9.5). This code accumulates customer service times into a daily log, fixing the time interval at each 24-hour day.

Display 9.5 HPF Code for Transactional Data

```
proc sort data=time_series_example;
by newdate;
proc hpf data=time_series_example out=sasuser.outhpftransactionbyhour;
id newdate interval=hour accumulate=total;
forecast los;
run;
```

The first few values of the data set are pictured in Display 9.6, with the time modifications and the forecast depicted in Display 9.7.

Display 9.6 Original Transactional Data

Obs #	Customer S...	LOS	NEWDATE
1	SE	217	01Jul04:00:22
2	SE	371	01Jul04:00:36
3	SE	209	01Jul04:00:46
4	SE	409	01Jul04:00:57
5	SE	1190	01Jul04:00:59
6	SE	223	01Jul04:01:19
7	SE	855	01Jul04:01:34
8	SE	364	01Jul04:01:52
9	HS	493	01Jul04:02:05
10	SE	331	01Jul04:02:17
11	HS	347	01Jul04:03:14
12	SE	964	01Jul04:03:34
13	SE	361	01Jul04:04:04
14	SE	400	01Jul04:04:37
15	SE	490	01Jul04:05:53
16	HS	204	01Jul04:06:52
17	HS	225	01Jul04:07:22
18	HS	522	01Jul04:07:46

The time values here are at scattered, almost random times. The times (and dates) are collected by computer time stamp as soon as the customer enters the queue.

Display 9.7 Modified Time Points

Obs #	NEWDATE	LOS
1	01Jul2004	30919
2	02Jul2004	20056
3	03Jul2004	17057
4	04Jul2004	11981
5	05Jul2004	23613
6	06Jul2004	24450
7	07Jul2004	30432
8	08Jul2004	21478
9	09Jul2004	27497
10	10Jul2004	18559
11	11Jul2004	24768
12	12Jul2004	31782
13	13Jul2004	19752
14	14Jul2004	21380
15	15Jul2004	31729
16	16Jul2004	26656
17	17Jul2004	26172
18	18Jul2004	19197

Note that NEWDATE includes only days (for example, 01Jul2004) instead of times within the days. The time series graph (generated using the **Explore** button) appears in Output 9.10.

You could also collect the average LOS by slightly modifying the code in Display 9.5 with a different accumulation interval.

Output 9.10 Time Series by Day

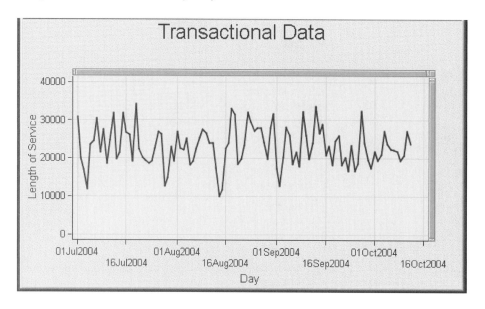

To collect the data on an hourly basis, modify the ID statement as follows:

```
id newdate interval=hour accumulate=total;
```

Output 9.11 shows the results. The graph is difficult to read and too crowded to be meaningful. To make it meaningful, you want to graph only a portion of the scale.

Output 9.11 Time Series by Day

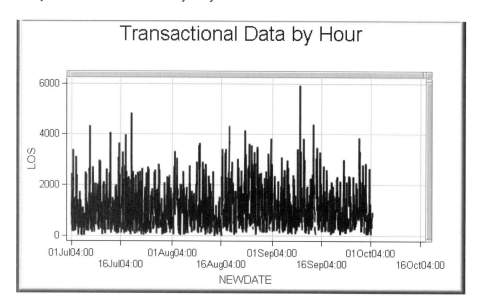

SAS Enterprise Miner 5.2 offers the ability to reduce the graph to a smaller subset (Display 9.8) when you are creating scatterplots. You identify the variable in the pull-down menu, as well as any WHERE clause restrictions. Output 9.12 shows the resulting graph.

Display 9.8 Graphing a Subset of the Data

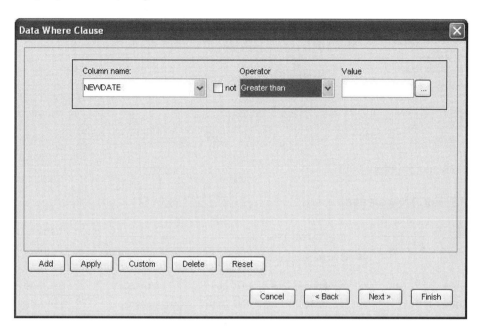

Output 9.12 Graph of Reduced Data Set

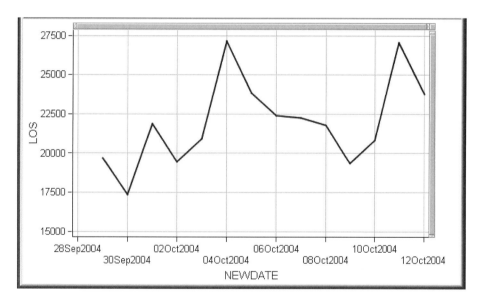

Using the following code to extract the hour from the time series:

```
data sasuser.newtimeseries;
   set sasuser.time_series_example;
   hour=hour(newdate);
run;
```

With this information, it is possible to look at the average values over the course of a 24-hour day:

```
proc means data=sasuser.newtimeseries n mean std min max;
   var LOS;
   class HOUR;
   output out=sasuser.hourlyaverage
          MEAN =
          / autoname;
   attrib _all_ label='';
run;
```

The result appears in Output 9.13.

Output 9.13 Hourly Averages

The MEANS Procedure

Analysis Variable : LOS

hour	N Obs	N	Mean	Std Dev	Minimum	Maximum
0	216	216	295.2638889	191.7943419	37.0000000	1190.00
1	176	176	268.8295455	158.2491144	39.0000000	915.0000000
2	117	117	299.8547009	168.6052452	42.0000000	795.0000000
3	138	138	302.5724638	201.9662792	42.0000000	964.0000000
4	119	119	301.1344538	186.2934592	19.0000000	955.0000000
5	108	108	289.9074074	189.5528204	17.0000000	1098.00
6	129	129	329.8217054	207.9158277	50.0000000	1228.00
7	163	163	325.1901840	179.3000641	39.0000000	1065.00
8	249	249	300.4457831	162.2091133	57.0000000	949.0000000
9	299	299	340.8929766	191.4231633	46.0000000	1192.00
10	370	370	343.1027027	179.7788471	25.0000000	1467.00
11	383	383	345.5143603	180.4529327	48.0000000	1754.00
12	399	399	365.1654135	182.7970776	48.0000000	1310.00
13	406	406	336.9655172	159.1141489	20.0000000	1146.00
14	389	389	336.4293059	145.3649274	36.0000000	789.0000000
15	407	407	339.5307125	182.6258212	27.0000000	1639.00
16	333	333	335.2672673	179.1966781	35.0000000	1329.00
17	336	336	343.4851190	197.7376969	17.0000000	1468.00
18	290	290	291.6793103	143.9887920	13.0000000	989.0000000
19	335	335	309.8179104	170.9751172	50.0000000	1282.00
20	355	355	304.7605634	172.0762596	32.0000000	1105.00
21	309	309	308.6181230	200.3016308	36.0000000	1293.00
22	296	296	318.8108108	189.4315440	32.0000000	1348.00
23	244	244	294.1680328	184.4520760	29.0000000	1078.00

Note that the average length of service tends to increase during the day, reaching a peak about 12 noon. A line graph of the hourly values tends to reinforce that prediction (Output 9.14). Alternatively, you could code PROC HPF by specifying the ID statement with the following options: NEWDATE, INTERVAL=**hour,** and ACCUMULATE=**average**.

Output 9.14 Line Graph of Hourly Averages

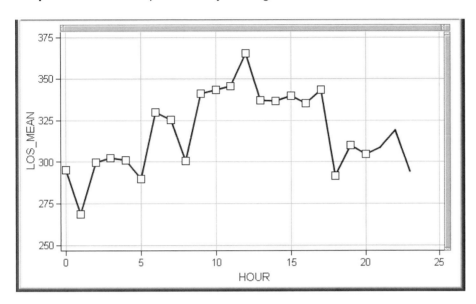

According to the graph, it takes longer to serve customers from about 9 a.m. to 5 p.m. By adding code to examine the number of customer arrivals each hour, you can determine if the excess service time is due to increased customers. Then you can recompute the average:

```
data sasuser.numberofarrivals;
   length  Server $ 16  Arrival 8  LOS 8  newdate 8  hour 8;
   set sasuser.newtimeseries;
        Arrival=1;
run;
```

In this case, you want to know the sum of arrivals each hour:

```
proc hpf data=sasuser.newtimeseries out=sasuser.hpfnumberofarrivals;
   id newdate interval=hour accumulate=total;
   forecast arrival;
run;

data sasuser.arrivalsbyhour;
   set sasuser.hpfnumberofarrivals;
   hour=hour(newdate);
run;
```

Then you can submit the following code:

```
proc means data=sasuser.arrivalsbyhour n mean std min max;
   var ARRIVAL;
   class HOUR;
   output out=sasuser.totalnumberofarrivals
          MEAN =
          / autoname;
   attrib _all_ label='';
run;
```

Output 9.15 shows the results.

Output 9.15 Number of Customer Arrivals by Hour

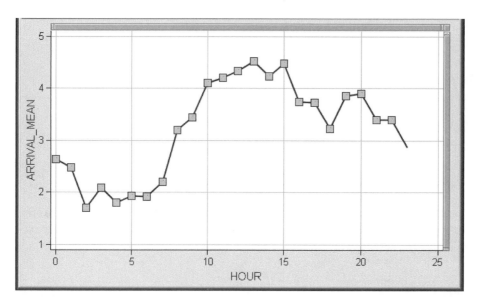

It appears that the increased service time is directly related to an increased number of customer arrivals. Thus, you can conclude that more personnel are needed at the peak hours between 9 a.m. and 5 p.m. to optimize customer service.

An alternate coding to achieve the same result follows:

```
proc hpf;
   id newdate interval=hour accumulate=nobs;
   forecast all;
run;
```

The **NOBS** value of the ACCUMULATE= option counts the number of arrivals in the specified time interval. Table 9.3 lists other values for the ACCUMULATE= option.

Table 9.3 ACCUMULATE= Option Values

Value	Result
None	No accumulation occurs; the time values must be equally spaced.
Total	Total sum of values in the interval.
Average	Average of all values within the given time interval.
Minimum	Minimum time value within the time interval.
Median	Median time value within the time interval.
Maximum	Largest time value within the time interval.
N	Number of nonmissing observations in the time interval.
NMISS	Number of missing observations in the time interval.
NOBS	Total number of observations within the given time interval.
First	First value within the time interval.
Last	Last value within the time interval.
STDDEV	Standard deviation of all values within the time interval.
CSS	Corrected sum of squares of all values within the time interval.
USS	Uncorrected sum of squares of all values within the time interval.

If you need to use a dynamic regressor along with the time series, add the following code:

```
proc hpf data=sasuser.time_series_with_regressors;
   out=sasuser.hpfwithregressors;
   id defineddate interval=hour;
   forecast _all_;
run;

proc autoreg data=sasuser.hpfwithregressors;
   model los=number_of_customers cumulative_entry_by_day
   cumulative_completion_by_day;
   output out=sasuser.losdynamic p=predicted;
run;
```

In this example, the initial time series analyzed deals with one shop service stall where problems are evaluated, minor problems fixed, and major problems transferred to another section of the shop. If the other section is full, then the items must wait until they can be moved. The total time in the initial service stall, then, also depends on the status of the rest of the shop.

The first step is to forecast all series in the data set using PROC HPF.

The next step is to run the AUTOREG procedure, which allows the development of a model (Output 9.16).

Output 9.16 PROC AUTOREG Results

```
                        The AUTOREG Procedure

                    Dependent Variable      LOS
                                            LOS


                    Ordinary Least Squares Estimates

        SSE             81845553.9    DFE                      559
        MSE                 146414    Root MSE           382.64112
        SBC             8315.47545    AIC                8298.14233
        Regress R-Square    0.7351    Total R-Square        0.7351
        Durbin-Watson       1.3314


                                      Standard           Approx
Variable                    DF   Estimate    Error  t Value  Pr > |t|  Variable La

Intercept                    1  -106.9042  37.4294    -2.86    0.0044
Number_of_Customers          1   355.4167   9.3650    37.95   <.0001   Number of V
Cumulative_Entry_by_Day      1     0.6167   1.0992     0.56    0.5750  Cumulative
Cumulative_Completion_by_Day 1    -1.2455   0.9357    -1.33    0.1837  Cumulative
```

The number of visits is statistically significant, but the cumulative values are not. Output 9.17 compares the predicted length of service values to the actual length of service values.

Output 9.17 Predicted Values versus Actual Values

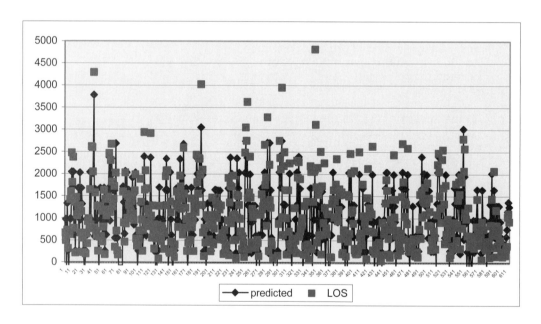

Even if you use dynamic regressors, extreme outliers will not be included in the model.

9.5 Exercises

1. Convert the monthly electricity usage information to yearly and forecast 10 years ahead.

2. Write a summary of your results.

Written Presentations

10.1 Introduction to Technical Reports

Technical reports communicate your results. When you write technical reports, use clear, concise English that avoids jargon as much as possible. Do not assume that your reader is familiar with the topic or the statistical methodology you used. Keep papers as brief as possible, but ensure that everything important is adequately covered. Have a friend or colleague read the paper and revise it for clarity as appropriate.

Technical papers or reports are self-contained reports that communicate to readers the purpose of your experiment as well as its conclusions. Include all pertinent project information. Do not include attachments or references to other papers unless they justify or offer evidence that supports your conclusions. Never refer to statistical output that is not discussed in detail. All the information needed to understand the statistical output should be contained within the technical paper itself.

Although technical reports should be objective and carefully report actual results, they generally have a point of view that is indicated by the summary of those results. In effect, the data that are analyzed tell a story, and it is up to the writer to determine just what that story is through the data mining process. Then, the writer must tell the story so that the reader accepts the conclusion as plausible. Therefore, the paper's narrative should lead the reader to the same conclusion.

Another consideration is the use of color versus black and white. In the end, color more clearly demonstrates data outcomes. However, many publications are printed in black and white. Therefore, the graphics should reflect the needs of the final publication medium. Fortunately, more publications are shifting to color. SAS Enterprise Miner graphics are designed for color. Note that although this book is not printed in color, a CD has been included with a full-color version of this book.

Technical reports generally have a standard format that uses the following sections. Each section provides a standard type of information:

- Abstract
- Introduction
- Method
- Results
- Discussion/Conclusion
- References

Insert a title page before the body of the report. Choose a descriptive statement for the title to help the reader determine whether to read further. The title page should also contain the name of the investigator and any co-investigators. Place the abstract on the second page. The abstract should concisely state the purpose of the paper and briefly summarize the results. Divide the abstract into four components: objective, method, results, and conclusion. Include a sentence or two for each component.

Caution: Spelling and punctuation errors greatly reduce the reader's ability to comprehend your writing. Use all of the tools available, including word processor spelling and grammar checkers, to ensure that you catch these errors. As helpful as they are, spell checkers still cannot distinguish among to, too, and two. Therefore, proofreading is absolutely necessary, both by you and by another person who is not familiar with the work. If the second reader is confused, the writing needs to be improved.

Even with proofreading, errors happen. You should take all precautions to avoid them while recognizing that errors may still be in the manuscript. The intent, then, is to minimize errors as much as possible through the proofreading process.

10.2 Abstract

If your technical report will be reviewed internally only, you do not need to provide an abstract. However, for any other paper, an abstract is required. Keep the abstract brief—approximately 250 words—unless shortening it makes it incomprehensible to a general audience. Reserve specific details for the body of the paper. Some journals have word limits on the abstract, and they should be respected. Other journals have specific formatting requirements for the abstract. Consider some examples of abstracts taken from the SAS Users Group International (SUGI) proceedings (re-named SAS Global Forum for 2007; see http://support.sas.com/events/ sasglobalforum/previous/index.html. The word limit here is 200 words.

Deng and Liu (111-27) have written the following abstract:

> According to the example of Baosteel production, this paper introduces the way of using data mining technology-SAS/EM to discover the rules that we don't know before and it can improve the quality of products and decrease the cost.

This abstract is very brief (38 words). It contains the word *Baosteel*, an unfamiliar term to a general audience. It would have been better to provide a longer, more general abstract that avoids unfamiliar terminology.

Another example is given by Kallukaran and Kagan (127-24):

> IMS Health is the principal source of information used in marketing and sales management by health care organizations through the United States. Of the various potential applications of neural networks, pattern recognition is considered one of major importance. This paper presents the results of using neural networks to classify time-series data into several trend pattern classifications [e.g., Increasing Trend, Decreasing Trend, Shift Up, Shift Down, Spike Up, Spike Down, and No Pattern], and the information generated from the classifier is used to detect various marketing related phenomena [e.g., Brand Switching, Brand Loyalty, and Product Trends].
>
> The data used for the test consisted of prescription data for 12 months, for 600,000 prescribers writing four drugs in the Anti-ulcer market. Using the neural network classifier and brand switching algorithm, the system was able to detect 2500 prescribers who were changing their prescribing behavior. The model is a promising formula for analyzing times-series information from extremely large databases, and presenting the user with only information relevant for decision making. This data-mining system, designed as part of the IMS Xplorer® product, uses SAS® System components for data retrieval, data preparation, graphical user interface, and data visualization. The IMS Xplorer product is a sales and marketing decision support system based on commercially-available client-server technology created for pharmaceutical companies in their effort to fully utilize the mission critical information found in the Xplorer data warehouse.

At 229 words, this is a much longer abstract. It provides more information about the content of the paper, including a brief introduction of the purpose and methods and some details on the results. Moving the IMS Xplorer information to the body of the paper would reduce the word count to under the 200-word limit and keep the level of detail in the abstract broad enough to attract a more general audience.

Consider this abstract by Dymond (259-24):

> A data mining case study is presented illustrating exploration for hidden inpatient subpopulations. Some of the major characteristics of data mining and their relation to business goals are reviewed.
>
> Six subpopulations are tentatively identified. Two subpopulations correspond to mental illness and alcohol/drug abuse. Four other subpopulations reflect medical and surgical diseases, segregated along lines of major diagnostic category, age, numbers of other diagnoses, and income.

Some suggestions are presented for using cluster analysis to find potential hidden groups, and for the interpretation and validation of these groups using visualization and discriminant analysis techniques.

This abstract contains 92 words and 3 paragraphs. The first paragraph could be expanded to further detail the techniques used. Or, better yet, the third paragraph could be moved to the end of the first. Brief results are given in the second paragraph, which could then be moved to the end of the abstract.

In another example, consider Fedenczuk (123-28):

> During a waterflood, large amounts of injected water are used to maintain and/or increase oil production from a petroleum reservoir. This paper shows how comparing the changes in oil, gas, and water production (relative to the water injection changes) helps assess fluid communication through a reservoir. The results are presented with special diagrams and contour maps, which show up to six communication parameters.
>
> The communication parameters are integrated with other geological parameters and used to develop predictive models. These predictive models help estimate the production capacity or production probability in waterflooded reservoirs.
>
> This paper also shows how decision tree models support a two to four times more accurate selection of high production wells than historically implemented selections.
>
> Finally, this paper shows the implementation of a profit matrix in a decision process for outcome optimization.

The total word count for this abstract is 134. The last two paragraphs contain only one sentence each and should be combined. Note that the first paragraph contains a theme statement, "This paper shows… ." Such a statement directs the reader to the overall content of the paper and helps them decide whether to read it. As much as possible, include a theme statement in every abstract.

The next example demonstrates the required format provided by a journal:

> **Objectives:** To investigate the relationship between heparin dose and patient outcome. To demonstrate the effectiveness of data mining to investigate variation in physician practice.
>
> **Methods:** The pharmacy database containing information about heparin dose prior to angioplasty was merged with a clinical database containing information about patient weight and length of stay. The data were analyzed using data mining and kernel density estimation.
>
> **Results:** Cardiologists practice different methods for administering heparin doses. This variability has impact on patient length-of-stay. Patients receiving greater than 80 mg/kg stay longer than patients receiving less ($p<0.0001$). This is independent of the number of vessels treated during angioplasty.
>
> **Conclusions:** Data mining is an effective tool that can be used to exploit the pharmacy database for research into physician practice.

The format requires the author to provide the necessary statements that should be in any abstract: objectives, methods, results, and conclusions.

10.3 Introduction

The introduction is an expanded summary of the purpose of the paper. It should also contain a summary of the study's conclusions. A good technical report always begins at the end. Normally, the introduction is no longer than a page, but it should be long enough to give the reader a complete idea of what the rest of the paper contains.

Deng and Liu (111-27) define the term *Baosteel* in the introduction, not in their abstract:

> Over a long period, Baosteel adopted the chemistry design of 'high manganese and low carbon' to produce the hot rolling plate used by welding pipe which steel grade is SP. In recent years as we communicated with other corporations, we found that the content of manganese of the same steel grade of other corporations is lower than ours, but its mechanical property is better than ours. The discovery attracted our attention. So we started to study the chemistry design and process of SP deeply.

Like the abstract, the introduction is short (84 words). However, the abbreviation SP is used twice without definition. Again, keep the introduction general, depending upon your knowledge of your audience.

Here is an introduction from Redlon (223-28):

> Market basket analysis is a common mathematical technique used by marketing professionals to reveal affinities between individual products or product groupings. Decision Intelligence, Inc. (DII) has prepared an open source SAS Market Basket Analysis Macro and made it available for download at www.dii-online.com. The purpose of this paper is to run through data preparation, program execution and, in an effort to explain the results, one potentially valuable application.

The introduction is short (68 words). A thematic statement is clearly identified by the beginning of the sentence, "The purpose of this paper... ." However, the statement could be improved by adding the following ending: "…to demonstrate the use of this market basket macro." The abstract is an expanded version of the introduction, so it would be better to reverse the two because the introduction usually expands upon the abstract.

A more expanded introduction is provided by Rinkus and Skee (164-24):

> In the credit card industry, many of our prospects are solicited via 'preapproved' offers. These offers are extended based on a priori knowledge of creditworthiness and financial behavior derived from an analysis of data obtained from a credit bureau. However, some credit card issuers also buy prospect names through list brokers. Since there is little or no credit or financial behavior data on these prospects, they do not receive a preapproved offer.

> List brokers are an important source for prospect names that have demonstrated some interest or behavior which can be tied into a marketing campaign. For example, subscribers to selected travel magazines may receive card offers featuring the opportunity to accumulate frequent flier miles based on card usage. Or, supporters of an environmental cause may have the opportunity to receive a credit card which will generate a donation to that cause based on card usage.

> Direct mail marketing campaigns typically include deliberate testing of random samples of names from many list courses. Analyses identify the best performing lists and categories of lists, and this knowledge drives business decisions effecting subsequent campaigns.

The word count is 182 words. The introduction defines the problem well; however, there is no clear statement of the purpose of the paper nor a brief summary of the problem. The reader does not know the value of the paper because of the missing content. In addition, a spelling error should be corrected prior to submission (*effect*=noun, *affect*=verb).

Sarma (250-26) provides a clear statement of purpose:

> This paper shows how to use SAS Enterprise Miner™ to develop forecasting models. As an illustration, a model is presented to forecast the entire current quarter's Gross Domestic Product (GDP) based on monthly indicators available during only the first half of the quarter.
>
> The paper shows, step-by-step, how to set up a forecasting project, use different nodes of the SAS Enterprise Miner™ to train and validate the models, and display the results. SAS Enterprise Miner™ consists of a number of nodes for data cleaning, exploratory analysis, model development and validation, scoring and forecasting. Only a few of these nodes are used in this project. In particular, the focus here is the Neural Network node. The Decision Tree node can also be used for exploratory data analysis and modeling, but it is not included in the discussion due to space limitation. It is hoped that the material presented here serves as an introduction to the SAS Enterprise Miner™. The methodology can easily be extended to other applications such as predicting response to direct mail in marketing, forecasting, potential losses of prospective credit card customers, etc.

This introduction contains 184 words. The first paragraph identifies the theme and purpose of the paper. The second paragraph introduces the capabilities of SAS Enterprise Miner software. Most of the material should be moved to the background section of the paper and results added instead. Note the use of the ™ symbol to designate a trademarked product. However, the trademark should be used only once.

Consider Karp (255-25):

> Logistic Regression is an increasingly popular analytic tool. Used to predict the probability that the 'event of interest' will occur as a linear function of one (or more) continuous and/or dichotomous independent variables, this technique is implemented in the SAS® System in PROC LOGISTIC. This paper gives an overview of how some common forms of logistic regression models can be implemented using PROC LOGISTIC as well as important changes and enhancements to the procedure in Releases 6.07 and above of the SAS® System.

Although short (84 words), this introduction has a statement of purpose. It does not describe the results because it is intended to show how to use a technique. One final example of an introduction follows:

> A hospital pharmacy database can be examined to find best practices in the absence of specific guidelines. The analysis presented in this paper concerns use of the drug, Heparin. Heparin is the drug of choice for maintaining therapeutic anticoagulation in patients prone to thrombosis, especially in the cardiac catheterization laboratory. Accuracy in heparin dosing is essential. Under-treatment can lead to life-threatening clot formation, whereas over-treatment can lead to hemorrhage. Unfortunately, there is tremendous variation between individuals in the heparin dose required to achieve therapeutic anticoagulation. The majority of current protocols are based on patient weight. Therefore, some patients are either below or above the target range after dosing. There is currently no reliable algorithm for predicting the optimal dosage for an individual.

Although many patients achieve rapid therapeutic anticoagulation, some do not, and, in that case, a second dose of Heparin is administered. In contrast, some patients receive too much heparin and incur bleeding complications. Recent studies have emphasized the importance of reducing heparin doses used for percutaneous coronary interventions, especially when combined with platelet inhibitors, to reduce bleeding complications.

Studies have shown that examinations of physician practices and variation can improve patient care while reducing costs. However, most of the studies rely more on physician consensus than on data analysis. The consensus is then examined in relationship to compliance rather than to compare practice to outcomes. There is also an issue of reliability of models. For this reason, the definition of quality has been reduced to a determination of compliance with guidelines. Unfortunately, not all practice habits have readily available guidelines. Therefore, data analysis must examine the relationship between physician practice and outcome using observational data.

 Practices in the Cath Lab are extremely variable. Heparin Doses range from 50 units/kg weight to 100 units. A second dose is routinely given by some cardiologists but not others. The purpose of this first study was to examine the relationship between Heparin dosing and patient outcomes. It was found that the Heparin dose can impact patient length of stay. Therefore, the development of a protocol specifying heparin dosing can lower costs.

This example is the longest introduction (349 words). The four paragraphs correspond to objective, method, results, and conclusion. Although the total size of the paper is often restricted, rarely is there a specific restriction on the introduction. As a general rule, introductions should be long enough to adequately describe the paper's content, but short enough to read quickly.

10.4 Method

This section explains the means of data collection. For a survey, the method of acquiring a valid random sample is important. Explain any measurement devices used and note if permission was needed to investigate files. Describe any difficulties encountered while collecting the data. For example, identify the nonresponse rate of a survey. If the nonresponse rate is significant, describe any efforts made to improve it. Consider a method section that discusses data collection problems:

It should be noted that there were a number of problems dealing with the establishment of the database. Patient record acquisition and translation were among the most daunting and immediate hurdles. For example, it took a week of time just to get a list of patient names. The only electronic list in existence was in the billing files. An attempt was made to narrow the list by diagnosis code, but it contained all patients for any problem for any physician working in the clinic. The foot ulcer patients comprised approximately 10% of the total list. There are multiple users of patient files and multiple locations required for each file. This made the acquisition of the files somewhat difficult. These difficulties clearly point out a need for an electronic database of patient information.

Other problems encountered and subsequently overcome within the patient files were gaps and inconsistencies. Sometimes missing information existed elsewhere and was found after diligent searching. In other cases, the information did not exist anywhere else. For example, there were times when one visit would conclude that the patient was doing fine; the next visit would mention that the amputation was healing with no intervening data concerning the need for or the scheduling of an amputation. There were surgical reports inserted in the patient records but they contained no information as to why an amputation was performed. Another hurdle had to do with language coding. It is helpful to the physician to be able to add comments, but these comments have to be coded in very standard language for the database. This is a standard problem in the area of medical informatics.

Many of these problems were expected, since patient records cover not only a variety of patient illnesses but are also available to many different physicians attending to sometimes very different aspects of a patient's condition. Another factor is the nature of the patients the clinic is concerned with; diabetic patients have many possible complications due to their underlying illness.

When problems are identified, solutions or potential solutions should also be identified:

Personnel within the clinic were extremely helpful in overcoming the patient record acquisition problems, but three weeks were still required to get into a routine process that was acceptable to everyone.

The data gaps encountered from time to time were generally one of two types: incomplete or omitted. The incomplete data could usually be found within post-operative notes or subsequent records; there was no recovery possible for the omitted data.

Translation of records into a form suitable for the database was a task that could only be tackled by developing a working knowledge of the necessary medical terms and the physicians' shorthand for that terminology. Again, the clinic personnel proved to be invaluable in regards to this task. Also aiding in this pursuit were the forms that were used on newer patients; these forms narrowed the doctors' responses, and were very helpful with the transition from chart notes to database entries.

The language coding problem was not as enormous a problem as expected, due in large part to the preprinted forms that some of the newer patient files contained; they indicated what was considered essential information on patient condition, and helped structure the language. The development of paper forms is an essential initial step in the development of electronic patient files.

The following example provides a methods section:

In the year 2000, a protocol for insulin/glucose treatment was initiated for all patients undergoing CABG surgery who had a fasting glucose blood sugar level greater than 126. The primary purpose of the protocol was to reduce infection rates in patients with diabetes, including those who were not previously diagnosed as diabetic. The protocol required blood glucose testing every hour before and after surgery, and every 30 minutes during surgery.

For a 4-month period, 223 patient records were examined retrospectively. The compliance levels with the protocol were ranked as follows:

1 = On protocol / Compliant

2 = Partial compliance: Ins. drip initiated with monitoring & some adjustments made BUT timing was not correct and protocol was not exactly followed &/or not aggressive enough to decrease blood glucose and bolus was not given.

3 = Not Compliant: Did nothing, no glucose records during surgery, skipped more than 2 hrs without glucose readings done during OR. Did Insulin bolus only and no drip started.

The emphasis here is on the method of data collection and on the variable definitions. It does not discuss data analysis methods. You can omit specific techniques if they are fairly descriptive and routine and scattered throughout the results section. A second example of method description follows:

To examine the usage of electricity for the past ten years with the data collected on a monthly basis, ARIMA time series models were used. Because electricity usage tends to be seasonable, we used a seasonable ARIMA model. A dynamic regressor was included in the model to measure monthly weather patterns since it is assumed that the amount of electricity consumed is dependent upon weather temperatures.

A third example follows. This example discusses the specific statistical method used because it is somewhat unusual. Depending on the audience, the definition of an ARIMA model can be expanded. For a general audience, focus on a nontechnical, informative discussion of the models. For a more technical audience, the actual ARIMA equations can be given.

To demonstrate just how variable the term "often" can be, the criteria for the diagnosis of ADHD were provided to a sample of students. Collective gathering points were chosen at various times of day to ensure a representative sample of students. As given in the appendix, the students were asked to give a value on a sliding scale from 0 to 100, and to give a verbal description of each phrase. Consider the distribution of three of the questions:

1. Often has difficulty sustaining attention in tasks _____ times each ¤ day ¤ week ¤ month.

2. Is often easily distracted _____ times each ¤ day ¤ week ¤ month.

3. Often fidgets and moves around _____ times each ¤ day ¤ week ¤ month.

A graph of the three distributions of continuous responses (asked as a percent of time) demonstrates relative consistency across questions while showing considerable variability across respondents (Figures 1, 2, 3). However, the discrete responses were not so consistent, but were equally variable. Each response was standardized to the number of times in a month the respondent suggests an activity needs to occur for it to happen "often." In the responses there is a higher standard for question 1; that is, that action has to occur more times per month than for question 2. There is a higher threshold still for question 3.

Figures 1, 2, 3 give the general distribution for questions 1, 2, 3.

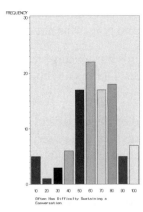

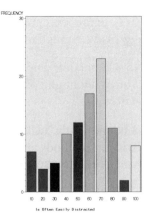

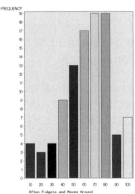

Cronbach's Alpha for the questions concerning the diagnosis of ADHD had a score of 0.68. Factor analysis via the varimax rotation identified only two factors. All but question 25 were contained in factor 1; question 25 was the only response loaded in factor 2. Question 4 also did not correlate with the total:

4. Often interrupts a conversation _____ times each ¤ day ¤ week ¤ month.

The figure shows considerable discrepancy with the other discrete responses, particularly question 3. This gives a strong indication of the variability in responses. Therefore, it becomes highly possible that any defining threshold value to define ADHD will include many false positives simply because of the different individual threshold values within the general population. Cronbach's Alpha for the continuous responses was much higher, at 0.955. A factor analysis on the continuous responses only identified one factor. It is clear from this analysis that individual respondents are consistent with themselves in their view of "often" but can vary considerably from respondent to respondent.

This example carefully documents the statistical methods used in the analysis. Although including figures in a methods section is unusual, you can do it as long as the need for the graphics is justified. Otherwise, graphics are generally confined to the results section. This example combines some features of the methods and results section. Use this format if the intended journal allows it. This format is also acceptable for a white paper intended for internal review only.

Cronbach's alpha is not defined in this section. It is assumed that the audience understands the concept. If that is not the case, explain it.

10.5 Results

It is important to summarize the main conclusions of the paper. Tell the reader exactly what was demonstrated in the analyses of the previous section. Indicate how the objective was satisfied. The statistical analysis must prove or disprove the hypotheses. It must also be convincing to the audience. Graphs, when reinforced by statistical analysis, tend to be convincing. Again, match the level of sophistication in the document with the intended audience.

When using data mining, a somewhat nontraditional technique, include the more expected, traditional statistical methods and explain why data mining provided superior results.

10.5.1 Data Summary

The data summary is critical to the paper and should *never* be omitted. It is essential to give the reader a visual representation of the data. Although a summary never constitutes proof, it can convince the reader of the reasonableness of your analysis. Use graphs for continuous data and tables for categorical data. Use a variety of different types of displays. You can combine this section with the data analysis section if this works better for the content of the paper.

Define and describe every variable collected in the data summary. For a survey, list the questions along with the percentage of each response. Never list the raw data. Graphs can be exported in TIF or JPEG format and inserted into a word processing document for integration in the report. Graphs can be exported in PS format for direct printing. Explain every graph and table used.

10.5.2 Data Analysis

Briefly outline the type of analysis used and provide a justification of your choice of method. Ensure that this section is complete. Discuss your assumptions and their validity. Describe the performance of any validity tests of the assumptions.

Briefly summarize the analysis. *Never* depend on computer output as a substitute for explanation. *Never* refer to computer output in the body of the paper. Use the cut-and-paste tools of your word processor. Ensure that any information in the analysis is self-contained.

Include all computer output required to satisfy the objective of the paper. Explain all parts of the computer output included in the paper. Do not assume that the reader understands the output. Explain each analysis as presented. Do not list a series of analyses and then summarize them collectively at the end. Develop your analyses linearly so that the reader can easily follow the logic.

Data analysis and summary sections can be combined and integrated into the results section.

10.5.3 Examples of Results

The results for the next example relate to the first example in Section 10.4 on staff compliance with an insulin protocol:

> The glucose data contained a ranking of protocol compliance. Using this ranking for only protocol patients (defined with fasting glucose value of 126 or better), an analysis was performed to determine the relationship between glucose level, compliance level, and infection rate. Table 1 indicates this relationship (p=0.0008).

Table 1 Number of Patients at Full, Partial, and No Compliance to Protocol by Infection Rates

Compliance Level	Non-Infection	Infection
Full Compliance	49 (94%)	3 (6%)
Partial Compliance	97 (92%)	9 (8%)
No Compliance	48 (74%)	17 (26%)

> There is a statistically significant increase in the infection rate as the compliance level decreases. Figure 1 demonstrates that the maximum glucose level remains within a narrow range from 180 to 280 for full compliance. However, for partial and no compliance, the maximum glucose level can range from 100 to over 300.

Figure 1 Comparison of Protocol Compliance Levels by Patient's Peak Glucose Levels

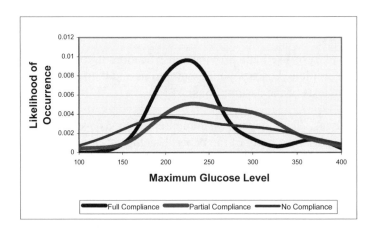

> Patients with no compliance were 13 times more likely to have an infection than the full compliance group; patients in the partial compliance group were 9 times as likely to have an infection. An examination of the partial compliance group demonstrates that infected patients are more likely to have higher maximum glucose levels. As noted in Figure 2, patients with infection are more likely to have a maximum value in the range between 220 and 279; patients without infection are more likely to have a peak level at 200.

Figure 2 Comparison of Protocol by Infection for No Compliance Group

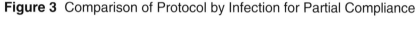

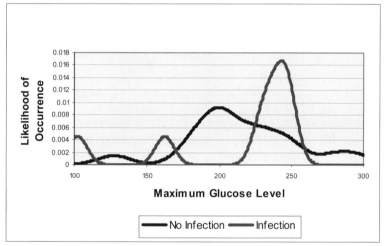

Virtually no patient with infection had a peak glucose level less than 200. With partial compliance, the differential in glucose level is also significant (p<0.0001, Figure 3).

Figure 3 Comparison of Protocol by Infection for Partial Compliance

In addition, data were compared for the same 4-month period when the protocol called for a 3-day insulin drip after surgery to the data from historical data in 1999 to determine whether the 3-day insulin drip resulted in a further reduction in infections compared to a 1-day insulin drip. Only patients with no compliance were compared (Figure 4) as patients with full compliance had virtually no infection rate (Table 2).

Figure 4 Comparison of 1-day and 3-day Protocols for Full Compliance

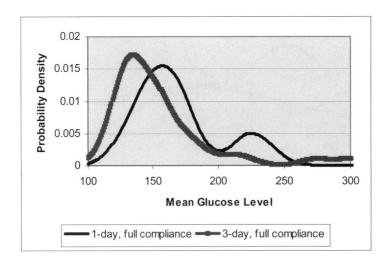

Table 2 Number of Patients with 3-day Insulin after Surgery Compared to 1-day Protocol

Protocol	Full Compliance	Partial Compliance	No Compliance
1-day	34 (16%)	15 (7%)	16 (8%)
3-day	33 (20%)	73 (44%)	36 (21%)

The more recent data have a lower overall level of compliance with the protocol. The result is statistically significant (p<0.0001, chi-square). Because of the small numbers of infection, Fisher's Exact Test was used to determine statistical differences between the two sets of data. Overall, the 1-day protocol had an infection rate of 9%; the 3-day protocol had a rate of 2% (p=0.0131). Restricting the data to the patients with full compliance to the protocol, the rates were 3% (1-day) and 6% (3-day) with a p-value of 0.6135. It should be noted that the small number of patients in this category yields insufficient power to declare that there is no difference in the rate. Similarly, there is insufficient power to compare the partial compliant patients (7%, 1-day; 0%, 3-day; p-value=0.1705). For patients with no compliance, the overall infection rate is high (25% 1-day; 14%, 3-day; p=0.4312).

With the 1-day protocol, there is a higher probability that the maximum glucose level will exceed 270 when compared to the 3-day protocol. With no compliance, the difference is a slight shift in mean glucose levels. There is a statistically significant increase in the infection rate as the compliance level decreases.

Kernel density estimation is still a fairly nonstandard technique. Therefore, this paper combines an examination using kernel density with the more standard analysis of variance. The graphs are carefully explained since they are unfamiliar to most readers.

10.6 Discussion/Conclusion

The final section of the paper should look ahead. Discuss the limitations of your study and describe further approaches that can build upon your work. Explain how your results can be applied. Discuss your work in a larger context.

Consider Aaron Lai (121-28):

> This is a preliminary study on the touch point interaction strategy. Just by knowing what kind of interactions are effective could provide the company an edge in promotion. The proposed analytical approach is easy to use and intuitive, future research could be done to understand why the prospect will behave in different situations.

Contrast the discussion with the introduction to the paper:

> Customer Relationship Management, or CRM, is an approach in improving the customer experience. The idea behind CRM is to provide a comprehensive strategy in customer solicitation, acquisition, retention and collection. It is particularly important to sales force automation (SFA). Many companies, such as Siebel and Oracle, have rushed to develop sophisticated software to help others achieve this goal. The most basic requirement for the system is to record every interaction between the customer or prospect and the company. Since the customer will have many interactions before a successful or a fail sale (e.g., not returning call), it would be useful to know how does the interaction affect the chance of outcome. Since the order of interaction will play a significant role in affecting the outcome (i.e., mail and then call will be different from call and then mail), it will be difficult to estimate the probability of success due to the fact that there are so many different kinds of interaction combinations. In this paper, I am going to propose a simple Bayesian prediction method that could tackle this problem.

This introduction focuses on CRM, yet the conclusion section never mentions the term. The discussion should indicate how the objective was met and summarize the results.

Consider Brocklebank, Lee, and Leonard (260-24):

> These examples demonstrate how Enterprise Miner™ will handle time series data sets with cross sections. The forecasting node in Enterprise Miner™ generates dummy variables and extends future observations for non-deterministic input variables for the purposes of forecasting. The forecasting node provides a predictive modeling mechanism based on linear regression models with autocorrelated errors or heteroscedastic errors. You can also perform several kinds of exponential smoothing techniques for a single time series. Finally, you can obtain predicted values and their corresponding confidence intervals to assist users in making business decisions. The forecasting node will be provided in a future release of SAS Enterprise Miner™.

The conclusion relates closely to the problem identified in the introduction:

> Time dependent data is very common in practice and usually manifests itself with several related components like different products, locations, SKU number, etc. Economists and statisticians have faced challenges associated with processing vast amounts of time series data long before the concept of data mining became in vogue. A wide class of analytic methods supports techniques to handle these problems ranging from simple forecasting methods like exponential smoothing to very advanced multivariate methods like Kalman Filtering and Statespace modeling. Data mining without forecasting is tantamount to

knowledge discovery without SAS software. This concept has also been reinforced by Thearling (1998) who documents the need to integrate forecasting methods into the data mining selection of offerings.

10.7 References

If you cite other works in your paper, you must include a references section. There are many different formats for references, depending on the submission journal. For example, the Modern Language Association (MLA), the American Psychological Association (APA), and the American Medical Association (AMA) all publish guidelines on paper formats, including references. Because interdisciplinary work frequently requires submission to a variety of journals with differing requirements, use a software add-on program that can manage the references. There are many available. They help you create and store a bibliographic list in almost any desired format.

If you intend to publish your paper, you should use references liberally instead of relying on common knowledge. White papers (frequently containing confidential material) not intended for outside publication rarely require formal references.

Because the fair use provision of copyright laws has differing interpretations, many journals have different policies on using direct quotations versus paraphrasing. Read submission requirements for authors carefully, and comply with those requirements as closely as possible.

10.8 Example Papers

This section presents several example papers demonstrating the writing techniques discussed here. The first paper is a literature review on ulcers. It shows the purpose, background, results, and conclusion. There is no method because the paper does not analyze results. The second paper gives the results of a text mining investigation of the content of dissertations by Web crawling through the repository of digital dissertations. The third example uses survey data and demonstrates a white paper rather than a paper intended for publication.

Example Review Paper: A Qualitative Examination of Medical Research

Introduction
It is generally assumed that medical research follows the scientific method and is based upon objective observation and data collection. However, the choice of what to study is generally a matter of philosophy and medical orthodoxy. There are trends in virtually every aspect of medical care. For example, only recently has quality of life become a valid topic of study in clinical trials (Fitzpatrick, 1999).

Because of the importance of published conclusions in patient treatment, it is useful to examine the process of medical research, and to examine the assumptions used in medical investigations. The example to be used here is that of gastric ulcers.

It was discovered in 1982 (Graham and Graham, 1998) that Helicobacter pylori (H. pylori) was responsible for most cases of gastric ulcers, with most of the remaining cases caused by medication treatment for other ailments, particularly arthritis. However, it was not until almost ten years later that eradication of the bacteria became the standard of care, even though the medications used for treatment had been readily available for almost ten years before the discovery of H. pylori.

The issues discussed in this paper are of a philosophic nature: what may hamper scientific discovery and the lack of desire to perform long term follow up that can hamper the discovery of adverse effects of treatment. Decision models based upon cost tend to ignore the impact of long-term adverse effects because they remain unknown and uninvestigated.

The introduction indicates that the article is not a research article; rather, it is a review of the philosophy of ulcer treatment. The last paragraph is somewhat confusing and should be rewritten. Does the article have more to do with things that hamper scientific discovery or the lack of long-term studies?

Following is a paper's background section, divided into five-year periods. The paper gives a brief summary of clinical studies over these five-year periods of time and demonstrates the trend in study for the same diagnosis, gastric ulcers. The background information is both concise and clear.

Historical Summary
It is important to examine the trend of treatment for gastric ulcers to understand the philosophical underpinnings that led to those treatments. Ulcers have been a problem for a substantial period of time. As the medical research papers are examined using an historical timeline, it is very apparent that the trend in treatment went from surgery to medication for reducing stomach acid to treatment of a bacterial infection. Terminology changed in the process and the focus of research altered as well.

Papers published in the medical literature were examined from 1966 to the present via Medline. Five-year intervals were examined using the keyword, "gastric ulcers." The numbers of papers published in each five-year interval from 1966 are given in Figure 1.

Figure 1 Number of Articles Published and Referenced in Medline

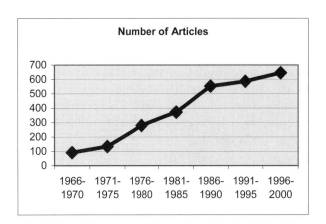

Note that the numbers continuously increase. This is probably due to the increased pressure to publish, and the increased availability of journals in which to publish.

Summary of 1966–1970
The papers in this time interval focused on two issues: surgical treatment of gastric ulcers and studies of animal models. The majority of the animal models involved rats and dogs, but arguments were made to use swine. A distinction was made between benign and malignant ulcers. There was virtually no discussion of drug treatment for the ulcers. It is apparent that the cause of ulcers was not well understood as there are also papers examining the underlying body structure that can be associated with ulcers. There are studies of muscle, mucosa, and blood sugar among others.

Summary of 1971–1975
Studies attempted to find effective means of distinguishing between benign and malignant ulcers. Many papers still examined surgical treatment of ulcers, although some studies began to examine the impact of medications on ulcers. The focus was on zinc sulphate and similar drugs. There was speculation on whether benign ulcers could become malignant. One study performed a 5-10 year follow up of surgical patients with the conclusion that the ulcers recurred in approximately 20% of the patients. Most of the animal models focused on rats with an occasional study on swine.

Summary of 1976–1980
Toward the end of this period, treatment studies were more focused on medications than surgery, concentrating almost exclusively on Cimetidine. The studies still compared drug treatment to placebo as there was no standard drug treatment in this time period. Other drugs were studied earlier in this time period. However, most of the studies involved very short periods of time. The results appeared to be successful in that within 6-10 weeks, the ulcer disappeared. One study (of less than 1 year) proposed a maintenance dose of Cimetidine to prevent recurrence. Some studies also examined socioeconomic factors that would be associated with the onset of ulcers. The term "malignant ulcer" faded in the literature.

Summary of 1981–1985
The medical treatment of ulcers continued with considerable research using two additional medications, Ranitidine and Omeprazole. Another drug that appeared in several papers was Acetazolamide. There was some preliminary research using rats to examine the impact of other medications on ulcers. The term "benign ulcer" was still in use, but fading as well.

Several review articles were written to examine the general issue of ulcer treatment. There were some papers comparing treatment by medication to treatment by surgery. There was a general consensus that surgery should be reserved for ulcers that did not respond to medical treatment. Cost effectiveness made an initial appearance.

Although disregarded by the mainstream of medical research, the existence of bacteria (H. pylori) in the stomach was discovered by an Australian, Dr. Barry J. Marshall in 1982. According to Medline, the discovery was first documented in Lancet (Marshall and Warren, 1984). There was dissent from other members of the community, denying the existence of H. pylori (Mueller et. al., 1986) but no confirmation or any attempt at confirmation from any other study. Barry Marshall and his colleagues stood alone in claiming the existence of a bacterial infection in the stomach.

Summary of 1986–1990

The focus of the papers remained on the use of medications to reduce acid levels. The drugs introduced previously, Ranitidine, Omeprazole, and Cimetidine, continued to be studied. However, toward the end of this period, papers appeared to determine the impact of the bacteria, H. pylori, on gastric ulcers. It was only in 1987, five years after the discovery of the bacteria, that its existence was accepted by the medical community. There was some shift of treatment to Amoxicillin and bismuth subsalicylate to treat the bacteria. However, most of the papers dealing with H. pylori focused on prevalence rather than treatment. Only a handful of papers discussed surgical treatment of ulcers, and those papers appeared primarily in Russian journals. Animal experiments focused on stress induced ulcers in rats. One paper did discuss the question of whether a "healed" ulcer was in fact healed. An occasional paper on long term follow up appeared, indicating a high degree of ulcer recurrence using the standard drugs. More discussion of maintenance doses to prevent recurrence appeared.

Summary of 1991–1995

Papers discussed the use of endoscopy in the diagnosis of gastric ulcers. The literature indicated that the medical community was generally convinced that H. pylori was the main cause of most gastric ulcers. A distinction began to appear concerning different causes. Another cause was attributed to the use of NSAIDs (non-steroidal anti-inflammatory drugs) such as aspirin and ibuprofen. A triple therapy, involving two antibiotics and one proton pump inhibitor (Omeprazole generally), became a standard treatment to eradicate H. pylori. Some long term follow up indicated that eradication of the bacteria did reduce recurrence.

Summary of 1996–2000

Publication of papers discussing treatment with triple therapy continued during this time period. Genetic research was employed to further investigate the properties of H. pylori to determine why some individuals were more susceptible to ulcers than others when both were infected with the bacteria. This problem led to at least one paper questioning the impact of H. pylori on ulcer formation. At the same time, a handful of papers were published questioning the impact of mental illness on stomach complaints. A greater number of papers appeared differentiating treatment between ulcers induced by H. pylori and ulcers induced by NSAIDs.

The trend is unmistakable. The general path of treatment was surgery in the 1960's followed by treatment for acid reduction in the 1970's and early 1980's. The discovery of H. pylori dramatically changed the direction of treatment, although this was not fully recognized until approximately 1995. At the present time, eradication of H. pylori is standard treatment. It will be shown that certain philosophical assumptions prevented an earlier discovery of H. pylori.

In the investigation of the literature, each summary gives a brief description of the trend, together with some typical references. The next section focuses on why the particular studies were chosen and describes some of the problems that working with narrow, inferential objects can cause; broad patterns that exist in the data can be missed.

In fact, this paper offers many arguments for data mining clinical data to improve patient outcomes.

Philosophical Assumptions

The general assumptions that governed the gastric ulcer research over the years are as follows:

1. The stomach acid will not allow bacterial growth.

2. Patient lifestyle is the primary cause of ulcers.

3. Long term follow up is not absolutely necessary.

Although few papers were published to examine the relationship of patient lifestyle to the onset of ulcers, it was frequently assumed that ulcers resulted from stress. Therefore, recurrence of ulcers was attributed not to treatment failure but to patient failure to reduce stress. If the stomach is too acidic to accommodate bacterial growth, there is no reason to investigate the stomach for the presence of bacteria.

However, there are more general philosophical reasons for research into ulcers. Why did medical research for so long fail to investigate the possibility of infection as a cause of ulcers? There are several reasons.

At this point, the paper shifts from discussing philosophical issues to analyzing statistical problems. It gives examples of poor statistical method and design. The writer should be careful in presenting the statistical design used in the study and some of the potential problems and flaws.

1. Research projects designed to answer very narrow questions.

Patients who need to take NSAIDs (for example, aspirin or ibuprofen) on an ongoing basis (for example, for arthritis) might need to continue therapy to offset the effects of the NSAIDs. However, the total problem for these patients was not examined; the study was only continued for eight weeks. The study was not designed to examine long-term results. Also, the paper doesn't address the question of why the medication did not work in more than 25% of the patients, even with the most effective drug. Yet the paper did not provide any discussion of the large number of patients for whom treatment failed; it focuses only on the higher rate of success.

2. Research projects focusing on only short-term results with no follow-up and, small sample sizes.

During the 1980's, when treatment shifted from surgery to medication, there were virtually no long-term or follow-up studies. Consider, for example, Collen et. al. (1980): Six weeks was the standard length of a study. Note that there were a total of 24 patients in the study, 11 and 13 in each group under consideration. Many of the studies relied upon such small samples. This tends to demonstrate another clear trend in medical research: insistence on a p-value of 0.05.

3. The dependence on a p-value of 0.05.

P-values represent just one measure of difference. Without a statistical power analysis to demonstrate that the number of patients is adequate, the lack of a p-value of 0.05 makes the study inconclusive (Cohen, 1988). In addition, not all statistical tests lend themselves to power analysis.

The p-value of 0.05 is not magical. It means that the probability of making an error when rejecting a null hypothesis is less than 0.05. The standard null hypothesis tested is that there is no difference in outcome between a group of patients receiving a treatment and a group a patients not receiving a treatment. Alternatively, the study may address a comparison between two different treatments, in which case, the null hypothesis states that there is no difference. It is valid to make such a test when the study is randomized, and there is a sufficiently large patient group studied. It is not particularly valid when the study is observational only. There are too many possible conflicting factors that can confound the outcome.

If an error rate of 5% is acceptable, why not 6% or 5.5%? Acceptable error should vary with the need. In a life threatening illness, a 10% chance that the medication is not effective could be acceptable. However in a relatively non-threatening illness, only a 0.001 chance that the medication will have very serious side effects may be acceptable.

Still, the main problem with using a p-value to come to a conclusion is that the conclusion can rarely be applied to an individual. The application of a screening test provides the following example:

$$\text{Sensitivity of screening test} = \frac{\text{Prevalence of Illness}}{\left[\text{Prevalence of Illness}\right] x \left[\text{Specificity of screening test}\right] + \left[1 - \text{Prevalence of Illness}\right] x \left[1 - \text{Specificity of screening test}\right]}$$

Suppose that a hypothetical screening test has a sensitivity of 95%, a specificity of 95%, and an illness prevalence of 5%. Then the probability of a correct positive diagnosis in the population is equal to:

$$\frac{0.05}{(0.05 \times 0.95) + (0.95 \times [1 - 0.95])} = 0.526$$

This equation is the standard Bayes' formula. Therefore, the application of the screening test to any one individual is questionable without additional verification. An initial screening should lead to a second diagnostic test to validate the outcome of the first screening test.

Human beings are very complex. It is next to impossible to reduce this complexity to one score or risk factor. However, this reduction is frequently done in medical research because simplistic statistical models are used that exclude the possibility of examining complexity.

4. Research projects that continue trends in already developed treatment instead of looking to new directions.

The tendency of inertia—to keep going in the same direction unless an opposing force is encountered—is very true of medical research. When surgery was the norm, most research studies focused on surgery. When medication became the norm, the research studies shifted to medication. It took approximately ten years to shift research from the reduction of symptoms to the eradication of H. pylori bacteria. The truly innovative tends to be ignored in part because innovation is somewhat risky.

At many medical schools, faculty are promoted and tenured almost solely on the basis of their ability to acquire external funding. An NIH grant submission requires the availability of preliminary data. The submission is reviewed by others in the discipline. The reviewers are usually permanent members of study sections. The criteria for tenure and promotion at the School of Medicine at the University of Louisville include the following:

> "An independent research program requires current extramural funding; federal funding support as principal investigator is preferred, or failing that, nationally peer-reviewed funding will be acceptable if evidence for recent submission and resubmission to federal sources is provided. Reviews of the research via extramural letters must be obtained and should support the rating of excellence.... For promotion to professor based on excellence in research, annual publication as major author will suffice only if the journal is judged by peers to be in a top, high visibility, journal in the field. In addition for promotion to professor based on excellence in research, sustained, renewed, federal funding as principal investigator will be required."

This can be seen as a general trend required of medical school faculty (Glazer, 1999):

> "This policy included productivity requirements that made revenue generation the principal function of faculty and demeaned the importance of teaching and service. It stipulated that faculty members would face salary reductions of up to 30 percent each year if they did not provide 70 percent of their salary through external funding."

The pressure to maintain a position by external funding mandates that the faculty member conform to fairly standard protocols and research hypotheses. The reliance on external funding and revenue production has actually resulted in a decline in medical research (Andreoli, 1999):

> "Thus, there has been an alarming fall in National Institutes for Health applications from physicians since 1995; there has been a drop in the number of applicants to distinguished academic societies, there has been a reduction of about 50 percent in interest in research careers, and contributions to well-known research journals from U.S. medical schools are in relative decline."

The paper builds a case. Is it persuasive? How should a reader judge? The paper does build an argument about the problem of assumptions. They should never be ignored by investigators.

5. Research projects that tend to generalize beyond reasonable scope.

Sometimes medical studies focus on groups that are too small, focus on only one gender, race or ethnic group. In some cases, the investigator attempts to generalize such a study to the entire population. Can a study of 10 patients be generalized to the entire population? Can a study performed exclusively on one gender, race, or ethnic group be generalized to the population at large? Should a medication approved for adults be prescribed for children? For example, consider the study cited in Wu et. al. (1999): It was a hospital-based, age- and sex-matched case-control study. Multivariate and stratified analyses were performed. Ninety-seven patients (52 gastric ulcers, 45 duodenal ulcers) and 97 non-ulcer controls were enrolled in the study.

Consider the location of the study: Department of Internal Medicine, Taichung Veterans General Hospital, Taiwan. The patients were age- and sex- matched but still did not represent the general population. For example, it is not in any way representative of the population of the United States. However, consensus panels, as reported by Gold (1999), make decisions on medical treatment on the basis of studies such as the one reported above.

6. Research projects that tend to accept results of observational studies with limited examination of confounding factors.

Consider the following study (Cheng Y. Macera CA. Davis DR. Blair SN.,2000): The participants were men who attended the Cooper Institute for Aerobics Research, Dallas, Texas, between 1970 and 1990. The presence of gastric disease was determined from a mail survey in 1990. Participants were classified into 3 physical activity groups according to information provided at the baseline clinic visit: active, those who walked or ran 10 miles or more a week; moderately active, those who walked or ran less than 10 miles a week or did another regular activity; and the control group consisting of those who reported no regular physical activity.

There are several possible confounding factors in this study: medical treatment has changed significantly between 1970 and 1990, including the treatment of stomach upset. There is substantial difference between the three identified categories, which could have been defined at 5-mile increments, or even 1-mile increments.

The study concluded that active men had a significantly reduced risk for duodenal ulcers (relative hazard [95% confidence interval] for the active group, 0.38 [0.15-0.94], and 0.54 [0.30-0.96] for the moderately active group). No association was found between physical activity and gastric ulcers for men or for either type of ulcer for women.

The final discussion section in this example attempts to generalize the results of the specific study of ulcers to the more general process of medical research. In the end, the discussion suggests that studies concerning other treatments will find similar results.

Discussion

Medical research papers tend to have a logical development (Velanovich, 1993). However, without sufficient knowledge to examine the statistical foundation of the clinical study, erroneous conclusions can easily be made (DeMets, 1999). A study result may be used as valid when it is in fact an incorrect generalization of a very narrow result.

Randomized, controlled clinical trials have always been accepted as the "gold" standard of medical research (Susser, 1996) with observational studies of lesser value. To avoid confounding, dependence upon case-control matching, historical controls, or longitudinal assessment are used. However, none of these can avoid the possibilities of confounding factors. Therefore, conclusions should always be conjectural with the allowance for additional studies. Unfortunately, results of observational studies are used as if they were just as valid as randomized, controlled trials. This is particularly true of studies of surgical procedures, which are almost totally lacking in randomization and gold standards.

Medical research does not take place in a vacuum. Decisions are made concerning what to study and how to study it. Those decisions have an impact on what is discovered. They also have an impact on the types of errors made when performing research. In the case of ulcers, it took ten years for research to shift to a different direction from surgery to controlling acid levels and another ten years to shift to treatment of an infection.

It is useful to examine the historical trend of medical research on one treatment topic. In this way, it is possible to look at how treatment changes with respect to the research, and how long it takes for treatment to change given new results. Even now, there are debates concerning whether to use antibiotic treatment or acid-reduction therapy (Fairman, 2000), nearly twenty years after the discovery of H. pylori.

Example Professional Journal Submission: An Investigation of the Content of Mathematics Dissertations

In the introduction to this example paper, the author advocates examining dissertation content. The paper does not follow the standard purpose, method, and results format because it focuses on persuasion. Is this the proper format for the introduction or should it use a more standard format, moving the rationale for the study to the background section?

Introduction

Several professional mathematical societies have called for mathematics to be more integrated with other disciplines, and to create more interdisciplinary degrees. Still others have speculated on the nature of a dissertation in a program oriented toward industrial rather than academic employment. For example, a report provided by the National Academies states that students more interested in nontraditional careers should design dissertations that meet high standards for originality but require less time than the more standard dissertation. Similarly, in a paper published in the Notices of the American Mathematical Society, it states, that interaction with at least one other science should be required for doctoral training in mathematics. The paper goes on to list several changes that should be made. Among them is to shorten the time to degree by streamlining qualifying examinations, offering more summer courses, and to start research as soon as possible.

There exists very little information in the mathematics literature discussing the nature of a mathematics dissertation. Guidelines for the dissertation are virtually non-existent. Successful completion, then, is determined by the decisions of the student's advisor and committee. A keyword search on Google using "mathematics dissertation content" yields sites for various PhD programs. A similar search in Education Abstracts yielded one paper on the actual content of dissertations—but that was in the field of management.[3] The ERIC database yielded no articles at all. Specific searches in the American Mathematical Monthly and the Journal of Statistical Education also were not profitable. While there is a constant demand for proof and documentation concerning mathematical ideas, there is almost no call to discuss methods for examining dissertation content and mathematics quality.

It is the purpose of this paper to examine the content of applied and interdisciplinary dissertations to determine how they should change in content so that the time to degree can be shortened, and so that students can get involved in research early in their careers. Suggestions concerning qualifying examinations will also be given.

The next section of the paper gives details of a text analysis from one particular source, Dissertation Abstracts (http://www.dissertationadvice.com/dissertationadvice/index.htm?gclid=CMeIwOfgyYcCFRieWAodGjNFbQ). This source makes available complete abstracts of dissertations and full text for a fee. Because SAS Text Miner software works best with smaller documents, it was only necessary to use the abstracts.

Dissertation Content

The problem with analyzing dissertation content is that the content is primarily text. It is possible to count the number of equations, theorems, and proofs in the body of the text in order to quantify what is essentially qualitative information. However, text analysis has been developed in order to examine the information more directly. The database, Dissertation Abstracts, was used to find the dissertations. The first keyword searches were for "applied mathematics" and "applied statistics." This search yielded 146 dissertations dating from 1986, of which 27 were identified as statistics. Text analysis found a total of 5 different clusters (Table 1). Misspellings can occur when using Web crawl, and can show up in the text cluster lists.

Table 1 Clusters of Terms in Applied Dissertations

Cluster Number	Descriptive Terms	Frequency	Label
1	High school, achievement, education, curriculum, score, teacher, vocational, instruction, secondary, edd, significant, grade, attitude, enroll, teach, prog	39	Education content, primarily for EdD and PhD in education
2	Equation, solve, numbericcal, solution, differential, stability, domain, aprtial, nonlinear, system, condition, boundary, approximation	27	Modeling content primarily with numerical analysis and differential equations
3	Wavelet, nonparametric, signal, applied statistics, distribution, test, function, discuss, perform, technique, theory	30	Statistics content, including application of statistical technique and development of statistical models
4	Tool, model, simulation, structure, science, property, statistics, approach, technique, develop, obtain, base, theory	35	Simulation models, some of which are statistics
5	Matrix, graph, network, architecture, parallel, algorithm, efficiency, computation, computer, implement	15	Computer science models

Concept links (Figure 1 and 2) reinforce this grouping of dissertations. Concept links are a method of investigating the content of text information. Text mining software uses the technique of association rules to create the concept maps. The term "mathematics" linked primarily to terms involving education. It seems clear that most of the dissertations that have the keywords "applied mathematics" in fact are in the area of mathematics education. In contrast, dissertations linked to "statistics" tend to focus on the type of model.

Figure 1 Concept Links for **mathematics**

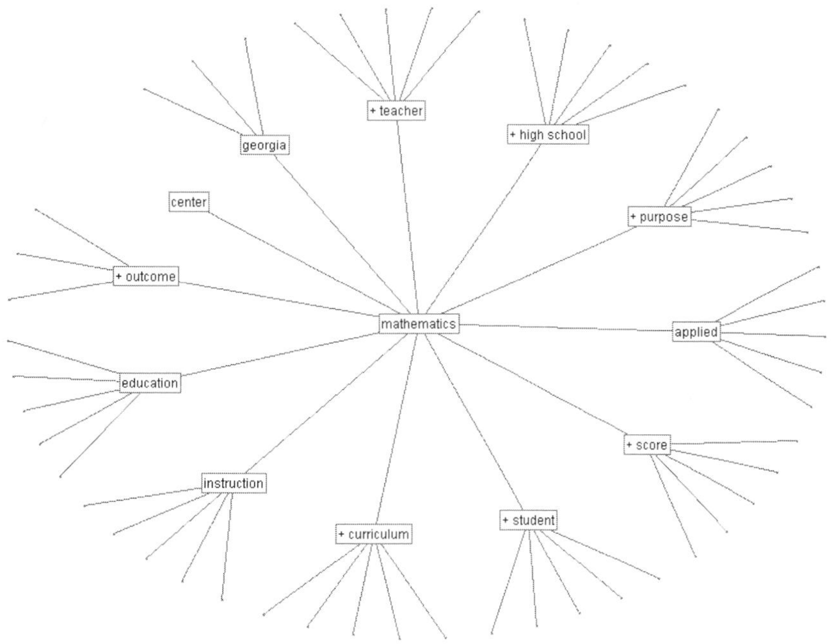

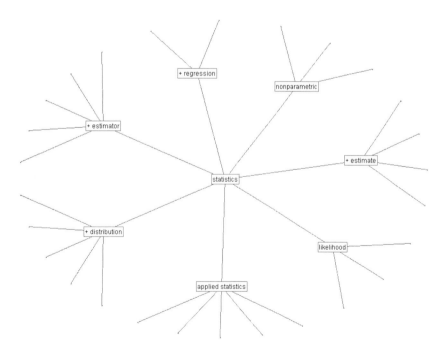

Figure 2 Concept Links for **statistics**

Contrast this table with Table 2, clustered using the terms "logistics", "actuarial science", "data mining", and "biostatistics" where the dissertations are based upon particular topics.

Table 2 Clusters of Terms in Application Area Dissertations

Cluster Number	Descriptive Terms	Frequency	Label
1	Biostatistics, statistics, gene, biology, distribution, parameter, regression, method, simulation, model, variable, study, function	51	Biostatistics, including examination of genes
2	Business, product, chain, firm, manufacturer, administration, market, supply, customer, relationship, logistics, management, performance	37	Logistics and supply-chain management
3	Structure, database, application, computer	3	Data mining; investigations of the database
4	Transportation, solution, facility, operations research, optimal demand, logistics operation, optimization, cost, decision, supply	25	Logistics and transportation issues
5	Computer, rule, discover, data mining, database, pattern, knowledge mining, algorithm, technique, data, application	86	Data mining techniques
6	Health, education, clinical, health sciences, group, response, practice, field, science, environment	66	Biostatistics and clinical trials
7	Political science, political history, century, policy, engage, United States of America, theory, implication, power	20	Applications to history and political science

To examine the clusters in Table 2, a table analysis was performed (Table 3).

Table 3 Chi-Square Analysis of Cluster by Application Topic

Cluster	Actuarial Science	Biostatistics	Data Mining	Logistics
1	11 (48%)	18 (35%)	21 (18%)	1 (1%)
2	2 (9%)	1 (2%)	3 (2%)	31 (33%)
3	0	1 (2%)	2 (2%)	0
4	0	0	3 (2%)	0
5	0	3 (6%)	82 (68%)	1 (1%)
6	7 (30%)	28 (54%)	9 (8%)	22 (24%)
7	3 (13%)	1 (2%)	0	16 (17%)

It is of interest to note that most of the dissertations defined by topic appear to be more concerned with outcome than with method. Again, the concept links reinforce the relationship of the concept to the outcome (Figure 3 and 4).

Figure 3 Concept Links for **logistics**

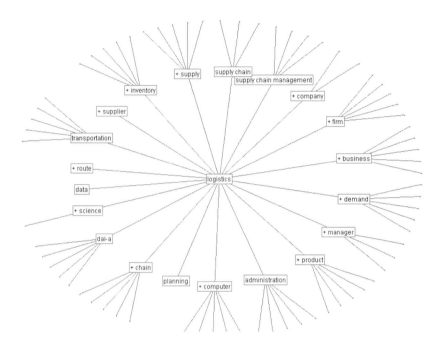

Figure 4 Concept Links for **data mining**

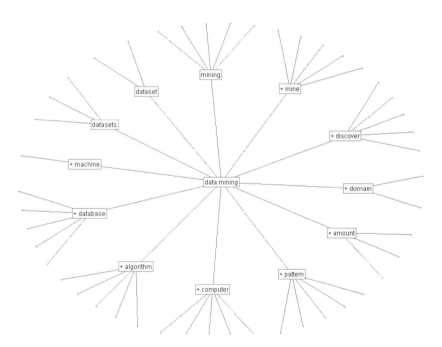

Biostatistics and actuarial science are more directly related to mathematics. However, they, too, are concentrated on outcomes rather than method.

Dissertation Abstracts does not identify the authors by individual department or discipline. Therefore, it is not possible to determine the proportion of the papers listed in Table 3 that were completed by mathematics students. However, the papers on logistics that focus on "supply chain management" indicate a business major while the data mining papers indicate computer science. It is clear that there is much mathematics being examined outside of mathematics departments.

This section of the paper returns to the rationale, or the purpose of the paper. In this case, the purpose is to determine content of dissertations related to statistics and data mining. This information should also be included in the introduction to clearly state the objective of the study. Then an introduction could be written in the standard format.

Qualifying Examinations

Similarly, there is almost no information in the mathematics literature pertaining to qualifying examinations. Ordinarily, the purpose of examinations such as the SAT and GRE are to compare to a standard. There are no national or international standards for qualifying examinations. According to Joseph Seidlin, there are two injunctions generally associated with high standards: 'keep them out' and 'put them out'. But the higher the standards, the greater the 'out-put' with many failures. Therefore, it seems to follow that many failures establish high standards.

The primary differences between the master's degree and the doctorate currently are the qualifying examinations and the research. Students should have sufficient coursework to signify a strong basis in mathematics without making the examinations so unduly burdensome that they dominate the student's early years in doctoral study to the exclusion of the research, as is often currently the case at many institutions. Because of the amount of time required to study for the examinations, research often waits until after the examinations are concluded, thereby extending the length of time a student spends in doctoral studies.

What then is a reasonable pass rate for qualifying examinations? Should the examinations be the sole gatekeeper to the completion of a doctoral degree? For a mathematics degree with its goal to graduate students for industrial employment, the focus should be on solving industrial problems. As the degree should focus on problem-solving, so should the assessment.

As an alternative to the qualifying examinations, we propose that students be given a series of industrial problems that need to be solved through analysis and judgment. The students should be allowed access to all resources that they might need to solve the problems, including textbooks and faculty members. A 10- or 30-day deadline should be established so that the student finds the best solution in the time given, and then defends the final decisions. Each student should be given different problems, but they should be able to discuss them amongst themselves. In other words, the examinations should be set up as students should expect to find problems in the industrial setting.

The discussion summarizes both the results and the rationale. Note, then, the paper's organization. Rationale and study are interwoven throughout the paper, with the data results providing support for the rationale. It is not the standard format for a technical paper, but it is effective in a situation where philosophical assumptions are an obstacle for examination of the data.

Discussion

Additional examinations of dissertations with mathematics content clearly show that there is significant mathematical content. Students who seek employment in industry can clearly demonstrate expertise without completing a mathematics doctorate. It becomes imperative that mathematicians carefully examine the content of dissertations that are expected by industrial employers, and to fashion an industrial degree that is in line with those expectations.

All aspects of the student's doctoral career should focus on industrial employment, including examinations and research. Otherwise, much of mathematics will continue to be developed outside of mathematics departments, and the departments themselves could become irrelevant.

Example White Paper: Analysis of Student Survey Data

This paper's format differs from the previous two because it is a white paper instead of an article intended for publication. As a white paper, it contains no background section. The introduction section has been omitted under the assumption that its limited readership is familiar with the study's purpose. The paper examines the content of the study as opposed to a specific hypothesis.

A total of 190 student survey forms were collected: 130 in courses numbered 200–300 and 60 in courses numbered 400 and above. The distribution by course level is below:

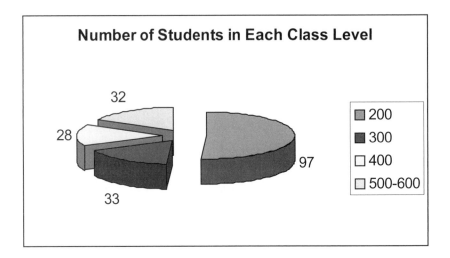

Of that number, the following percentages of students expressed interest in pure and applied mathematics (students could check both categories if they desired):

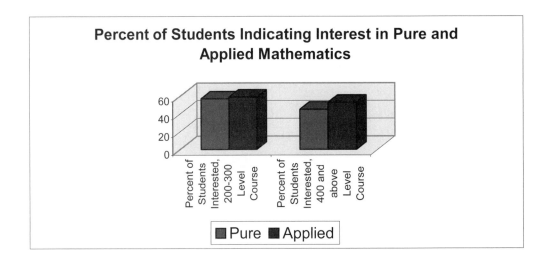

Note that in general categories, the students are relatively split between the two categories. However, when they are broken down by individual mathematical discipline, there are differences:

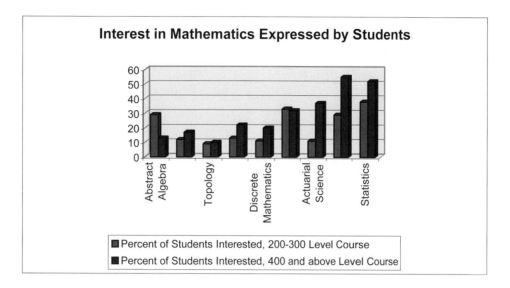

Students express greater interest in the applied mathematics sequences, particularly probability, statistics, and actuarial science. This interest increases for students in higher level mathematics courses.

On the average, students in courses 200–300 had taken one mathematics course previously to the one enrolled and expressed an interest in one and half additional courses (on average).

For students in upper-level courses, this average increases to 2. The overall distribution is equal to

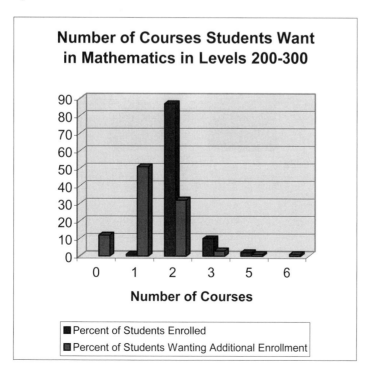

For students in lower-level courses and in upper-level courses:

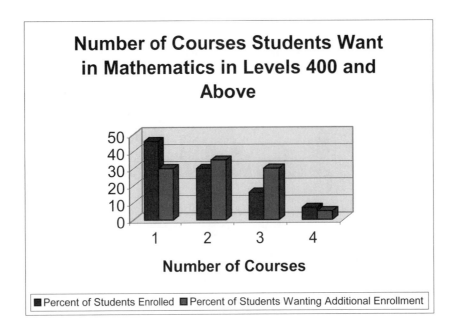

In order to succeed in mathematics courses, students need to invest in study time. Therefore, students were asked to estimate the amount of time they studied. Overall, the distribution is as follows:

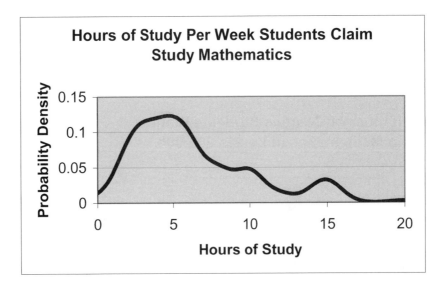

For a 3-hour course, students should study 9–10 hours outside of class and for a 5-hour course, they should study approximately 15 hours per week. Students on the average are investing half that amount of time. If the study times are compared by course level, it is noticeable that students in 200–300 level courses are investing less than 5 hours per week. As these are largely 5-hour courses, they are studying approximately 1/3 of the time needed. Students in upper-level courses have increased the number of hours but these are spread across more than one mathematics course.

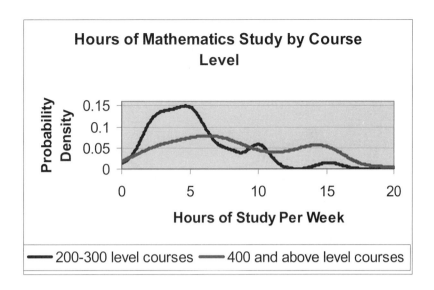

The Department of Mathematics has recently added a Maple lab to all calculus courses. Statistical software has been required in all statistics courses for quite some time. It is an essential part of the modeling sequence. Student opinions concerning the use of computers were also solicited:

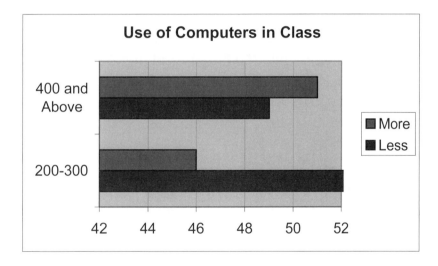

Note that the majority of students in 200–300 level courses (with the required Maple lab) want less use of the computer; this trend reverses in upper level courses. Students were also asked specifically about the use of Maple in calculus:

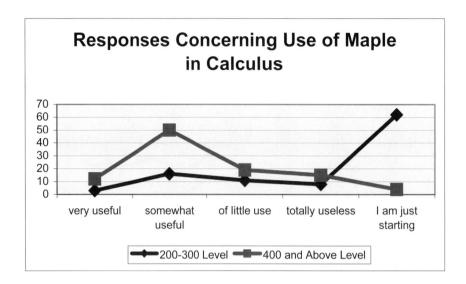

Again, note that students in upper-level courses found the Maple to be useful, with a substantial minority (25%) believing that the calculus lab had little use. Students in lower-level courses were evenly divided in their estimation of the use of the lab.

Restricting attention to those students with experience in Maple indicates that a sizeable proportion (50%) find the Maple lab of little use:

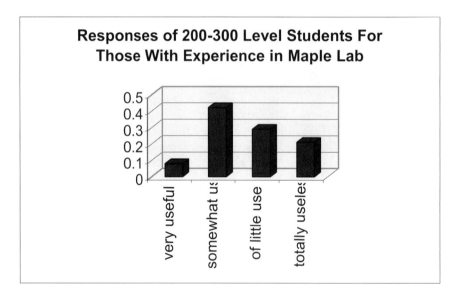

Since the Department of Mathematics is contemplating the development of a Master's and PhD program in industrial and applied mathematics, students were asked about their experiences in applied courses. Applied courses can focus on computation, manipulating numbers and variables, or they can focus on concepts using computational or statistical software to perform the computations. Students preferred that these courses focus on concepts but found that they primarily focused on computations:

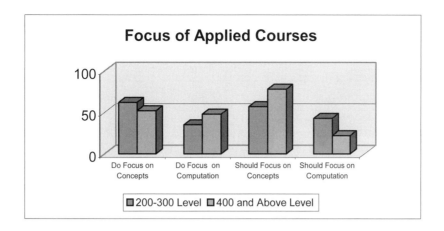

Students in the upper-level courses have a strong opinion that the courses focus on computations but should focus on concept. With the use of Maple and other computer software, computations can be performed with the aid of the computer so that it is possible to focus on concepts.

Students also have an interest in internships, ranging from 52% in beginning level courses and increasing to 64% in upper-level courses:

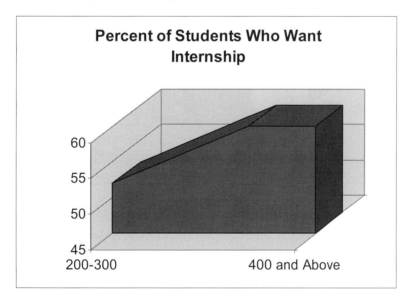

Students were asked if they had difficulties enrolling in mathematics courses. In the 200–300 level courses, a small percentage (13%) did have difficulty:

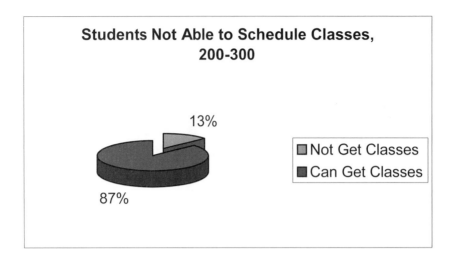

However, this percentage climbed to 34% for students in upper-level classes:

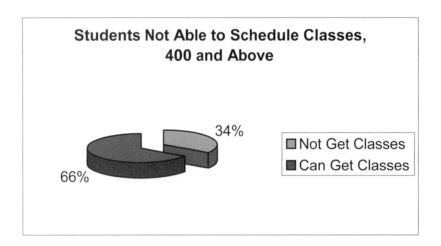

Note that this white paper also does not include a discussion section and a summary of the results. The paper was written to be discussed and reported by a committee and the results summary left for the general discussion.

Read these papers carefully, and note their style. Aim for clarity and understanding on the part of your audience.

10.9 Exercises

1. Go to an electronic abstract database (such as ERIC at http://www.eric.ed.gov/ ERICWebPortal/Home.portal or PubMED at http://www.pubmed.gov/) and find five abstracts on a specific topic of your choice. Examine them carefully and determine whether a specific format was required for the abstract. Evaluate the abstract by commenting on the following:

   a. The length of the abstract

   b. The completeness of the abstract.

2. Write an evaluation of each paper in Section 10.10. If you see room for improvement, rewrite the relevant sections.

Example Data Mining Papers

11.1 Introduction

This chapter contains four papers written by the author that analyze several of the databases in this book using data mining techniques. These papers present this author's decision-making process and reported results.

- The first paper analyzes the medication data set introduced in Chapter 4.

- The second paper analyzes the faculty workload data set introduced in Chapter 1.

- The third paper analyzes the student database on grades and enrollment as restricted to one department, as discussed in several chapters previously.

- The fourth paper is a text analysis of the content of Web pages related to vaccines.

These papers are examples of how to assemble information derived from data mining into a cohesive unit. Keep in mind that papers written for an external audience must use the format presented in Chapter 10: abstract, introduction, background, method, results, discussion/conclusion, and references. Papers written for an internal audience, such as technical reports, do not need to include background and references sections.

Ultimately, you (the author) choose what to mine, labeling variable fields as target or input. No single data mining project can find all of the information contained in a database. Base your choices on knowledge of the domain. There is never one right answer to a data mining project, which makes it difficult to provide solutions to exercises. You should examine the data sets used in this text and write your own results. Or, choose a data set that is significant to you and complete a data mining project on it. Remember to document your findings in a technical report.

There are many opportunities to present interesting data mining results. Regional SAS users groups hold annual meetings and there are several related to specific industries. The SAS Global Forum is another avenue to present your results. You are strongly encouraged to submit papers to these conferences.

11.2 Analysis of Multiple Drug Purchases and Consumer Drug Costs

Abstract

When you define an observational unit in a data set by one field, defining a different observational unit becomes difficult. For example, customer drug purchases are usually defined by the purchase rather than by the customer. The Association node in SAS Enterprise Miner 5.2 uses a customer identifier to link purchases when the purchase is the observational unit. However, the Association node is inadequate when there are too many different purchase choices. An alternative method is to change the observational unit to the customer using the TRANSPOSE and CONCAT procedures. In this way, all customer purchases are linked in a text string that can be examined using SAS Text Miner software. A second method is to reduce the number of choices by defining larger classes that combine similar choices. The methods demonstrated in this paper are applied to a public data set similar to those collected in any retail pharmacy.

Introduction

Retail pharmacy is different from other retail businesses because the consumer does not make the medication choice; that choice is made by the physician. The insurer sets the price paid by the consumer. There are no drug specials with special rates at a retail pharmacy. Nevertheless, consumers with chronic medication needs can be identified through a market basket analysis.

Such a market basket analysis is usually performed using association rules available in SAS Enterprise Miner software. However, if there are too many possible choices, association rules tend to fail. Given the number of medications available, association rules don't provide meaningful results. This paper examines alternative techniques for market basket analysis in the presence of thousands of possible choices.

The data used for this example are in the public domain, downloaded from http://www.meps.ahrq.gov/mepsweb/data_stats/download_data_files.jsp. The data set, named the MEPS HC-059A: 2001 Prescribed Medicines File, provides information on household-reported prescribed medicines for a nationally representative sample of the noninstitutionalized U.S. population. The data set helps users estimate prescribed medicine usage and expenditures. These data could be collected in any retail pharmacy.

Each record in the data set represents one prescribed medicine that was obtained during 2001. There are codes for individual households and for individuals within each household. The data set contains approximately 277,000 records. With a total of 3,837 medications on the list, 2,639 were prescribed for two or more households. A partial list of the medications appears in Figure 1.

Figure 1 Partial List of Medications in the Data Set

```
                      MEDICATION NAME (IMPUTED)

                                                    Cumulative  Cumulative
RXNAME                          Frequency  Percent  Frequency   Percent

-7                                   201     0.07        201      0.07
-9                                  3246     1.17       3447      1.24
7 CYCLES NORDETTE                      1     0.00       3448      1.24
A & D OINTMENT                        11     0.00       3459      1.24
A/B OTIC                              36     0.01       3495      1.26
ABSORBASE                              8     0.00       3503      1.26
ACCOLATE                             146     0.05       3649      1.31
ACCU-CHEK                              3     0.00       3652      1.31
ACCU-CHEK ADVANTAGE                    5     0.00       3657      1.32
ACCU-CHEK ADVANTAGE (STRIP)            8     0.00       3665      1.32
ACCU-CHEK ADVANTAGE (STRIP,2X50)       5     0.00       3670      1.32
ACCU-CHEK ADVANTAGE CARE               6     0.00       3676      1.32
ACCU-CHEK COMFORT CURVE (STRIP)        5     0.00       3681      1.32
ACCU-CHEK COMFORT CURVE STRIPS         7     0.00       3688      1.33
ACCU-CHEK INSTANT                      1     0.00       3689      1.33
ACCU-CHEK SIMPLICITY CARE (COMPLETE MONITORING)  4  0.00  3693  1.33
ACCU-CHEK TEST STRIP                   7     0.00       3700      1.33
ACCUPRIL                            1507     0.54       5207      1.87
ACCURETIC (10X3)                      29     0.01       5236      1.88
ACCUTANE                              72     0.03       5308      1.91
ACCUTANE (RX PAK, 10X10)              42     0.02       5350      1.93
ACCUZYME                               1     0.00       5351      1.93
ACEBUTOLOL HCL                        89     0.03       5440      1.96
ACEON                                 42     0.02       5482      1.97
ACEPHEN                                6     0.00       5488      1.98
ACETAMIN                              19     0.01       5507      1.98
ACETAMIN W/COD                         1     0.00       5508      1.98
ACETAMIN/COD3                         28     0.01       5536      1.99
ACETAMINAPHEN                          1     0.00       5537      1.99
ACETAMINOPHEN                        358     0.13       5895      2.12
ACETAMINOPHEN (A.F.,CHERRY)            8     0.00       5903      2.12
ACETAMINOPHEN (DROPS)                  4     0.00       5907      2.13
ACETAMINOPHEN (DROPS, A.F.)            1     0.00       5908      2.13
ACETAMINOPHEN (INFANT)                 1     0.00       5909      2.13
ACETAMINOPHEN E.S.                     1     0.00       5910      2.13
ACETAMINOPHEN INFANTS                  1     0.00       5911      2.13
ACETAMINOPHEN INFANTS (DROPS,A.F.,FRUIT)  1  0.00    5912      2.13
ACETAMINOPHEN W/ CODEINE              10     0.00       5922      2.13
ACETAMINOPHEN W/COD                   36     0.01       5958      2.14
ACETAMINOPHEN W/CODEINE               25     0.01       5983      2.15
ACETAMINOPHEN W/CODEINE #3            24     0.01       6007      2.16
ACETAMINOPHEN W/CODEINE ELIXIR         1     0.00       6008      2.16
ACETAMINOPHEN W/CODEINE#3              1     0.00       6009      2.16
ACETAMINOPHEN WITH CODEINE             1     0.00       6010      2.16
ACETAMINOPHEN/APAP                     1     0.00       6011      2.16
```

A quick review of the different medications demonstrates that many medications are virtually identical. Some of the drug names are standard, but there are many variations. Misspellings or abbreviations are also apparent, for example *acetamin*. Numeric codes are used for unknown or missing medications (-7,-9). Finding an easy way to simplify the list would be helpful. For the most part, the difference in drug names occurs because of the level of detail provided at data entry.

Creating Linkages with SAS Text Miner Software

SAS Text Miner software offers a number of analysis methods. Some data preprocessing is required to define linkages. All medications for one household (or one patient) must be linked, and the observational unit must be changed from medication to household. Table 1 lists the clusters defined by the software.

Table 1 Clusters of Medications

Cluster Number	Cluster Description	Cluster Label
1	glucophage, furosemide, zestril, synthroid, softclix	Diabetes, heart
2	allegra, claritin, flonase, nasonex, hydrochlorothiazide	Allergies
3	lipitor, vioxx, allegra, claritin	Lipitor, arthritis, and allergies
4	augmentin	Children's antibiotic
5	vicodin, apap/hydrocodone_bitartrate, celexa, naproxen, vioxx	Pain
6	zoloft, triple_antibiotic, paxil, zyrtec, naproxen	Depression, allergies
7	synthroid, premarin, augmentin, zithromax, amoxicillin	Post-menopause and antibiotics
8	levoxyl, synthroid, premarin, lipitor, zoloft	Post-menopause, cholesterol, and depression
9	hydrochlorothiazide, lipitor, norvasc, furosemide, zestril	Cholesterol, hypertension
10	estradiol, prednisone, prempro, zocor, zyrtec	Post-menopause, allergies, cholesterol
11	glyburide , aspirin, glucophage, lisinopril, simvastatin	Diabetes, cholesterol
12	lanoxin, coumadin, pravachol, furosemide, norvasc	Heart, cholesterol
13	atenolol, hydrochlorothiazide, lipitor, zestril, premarin	Heart, cholesterol
14	fosamax_(unit_of_use, blister_pck, fosamax_(unit_of_use), fosamax, celebrex	Ulcer, arthritis
15	fluoxetine_hcl, prozac, zithromax, augmentin, cephalexin	Antibiotic, depression
16	singulair_(unit_of_use), albuterol, serevent, flovent, singulair	Asthma
17	celebrex, ultram, hydromet, vioxx, ibuprofen	Arthritis
18	premarin, medroxyprogesterone_acetate_(unit_of_use), allegra, triple_antibiotic, cephalexin	Post-menopause, antibiotics
19	prevacid, cephalexin, amoxicillin, ibuprofen, celebrex	Ulcer, antibiotic, arthritis
20	triple_antibiotic, augmentin, ibuprofen, motrin, amoxicillin	Antibiotic, pain
21	paxil, paxil_(unit_of_use), alprazolam, lorazepam, amoxicillin	Depression, antibiotic

The clusters represent combinations of diagnoses. Recall that the examination is by household, and different household members might have different diagnoses. Also, patients with severe, chronic illnesses often suffer from related co-morbidities. Patients with diabetes often have heart problems. Patients with arthritis can have gastric problems related to their arthritic medications.

Examining Payments by Clusters

Because the clusters are defined by analyses, they must be considered random effects and the linear mixed model (the MIXED procedure) used. Figures 2 through 11 show the total paid by each patient (or third party) in the 21 defined clusters as well as the kernel density estimators of several selected clusters to illustrate the entire payment distribution. Note that the highest self-pay cluster shown in Figure 2 is for patients with ulcers and arthritis. A number of recently introduced medications are not yet on third-party formularies, which could account for this result. The cluster with the next highest payment is for patients with diabetes and heart problems. The highest average self-pay for a year is $1,300. The highest average payment by private insurance is $1,400 per year. Figures 12 and 13 give an overall framework for the payments.

Figure 2 Payment by Customers for Medications by Cluster

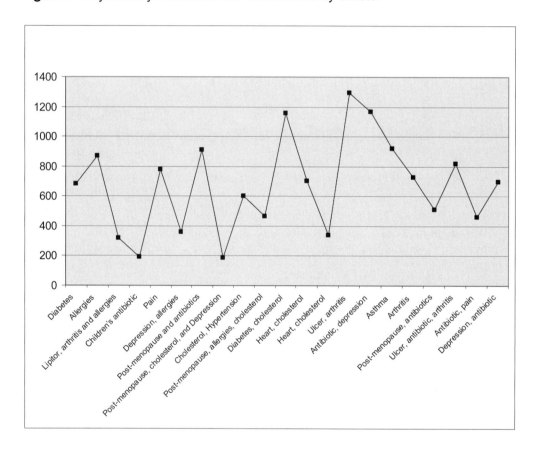

Figure 3 Kernel Density Estimation of Selected Clusters for Self-Pay

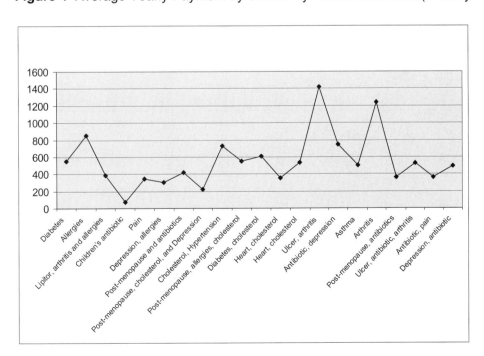

Use kernel density estimation to examine differences within clusters. Cluster 2 (allergies) has a high probability of low self payments. In contrast, Cluster 14 (arthritis and ulcers) has a fairly high probability of payments in the $500 to $1,000 range.

Figure 4 Average Yearly Payment by Cluster by Private Insurance (Primary Insurer)

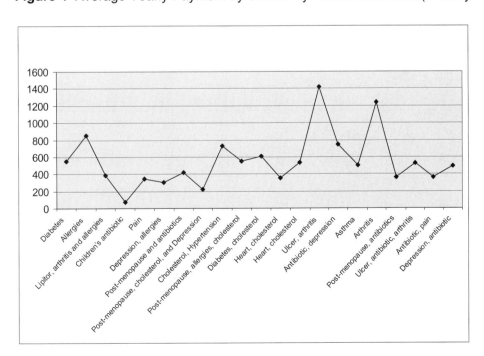

The two highest payments by private insurance are for ulcers and arthritis or for arthritis alone. The next highest cluster is for allergies.

Figure 5 Kernel Density Estimation of Selected Clusters for Private Insurance

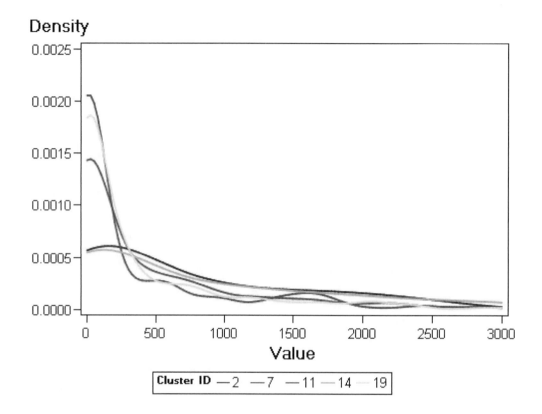

Insurance payments for post-menopause drugs and antibiotics are relatively small but consistent across insurers. This is also true for diabetes and cholesterol (Cluster 11) and antibiotics (Cluster 19). However, for arthritis and allergies, the payments by different insurers vary widely.

Figure 6 Average Yearly Payment by Cluster by Medicare

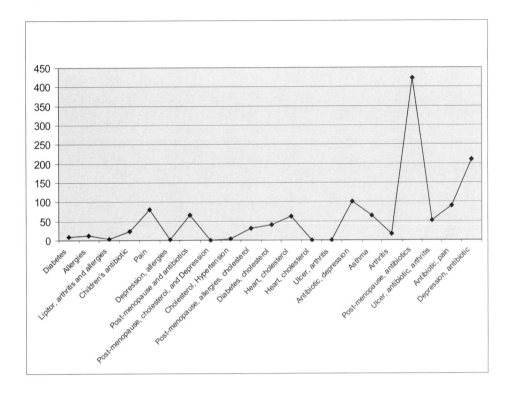

Figure 7 Kernel Density Estimation of Selected Clusters by Medicare

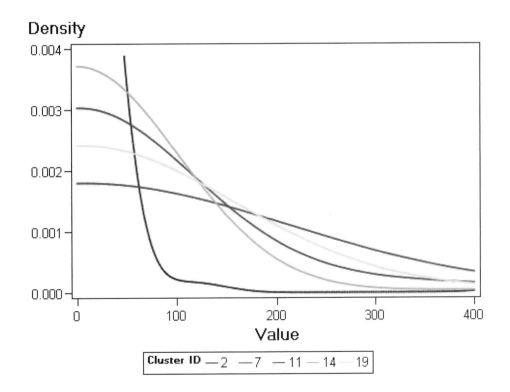

As noted in both Figures 6 and 7, Medicare pays for very few medications; its highest average payment is for post-menopause drugs. It will be interesting to compare results before and after the passage of legislation to include medications in Medicare coverage.

Figure 8 Average Yearly Payment by Cluster by Medicaid

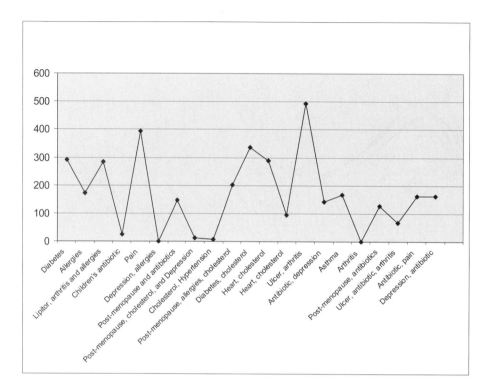

Figure 9 Density Estimation of Selected Clusters by Medicaid

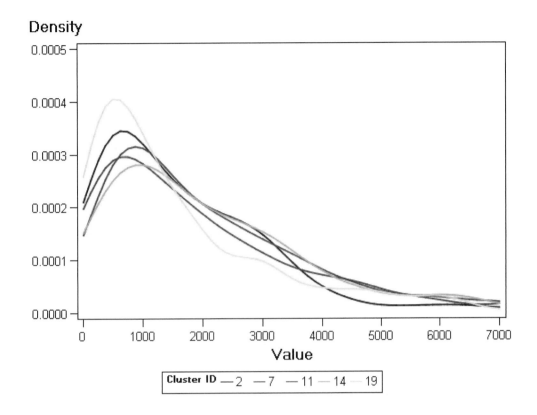

In Medicaid payments, the highest payments are also for arthritis and ulcers. The second highest is for pain.

Figure 10 Average Yearly Payment by Cluster from All Sources

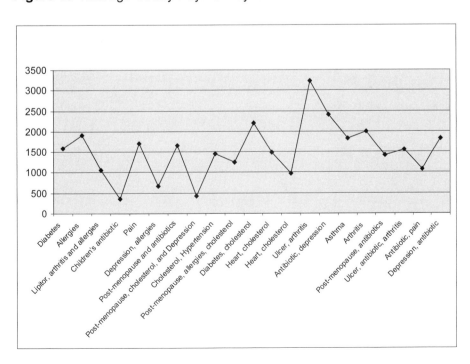

Figure 11 Density Estimation of Selected Clusters by All Sources

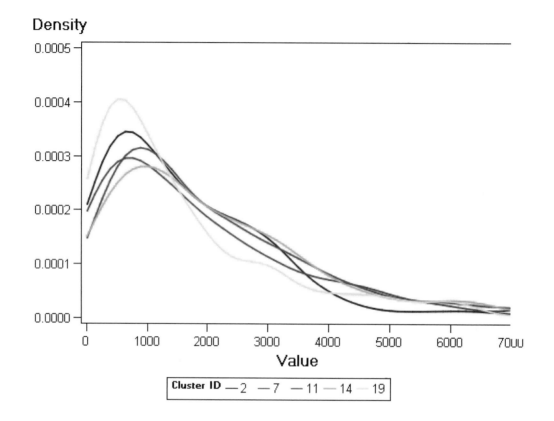

For total payments, the highest are again for ulcers and arthritis. The peak payment for a year is under $1,000.

Figure 12 Kernel Density Estimation for Most Clusters for Private Insurance

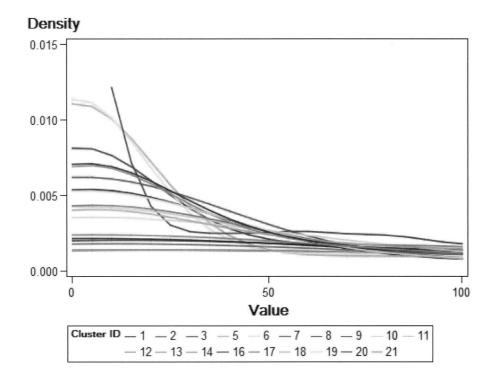

Most of the remaining clusters reflect a hierarchy of costs. For example, Clusters 5, 6, and 8 have the highest probability of low cost; Clusters 9 and 14 have the lowest probability of low cost. Clusters not pictured have little variability beyond the 0 point.

Figure 13 Kernel Density Estimation for Most Clusters for Self-Pay

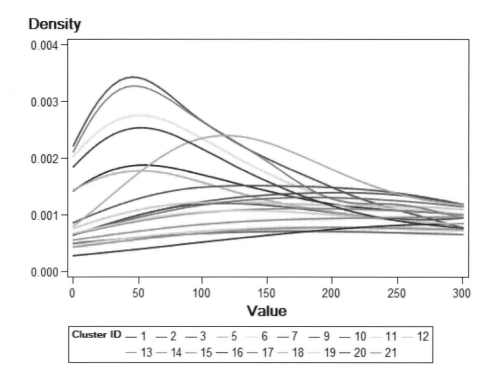

The hierarchical pattern in Figure 12 is not present here. In fact, for many of the clusters, the probability of higher payment increases rather than decreases; only Clusters 3, 10, 6, 20, 1, and 5 have a probability of lower cost, with the probability decreasing for higher payments.

Defining Concept Links with Association Rules

In addition to clusters, you can use concept links to find relationships. SAS Text Miner software uses association rules to define the concept links. The relationship between terms is assumed by default to be highly significant. That is, the chi-square statistic is greater than 12. Figure 14 shows the concept links for the medication Celexa.

Figure 14 Concept Links for Celexa

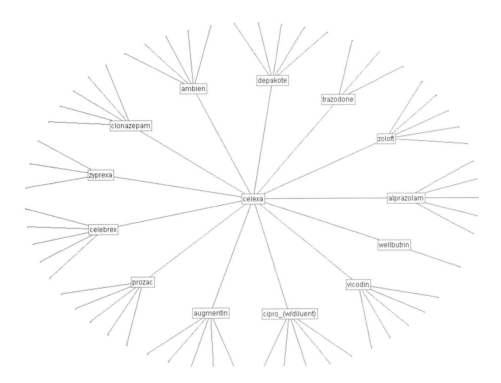

The concept links provide the confidence value for the association. Medications, such as Prozac and Zoloft, are listed as associated with Celexa. These links indicate that patients often switch from one drug to another either because the drug is not effective in treating the condition or there is a change in insurance formularies. Also, note that Vicodin (a pain killer) is listed.

Figure 15 Concept Links for Zestril

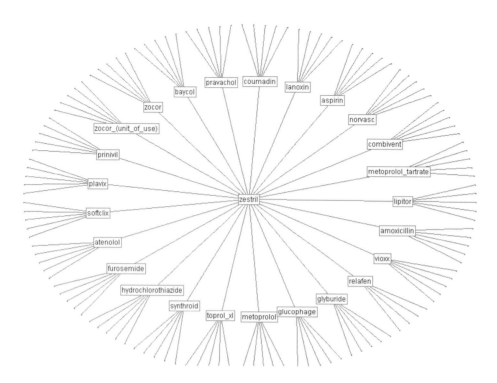

There are many links to Zestril. They include many heart and diabetes medications, indicating a strong link. Zestril is often used to treat heart problems in combination with other medications.

Figure 16 Concept Links for Albuterol

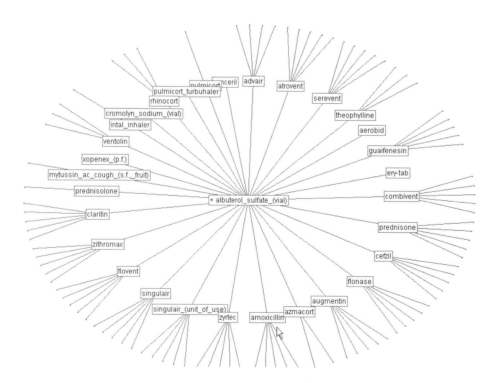

Albuterol is related to various other asthma medications such as Singulair, Zyrtec, and Serevent. It is also related to antibiotics such as Zithromax. There is a relationship between Albuterol and Flovent.

Validating Text Clusters

The example data set includes ICD9 codes that give the patient diagnosis associated with a medication. You can use these diagnosis codes to validate the text clusters. The Association node in SAS Enterprise Miner 5.2 was used to examine all ICD9 codes for patients in any one text cluster. Figure 17 gives the linkages for codes for patients in Cluster 16, asthma. In a link analysis, the most common codes have the largest shape; the most prominent linkages have the widest lines. Table 2 gives the most prominent codes. With the exception of depression, the most prominent codes are associated with asthma and upper respiratory tract diseases.

Figure 17 Diagnosis Codes Associated with Cluster 16

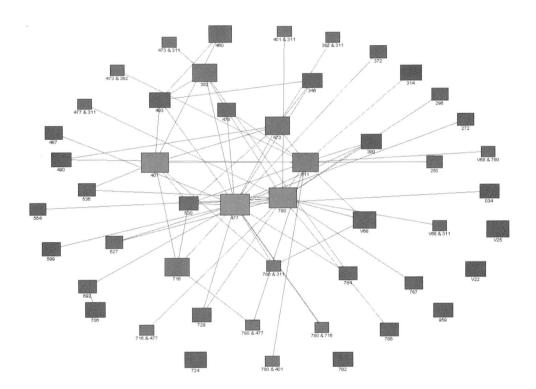

Table 2 ICD9 Codes Associated with Asthma Cluster

Code	Representation
780	Sleep disorder, dizziness
401	Essential hypertension
477	Allergic rhinitis
311	Depression
473	Chronic sinusitis
530	Diseases of the esophagus
476	Upper respiratory tract diseases
493	Asthma
382	Otitis media

Similarly, the diagnosis codes associated with Cluster 1, diabetes and heart, were examined (Figure 18) with the codes defined in Table 3. While codes 715 and 716 don't seem to fit immediately, joint stiffness is commonly associated with diabetes.

Figure 18 Diagnosis Codes Associated with Diabetes and Heart

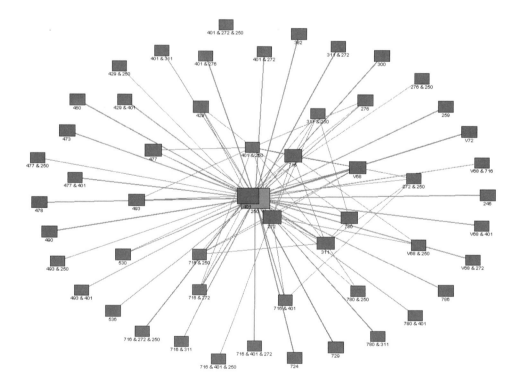

Table 3 Diagnosis Code Definitions

Code	Representation
250	Diabetes
401	Essential hypertension
272	High cholesterol
715	Osteoarthrosis
716	Other arthropathies
V58	Convalescence and palliative care
311	Depression
780	Sleep disorder, dizziness
429	Complications of heart disease

Conclusion

Association rules work best when there are only a few possible consumer choices. When there are thousands of choices, you need to find methods to reduce the choices to classes of choices. SAS Text Miner software can automate the reduction by defining clusters of choices based on the rules of grammar, stemming, and context. The association is preserved by defining the observational unit as one consumer and defining a text string of possible choices.

SAS Text Miner software applies association rules through concept links. Linkage between items in a market basket is preserved through the construction of a text string where all purchases are contained within the string. The method is successful when items in the market basket are *stemmed* so that similar items have similar base words. You must validate the clusters found using additional variables in the data set.

11.3 Analysis of Faculty Workloads and Instruction Costs

Introduction

Instruction is more cost-effective when part-time instructors are used as often as possible, full-time faculty can buy out as many courses as possible, and fewer courses are offered by maximizing enrollment in each course. For example, if a full-time faculty member earning $80,000 per year has a grant buy out of 20% ($16,000) for one course, then paying a part-time instructor $5,000 to teach that course saves the university $11,000. That figure does not include the overhead that is also returned to the university for the grant. Hiring postdoctorate candidates, who often draw half the salary of full-time faculty members, to replace faculty members on leave is also cost-effective. Hiring graduate students is costlier than hiring part-time faculty and postdoctorates once tuition levels, particularly out-of-state rates, are computed. However, graduate students still cost less compared to full-time faculty members. Strict cost guidelines cannot be followed, however, because there are tradeoffs in quality, including high instructor turnover and instructors with fewer credentials teaching in the place of instructors with more credentials.

The following variables were analyzed in the data set:

- faculty workloads
- faculty course assignments
- faculty leaves
- courses scheduled
- course enrollment
- cost factors

Investigating average values is not adequate. Enrollments vary from fall to spring and from year to year. Therefore, you must examine the problem of variability and account for it when analyzing cost, enrollment, and scheduling. Otherwise, the department will have insufficient funds in high demand years and extra funds in low demand years. Using funds available during low demand to cover courses in high demand would be ideal. However, that would mean carrying over continuing funds.

We defined the variables needed to complete the analysis, and a process flow diagram was developed in SAS Enterprise Guide to continually update the results. SAS Enterprise Guide was chosen because it can automate the graphing process and it can be modified easily by non-SAS programmers.

Results

Figures 1 and 2 give kernel density estimates of overall time committed to instruction. Figure 1 demonstrates the difference between actual course allocation and total instruction (involving supervision of students). Note that most of the distribution is between 40% and 60% for instruction, with some outliers. However, Figure 2 gives a three-year distribution. It is clear that classroom time is declining.

Figure 1 Difference between Course Time and Instruction Time

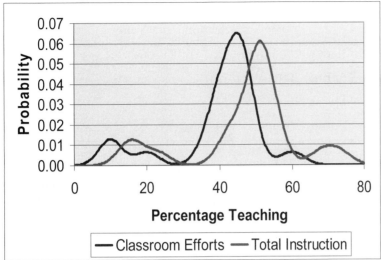

Figure 2 Examination of Classroom Time over Three-Year Period

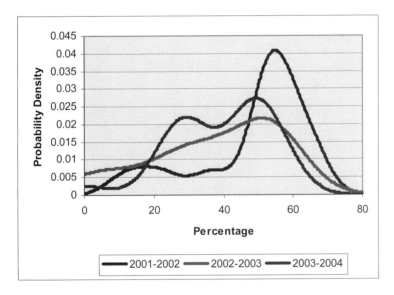

From 2001–2002 to 2002–2003, teaching percentages dropped dramatically in the Mathematics Department. The trend continued in 2003–2004, although there is an obvious tendency toward a bimodal curve, indicating a split in the department between those with 45% allocations and those with 25% allocations. The longitudinal trend should be considered during departmental requests for more teaching resources.

The department has 25 full-time tenured and tenure-track faculty members. Each is responsible for teaching two courses per semester. However, an examination of the last four years indicates that the faculty members teach approximately two-thirds of this amount (Table 1).

Table 1 Course Sections Taught by Tenured Faculty

Semester	Number of Section	Semester	Number of Section	Total for Year
Fall, 2000	31	Spring, 2000	38	69
Fall, 2001	35	Spring, 2001	31	66
Fall, 2002	35	Spring, 2002	34	69
Fall, 2003	34	Spring, 2003	34	68

The additional 30 courses must be taught by part-time and term faculty. Term faculty are not in tenure track positions and are given short-term contracts that can be renewed. Therefore, it is worth examining the reasons that those courses are not taught (Table 2).

Table 2 Reasons Faculty Have Lower Teaching Requirements

Course Sections	Explanation	Reimbursement to College
68	Taught by full-time	Salary base
9	Reductions for administration	None
4	Grant buyout	90% salary base
3	Reduction for assistant professors	None
12	Unpaid leave	100% salary base
8	Paid leave	50% one salary base
2	Emergency medical leave	50% one salary base

The paid leaves and grant buyouts provide the department with $182,000 in salary dollars, which is fairly consistent from year to year. This money can be used to pay for term and part-time instruction, including postdoctoral positions. One term faculty member can teach 10 course sections per year of general education, while 2.5 term positions can cover the courses not taught by faculty members.

Therefore, the paid leave results in a net gain for the department of almost $100,000, and paid reductions in teaching yield a net gain to the department because of salary differentials between full-time, part-time, and term faculty members.

The number of faculty members teaching the standard four courses has declined from 16 to 10 while the number of faculty members on reduced loads of two has increased from 2 to 7 and reduced loads of three from 3 to 4. Therefore, 10 members of the faculty teach a full load; 11 teach a reduced load. The total number of courses taught by faculty has declined from 77 to 68 (see Figure 3).

Figure 3 Number of Courses Taught by Faculty Member

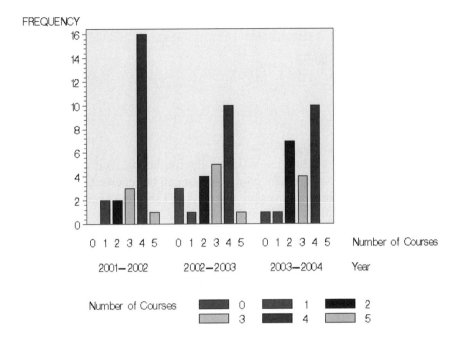

Figure 4 contrasts the number of courses taught by full-time faculty members to the number taught by part-time and term faculty members.

Figure 4 Courses Taught by Part-Time and Term Faculty Members

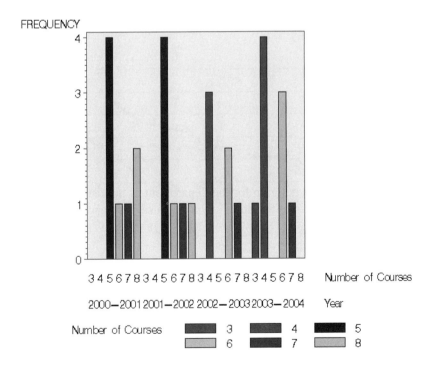

In 2000–2001, term instructors taught a total of 49 sections. This declined to 44 sections in 2003–2004. In 2000–2001, term and full-time faculty members taught a total of 126 courses; this declined to 102 in 2003–3004.

Another important consideration is the area of expertise for each faculty member and the courses taught. A simple ratio was used, equal to the number of courses in a discipline divided by the number of faculty in that discipline. Figure 5 shows the disparities in the specific needs of the department.

Figure 5 Ratio of Faculty to Discipline

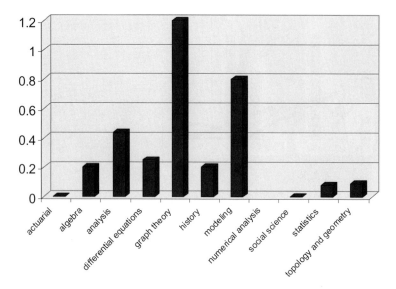

If students wanted more courses in graph theory and modeling, it would be beneficial to have more faculty in those areas. Therefore, students were surveyed to determine their preferences (see Figure 6).

Figure 6 Results of Student Survey

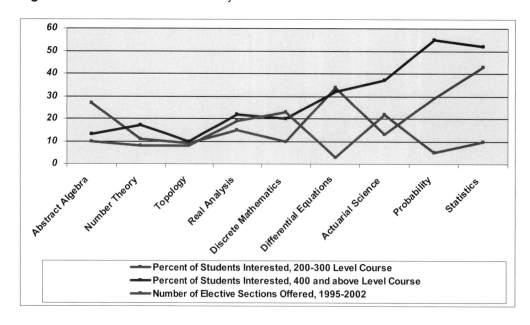

Another resource allocation concerns the amount of time spent performing research, as Figure 7 illustrates. The total time allocation should be a sum of instructional time, research, and service.

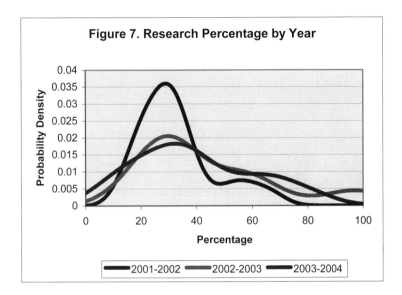

Figure 7. Research Percentage by Year

In 2001–2002, research allocation peaked at about 25%, with a small subpeak at 60%. However, in 2002–2003 and 2003–2004, research allocations became more variable, and more faculty members had allocations higher than 45%.

Discussion
Cost and faculty productivity can have a cost benefit through the acquisition of course buyout from grant activity. The question is whether the cost benefit affects the quality of instruction. Basic general education can be taught by experienced term faculty with no loss of quality.

11.4 Analysis of the University Database for Mathematics

Analysis of General Education Requirements

Introduction

Many resources are used to teach remedial courses to students unprepared for university work, particularly in mathematics. However, student course choices are often not examined to see if there are specific pathways to greater success. This paper examines student transcripts, including courses chosen and grade point average (GPA) in those courses, to determine which pathways are more successful than others.

Method

All information on enrollment, degrees earned, and grades received were downloaded from the Registrar's database from 2000 to the present (August 2005). There were a total of 78,000 student records and almost 300,000 student enrollments. Information from multiple tables was linked using the student identification number. The study was submitted to and approved by the Institutional Review Board (IRB) for human studies review before examining the data. The Registrar's database contains information on courses. The downloaded data file has an observational unit defined as course, so each student has multiple entries. It is possible to change the observational unit to student. However, how do you best record all courses for an individual student into one observational unit? One way is to create a text string that contains all courses of interest for any student and then to create a field for the average GPA for those same courses. The text string contains the entire student pathway through the curriculum. Once the text strings are defined, you can examine them using text analysis. In particular, associations of courses can be determined, and clusters can be defined as specific patterns of student choice.

Results

Courses by Department

First, there is considerable difference between disciplines related to student success. Figure 1 shows the proportion of grades by selected discipline for general education courses.

Figure 1 Proportion of Grades by Selected Disciplines

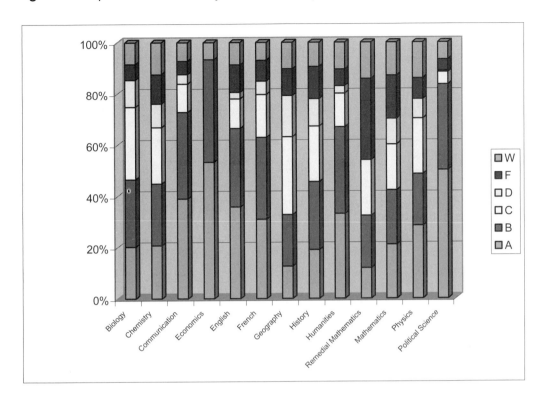

Economics and political science have awarded the highest proportion of A's, followed by communication and English. Remedial mathematics and geography have awarded the lowest proportion of A's, followed by history, biology, chemistry, and mathematics. Combining the proportion of W's and F's, the highest proportion is awarded by remedial mathematics, followed by mathematics; the fewest W's and F's are awarded by communication and political science. The graph demonstrates that the reputation of mathematics as a gatekeeper to success at the university is well-deserved. Figure 2 shows the grades by mathematics course.

Figure 2 Grades by Mathematics Course

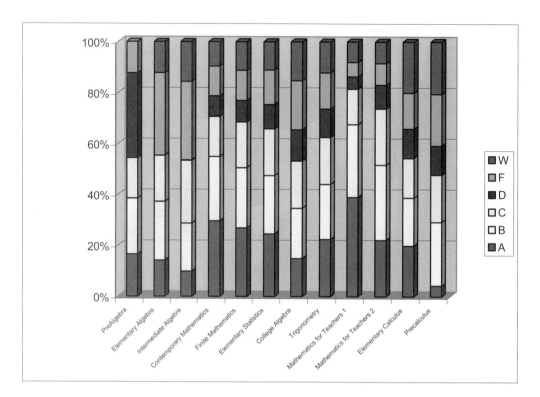

The highest rate of success is for contemporary mathematics, which is not an algebra-based course, and for the courses for teachers; the lowest is for the algebra sequences: elementary, intermediate, college algebra, and precalculus. Therefore, students in a position to avoid the algebra-based courses will have a higher rate of success in the gatekeeper discipline.

Clustering of Mathematics Performance

Figures 1 and 2 use course as the observational unit instead of student. To examine individual performances in mathematics courses, you must examine all of the mathematics courses attempted by an individual student. First, all enrollments for one student are translated and then concatenated. Figure 3 shows the proportion of students in each unit of the university by mathematics cluster.

Figure 3 Proportion of Students by Mathematics Cluster

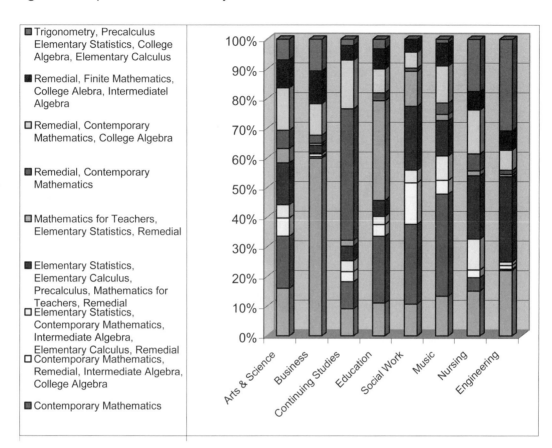

Most business majors enroll in the college algebra, finite mathematics sequence; the majority of continuing studies students begin in the remedial courses. Figure 4 shows the proportion of graduates to mathematics cluster.

Of the 1,009 engineering majors beginning at the general education level (precalculus and below), only 8 completed a degree in the same time frame. The results suggest that students who do not score on the ACT test as ready for calculus should be discouraged from declaring an Engineering major. Similarly, while college algebra and finite mathematics account for 59% of enrollment from the School of Business, the same cluster accounts for 76% of degrees. All continuing studies students must transfer to a different unit to graduate, so none of those enrolled are included in the degree list.

Several clusters contain contemporary mathematics; all but one also include remedial mathematics. The primary units include arts and sciences, education, social work, and music, disciplines that do not focus on mathematics. In Cluster 2 without remedial mathematics, enrollment is at 18%, 27%, 22%, and 34%, respectively. However, that same cluster accounts for 25%, 38%, 38%, and 34%. It shows that the likelihood of graduation is less (except for music) when students begin at the remedial level (see Figure 4).

Figure 4 Likelihood of Graduation by Cluster

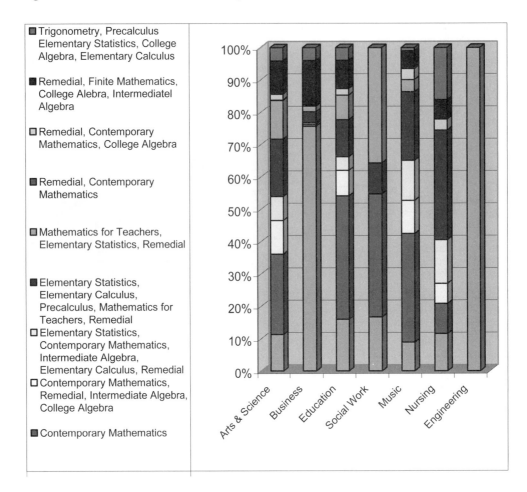

Students sometimes repeat the same course to improve the final grade and to advance. Therefore, the average grade on a 4-point scale was computed for each individual student. Figure 5 offers a kernel density estimation of grade point average by cluster.

Figure 5 Distribution of Grade Point Average by Cluster

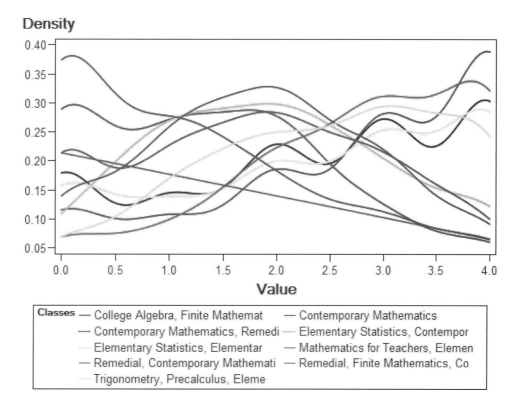

Classes — College Algebra, Finite Mathemat — Contemporary Mathematics
— Contemporary Mathematics, Remedi — Elementary Statistics, Contempor
— Elementary Statistics, Elementar — Mathematics for Teachers, Elemen
— Remedial, Contemporary Mathemati — Remedial, Finite Mathematics, Co
— Trigonometry, Precalculus, Eleme

There are two readily identifiable trends in Figure 5. Courses in contemporary mathematics, college algebra and finite mathematics, elementary statistics, and mathematics for teachers have increasing probability from left to right toward the higher grade point averages. Remedial mathematics has decreasing probability toward the higher grade averages. Figure 6 restricts the probability distributions to students who have completed degrees.

Figure 6 Distribution of Math GPA by Clusters for Graduating Students

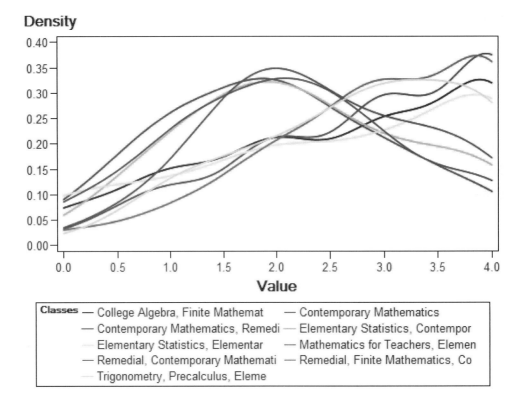

The distributions for those clusters that had increasing probability of higher grade points remain similar, indicating that those who graduate have similar probability compared to all students enrolled in those mathematics clusters. However, graduates beginning in the remedial groups have a peak probability of a C-average grade point in mathematics. Contrast Figure 6 with the distributions in Figure 7 of students who have not completed a degree.

Figure 7 Distribution of Math GPA by Clusters for Non-Graduating Students

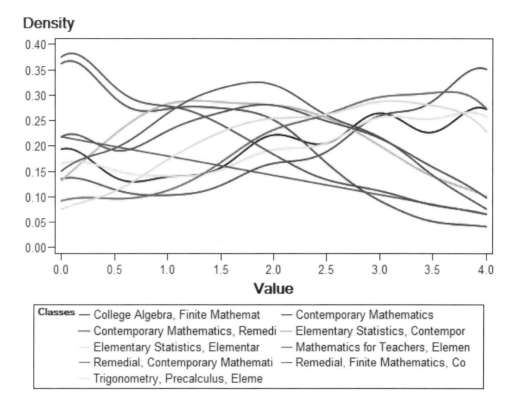

By comparing Figures 6 and 7, it is clear that students in remedial courses who average less than a 2.0 have a high probability of not graduating. Most students who enroll in remedial courses have a low grade point average, indicating that the prognosis of remedial students is poor.

Both grade average and mathematics cluster were used to predict graduation outcomes. Predictive modeling in SAS Enterprise Miner 5.2 was used to investigate the relationship. To validate the results, the data were partitioned into training, validation, and testing data sets. For logistic regression, the misclassification rate for the testing set is 19%, indicating that the model can predict more than 80% of student outcomes correctly. Figure 8 shows the corresponding decision tree to predict outcomes. Three input variables were used in the model: Enrollment College, Mathematics Cluster, and Mathematics Grade Point Average.

Figure 8 Decision Tree for Predicting Student Success

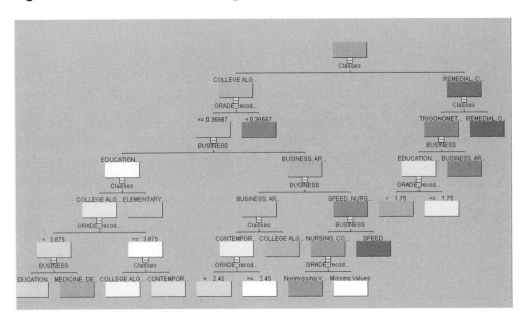

A white block indicates the prediction of successful graduation—the darker the block, the less likely the graduation. Note that those in education can succeed with a grade point average of 1.75 or above in the remedial track; those in business require 2.45 or above in the college algebra track. An F performance in the college algebra track indicates non-graduation. SAS Enterprise Miner software also prints English rules corresponding to Figure 8. Some of the rules follow:

```
IF  GRADE_recoded_Mean  < 0.3666666667
AND Classes IS ONE OF: COLLEGE ALGEBRA, FINITE MATHEMAT
    CONTEMPORARY MATHEMATICS CONTEMPORARY MATHEMATICS, REMEDI
    ELEMENTARY STATISTICS, CONTEMPOR ELEMENTARY STATISTICS, ELEMENTAR
    MATHEMATICS FOR TEACHERS, ELEMEN REMEDIAL, FINITE MATHEMATICS, CO
THEN
    NODE    :        4
    N       :     2970
    NO DEGRE:    91.0%
    DEGREE  :     9.0%


IF  Classes EQUALS REMEDIAL, CONTEMPORARY MATHEMATI
THEN
    NODE    :        7
    N       :     5912
    NO DEGRE:    98.2%
    DEGREE  :     1.8%


IF  Major  IS ONE OF: BUSINESS ARTS & SCIENCES SPEED NURSING
    CONTIN. STUDIES
AND Classes EQUALS TRIGONOMETRY, PRECALCULUS, ELEME
THEN
    NODE    :       13
    N       :     2382
    NO DEGRE:    90.2%
    DEGREE  :     9.8%
```

```
IF  Classes IS ONE OF: ELEMENTARY STATISTICS, CONTEMPOR
    ELEMENTARY STATISTICS, ELEMENTAR
AND Major  IS ONE OF: EDUCATION MEDICINE DENTISTRY ALLIED HEALTH
    LAW - DAY KENT
AND 0.3666666667 <= GRADE_recoded_Mean
THEN
   NODE    :      20
   N       :     281
   NO DEGRE:   28.8%
   DEGREE  :   71.2%


IF  GRADE_recoded_Mean  <        1.75
AND Major  IS ONE OF: EDUCATION MUSIC
AND Classes EQUALS TRIGONOMETRY, PRECALCULUS, ELEME
THEN
   NODE    :      24
   N       :      39
   NO DEGRE:   76.9%
   DEGREE  :   23.1%


IF           1.75 <= GRADE_recoded_Mean
AND Major  IS ONE OF: EDUCATION MUSIC
AND Classes EQUALS TRIGONOMETRY, PRECALCULUS, ELEME
THEN
   NODE    :      25
   N       :      61
   NO DEGRE:   44.3%
   DEGREE  :   55.7%
```

At some values, such as when the grade point average is less than 0.367, the likelihood of graduation is extremely small. Similarly, if the cluster is remedial and contemporary mathematics, then the non-degree is approximately 98% of the group. However, for another track, the degree rate climbs to 56%. The score rankings graph (Figure 9) also indicates that some individuals can be predicted with greater confidence than others.

Figure 9 Score Rankings for Predicting Student Success

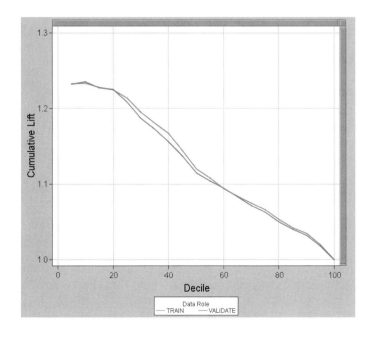

For a binary target, all observations in the scored data set are sorted by the posterior probabilities of the event level in descending order. Then the sorted observations are grouped into deciles where observations in a decile are used to calculate the statistics. The *x*-axis of a score rankings chart displays the deciles (groups) of the observations. The *y*-axis displays the cumulative percent response. For this example, responders are identified as non-degree. Observations with a posterior probability of non-degree greater than or equal to 0.5 are classified as responders. Note the decreasing level across the deciles. The students most at risk for not graduating can be predicted early in their academic careers based on their performance in mathematics courses.

College Algebra

Recently, the algebra offerings were reorganized. The University of Louisville now teaches college algebra, while pre-algebra and intermediate algebra are taught by community college faculty. This is an expensive method. Currently, students need a score of 23 on the mathematics ACT examination to enroll in college algebra. Special sections of college algebra were developed requiring 5 contact hours for students at the 20–22 ACT level to see if the extra time would enable them to succeed. Figure 10 shows the distribution of ACT scores by type of course enrollment.

Figure 10 ACT Level by Course Enrollment

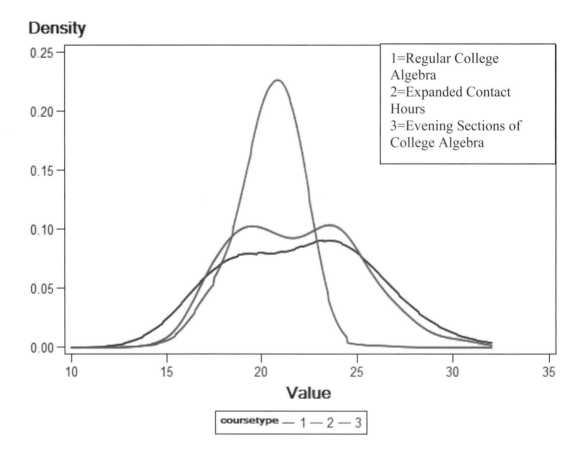

The math ACT in the college algebra sections with expanded contact hours has less variability compared to the others, with students above the value of 23 ineligible. However, many students with an ACT score lower than 23 are still enrolled in regular sections of college algebra. Figure 11 shows a breakdown of grades by ACT scores.

Figure 11 Student Grades by ACT Scores

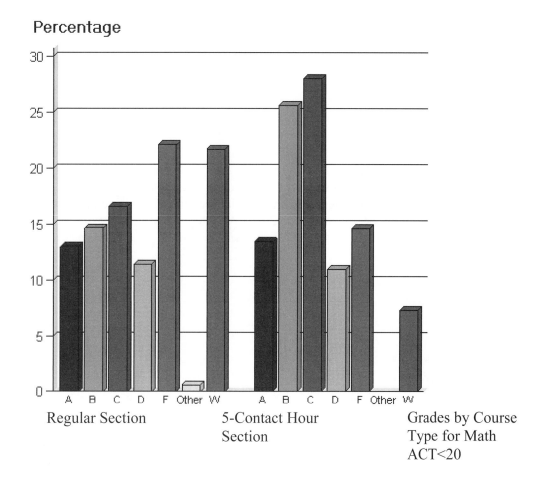

For students with an ACT score less than 20, there is a higher proportion of A, B, and C grades and a lower proportion of F and W scores compared to the regular section of college algebra. Figure 12 shows a similar graph for students with a math ACT score between 20 and 23.

Figure 12 Proportion of Grades for Students with ACT Score between 20 and 23

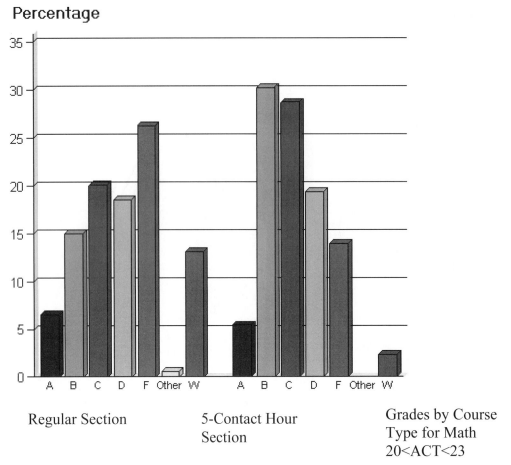

Percentage

Regular Section   5-Contact Hour Section   Grades by Course Type for Math 20<ACT<23

Again, there is considerable improvement in the sections with 5 contact hours. Note that there is no real difference in ACT scores for students who pass (A, B, or C), and those who fail (see Figure 13).

Figure 13 Comparison of ACT Scores for Passing and Failing Students

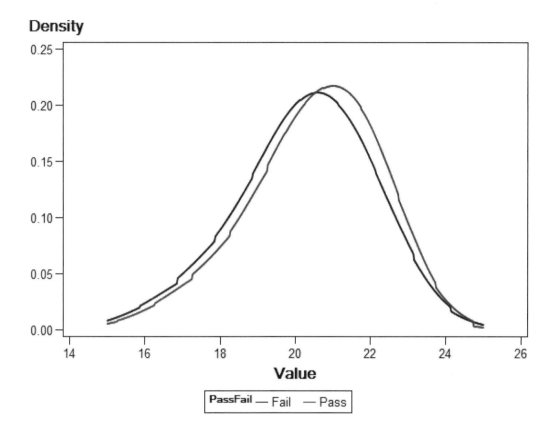

Discussion

There is a strong relationship between performance in mathematics courses and final success in graduation. The relationship depends on choice of major as well as choice of mathematics course. This information can be used to advise students to shift majors if their mathematics performance is inadequate to succeed in their current choice of major. If the performance in mathematics is too low, the likelihood of graduation is almost non-existent. This should be considered when discussing future student choices.

It is also clear that more contact hours with the instructor results in greater success for students in college algebra. Because the regular sections are taught at large lectures, should all college algebra be taught in small sections?

Analysis of Undergraduate Courses and Program

Introduction

Currently, once students are admitted to the College of Arts and Sciences at the University of Louisville, they may choose any major. However, some majors require greater background knowledge than others. The choice of major can itself be an impediment to retention if the student is enrolled in courses beyond their skill level. It would be helpful to tell students the estimate of success for their chosen major given ACT scores.

This paper investigates the relationship between ACT scores, courses attempted, and retention for students who declare a major in mathematics. It was found that students with low ACT scores who declare as mathematics majors generally change majors or do not graduate. It was also found that there is a change in the proportion of high grades assigned by course level. Reasons for different grade patterns should be examined.

Methods

An examination of the institutional database from 2000–2004 showed a total of 172 students with a declared major of mathematics sometime in their first year of enrollment. Of that number, 40 took mathematics courses at the general education 100 level (precalculus). To complete the analysis, several queries were required from the course enrollment database. In particular, comparing course grades to admission ACT scores has proven to be a difficult extract.

Levels of course entry are defined as follows:

- 100: general education with a prerequisite of a 23 ACT score
- 190: precalculus with a prerequisite of a 25 ACT score
- 205: first semester calculus with a prerequisite of a 27 ACT score
- 206: second semester calculus with a prerequisite of a 27 ACT score and AP calculus examination or math 205

Results

Table 1 shows the relationship among choice of mathematics, change in major, and retention after the first year of registration. While students who start at the 190, precalculus level seem to be retained more than students who start at any other course level, it is troubling that 32% of students in calculus II change their major and 21% leave the university altogether.

Table 1 Proportion of Students Changing Majors or Leaving after One Year

Starting Course Level	Proportion Changing Majors	Proportion Leaving University
100	53%	18%
190	10%	15%
205	20%	23%
206	32%	21%

Table 2 shows student grades by course level. The course levels represent the following:

- 300: calculus III, linear algebra, introduction to proof
- 400: differential equations, numerical analysis
- 450: actuarial courses
- 500: modern algebra, analysis, probability and statistics
- 550: actuarial courses
- 600: graduate mathematics

Actuarial courses were coded separately because they are taken more by part-time students in the community preparing for actuarial examinations than full-time mathematics majors. The percentages in Table 2 do not add to 100% because of miscellaneous other grades not listed (audits).

Table 2 Comparison of Grades by Course Level

Course Level	A	B	C	D	F	W
100	25%	23%	17%	8%	17%	10%
190	26%	16%	10%	21%	21%	5%
205	23%	13%	13%	13%	13%	23%
206	28%	12%	12%	16%	12%	20%
300	26%	19%	19%	7%	16%	12%
400	48%	22%	12%	2%	5%	10%
450	54%	17%	8%	1%	8%	12%
500	32%	20%	9%	5%	10%	21%
550	80%	0%	0%	0%	10%	10%
600	71%	11%	2%	1%	1%	8%

Note the sharp increase in the proportion of A grades between the 300-level and the 400-level, while the proportion of F's and W's is cut almost in half. However, the A's decline while the F's and W's increase at the 500-level, increasing again at the 600-level. At the 500-level, senior undergraduates are enrolled along with graduate students. Who is more responsible for the lower grade levels: graduate or undergraduate students? Table 3 drills down into the 500-level courses by degree pursued.

Table 3 Grades for 500-Level Courses by Degree

Grade	BA Degree	BS Degree	MA Degree
A	25%	21%	60%
B	26%	11%	18%
C	11%	13%	3%
D	5%	3%	0%
F	12%	15%	1%
W	21%	37%	14%

Contrast these percentages with those in Table 4 for the undergraduate level.

Table 4 Grades for 400-Level Courses by Degree

Grade	BA Degree	BS Degree
A	43%	30%
B	26%	30%
C	17%	10%
D	4%	0%
F	9%	0%
W	0%	30%

The lower percentage for the A grades is caused by missing values for degrees pursued. However, it is clear that the percentage of A grades drops considerably from the 400-level to the 500-level for undergraduate students when a substantial number of graduate students are in the courses. One explanation for this change could be that graduate students increase the expectations of faculty members disproportionate to the increased maturity levels of the undergraduate students. It is a hypothesis that should be examined. Figure 14 gives the proportion of A grades by degree (BA, BS, MA). First, note that undergraduate mathematics students take very specific 500-level courses that correspond to degree requirements; graduate students take many more of the 500-level courses. It is also apparent that undergraduates tend to be at the extremes, with all or none receiving A grades in courses.

Figure 14 Proportion of A Grades by Degree Pursued

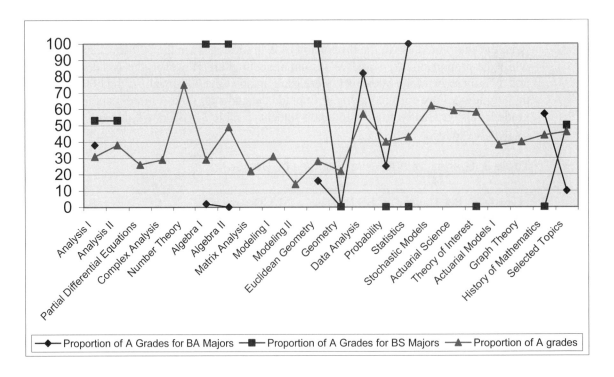

If the proportion of A grades is compared for graduate and undergraduate students only in the courses that have both graduate and undergraduate students, the difference becomes 45% for graduate students and 33% for undergraduate students. For courses taken only by graduate students, the proportion of A's drops to 41%. The overall graduation rate by course level is shown in Table 5.

Table 5 Graduation Rate by Course Level and Grade for Mathematics Majors

Course Level	Graduation Rate for A grades	B grades	C grades	D, F grades	W grades
100	36%	30%	18%	0%	50%
200	65%	0%	0%	41%	0%
300	76%	49%	37%	20%	46%
400	100%	0%	0%	0%	0%
500	80%	76%	100%	27%	20%
600	100%	100%	100%	None given	None given

The graduation proportion steadily increases as the course level increases. At the 400-and 500-levels, these percentages occur even though the proportion of A grades decreases. For graduate students enrolled at the 600-level, a C grade is equivalent to a D or F at the undergraduate level because of the requirements that students have a 3.0 GPA.

Figure 15 shows the relationship between ACT math scores and course levels. There is a shift toward higher values. Figure 16 shows a smoothed histogram with the different course levels overlaid. The probability for 100-level and 190-level courses is near the lower end of 22–24, while more advanced courses are at the higher end of 30+. The dividing point appears to be between 205 and 206 (calculus I and II), where the peak for calculus I is at 27 but shifts to 31 for calculus II. Beyond the level of calculus, students with a low ACT score have almost no likelihood of enrolling. It appears that students with lower ACT scores do not continue on to more advanced mathematics courses.

Figure 15 ACT Math Score by Course Level

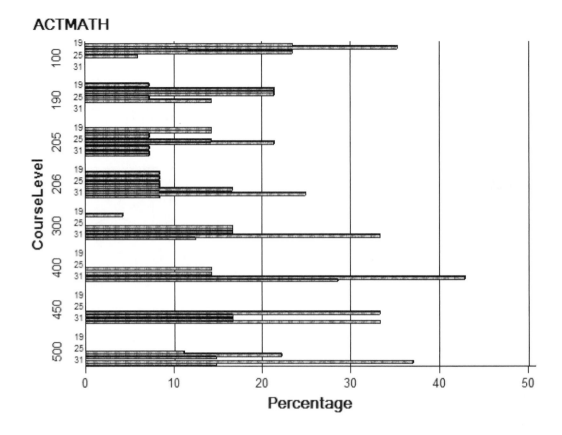

Figure 16 Smoothed Histogram of ACT Levels

Figure 16 also shows that the peak ACT level for the 100-level general education courses is below the minimum prerequisite value. A second peak occurs at 24, just above the requirement of 23. Similarly, most of the ACT values for the 190, precalculus level are lower than the prerequisite value. It appears that too many students are enrolled in courses for which they are not prepared.

Discussion

Focus of student enrollment versus ACT scores should move beyond those at risk who require remedial mathematics and those who enroll as at-risk students. Students who pass the university requirement of a 21 composite ACT score are also at risk. Although it has always been clear that students with low ACT scores are at risk at the university, specific cutoff values are not as obvious because dedicated students can overcome barriers. However, as shown in Figures 15 and 16, students with ACT mathematics scores below 30 are at risk if they declare as mathematics majors. Students with ACT scores below 30 should be discouraged from declaring mathematics majors, or the requirement for mathematics majors should be a math ACT score of 30 or greater or completion of math 206, calculus II.

Students enrolled at the 400-level have a mathematics ACT score above 30, as shown in Figure 15. However, as the students move from the 400-level to the 500-level, grades decrease for undergraduate students. It is apparent from Table 3 that enrollment in these courses by graduate students changes performance expectations. The department should consider whether it wants to maintain these expectations at the 500-level or whether undergraduate students should be held to a standard more in line with the expectations at the 400-level.

There are some limitations to this study. Extracts from the institutional database leave too many missing values at crucial points in the database. This study relies on report tables that could be downloaded from the PeopleSoft database used to store institutional data. However, because this study is primarily exploratory rather than inferential, it does provide several results that require follow up.

Analysis of Graduate Courses and Program

Introduction

A typical university makes a considerable investment in graduate students in mathematics. Many universities offer stipends and tuition remissions, which are increasing regularly to remain competitive for quality students. Although the university will receive some return on investment (ROI) in teaching responsibilities, graduate students in many cases cost more than adjunct faculty members who do not normally require tuition benefits. At the University of Louisville, postdoctoral positions are more cost-effective than graduate student positions. A more important ROI is for graduate students to complete their degrees. To do so, students must complete courses successfully (A or B). Often they are required to take comprehensive examinations in addition to completing their coursework.

This paper examines the relationship between variability in course instruction, testing, and grading and retention of students. At the graduate level, examinations are not validated, nor are multiple graders used to investigate the issue of reliability of grading habits. Graduate faculty members usually enjoy complete autonomy in assigning grades, in selecting course content, and in developing examinations. Autonomy leads to variability of practice, which leads to variability of results. This paper examines the relationship between the variability of practice to the variability of retention of graduate students.

Method and Background

Information was solicited using ERIC and Education Abstracts, two electronic databases that contain references to publications in education, including higher education. With one exception, the author found no papers related to examinations of the variability in grading in higher education. This variability is commonly known to exist, but it is not documented through statistical analysis. Monetary cost of this variability is also not examined, particularly in departments where most, if not all, of the graduate students are given stipends and tuition remission.

The questions that must be considered in terms of higher education policy are as follows:

1. Is the university investing in instructors or in students when providing stipends and tuition?

   a. At the University of Louisville, graduate students represent a higher cost per credit hour taught compared to adjunct faculty.

2. What is the cost per graduate as defined by the ratio of the number of graduate students hired to the number of students graduated?

   a. Just how many resources is the university willing to spend per graduate?

3. When hiring employees, most businesses in the private sector assume that the new hire can perform the job required.

   a. Should universities admit graduate students with the assumption that they will succeed in their degree program? Or do they admit them with the assumption that over 50% will not succeed?

To investigate these questions, data for 2000–2004 on enrollment and grades were collected from the university's PeopleSoft database. The information was supplemented with information in paper files from the Department of Mathematics. Descriptive statistics, data visualization, and data mining techniques were used to investigate the data.

Table 6 lists the MA and PhD degree requirements in the Department of Mathematics at the University of Louisville. Although the MA degree does not require specific courses, students must enroll in available course sequences. Six are available. Many MA students take 500-level prerequisites to the sequences to complete their 30 credit hours.

Table 6 Graduate Degree Requirements at the University of Louisville

Degree Requirements	MA	PhD
Total Credit Hours	30	66–72
600-Level Courses	Two 6-hour course sequences One additional 3-hour course	Two of Analysis, Combinatorics, Algebra Two of Modeling, Applied Statistics, Probability and Statistics
Applied Courses (can be in a related discipline)	12 hours as approved by advisor	18 hours as approved by advisor
Internship	Optional	Required
Additional Requirements		Computer project
Exit Requirements	Comprehensive written examination or two PhD qualifying examinations or MA thesis	Two theoretical qualifying examinations, 1 applied qualifying examination, candidacy examination, dissertation

Results

First, retention from the first semester to the second semester was considered, both for the 500-level prerequisite courses and for the 600-level courses (Table 7). There is considerable variability in the drop-off from semester I to semester II, which can be as high as 60% of the students enrolled in semester I. For graduate students in the PhD program, this drop-off can result in a one- or two-year delay in completion of degree requirements (since courses are not offered every year). Not all students are willing to accept this delay, and some will leave the program.

Table 7 Retention in Sequence Courses

Course	Academic Year	Semester 1	Semester 2	Percentage Drop-off
Analysis I, II (500-level)	2002–2003	30	21	30%
	2003–2004	35	15	57%
	2004–2005	33	12	64%
Algebra I, II (500-level)	2002–2003	30	17	43%
	2003–2004	19	16	16%
	2004–2005	21	14	33%
Probability and Statistics (500-level)	2003–2004	23	22	4%
	2004–2005	23	20	13%
Modeling (500-level)	2003–2004	9	6	33%
Analysis I, II (600-level)	2003–2004	16	9	44%
	2004–2005	13	7	46%
Algebra I, II (600-level)	2002–2003	15	8	47%
	2004–2005	16	13	19%
Combinatorics I, II (600-level)	2002–2003	11	7	36%
	2004–2005	23	17	26%
Probability and Statistics (600-level)	2002–2003	20	12	40%
	2004–2005	9	13	Increase
Modeling I, II (600-level)	2003–2004	25	23	8%
Applied Statistics (600-level)	2003–2004	20	13	35%

To examine the relationship between drop-off and grades, Table 8 lists the grades for the sequence courses. Table 9 examines the relationship specifically for Modeling I and II because the 500-level and 600-level courses are taught simultaneously.

Table 8 Grades by Course

Grade	Analysis I	Analysis II	Algebra I	Algebra II	Probability	Statistics
A	30%	41%	23%	55%	29%	42%
B	23%	32%	23%	17%	33%	18%
C	11%	8%	14%	1%	15%	4%
D	5%	18%	9%	11%	2%	4%
F	11%	3%	7%	4%	10%	5%
W	19%	15%	24%	10%	10%	22%

Analysis I has a 64% success rate (grades A, B, or C), yet the drop-off is higher than the failure rate. It is clear that combining the 500-level and 600-level modeling classes penalizes those enrolled at the 500-level because the success rate is half that of the 600-level for Modeling I and only 35% for Modeling II.

Table 9 Grades for 500-Level Modeling Contrasted with 600-Level Modeling

Grade	Modeling I (500)	Modeling I (600)	Modeling II (500)	Modeling II (600)
A	12%	60%	7%	83%
B	33%	33%	21%	14%
C	30%	0%	7%	0%
D	0%	0%	57%	0%
F	0%	0%	7%	0%
W	26%	5%	0%	3%

Figure 17 shows the linear relationship between success rate and drop-off ($p=0.0054$, $r^2=38\%$). It is clear, then, that the drop-off depends on the success rate in the first semester classes. Figure 18 shows how much the success rate can vary from year to year. The peak success is 90% and the lowest success is 35%.

Figure 17 Relationship between Success and Drop-off in First Semester of Sequence

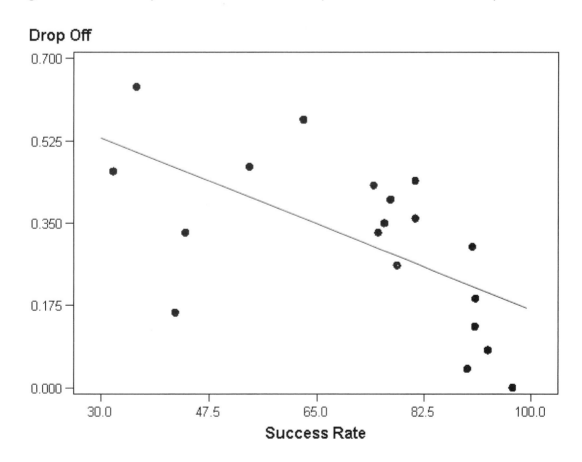

450 Introduction to Data Mining Using SAS Enterprise Miner

The issue is whether the success rates are reasonable for these courses and whether the students or the instructors are responsible for the differential success rates from semester to semester. Although it is possible that differences in student competencies could explain the differences in grading, it is far more likely that grade variability is the result of different faculty members teaching the courses. They can vary course material and test difficulty. Therefore, it is reasonable to conclude that differences in grading can have considerable impact on student retention.

Figure 18 Variability in Success Rate for Analysis I and II at the 500-Level

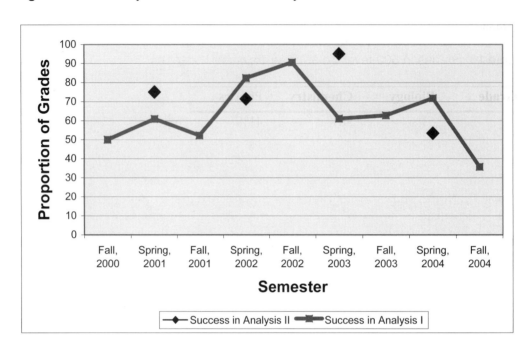

In the fall semester 2003, 600-Level Analysis I had 76% A grades, which fell to 9% in the fall of 2004. In the fall of 2004, the success rate was only 32% compared to 81% the year before. Similarly, the success rate in 600-Level Algebra I was 54% in 2002 compared to 91% in 2004. The same inconsistency occurs in 600-Level Combinatorics (66% success in 2000 compared to 81% in 2002 and 78% in 2004).

Students in the MA program are required to complete two 600-level sequences. It is clear that students who choose to take two of Modeling, Applied Statistics, or Probability and Statistics will have a higher success rate compared to students who choose two of Analysis, Algebra, and Combinatorics. Some students have begun to realize this as they have passed two of the qualifying examinations in the applied sequences to complete the MA.

If students enroll for the minimum of 9 credit hours per semester, they will need a total of 54 credit hours for the first three years. The core mathematics requires 24 credits; the application area requires 18 for a total of 42 of the 54. That leaves 12 hours (four courses) minimum. If students take three and a half years for the qualifiers, that requires an additional three courses for a total of seven. Since fall 2002, the Department of Mathematics has offered a total of four 600-level courses that are not part of the core curriculum (excluding actuarial courses, which are geared toward non-majors).

The combined enrollment in these courses was 41. Students, therefore, are supplementing their courses with independent study. There were 27 sections of independent study offered in 2005 alone. That indicates a minimum of 27 students, which could increase if more than one student was enrolled in some of the sections. Nevertheless, if a faculty workload is 2% for each independent study, these sections account for over 50% of one full-time equivalent (FTE).

In addition to the internal comparisons within the Department of Mathematics, success rates were computed for other science departments (Tables 10 and 11). These tables demonstrate that success rates are higher in biology, chemistry, and physics compared to the success rates in mathematics courses.

Table 10 Grades in 500-level Courses for Science Disciplines

Grade	Biology	Chemistry	Physics
A	51%	36%	41%
B	27%	29%	25%
C	8%	13%	9%
D	3%	5%	2%
F	2%	4%	4%
W	8%	10%	12%

Table 11 Grades for 600-Level Courses in Science Disciplines

Grade	Biology	Chemistry	Physics
A	55%	50%	48%
B	23%	34%	20%
C	2%	7%	6%
D	.4%	1%	0%
F	2%	.5%	.4%
W	6%	7%	3%

It is clear that reduced course enrollment affects graduation rates. From 2000-2002, the Department of Mathematics had 22 graduate students. From 2002 to the present, that number increased to 30. Yet the number of MA students remains low (Figure 19), no higher than 8 in any one year. Salary and tuition for 30 students at approximately $30,000 per year per student yields a total of $900,000. The cost of one instructor's time (salary and benefits) for one graduate course is approximately $10,000 per course per semester or $100,000 for five sequences. Additional costs include support personnel, computers, recruiting efforts, and administration. Therefore, the University of Louisville is spending a minimum of $1 million per year to educate graduate students. Given the average graduation rate of 6.3 students per year, the university is spending $158,730 per degree awarded. In contrast, the university hires adjuncts at a cost of $2,500 per credit hour or $7,500 per three-hour course. One graduate student teaches two courses per year, for a benefit to the University of $15,000 per year. Thus, the costs for the graduation greatly outweigh the benefits received.

Figure 19 Graduation Rates for MA Students

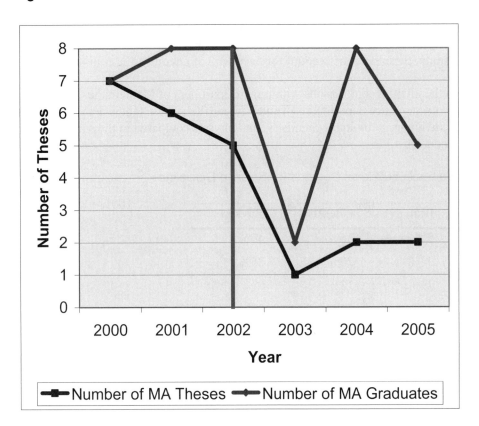

Qualifying Examinations

Because of the importance of qualifying examinations in advancing students, it is critical to examine them as well. Table 12 lists the passing rates for each examination by semester. Table 13 lists the prerequisites for each examination.

Table 12 Pass Rates for Qualifying Examinations

Exam	Algebra	Analysis	Combinatorics	Prob. & Statistics	Applied Statistics	Modeling
May 2003	80%	____	50%	100%	____	____
October 2003	50%	____	50%	____	____	____
May 2004	100%	75%	0%	____	100%	91%
October 2004	____	0%	0%	____	100%	____
May 2005	100%	75%	73%	____	____	____
October 2005	100%	100%	33%	____	____	____
# Students Attempted	21	16	20	1	8	11
# Students Passed	19	13	12	1	8	11
Percentage Passed	90%	81%	60%	100%	100%	100%

Table 13 Prerequisites for Examination Sequences

Course	Prerequisites
Algebra	500-Level Algebra I and II
Analysis	500-Level Analysis I and II
Combinatorics	500-Level Algebra I or 500-Level Graph Theory
Probability and Statistics	500-Level Probability and Statistics
Applied Statistics	500-Level Probability and Statistics
Modeling	Linear Algebra

Note that Combinatorics requires fewer prerequisite courses than the algebra course. One issue is whether a course with fewer expectations for class entry has greater expectations for class exit compared to other courses because fewer students do well in the qualifying examinations. Note that Combinatorics is the only examination that some students required a third attempt to complete. As the overall pass rate is 60%, and except for one good term (May 2005), the pass rate for the Combinatorics Exam is only 43%, it is clear that the Combinatorics examination is much more difficult than the other examinations. It has then become, more than any other exam, the gatekeeper to dissertation level in the PhD program.

Should Combinatorics be the gatekeeper to the program? Also, students who took the examination in May 2005 appear to be more fortunate compared to others because the pass rate was so much higher. Should students have such a random draw in terms of the examinations or should the pass rates be consistent across terms?

Students only need to take one applied exam and two theoretical exams. Therefore, it is expected that half as many students would take the applied exam. Yet when the number of attempts is totaled (44 versus 18), it is clear that more students than expected are taking the theoretical examinations. There are two possible reasons, as follows:

1. Fewer students pass the theoretical examinations, so the additional numbers reflect the extra attempts necessary to pass.

2. Student advisors tend to emphasize completion of the theoretical courses before completion of the applied courses.

An examination of the transcripts of individual students would determine which explanation is the more reasonable. However, examining the relationship of success in the courses to qualifying examinations indicates similarities across courses. There was only a 32% success rate in Analysis in 2004, which resulted in only four students attempting the Analysis examination. In contrast, there was a 78% success rate in Combinatorics, with 11 students attempting the exam. However, in 2002, there was an 81% success in Combinatorics, with only a handful of students attempting the qualifying examination with a very low probability of success.

Another reason that fewer students can take the applied examination is that courses are only offered every other year, while theoretical courses are offered every year, even though students need to complete two applied and two theoretical courses. More importantly, the Probability and Statistics sequence and the Applied Statistics sequence, which both depend on the 500-level Probability and Statistics prerequisite, run from fall to spring while the 500-level prerequisite runs from spring to fall. Therefore, if a student enters the graduate program needing to take the 500-level Probability and Statistics, they will be unable to complete either sequence until the third year of their graduate program (500-Level Probability in the spring of year 1, 500-level Statistics in the fall of year 2, and a sequence in the fall and spring of year 3). Scheduling classes, therefore, makes it impossible for students to choose both statistics sequences to complete core requirements because that would require four years in the PhD program. The remaining four sequences can be completed by the end of the second year of the PhD program. It is strongly recommended that the university revise the schedule for statistics courses.

Discussion

Course grading and content can be extremely variable, depending on the course instructor. This variability is highly related to the level of student success in the course, and the level of student success is highly related to degree completion. The university must decide whether to institute quality control policies to reduce outcome variability in graduate courses or whether to allow faculty to continue to enjoy complete autonomy in both course grading and content.

In the business environment, new hires are expected to succeed in their positions. It is evident from the variability in success rates (which can be as low as 35%) that graduate students are not necessarily expected to succeed. Because of the significant financial investment in graduate students, the graduate admissions process should be improved, again by implementing quality control measures, to ensure that the majority of students admitted successfully complete their degrees.

11.5 Investigation of Web-Available Information on Vaccines

Introduction
Vaccines are one of the most universally accepted medical treatments. However, a small, very vocal group opposes universal vaccination. Some members of the opposition hold strong medical credentials while most of those opposed have none whatsoever. When the smallpox vaccine was re-introduced, mostly for healthcare providers, few took it. Also controversial was the anthrax vaccine at one time required of military personnel.

This paper uses the SAS Text Miner software in SAS 9.1 to investigate Internet information related to vaccinations that is available to consumers. The software can examine unstructured text and develop meaningful structures from the patterns of words found within the documents.

Method
The first step was to collect documents referencing vaccines from different sources. The search engine Google was used for a keyword search of the term *vaccine*. The first 135 Web sites listed were saved in a local file folder. The SAS Text Miner macro %TMFILTER was used as follows to import the Web pages into a SAS data set:

```
%macro tmfilter(dataset=work.data, dir= , port = 5555,
host=localhost, url= , depth=2);
```

The macro imported text from 135 of the 150 Web pages into the data set. No additional preprocessing was used or needed. The default weights (entropy) were used for the clustering. Expectation maximization was used instead of hierarchical clustering because it tends to provide better groupings.

The results of exploratory analysis using concept maps, available in SAS Enterprise Miner 5.2, were also examined. A *concept map* organizes and represents information. Relationships between words in the text are indicated by connecting lines. In SAS Text Miner software, the user chooses a word to place at the center of the concept map. Words that are linked to the chosen word are organized in a circular fashion around it with lines indicating connections. A second set of connections is also provided from each of the initial connections to the chosen word. Beyond that, the user must choose a new central word. Behind each word is a list of documents that are connected to the central word so that you can identify the connections if needed.

Results
Table 1 lists the results of the text analysis on the 135 Web sites. A total of four clusters were identified in the data.

Table 1 Words Identifying Document Clusters in SAS Text Miner Software

Cluster Number	Cluster Contents	Frequency	Percentage
1	Cattle, find, frequently, friend, gloves, vaccines, active, centre, service, help	26	19
2	Access, aids, children, classic, clinical, cooperative, date, development, excellence, hiv, polio, release, report, smallpox, thimerosal, health, immunization, vaccination, collection	53	39
3	Child, information, mission, resources, statement, subscribe, web, wyeth, contact, feedback, page, book, email, center, directory, navigation, pharmaceutical, science, update, vaccination	43	32
4	Allergy, disease, harass, measles/mmr, mercola, reaction, symptom checker, vaccine reaction, contact	13	10

The word lists allow for the clusters to be labeled (Table 2).

Table 2 Cluster Labels

Cluster Number	Label
1	Vaccine supplies
2	General information about vaccinations
3	General information about childhood vaccination
4	Anti-vaccine information

The number of sites dedicated to risks and anti-vaccine information is large but does not outnumber the sites developed to provide general information. The labels can be validated by examining one or two Web pages contained within the cluster (Table 3). These web sites were accessed in 2004 and some may no longer exist.

Table 3 Representative Web Sites

Cluster Number	Beginning Text in Web Site	Web Site
1	Find it...boots & Gloves Carhartt Clothing Cattle Vaccines	PBS animal health cattle vaccines.html
	Welcome to New England Medical Supply, Inc.	Vaccinessupplier.htm
2	Immunizations Saves Lives. It is one of the most cost-effective....	844b8a807202a3d5852568e3006b2b5b.html
	Almanac-Science-Body Vaccine Source, The US FDA	A0876007.html
3	Vaccines for Children VFC Home Parents Providers State A Partnership for Children's Health	Default.htm
		GAVI the Vaccine Alliance.html
4	Vaccine reaction harassed for your views	autismap.htm
	Dr. Joseph Mercola, author of *The No-Grain Diet*	mercury.htm

However, it must be recognized that patients and parents have legitimate concerns about vaccinations that may need to be addressed by a medical professional. Patients who investigate vaccinations on the Internet will discover some of the risks, and they might have questions that need to be answered. Therefore, it is helpful to use text analysis to find the major topics of concern. SAS Text Miner software provides a list of all words that appear more than twice within the documents. The list can be ordered by frequency of appearance. Therefore, terms can be flagged that occur multiple times, indicating a level of interest. In this example, we specifically flagged the following terms:

- Polio
- Measles
- Autism
- Disease
- Immune system
- Smallpox
- Mercury
- Thimerosal
- Infection

Specifically, the term *autism* appeared in 19 documents. The concept map of terms related to autism appears in Figure 1.

Figure 1 Concept Links for **autism**

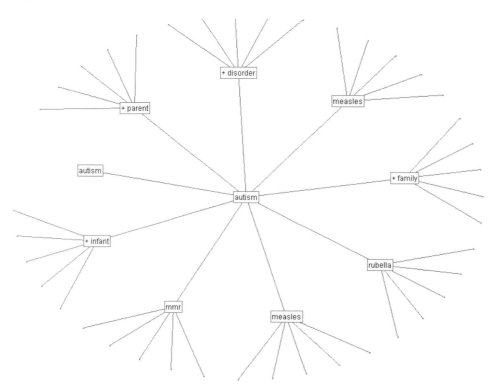

It is clear that the main concern about autism is related to the measles, mumps, and rubella (MMR) vaccine. Therefore, medical providers should be prepared to discuss this issue with their patients. Of even more concern is the impact of vaccination on the immune system. The search revealed the term *immune system* occurred in 26 documents with many more links (Figure 2).

Figure 2 Concept Links for **immune system**

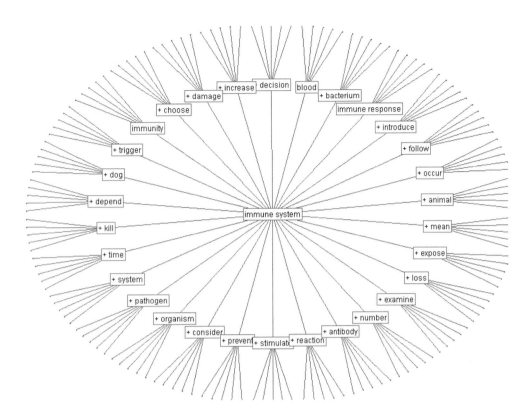

By looking at the related term *decision*, Figure 3 presents the second generation of the concept map. Most prominent are the terms *law* and *choose*. Patients interested in reading about this information are those considering refusing vaccination either for themselves or for their children.

Figure 3 Concept Links for **decision** related to **immune system**

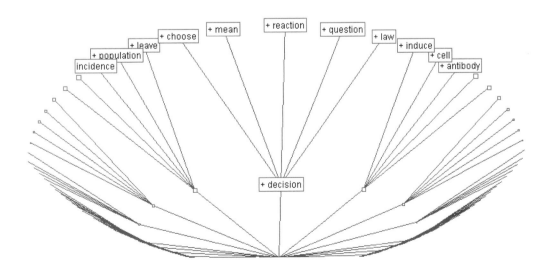

Discussion

Automatic examinations of Internet information using SAS Text Miner software can be more inclusive and more extensive compared to standard manual examinations. Hundreds of Web sites can be stored and examined easily to determine site content.

Because information on the Internet is uncontrolled and easily accessible, health care professionals must be aware of the information that exists because their patients will show it to them. Although this paper primarily addresses vaccine information, a similar search can be performed on virtually any topic. Physicians also should be prepared, using evidence from the medical literature, to discuss the Internet information with their patients.

Index

Books Available from SAS® Press

Advanced Log-Linear Models Using SAS®
by **Daniel Zelterman**

Analysis of Clinical Trials Using SAS®: A Practical Guide
by **Alex Dmitrienko, Geert Molenberghs, Walter Offen,** and
Christy Chuang-Stein

Annotate: Simply the Basics
by **Art Carpenter**

*Applied Multivariate Statistics with SAS® Software,
Second Edition*
by **Ravindra Khattree**
and **Dayanand N. Naik**

*Applied Statistics and the SAS® Programming Language,
Fifth Edition*
by **Ronald P. Cody**
and **Jeffrey K. Smith**

An Array of Challenges — Test Your SAS® Skills
by **Robert Virgile**

*Carpenter's Complete Guide to the SAS® Macro Language,
Second Edition*
by **Art Carpenter**

The Cartoon Guide to Statistics
by **Larry Gonick**
and **Woollcott Smith**

*Categorical Data Analysis Using the SAS® System,
Second Edition*
by **Maura E. Stokes, Charles S. Davis,**
and **Gary G. Koch**

Cody's Data Cleaning Techniques Using SAS® Software
by **Ron Cody**

*Common Statistical Methods for Clinical Research with
SAS® Examples, Second Edition*
by **Glenn A. Walker**

The Complete Guide to SAS® Indexes
by **Michael A. Raithel**

*Data Management and Reporting Made Easy with
SAS® Learning Edition 2.0*
by **Sunil K. Gupta**

*Debugging SAS® Programs: A Handbook of Tools and
Techniques*
by **Michele M. Burlew**

*Efficiency: Improving the Performance of Your SAS®
Applications*
by **Robert Virgile**

The Essential Guide to SAS® Dates and Times
by **Derek P. Morgan**

The Essential PROC SQL Handbook for SAS® Users
by **Katherine Prairie**

*Fixed Effects Regression Methods for Longitudinal Data
Using SAS®*
by **Paul D. Allison**

Genetic Analysis of Complex Traits Using SAS®
Edited by **Arnold M. Saxton**

A Handbook of Statistical Analyses Using SAS®, Second Edition
by **B.S. Everitt**
and **G. Der**

Health Care Data and SAS®
by **Marge Scerbo, Craig Dickstein,**
and **Alan Wilson**

The How-To Book for SAS/GRAPH® Software
by **Thomas Miron**

*In the Know ... SAS® Tips and Techniques From
Around the Globe*
by **Phil Mason**

Instant ODS: Style Templates for the Output Delivery System
by **Bernadette Johnson**

*Integrating Results through Meta-Analytic Review Using
SAS® Software*
by **Morgan C. Wang**
and **Brad J. Bushman**

Learning SAS® in the Computer Lab, Second Edition
by **Rebecca J. Elliott**

The Little SAS® Book: A Primer
by **Susan J. Slaughter**
and **Lora D. Delwiche**

The Little SAS® Book: A Primer, Second Edition
by **Susan J. Slaughter**
and **Lora D. Delwiche**
(updated to include SAS 7 features)

The Little SAS® Book: A Primer, Third Edition
by **Susan J. Slaughter**
and **Lora D. Delwiche**
(updated to include SAS 9.1 features)

The Little SAS® Book for Enterprise Guide® 3.0
by **Lora D. Delwiche**
and **Susan J. Slaughter**

support.sas.com/pubs

The Little SAS® Book for Enterprise Guide® 4.1
by **Lora D. Delwiche**
and **Susan J. Slaughter**

Logistic Regression Using the SAS® System:
Theory and Application
by **Paul D. Allison**

Longitudinal Data and SAS®: A Programmer's Guide
by **Ron Cody**

Maps Made Easy Using SAS®
by **Mike Zdeb**

Models for Discrete Data
by **Daniel Zelterman**

Multiple Comparisons and Multiple Tests Using SAS®
Text and Workbook Set
(books in this set also sold separately)
by **Peter H. Westfall, Randall D. Tobias,**
Dror Rom, Russell D. Wolfinger,
and **Yosef Hochberg**

Multiple-Plot Displays: Simplified with Macros
by **Perry Watts**

Multivariate Data Reduction and Discrimination with
SAS® Software
by **Ravindra Khattree**
and **Dayanand N. Naik**

Output Delivery System: The Basics
by **Lauren E. Haworth**

Painless Windows: A Handbook for SAS® Users, Third Edition
by **Jodie Gilmore**
(updated to include SAS 8 and SAS 9.1 features)

The Power of PROC FORMAT
by **Jonas V. Bilenas**

PROC SQL: Beyond the Basics Using SAS®
by **Kirk Paul Lafler**

PROC TABULATE by Example
by **Lauren E. Haworth**

Professional SAS® Programmer's Pocket Reference,
Fifth Edition
by **Rick Aster**

Professional SAS® Programming Shortcuts, Second Edition
by **Rick Aster**

Quick Results with SAS/GRAPH® Software
by **Arthur L. Carpenter**
and **Charles E. Shipp**

Quick Results with the Output Delivery System
by **Sunil K. Gupta**

Reading External Data Files Using SAS®: Examples Handbook
by **Michele M. Burlew**

Regression and ANOVA: An Integrated Approach Using
SAS® Software
by **Keith E. Muller**
and **Bethel A. Fetterman**

SAS® for Forecasting Time Series, Second Edition
by **John C. Brocklebank**
and **David A. Dickey**

SAS® for Linear Models, Fourth Edition
by **Ramon C. Littell, Walter W. Stroup,**
and **Rudolf J. Freund**

SAS® for Mixed Models, Second Edition
by **Ramon C. Littell, George A. Milliken, Walter W. Stroup,**
and **Russell D. Wolfinger**

SAS® for Monte Carlo Studies: A Guide for Quantitative
Researchers
by **Xitao Fan, Ákos Felsővályi, Stephen A. Sivo,**
and **Sean C. Keenan**

SAS® Functions by Example
by **Ron Cody**

SAS® Guide to Report Writing, Second Edition
by **Michele M. Burlew**

SAS® Macro Programming Made Easy
by **Michele M. Burlew**

SAS® Programming by Example
by **Ron Cody**
and **Ray Pass**

SAS® Programming for Researchers and Social Scientists,
Second Edition
by **Paul E. Spector**

SAS® Programming in the Pharmaceutical Industry
by **Jack Shostak**

SAS® Survival Analysis Techniques for Medical Research,
Second Edition
by **Alan B. Cantor**

SAS® System for Elementary Statistical Analysis,
Second Edition
by **Sandra D. Schlotzhauer**
and **Ramon C. Littell**

SAS® System for Regression, Third Edition
by **Rudolf J. Freund**
and **Ramon C. Littell**

SAS® System for Statistical Graphics, First Edition
by **Michael Friendly**

The SAS® Workbook and *Solutions* Set
(books in this set also sold separately)
by **Ron Cody**

Selecting Statistical Techniques for Social Science Data:
A Guide for SAS® Users
by **Frank M. Andrews, Laura Klem, Patrick M. O'Malley,**
Willard L. Rodgers, Kathleen B. Welch,
and **Terrence N. Davidson**

Statistical Quality Control Using the SAS® System
by **Dennis W. King**

A Step-by-Step Approach to Using the SAS® System
for Factor Analysis and Structural Equation Modeling
by **Larry Hatcher**

support.sas.com/pubs

A Step-by-Step Approach to Using SAS® for Univariate and Multivariate Statistics, Second Edition
by **Norm O'Rourke, Larry Hatcher,**
and **Edward J. Stepanski**

Step-by-Step Basic Statistics Using SAS®: Student Guide
and *Exercises*
(books in this set also sold separately)
by **Larry Hatcher**

Survival Analysis Using SAS®:
A Practical Guide
by **Paul D. Allison**

Tuning SAS® Applications in the OS/390 and z/OS
Environments, Second Edition
by **Michael A. Raithel**

Univariate and Multivariate General Linear Models:
Theory and Applications Using SAS® Software
by **Neil H. Timm**
and **Tammy A. Mieczkowski**

Using SAS® in Financial Research
by **Ekkehart Boehmer, John Paul Broussard,**
and **Juha-Pekka Kallunki**

Using the SAS® Windowing Environment: A Quick Tutorial
by **Larry Hatcher**

Visualizing Categorical Data
by **Michael Friendly**

Web Development with SAS® by Example, Second Edition
by **Frederick E. Pratter**

Your Guide to Survey Research Using the SAS® System
by **Archer Gravely**

JMP® Books

JMP® for Basic Univariate and Multivariate Statistics: A Step-by-Step Guide
by **Ann Lehman, Norm O'Rourke, Larry Hatcher,**
and **Edward J. Stepanski**

JMP® Start Statistics, Third Edition
by **John Sall, Ann Lehman,**
and **Lee Creighton**

Regression Using JMP®
by **Rudolf J. Freund, Ramon C. Littell,**
and **Lee Creighton**